OFFICIAL

Netscape Internet Starter Kit

WINDOWS & MACINTOSH

KIT

OFFICIAL

Netscape Internet Starter Kit

WINDOWS & MACINTOSH

KIT

An imprint of
Ventana Communications Group

Everything you need
to get started!

PHIL JAMES

CONTRIBUTING AUTHOR
MARK CHAMBERS

VENTANA

Official Netscape Internet Starter Kit

Library of Congress Catalog Card Number: 97-060680

First Edition 9 8 7 6 5 4 3 2 1

Printed in the United States of America

Published and distributed to the trade by Ventana Communications Group
P.O. Box 13964, Research Triangle Park, NC 27709-3964
919.544.9404
FAX 919.544.9472
http://www.vmedia.com

Ventana Communications Group is a division of International Thomson Publishing.

Netscape Publishing Relations
Suzanne C. Anthony
Netscape Communications Corporation
501 E. Middlefield Rd.
Mountain View, CA 94043
http://home.netscape.com

President
Michael E. Moran

Vice President of Content Development
Karen A. Bluestein

Director of Acquisitions and Development
Robert Kern

Managing Editor
Lois J. Principe

Production Manager
John Cotterman

Art Director
Marcia Webb

Technology Operations Manager
Kerry L. B. Foster

Brand Manager
Jamie Jaeger Fiocco

Creative Services Manager
Diane Lennox

Acquisitions Editor
JJ Hohn

Project Editor
Jennifer R. Huntley

Copy Editor
Beth Woodard

CD-ROM Specialist
Ginny Phelps

Desktop Publisher
Kristin Miller

Proofreader
Christopher Riffer

Indexer
Tim Griffin

Interior Designer
Patrick Berry

Cover Illustrator
Lisa Gill

About the Authors

Phil James has been wandering around cyberspace, often aimlessly, for more than a decade. He is a software design consultant, performance artist, part-time musician, and author of several Ventana bestsellers, including the *Official Netscape Navigator 3.0 Book* and the *Official Netscape Communicator Book*. As a literary writer, his stories have appeared in a variety of print and electronic zines. Currently, he is working on a series of one-note operas.

Contributing author **Mark Chambers** is a freelance author, BBS sysop, and game programmer who spends entirely too much time on the Internet. His work for Ventana includes contributing work on the bestselling *Official Netscape Navigator 2.0 Book*.

Acknowledgments

I can't tell you how many people helped out on this one. But I would like to thank all the hard-working Ventana people who made this my smoothest, most hassle-free project yet, especially JJ Hohn, Jennifer Huntley, John Cotterman, Jamie Jaeger, Laura Stalzer, and Kristin Miller.

I also want to thank everyone who helped on the earlier versions of this book: Dick Cravens, Mark Chambers, Clay Shirky, and Walt Bruce.

I couldn't have won this Academy Award without the unflagging dedication and support of my Internet Service Provider, Computerland. Oops, wrong speech. Anyway, their URL is http://www.computerland.net, and they're good people and they'd be happy to sell you stuff.

Lastly, a great big thank you to my wife and kids, who are always the light at the end of the tunnel of words.

—Phil James

I would like to thank the fine folks at Ventana for their help, especially Jennifer Huntley and JJ Hohn.

—Mark Chambers

Contents

Introduction

Just a couple of years ago I wrote in the introduction to a book that exploring the Internet made you a pioneer, a rugged individualist blazing new information trails. Well, you can take off that buckskin jacket now: the pioneering days are over. The territory has been surveyed and subdivided, the electronic carpenters are busy with their virtual hammers and saws, and that sure sign of progress—advertising—has sprung up all over the Net. Having an Internet connection these days is about like owning a TV in the late 1940s.

The mainstreaming of the Net, though, has in no way diminished its excitement. As content providers familiar with other media started moving in, they pushed the boundaries of what is possible on the Net. The world of monochrome text that I was used to suddenly became an electronic amusement park full of images, sounds, and interactivity. New ways of presenting information have demanded new technologies, and new technologies have inspired new ways of delivering information. This feedback loop between the content people and the technical people has sped up the pace of innovation so much that I don't even get a break between writing new versions of this book!

Netscape remains the leader when it comes to innovation. There are not many companies that have grown so quickly, and there are even fewer that have earned so much respect from the industry. If you wanted to start exploring the Internet three years ago, your head would have been buzzing with arcane terminology. (I even wrote a book or two full of arcane terminology!) But now a new Internet user needs to add only a few words to his or her vocabulary, and certainly the most prominent of these is *Netscape*.

Netscape's success is not simply an artifact of our celebrity culture, in which people and businesses step up to the plate for their 15 minutes of fame. No, in this case, there are more substantial factors. First of all, there's the "right time, right place" factor. The founders of Netscape knew that a graphical World Wide Web browser was the single most important piece of software you could produce right now. Secondly, they knew that to succeed, they must integrate a full range of Internet services. Netscape Navigator is aimed at a public that no longer wants—and will no longer tolerate—the dozens of little applications that used to be necessary to perform even the most routine Internet tasks. Finally, Netscape recognized the importance of open platforms. With its support for plug-ins and other extensions, Netscape Navigator 3.0 is positioned to follow the curving path into the future for many years to come.

Let's take a moment to look at what Netscape Navigator 3.0 means to you:

- You can browse through the enormous range of multimedia information available on the World Wide Web. You can do advanced research without flying off to some university library, you can read the latest stock quotes, you can listen to clips of songs before you go out and plunk down $15 for a CD, you can probably even learn to dance the lambada with animated step-by-step lessons. Remember the lambada?
- You can access all the older, less flashy repositories of information: specialized Gopher and Telnet sites, vast file archives, and databases full of bizarre and arcane data.
- You can exchange electronic mail quickly and reliably with Internet users around the world. You can even exchange messages with users of private online services connected to the Net. Fire up Netscape Navigator 3.0 and you are almost by default a "global citizen." And if you want to be a very flashy global citizen, Navigator lets you incorporate multimedia right into your e-mail messages.

Who Can Use This Book

This book is aimed at anyone who knows how to use Windows or Mac OS and wants to get busy on the Net. It's also aimed at anyone who's been on the Net for a while but wants to upgrade to Netscape Navigator 3.0. Here's what you need:

- A 386sx or better PC with at least 8MB of RAM and Windows 95, Windows 3.1, or Windows NT installed. (You might be able to get away with as little as 4MB of RAM using Windows 3.1, but I don't recommend it.)

- Macintosh owners, you'll need a Macintosh 68000 (68020 minimum) running System 7 or higher, or a more current Macintosh PowerPC or Power Macintosh, with at least 8MB of RAM for the most limited configuration of Navigator 3.0. Netscape's recommendation for minimum memory is 9MB of RAM, but you will want to operate with at least 16MB in order to use some of the new features and functions of this exciting product.
- If you haven't already installed Netscape Navigator 3.0, about 8MB of space on your hard drive for a full installation of the Windows 3.1 version and about 15MB for a full installation of the Windows 95 or Windows NT version.
- A CD-ROM drive.
- For home access via an Internet access provider, a modem, preferably one that can run at 33.6 or 28.8 kbps.

Chances are that unless you're a very ambitious and wealthy computer nerd (no longer an oxymoron in the age of Gates), you don't have a direct connection to the Net. That means you need a modem and an account with an Internet Service Provider. Neither is hard to get or very expensive any more. Of course, you should get the fastest modem you can afford, preferably one that can run at 33.6 or 28.8 kbps, but a 14.4 kbps modem will still do the job.

How This Book Is Organized

In **Chapter 1, "Getting Started,"** you'll choose an Internet Service Provider from your CD-ROM and actually install and configure the Netscape Navigator 3.0 software. This chapter goes pretty deeply into configuring Windows 95 for Internet access. Once you work through the instructions here, you'll be ready to start exploring.

Chapter 2, "The Net & the Web," provides an overview of the Internet: where it came from, some of its features, and where it's going. You'll learn what the difference really is between the Internet and the World Wide Web, and you'll learn enough about the technical underpinnings of the Net to understand any other technical discussions in the book. We'll even throw in some hints on using the Net so that the natives don't spot you as a "newbie."

Chapter 3, "A Quick Look Around," introduces you to the Netscape Navigator 3.0 interface and the basics of navigating the Web. In a few short minutes, you'll be cruising, surfing, or whatever the term is this year.

Electronic mail is one of the most important "meat and potatoes" Internet applications, and **Chapter 4, "Netscape Mail,"** covers it fully. Step-by-step tutorials guide you through the excellent e-mail facilities that are built right into Netscape Navigator 3.0, and in no time you'll be zipping off messages as if you'd been doing it for years. And with Navigator 3.0's advanced e-mail features, you can even make your messages look just like mini Web pages!

Chapter 5, "Newsgroups," introduces you to one of the most fascinating services available on the Net. Usenet newsgroups are forums where Internet users with particular interests trade information, insights, and even files. There are groups devoted to everything from astrophysics to zydeco, and with the excellent newsgroup functionality built right into the Netscape software, you'll be able to join in quickly.

In **Chapter 6, "Getting Files via FTP,"** you'll learn how to explore file archives and download files via FTP, the standard file transfer protocol on the Net. There are archives of informational files, technical files, shareware and freeware programs, games, graphics, video clips.... ***Warning:*** Get a bigger hard drive. You're not going to believe what's available.

Chapter 7, "Gopher & Telnet," introduces you to two old Internet friends: Gopher and Telnet. These Internet services have been around for quite a while, but are still useful tools in certain situations. Netscape Navigator 3.0 includes support for both.

Of course the real *fun* of the World Wide Web is its multimedia capabilities. **Chapter 8, "Graphics, Sound & Video,"** explains how Netscape Navigator 3.0 makes your computer screen look more and more like a TV screen. We show you some of what's available out there, and we walk you through configuring Netscape Navigator 3.0 so that it uses your system optimally in dealing with these new types of information.

In **Chapter 9, "Power Navigator 3.0,"** we go beyond the basics and show you some of the more forward-looking extensions to a forward-looking piece of software. Don't be scared off by the word "advanced": none of these features are difficult to use. In this chapter we explore VRML, Java, JavaScript, and plug-ins.

Stay Up-to-Date With Netscapepress.com

Netscapepress.com is the place to go for the latest information about Netscape Press. Connect via http://www.netscapepress.com to access a complete catalog of Netscape Press titles, technical support, and updated information related to this book.

Netscapepress.com is also the home of *Navigate!*—the official electronic publication of Netscape Press and your best source for articles and reviews aimed at Netscape users. *Navigate!* features interviews with industry icons and experts as well as articles excerpted from upcoming Netscape Press titles.

Netscape Press is a joint effort between Ventana and Netscape Communications Corporation and serves as the publishing arm of Netscape.

OK, enough introduction. Let's get busy exploring this vast new world of multimedia information!

Getting Started

If you've heard about all that the Net has to offer, you're probably eager to get busy exploring this vast new electronic world. Thanks to Netscape Navigator 3.0, it's easy. But first, we'll have to prepare your computer and select an ISP (short for *Internet Service Provider*) so that you can actually connect to the world of Cyberspace. In this chapter, we'll show you:

- How to select a service provider from the CD-ROM.
- How to make sure you have the necessary hardware and software.
- How to connect to the Internet (with extensive coverage of Windows 95's built-in connectivity features).
- For Macintosh owners, we'll discuss how you can set up your Internet connection as well.
- How to install Netscape Navigator 3.0.
- How to configure Netscape Navigator 3.0 so that it works the way you want it to.

OK, first things first. Where will you get your Internet connection? The simplest method, from the point of view of the end user of Netscape Navigator 3.0, is a permanent local area network (LAN) connection. But what about Internet access for the home, or for businesses that don't require a round-the-clock hardwired connection? That's where the ISP comes to the rescue!

ISP Options

What does an ISP provide? Basically, your service provider offers you an account and an Internet connection; once your account is in place, you can call from your computer and log on to your ISP, who then links you to the Internet.

Here's how it works: Whenever you want to be "live on the Net," you click an icon and your computer places a modem call to your service provider. After the remote computer determines that you are in fact a valid customer, it connects you to the Internet, and you communicate using Netscape Navigator 3.0 or any other Internet software just as if you were wired in directly via a local area network. The information you send and receive is in the correct format for communicating over the Net. In addition, each packet of data is "wrapped" with extra information that allows it to be transmitted or received by modem instead of coaxial network cable. This extra envelope is the Serial Line Internet Protocol (SLIP) or Point-to-Point Protocol (PPP). You need to use only the protocol your access provider supports.

SLIP & PPP Connections to the Net

If you don't have to be linked to the Internet all the time, you can get a Serial Line Internet Protocol (SLIP) or Point-to-Point Protocol (PPP) account with an Internet access provider. These are dial-up accounts that give you the same full access to the Net as hardwired connections, but you are online only during the time your computer is actually linked by phone with your access provider.

Most access providers charge by the hour for SLIP or PPP connectivity, but your bill will be much, much lower than with a leased line connection, sometimes as low as $20 a month.

TIP

Windows 95 gives you Internet support and PPP connectivity right out of the box, but SLIP will not work with Windows 95 unless you install the Internet components from Microsoft Plus! or the special SLIP client software that's available only on the CD-ROM version of Windows 95.

What About ISDN?

Normal telephone lines are low-bandwidth analog lines; compared to digital lines, they can't handle large amounts of information very quickly. An ISDN line is a special kind of all-digital line that your phone company may be able to run to your house or office. There are some hefty installation fees, and then you're usually charged by how much you use the line. This fee is in addition to whatever hourly rates you pay your Internet access provider.

In order to use your ISDN line for Internet access, you need a few pieces of specialized equipment and an account with an access provider that supports ISDN connectivity. Unfortunately, you still need to understand some complex terminology before even ordering a line from your phone company. It is beyond the scope of this book to address these issues, and for most individual users ISDN is not yet a cost-effective option. If you want to investigate this connectivity method further, there's lots of information available on the Net itself.

In this section, we'll cover the installation of the three ISP options provided with your CD-ROM: EarthLink, Sprint, and AT&T WorldNet℠ Service.

EarthLink

To install EarthLink, run the Setup program located in the EarthLink directory on your CD-ROM. Setup will prompt you for a destination directory where it can copy the required files, as in Figure 1-1. If you'd like to use another directory besides the default location, enter the path directly into the field or click on the button next to the path field to browse through your system for a suitable destination.

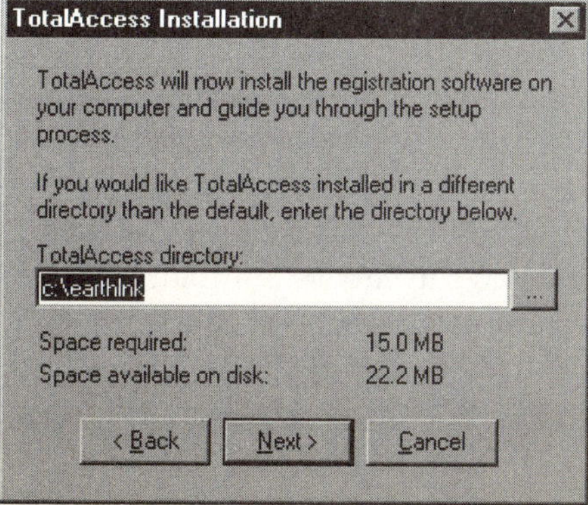

Figure 1-1: Selecting a default installation directory for EarthLink.

Setting up a new EarthLink account is easy:

1. Once the software has been installed, you'll be asked if you'd like to set up a new account—click on Yes to continue.
2. Enter your account information in the General Information screen and click on Next to continue.
3. On the User Information dialog, type a username and password for your account, as shown in Figure 1-2. Note that your EarthLink e-mail address is built at the bottom of this dialog as you enter your username—pretty neat! Click on Next> to continue.

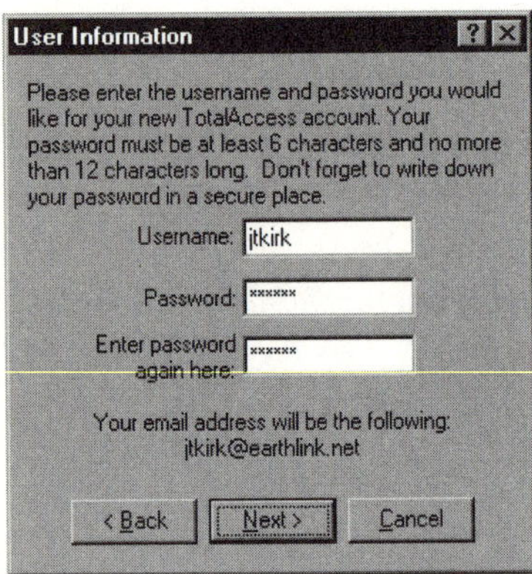

Figure 1-2: EarthLink will request account information on this screen.

4. If you were referred to EarthLink by a current subscriber, enable the checkbox on the Referral dialog and enter their username. Click on Next> to continue.
5. On the next screen, you should specify a payment plan; if you have a local number to call, EarthLink offers a less expensive plan called TotalAccess USA. To see if there is an access number in your local calling area, click on the View List button and scroll through the Dial-Up Number list. You can also update the list to display the latest access numbers from this dialog. If your location isn't within the local calling range of one of the access numbers, you can choose the TotalAccess 800 service instead and connect to a toll-free number—of course, this is more expensive. Once you've made your selection, click on Next> to continue.
6. Next you'll see the license display; after you've read the fine print, click on I Agree to continue.

7. Time to talk money! Enter your credit card information and click on Next> to continue.
8. On the next screen (Figure 1-3), select your modem from the drop-down list box and click on Modem Settings to make sure that it's correctly configured. If you've already used your modem under Windows 95, your modem should already be selected and all the settings should be OK. Click Next> to continue.

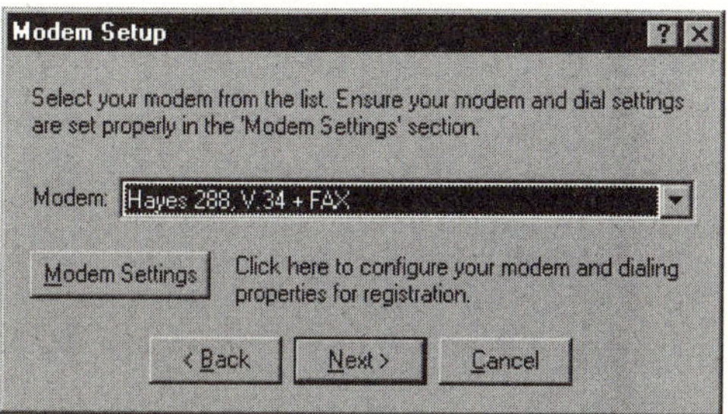

Figure 1-3: Selecting a modem for your EarthLink connection.

We're set! You've entered all the information you'll need, and all that remains is for you to click on the OK button to register your account with EarthLink.

Sprint

To begin the Sprint installation process, run the Setup program located in the Sprint directory on your CD-ROM. Setup will prompt you for a destination directory where it can copy the required files, as in Figure 1-4. If you'd like to use another directory besides the default location, enter the path directly into the field or click on the button next to the path field to browse through your system for a suitable destination.

Figure 1-4: Selecting a default installation directory for Sprint.

To set up a new Sprint account, follow these steps:

1. Once the software has been installed, your system will display the Sprint Account Registration welcome screen, as shown in Figure 1-5; to set up a new account, click Next> to continue.

Figure 1-5: The Sprint Account Registration welcome screen.

2. On the first registration screen shown in Figure 1-6, select the first option (*I need to create a new Internet account*) and click Next>.

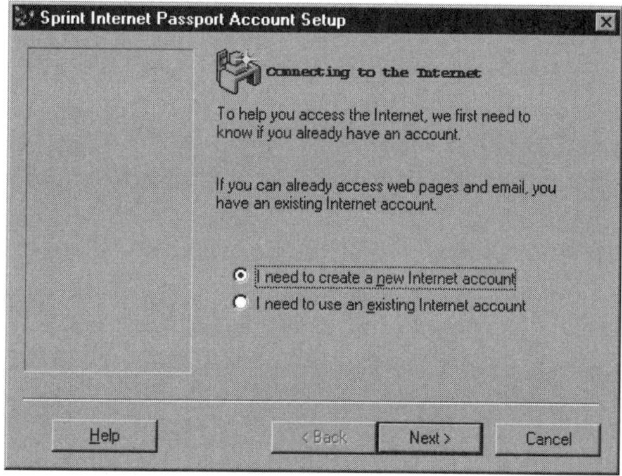

Figure 1-6: Selecting a new Internet account.

3. On the Personal Information dialog, enter your name and address as shown in Figure 1-7.

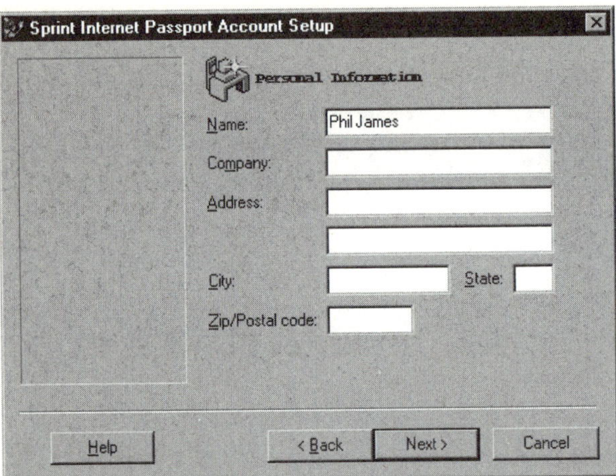

Figure 1-7: Enter your personal information for your Sprint Internet account on this dialog.

4. On the next screen, you should specify your billing information; enter your credit card information on the dialog shown in Figure 1-8 and click on Next> to continue.

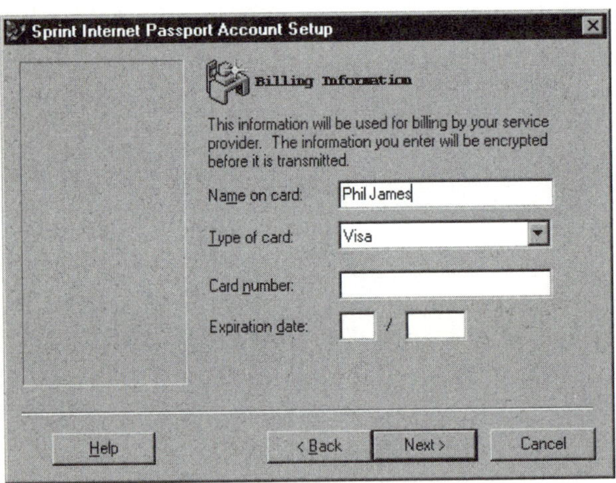

Figure 1-8: On this dialog, specify your credit card information.

5. On the next screen (Figure 1-9), the account program displays the modem connection it will use to connect to the Internet. If you'd rather use another modem connection, click the Rerun Modem Wizard button. If you've already used your modem under Windows 95, your modem should already be selected and all the settings should be OK. Click Next> to continue.

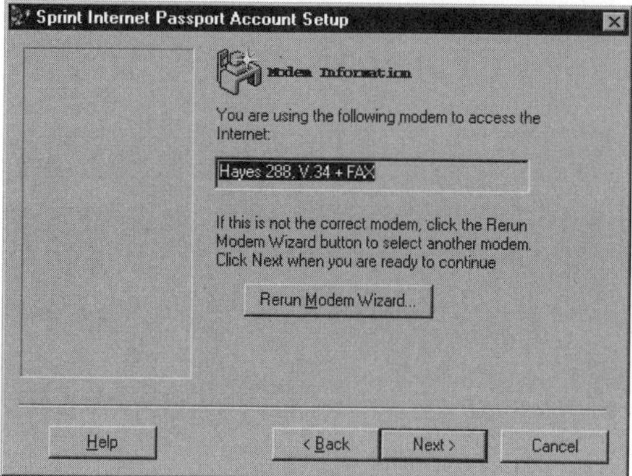

Figure 1-9: Sprint displays the default modem connection it will use.

6. On the next screen, enter your area code and telephone number and click on Next> to continue.
7. Next, enter the code necessary to disable call waiting; use an outside line or select pulse dialing, if necessary. In most cases, you can leave these settings at their default values. Click on Next> to continue.

Sprint will now connect to the automated registration center and launch Netscape Navigator. Depending on the information you've provided, the registration center may display additional questions on the Sprint Web site. Once you've answered these questions, registration is complete!

AT&T WorldNet Service

To install AT&T WorldNet Service, run the Setup program located in the AT&T WorldNet directory on your CD-ROM. Setup will prompt you for a destination directory where it can copy the required files, as in Figure 1-10. If you'd like to use another directory besides the default location, click on the button next to the path field to browse through your system for a suitable destination. You may be prompted to restart your computer before you begin the registration process—do not try to register until you've rebooted.

These instructions are for Windows 95 users. If you are using Windows 3.1x or Macintosh please see the vreadme.txt on the CD-ROM. If you are a Macintosh user the version of Netscape Navigator included with AT&T WorldNet Service is 2.02. It includes support for frames, tables, and plug-ins. Please note that you need a registration code to join AT&T WorldNet Service. If you are an AT&T Long Distance customer, enter LAK79N6A4. Use LAK79N6A5 if you use another long distance carrier.

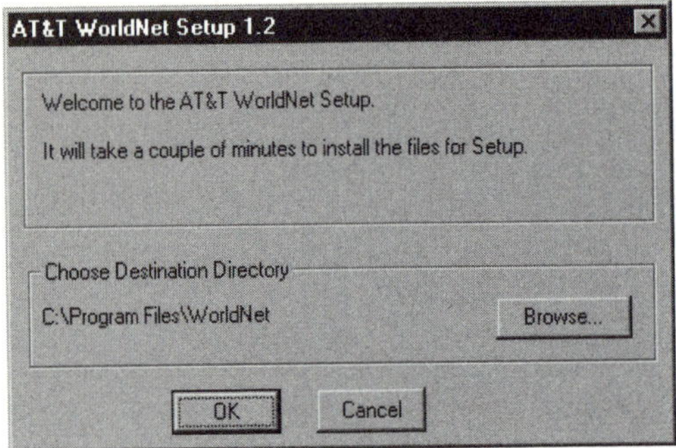

Figure 1-10: Selecting a default installation directory for AT&T WorldNet Service.

To set up a new AT&T WorldNet account, follow these steps:

1. Once the software has been installed, your system will display the AT&T WorldNet Setup welcome screen, as shown in Figure 1-11; to set up a new account, click Next> to continue. If Setup doesn't run, double-click on the AT&T WorldNet registration icon.

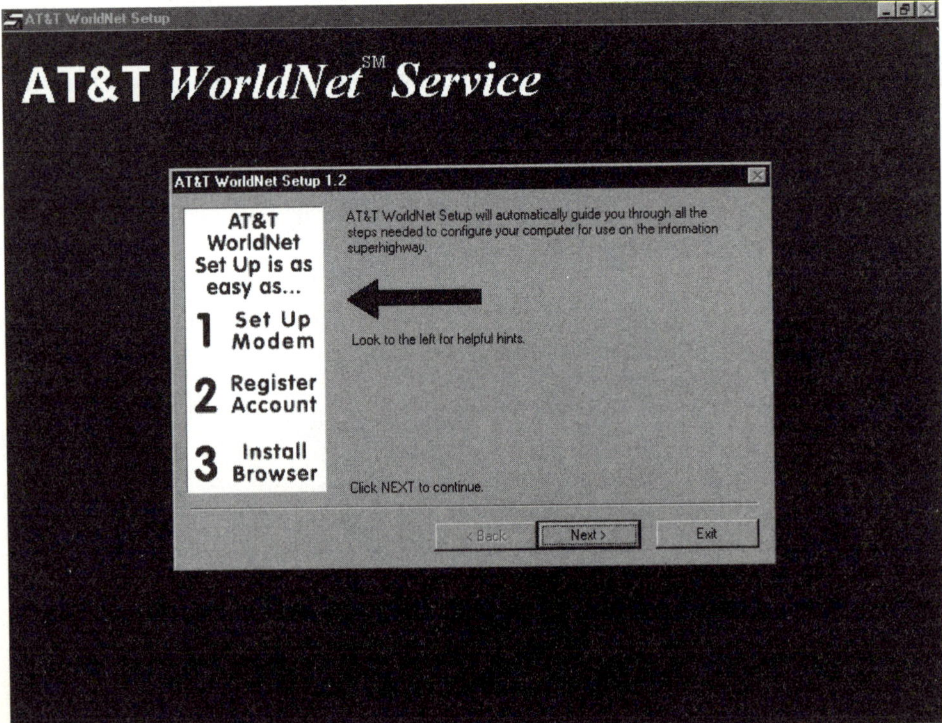

Figure 1-11: The AT&T WorldNet Setup welcome screen.

2. Your first step will be to select the modem connection AT&T WorldNet Service will use to connect to the Internet, as shown in Figure 1-12. If you'd rather use another modem connection, click the Change button to run the Windows 95 Install New Modem Wizard; if at the time of connection your modem will not dial, try the Hayes Compatible selection. If you've already used your modem under Windows 95, your modem should already be selected and all the settings should be OK. Click Next> to continue.

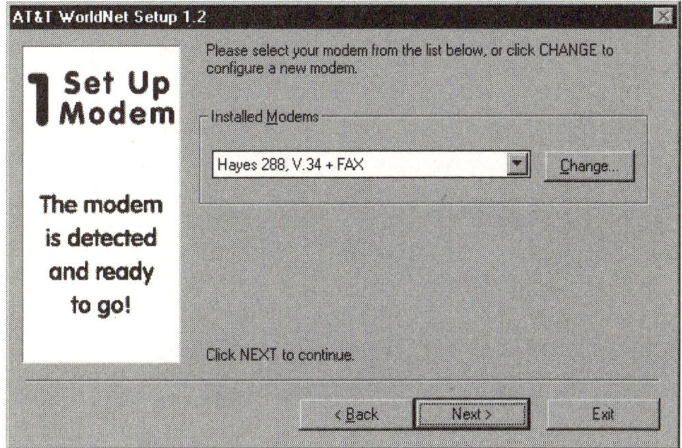

Figure 1-12: Selecting the modem to use for Internet connections.

3. Next, enter your area code, telephone number, and location as shown in Figure 1-13. Unless you've created a custom location, the value of Default Location will work fine. Click Next> to continue.

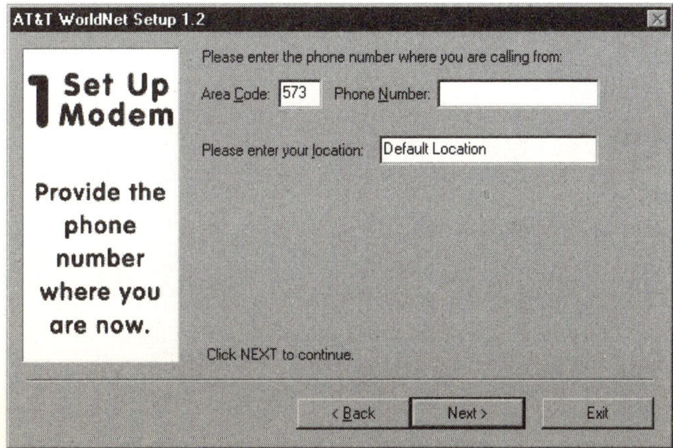

Figure 1-13: This dialog will prompt you for your telephone and location information.

4. On the next screen shown in Figure 1-14, the AT&T WorldNet Setup program prompts you for additional telephone information. Select tone or pulse dialing and enable any custom dialing properties you may need—for example, you can disable call waiting, or dial a number to use an outside line. In most cases, you can leave these settings at their default values. Click Next> to continue.

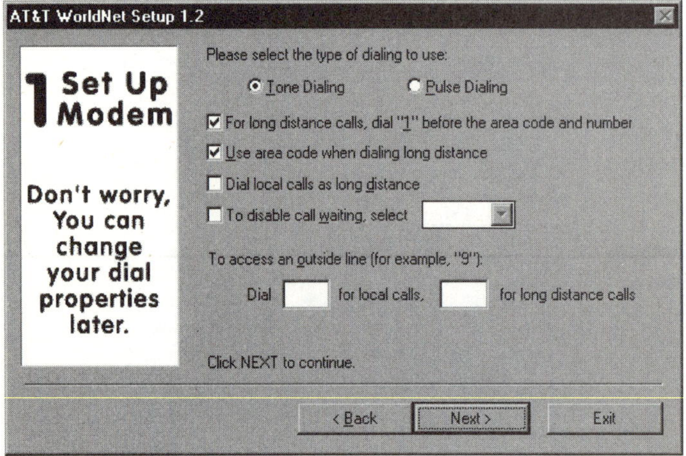

Figure 1-14: If you have custom dialing properties, you can enter them here.

5. On the next screen (Figure 1-15), you are prompted to select an account option. Since this is a new account, select the Create a New Account option and click Next> to continue.

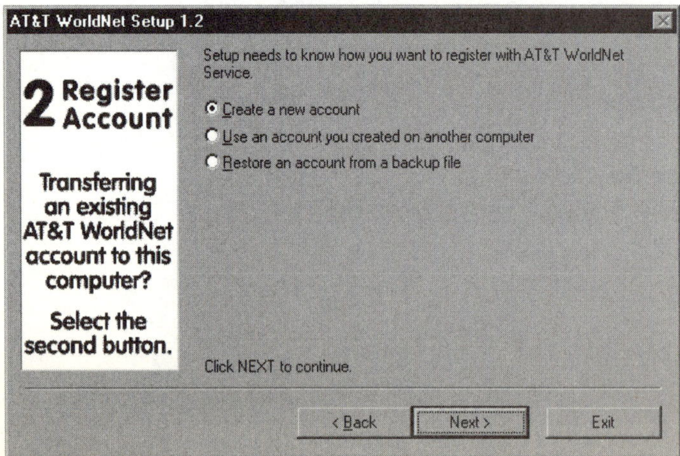

Figure 1-15: Selecting the Create a New Account option.

6. On the next screen, the 1-800 number that AT&T WorldNet Setup will use to register your account is displayed. Click on Next> to continue.
7. AT&T WorldNet Service will now automatically connect for the registration process. Once the connection has been made, Setup will display the primary local access number or 1-800 number to use for AT&T WorldNet connections, as shown in Figure 1-16. There is an additional hourly charge to use the 1-800 number. Click on the number to select it and click Next> to continue.

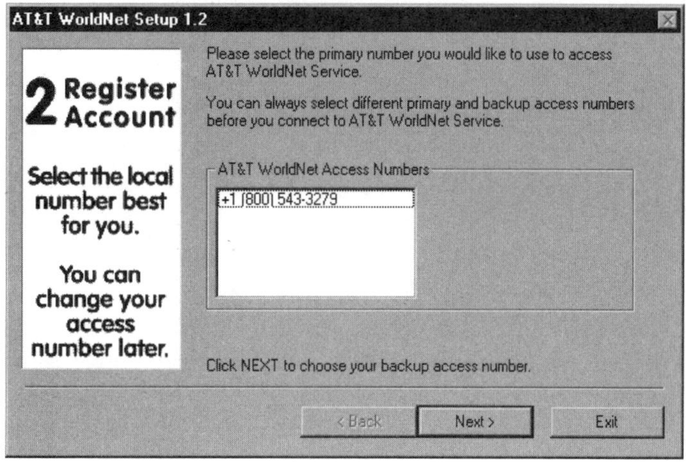

Figure 1-16: Selecting a primary access number.

8. Next, Setup will prompt you to select a backup number that can be called if the primary number is busy. If there is no local access number available, both your primary and backup numbers will be the same 1-800 access number. There is an additional hourly charge to use the 1-800 number. Click on the number to select it and click Next> to continue.
9. The next dialog will prompt you for a registration code. Enter one of the codes listed below and click Next> to continue. If you are an AT&T Long Distance customer, enter LAK79N6A4. Use LAK79N6A5 if you use another long distance carrier.
10. Setup will next display the Service Agreement dialog shown in Figure 1-17, where you can read the Service Agreement. If you accept the terms outlined in the Service Agreement, select the Yes option and click Next> to continue.

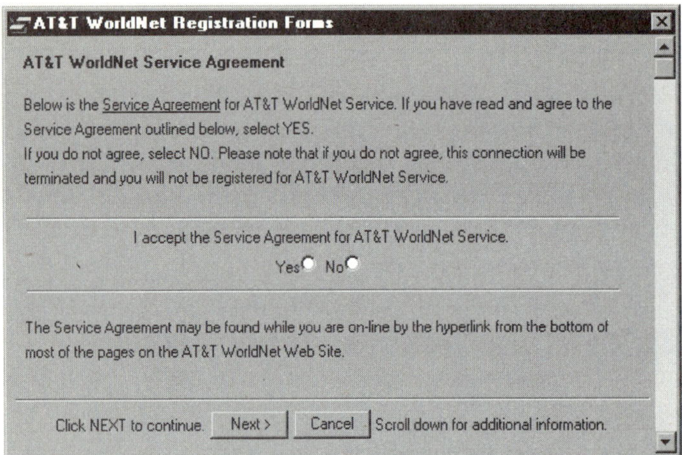

Figure 1-17: You must indicate your acceptance of the Service Agreement to continue.

11. On the next screen, it's time to select a payment plan. Click on the plan you'd like to use and click Next> to continue.
12. The next screen will prompt you for your personal and contact information, as shown in Figure 1-18. Enter your information and click Next> to continue.

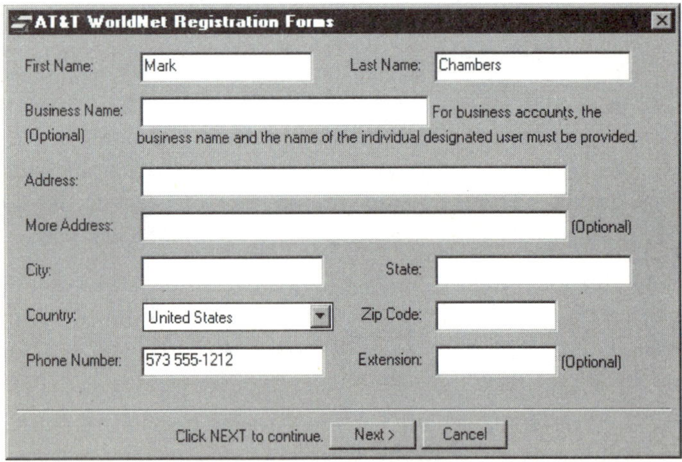

Figure 1-18: AT&T WorldNet Service prompts you to enter your personal and contact data.

13. Time to provide AT&T with your credit card information for billing (Figure 1-19). Enter your credit card information and click Next> to continue.

AT&T WorldNet Registration Forms

Special Offer: Register with your AT&T Universal Card and safeguard your Internet purchases.

Please verify that the cardholder information below is correct and modify as is necessary.

Credit Card: American Express
Expiration Date:
Card Number:
For example, 06/98.
Name On Card: Mark Chambers
Zip Code: 99999
Billing Address: 1313 Mockingbird Lane, Anytown, MO

By providing this information, you agree to pay all charges applied by AT&T in connection with your use of AT&T WorldNet Service to the credit card above in accordance with the card issuer agreement. You may provide any credit card you are authorized to use. **During this registration process, your credit card information is sent over a secure AT&T network.**

Click NEXT to continue. Next > Cancel Scroll down for additional information.

Figure 1-19: As a final registration step, Setup requests your credit card data.

The Setup program will now verify the credit card information you've supplied. Depending on the personal information and billing data you've provided, the registration program may display additional questions. Once you've answered these questions, registration is complete, and AT&T WorldNet Service will automatically install Netscape Navigator! If you have any problems during installation or registration, call the Customer Care number at 1-800-400-1447.

Billing Table

ISP	Unlimited Access Rate	Base Rate	Additional Hours
AT&T WorldNet Service*	$19.95/month	$4.95 for 5 hours/month for AT&T Long Distance customers $4.95 for 3 hours/month for non-AT&T Long Distance customers	$2.50/hour
Sprint	$19.95/month	$1.50/hour	
EarthLink	$19.95/month (local) or	$24.95/month (800 access) 5 free hours/month	$4.95/hour
* Telephone access and other charges and taxes may apply. Other terms and conditions apply. Prices quoted are effective as of June 1, 1997 and may be changed by AT&T at any time.			

Table 1-1: Billing rates for AT&T WorldNet℠ Service, Sprint, and EarthLink.

EarthLink provides 15 free days with unlimited access rate signup. Sprint provides 30 free days with unlimited access rate signup.

Hardware & Software Requirements

Now that you've registered with the Internet Service Provider of your choice, let's go over the hardware and software requirements for using Netscape Navigator 3.0 on both the PC and Macintosh.

Windows 3.1 or Windows 95

To run the Windows 3.1 or Windows 95 version of Netscape Navigator 3.0, you need:

- A 386sx or better computer running Windows 3.1, Windows for Workgroups, Windows 95, or Windows NT.
- At least 4MB of RAM for Windows 3.1 and at least 6MB for other operating systems. In my experience, everything will work much better with a minimum of 8MB.

TIP

If you are planning to use CoolTalk, Navigator 3.0's very cool new phone, chat, and white board utility, the requirements are a little stricter. You need a fast 486 (at least 50 MHz) and 8MB of RAM.

- At least 3MB of free space on your hard drive for a minimum installation under Windows 3.1 and at least 9MB for a minimum installation under Windows 95 or Windows NT. To use all program features effectively, you should have at least 8MB of free space under Windows 3.1 and at least 15MB under Windows 95 or Windows NT.
- A live connection to the Internet, either via your LAN or via a SLIP or PPP connection with an Internet access provider. If you're using SLIP or PPP, you also need:
  - A modem properly connected to your computer. The modem should be at least 14.4 baud.
  - An account with one of the Internet access providers featured on the CD-ROM.

Macintosh

To run the Macintosh version of Netscape Navigator 3.0 including the Audio Playback plug-in, you need:

- Mac System 7.1 running on a 68020, with QuickTime 2.1 and Sound Manager 3.1, or
- Macintosh PPC with a PPC 601 (66MHz) running System 7.1.2, QuickTime 2.1, and Sound Manager 3.1. Users of System 7.5 software will want to install Apple's System 7.5.3 System Update 2.0 which includes the latest version of Open Transport 1.1.
- A minimum of 6MB of free hard disk space.
- At least 8MB of RAM, preferably much more (16MB would be a better operating minimum with the Power Mac and System 7.5).
- If you expect to install the Live3D plug-in version of Navigator 3.0, you will need the Macintosh PowerPC with at least 24MB of physical RAM (16MB for Navigator 3.0 and 8MB for System Software) and be operating with virtual memory turned on. The Live3D version requires a minimum of 10MB free hard disk space during installation. The PPC 604 Power Macintosh is preferred, although Live3D will work satisfactorily on a PPC 601 or PPC 603 system.
- A live connection to the Internet, either via your LAN or via a SLIP or PPP connection with an Internet access provider. If you're using SLIP or PPP, you also need:
  - A modem properly connected to your computer. The modem should be rated for data transmission speeds of at least 14,400 bits per second (bps), and 28,800 bps is strongly recommended.
  - An account with one of the Internet access providers featured on the CD-ROM.

Internet Connectivity Software

So far everything's been pretty simple and straightforward, right? Well, here's where it gets a bit complicated. Don't worry, the information in this section is the hairiest stuff in the book. If you get through it without scratching your head a time or two you may be geekier than I am.

If the designers of PC operating systems had foreseen back in the dark ages (the eighties) that "Internet" would become a household word, they would have built a TCP/IP layer right into DOS. What is a TCP/IP layer? When you type a message into an e-mail program, for instance, it has to be formatted for transmission over the Net; in addition, it has to have an address attached so that it gets to the right destination. Conversely, incoming messages must have the addressing information stripped off and have to be reconstituted into something you can read. This process of packaging and unpackaging Internet information is the task of the Transmission Control Protocol/Internet Protocol (TCP/IP) layer.

Since the designers of PC systems software couldn't see into the future, you need an additional piece of software to provide this functionality—at least if you're running a pre-Windows 95 version of Windows. If you're directly connected to the Internet via a LAN, that's all you'll need. But to establish an active account with a SLIP or PPP access provider, you also need software that dials an access number and packages TCP/IP packets so that they can be sent out via modem. Fortunately, most TCP/IP software for Windows also includes a dialer and SLIP or PPP features.

And what if you have Windows 95? Well, you're lucky! Windows 95 has TCP/IP built right in, as well as PPP and a dialer. That's the good news. The not-so-good news is that you still have to configure the software, and Windows 95's Internet configuration is one of those tasks that gives writers like me a nice warm feeling of job security.

Whether you install separate Internet connectivity software on a Windows 3.1 system or configure Windows 95 for Internet access, there are a bunch of account-specific Internet addresses and other numbers you will need to enter. When you sign up with an Internet access provider, you are usually sent a data sheet that includes this configuration information.

Where to Get Internet Connectivity Software for Windows 3.1

As I already mentioned, Windows 95 has Internet functionality built right in. In a few minutes, I'll show you how to configure Windows 95 for getting on the Net, but what about you Windows 3.1 users? Where do you get software for Internet access?

The answer is, it's all over the place! Here are a few of your options:

- Netscape sells a special version of Netscape Navigator 3.0 called the Personal Edition. This software operates exactly like the program included on the CD-ROM that accompanies the CD-ROM Edition of this book, but also includes TCP/IP software as well as a dialer and SLIP or PPP options. It even includes a special introductory offer from an access provider.
- Ventana Communications Group has released several excellent products, such as the Windows Internet Membership Kit and the World Wide Web Kit, that include connectivity software and special offers from access providers.

- There are several shareware Internet connectivity products available from most large electronic bulletin board systems and online services. The best-known of these is Trumpet 2.0, which has almost become a standard for Windows 3.1 SLIP and PPP users.
- Microsoft offers a TCP/IP add-on for Windows for Workgroups (LAN only, no SLIP or PPP). Contact Microsoft for further information on this product.

Obviously, it's impossible to cover installing and configuring all these different pieces of software! If you're a Windows 3.1 user, you're on your own until we get into installing Netscape Navigator 3.0 itself. But don't worry: all of the products just mentioned come with pretty good documentation, and armed with the chart you filled out earlier, you should do just fine. You can also call your access provider for technical support. Most access providers are familiar with a broad range of connectivity software.

If you're a Windows 95 user, though, or if you're thinking about installing Windows 95, I can help you out a bit more. Read on!

Windows NT

It's beyond the scope of this book to cover Windows NT configuration for Internet or intranet access. Fortunately, Windows NT's own Help system is pretty good, and Microsoft provides a variety of documentation for specific tasks. Reading through the following sections may help you understand the principles, if not the exact details, of how to set up Windows NT. One thing to keep in mind, though: If you plan to use Windows NT to connect to the Net, you use the *Remote Access Dialer*. It looks a lot different from Windows 95's Dial-Up Networking, but it's pretty easy to set up and use.

Setting Up Windows 95

If you plan on spending a lot of time on the Internet, Windows 95 provides some advantages over previous versions of Windows:

- As I mentioned before, TCP/IP and PPP connectivity are built right into the operating system, so you don't need extra software just to get on the Net. (For SLIP connectivity, see the sidebar "Adding SLIP Support" later in this chapter.)

- Windows 95 lets you use 32-bit Windows applications such as the Windows 95 version of Netscape Navigator 3.0. 32-bit programs generally run faster, and they may include more features than their 16-bit counterparts. In addition, many vendors of Internet applications are now concentrating almost exclusively on Windows 95 versions.
- The Windows 95 user interface is easier for most users, so you can move around the Net more quickly.
- With Windows 95, you are less likely to experience crashes or other annoying software problems while connected to the Net.

If you're going to spend a lot of time on the Net and if you're considering installing Windows 95 anyway, I'd recommend you go ahead and do it now.

OK, let's assume you took my advice and just got through installing a brand new copy of Windows 95. (Or maybe you already had it installed and didn't even need my advice.) Now let's get your system set up for Internet connectivity.

Setting Up Windows 95 for a SLIP or PPP Connection

Although the three providers included on the CD-ROM will automatically help you set up a PPP connection, it never hurts to know how to perform this important process manually! In this section, we'll cover the necessary steps required to set up a SLIP or PPP connection using Windows 95. I'll take you through it from beginning to end. The main things you need are patience, the ability to follow directions carefully, and about 20 minutes. There are a few other requirements:

- Windows 95 successfully installed on your machine.
- A modem installed in or attached to your computer, preferably 33.6 kbps or 28.8 kbps, though 14.4 kbps is OK.
- Your original Windows 95 CD-ROM or disks (CD-ROM required for SLIP support, though not for PPP).
- A PPP or SLIP account with an Internet access provider.
- The following information, all of which you should have received from your PPP access provider:
    - Your user ID.
    - Your account password.

- The IP address assigned to you by your access provider. (***Note:*** Some access providers do not give you your own IP address, but dynamically assign you a new one each time your computer logs on. If you were not assigned an IP address, this is probably the way it works for you.)
- The DNS address(es) for your access provider.
- What kind of account this is (PPP, SLIP, or CSLIP).

Installing Your Modem

OK, got all your supplies? The first step is telling Windows 95 about your modem. (If you already configured your modem when you installed Windows 95, you can skip this section. I'll meet you around the bend, in the "Adding Dial-Up Networking" section.) I'll assume you've completed the physical part of the installation, attaching your modem to your computer and to a wall jack following the manufacturer's instructions. Now it's time to go to Windows 95's Modems facility. To install your modem:

1. Select Settings from the Windows 95 Start menu, and then select Control Panel from the cascading submenu.
2. Double-click the Modems icon. The Modems Properties dialog box appears, with the General tab selected as shown in Figure 1-20.

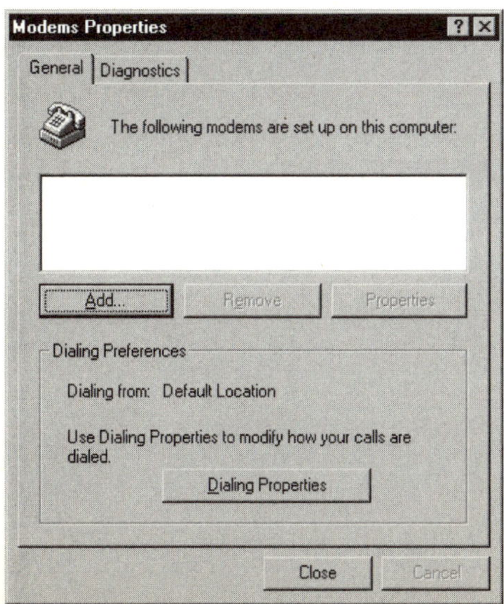

Figure 1-20: The General tab.

If your modem already appears in the list, Windows 95 has already installed it for you automatically. You can skip ahead to the section "Dialing Properties."

3. Click Add. The Install New Modem Wizard appears, as shown in Figure 1-21.

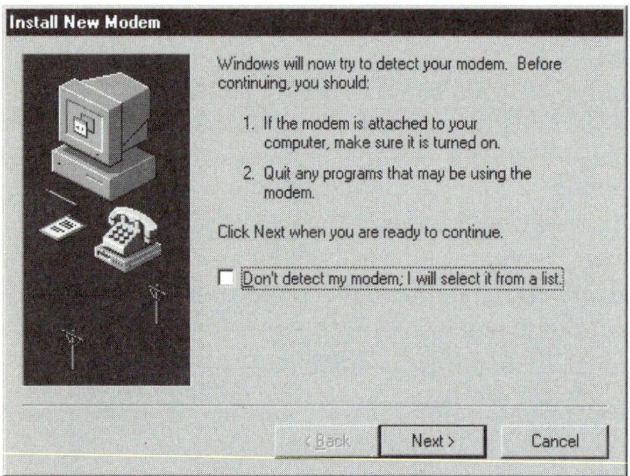

Figure 1-21: The Install New Modem Wizard.

4. Click Next. Windows 95 spends a few moments trying to detect your modem and then pops up the Verify Modem dialog box, as shown in Figure 1-22.

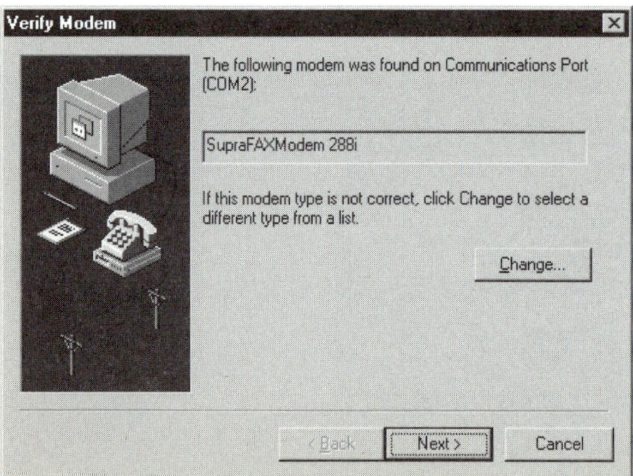

Figure 1-22: The Verify Modem dialog box.

5. If Windows 95 has not correctly identified your modem, you can click the Change button to select it manually. Otherwise, click Next and then Finish to exit the Install New Modem Wizard.

Now we'll configure your Dialing Properties. This configuration option is also accessed from the General tab of the Modems Properties dialog box, so stay right where you are!

Dialing Properties

The Windows 95 Dialing Properties tell your modem how to dial calls from your location. For instance, you may have to dial 9 to get an outside line, and you probably need to dial 1 for long-distance calls. Perhaps you even want to use a credit card for all your data calls. You may have already dealt with the Dialing Properties when you first installed Windows 95, but in case you didn't, or in case you want to change them, here's what you do:

1. In the General tab of the Modems Properties dialog box, as shown earlier in Figure 1-10, click the Dialing Properties button. The My Locations tab appears, as shown in Figure 1-23.
2. In the Where I am section of the tab, type in your area code and select your country from the drop-down list. Do not change the field that contains the words "Default Location."
3. In the How I dial from this location section, fill in all the fields appropriately for your phone system. For home phones, several of the fields can be left blank. If you check the Dial using Calling Card check box, you are prompted for further information.
4. If you will always log on to the Internet from this location, you're done. Simply click OK to return to the General tab and then click Close to save your changes and exit the Modems Properties dialog box. But let's say you're using a laptop that you transport between home and work, and you'll be accessing the Internet from both places. In that case you'll probably need to create a new location with its own dialing properties.

TIP

If you're using a laptop that you transport between home and work, or if you'll be accessing the Internet from more than one office, you can create a new location with its own dialing properties. Click the New button in the My Locations tab, enter the name of the new location, and type in any changes to the dialing properties. Dial-Up Networking will let you choose from among any new locations you add here. Click OK to save the new location.

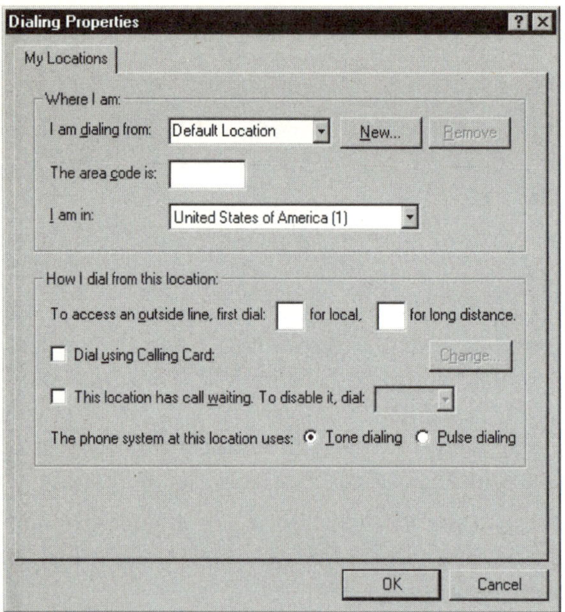

Figure 1-23: The My Locations tab.

Adding Dial-Up Networking

Dial-Up Networking is the Windows 95 component that lets you attach to your Internet access provider via SLIP or PPP. You may have installed it when you first installed Windows 95, but in case you didn't:

1. Select Settings from the Windows 95 Start menu, and then select Control Panel from the cascading submenu. The Control Panel folder appears.
2. Double-click the Add/Remove Programs icon. The Add/Remove Programs Properties sheet pops up.
3. Select the Windows Setup tab, shown in Figure 1-24.

TIP

As you can see by skimming ahead, setting up your Windows 95 system for SLIP or PPP Internet connectivity is not difficult, but it does *take some time. If you'd rather travel in the fast lane, pick up a copy of Microsoft Plus!, an excellent add-on to Windows 95. It includes an Internet Setup Wizard that will make this whole process much simpler.*

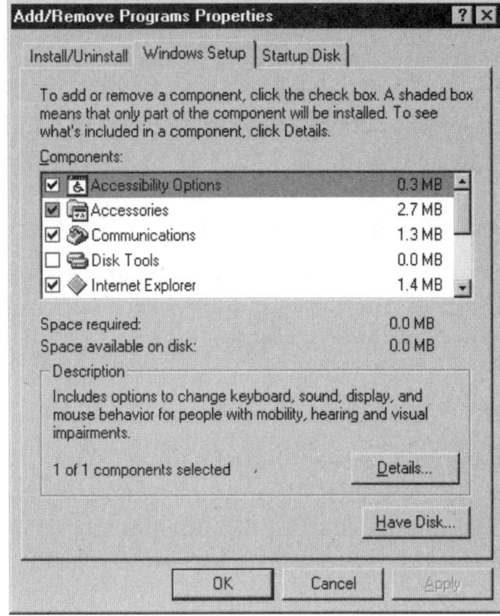

Figure 1-24: The Windows Setup tab.

4. In the list of components, highlight the Communications entry and click the Details button. The Communications dialog box appears, as shown in Figure 1-25.

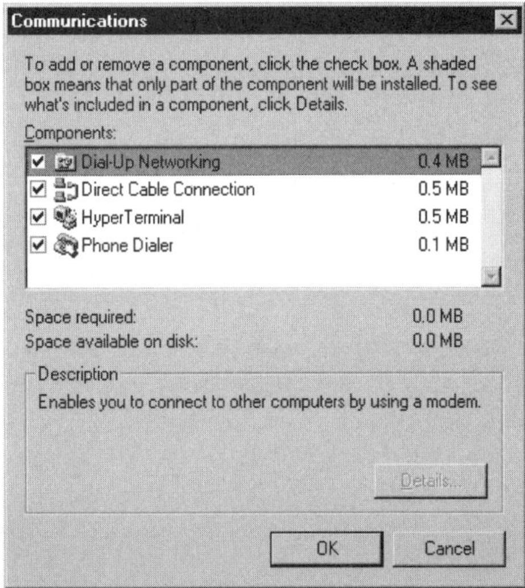

Figure 1-25: The Communications dialog box.

Follow any instructions for inserting or removing your Windows 95 CD-ROM or disk.

5. If Dial-Up Networking is already checked, skip ahead to the next section, "Adding TCP/IP." Otherwise, check Dial-Up Networking and then click OK. You are returned to the Windows Setup tab, with Communications now checked.

   If you want, you can add other components as well at this time.

6. Click OK. The Copying Files message box appears, and after a few moments Windows 95 informs you that you must restart your computer in order for the changes to take effect. Go ahead and do that now.

Adding TCP/IP

When you hook up your computer to the Internet, whether by cables or a dial-up connection, it must use the same TCP/IP protocols for sending and receiving data as every other entity on the Net. TCP/IP functionality is included on your Windows 95 CD or disks, but it is not installed automatically.

TIP

If you've already added TCP/IP for a network adapter card, you do not need to add it again. TCP/IP is TCP/IP, whether it's used on a LAN or with Dial-Up Networking. You can skip ahead to the section "Dial-Up Adapter Properties." If you don't know whether or not TCP/IP is already installed, read on.

To add TCP/IP to Windows 95:

1. Select Settings from the Windows 95 Start menu, and then select Control Panel from the cascading submenu. The Control Panel folder appears.
2. Double-click the Network icon. The Configuration tab pops up, as shown in Figure 1-26.

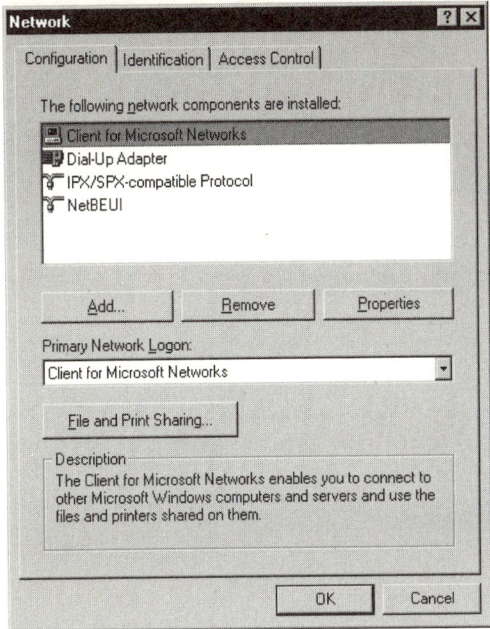

Figure 1-26: The Configuration tab.

Don't worry if you have other network components in the list. When you added Dial-Up Networking to Windows 95, the system added some components necessary for remote access to Novell or Microsoft LANs. If you are not currently on a LAN and are not planning to connect your machine to other computers, and if you only want to use Dial-Up Networking to connect to the Internet, you can remove these extra components. But whatever you do, *do not remove the Dial-Up Adapter!*

3. If TCP/IP already appears in your list, skip ahead to the section "Dial-Up Adapter Properties." Otherwise, click the Add button. The Select Network Component Type dialog box appears, as shown in Figure 1-27.

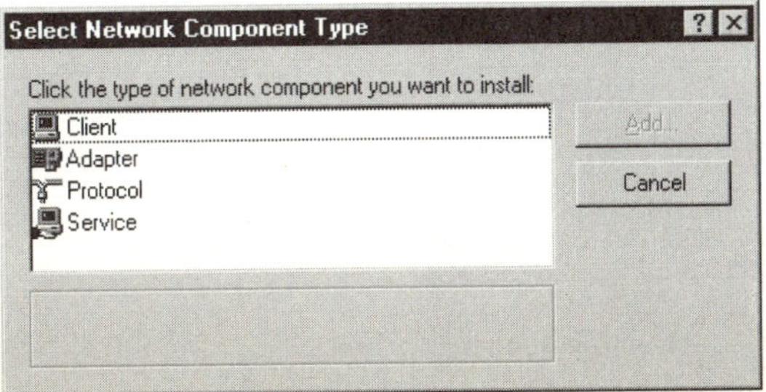

Figure 1-27: The Select Network Component Type dialog box.

4. Select Protocol and click Add. The Select Network Protocol dialog box appears.
5. Select Microsoft in the left panel, then TCP/IP in the right panel, as shown in Figure 1-28.
6. Click OK. You are returned to the Configuration tab, which should now contain TCP/IP, as shown in Figure 1-29.

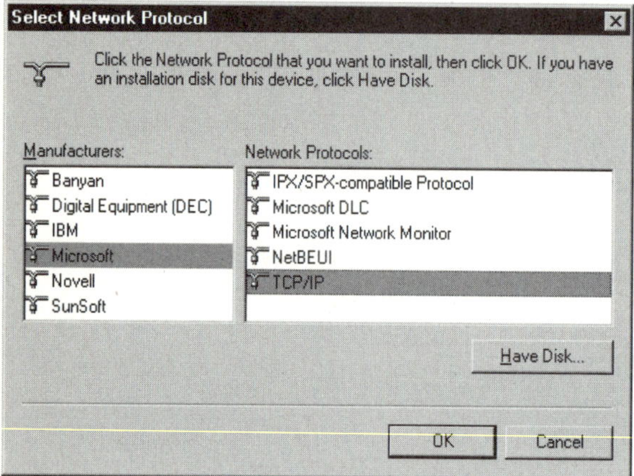

Figure 1-28: The Select Network Protocol dialog box with TCP/IP selected.

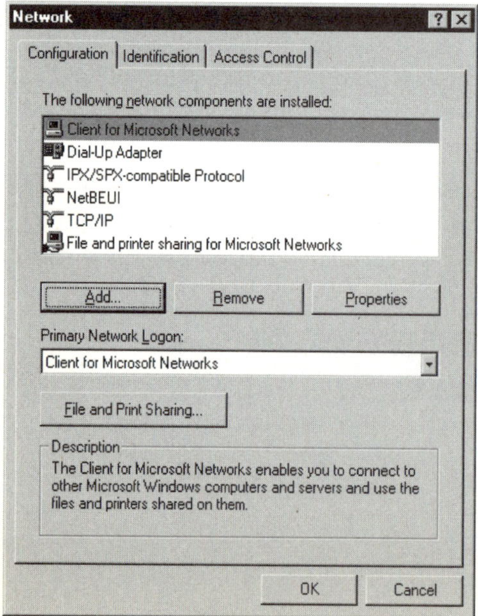

Figure 1-29: The Configuration tab with new TCP/IP component added.

Now we just need to make sure that the two network components we care about, the Dial-Up Adapter and TCP/IP, are configured properly. This part is easy.

Adding SLIP Support

As I mentioned before, some Internet access providers use PPP for dial-up access and some use SLIP.

The base Windows 95 product supports PPP, but it does not support SLIP (or CSLIP) connections right out of the box. Fortunately, if you have the CD-ROM version of Windows 95, you can add this capability very simply. Here's how:

1. Insert the original Windows 95 CD in your CD-ROM drive.
2. Select Settings from the Windows 95 Start menu, and then select Control Panel from the cascading submenu. The Control Panel folder appears.
3. Double-click the Add/Remove Programs icon. The Add/Remove Programs Properties sheet pops up.
4. Go to the Windows Setup tab, then click the Have Disk button. The Install From Disk dialog box pops up.
5. Click the Browse button, then in the Open dialog box navigate to the file ADMIN\APPTOOLS\DSCRIPT\RNAPLUS.INF on your CD-ROM drive. Click OK.
6. In the Have Disk dialog box, select SLIP and Scripting for Dial-Up Networking and then click Install. SLIP and CSLIP support are added to your system.

Dial-Up Adapter Properties

Let's quickly check the Dial-Up Adapter properties. You probably won't have to change anything, but since you're somebody who likes getting under the hood, you should know where to find these settings in case you need to adjust them later. To access the Dial-Up Adapter settings:

1. In the Configuration tab, select Dial-Up Adapter and then click the Properties button. The Dial-Up Adapter Properties sheet appears, with the Driver Type tab selected. Don't change anything in this tab.
2. Select the Bindings tab. This is where you associate the Dial-Up Adapter with a particular set of networking protocols. In this case, it should be associated with TCP/IP. Make sure that TCP/IP is checked, as shown in Figure 1-30. If it is not, check it.

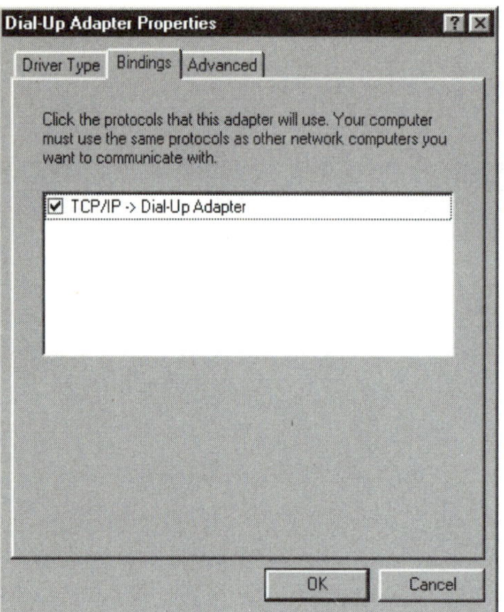

Figure 1-30: The Bindings tab with TCP/IP selected.

3. Now select the Advanced tab. The only setting that applies here is whether or not you want a troubleshooting log file recorded when the Dial-Up Adapter attempts to connect with your Internet access provider. The default is No, but if at some point you experience difficulties with your link, you might want to temporarily change this to Yes.
4. Click OK. You are returned to the Configuration tab.

TCP/IP Properties

Now let's take a look at the TCP/IP properties:

1. Back in the Configuration tab, select TCP/IP and click the Properties button. The TCP/IP Properties sheet appears, with the IP Address tab selected, as shown in Figure 1-31.

TIP

If you are on a LAN, you may have several bindings associated with TCP/IP. For instance, in the Configuration tab you might see listed TCP/IP-> Your Network Adapter Card as well as TCP/IP-> Dial-Up Adapter. If you plan to use SLIP or PPP for your Internet connectivity, select TCP/IP-> Dial-Up Adapter.

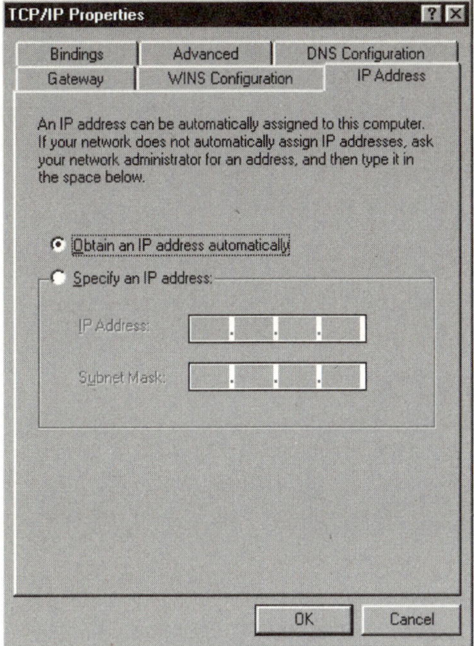

Figure 1-31: The IP Address tab.

2. If your Internet access provider assigns IP addresses dynamically, make sure the Obtain an IP address automatically radio button is selected. You can skip ahead to step 4.

Fixed & Dynamic IP Addresses

Some Internet access providers assign you a fixed IP address, and others let you obtain a different one automatically each time you log on. The second method, known as *dynamic address assignment*, is becoming more common for home and small business accounts. Which is better? It doesn't really matter a lot. The only reason you might need a fixed IP address is if you plan to set up any sort of server software on your computer—in other words, if you want to let Internet users log in to your machine to get files or view Web documents. Obviously, in this scenario, they'd need to know your Internet address, so your address couldn't be constantly changing! But for most uses of the Net, a dynamic address is just fine.

3. If your Internet access provider has assigned you a fixed IP address, click the Specify an IP address radio button and enter your assigned IP address. In addition, enter the subnet mask for this address.

TIP

Chances are good that the subnet mask is 255.255.255.0.

4. Now select the DNS Configuration tab, as shown in Figure 1-32.

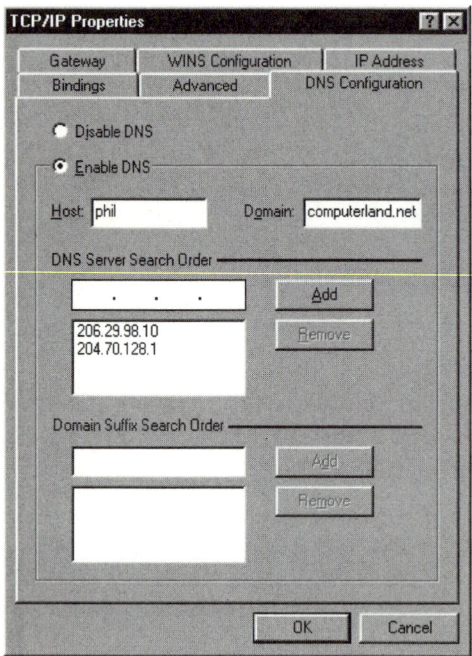

Figure 1-32: The DNS Configuration tab.

5. Unless you've received different instructions from your Internet access provider, enter the DNS address or addresses you've been given:
   - Click the Enable DNS radio button. Enter your username in the Host box and the domain name of your access provider's DNS server in the Domain box.
   - In the DNS Server Search Order box, enter the IP address for your access provider's main DNS server and click Add. If your access provider has given you an alternate DNS address, enter that now and click Add again.

- In the Domain Suffix Search Order box, type in the domain suffix for your access provider's DNS and click Add. (In many cases you will leave this field blank.) You can add several domain suffixes the same way you added entries in the DNS Server Search Order box.

6. Unless you're a serious propeller-head, leave the rest of the tabs in these Properties alone! Click OK to return to the Configuration tab, then click OK again to exit the Network properties sheet.

TIP

The one other tab you may want to look at is Bindings. If you are security-conscious, you should make sure that "File and printer sharing for Microsoft networks" is unchecked. Otherwise, it is possible that while you are connected to the Net somebody could access resources you've set up as shared resources on your system.

Windows 95 may copy some files from your CD-ROM or disks and then tell you that you need to restart your computer for these changes to take effect. If so, press the Restart button, and I'll meet you back here in an hour or two when your system is back up. (Just kidding.)

Adding a Dial-Up Connection

Now that you've got the Dial-Up Adapter and some network components installed, your computer is ready to behave itself on the Net, sending and receiving properly formatted information just like the zillions of other computers online right now. But first you have to tell Windows 95 how to actually connect to your Internet access provider. It's really pretty straightforward:

1. Double-click the My Computer icon on your Windows 95 desktop. The My Computer folder opens, revealing several icons.
2. Double-click the Dial-Up Networking icon. The Dial-Up Networking folder opens.
3. Now double-click the Make New Connection icon. The Make New Connection Wizard appears, as shown in Figure 1-33.
4. Enter the name of your access provider in the box labeled Type a name for the computer you are dialing. Since I use Computerland as my access provider, for instance, I'd type Computerland.

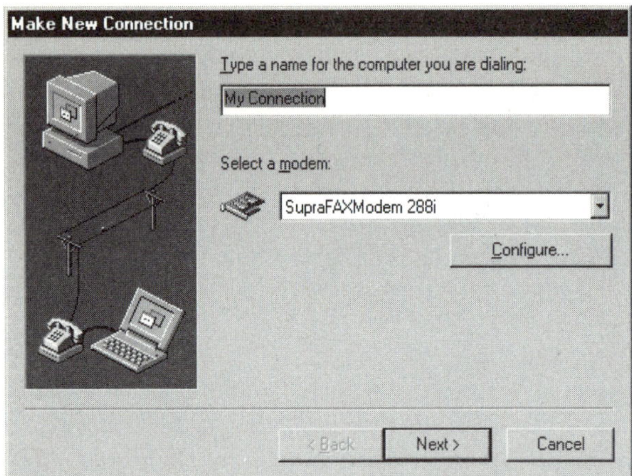

Figure 1-33: The Make New Connection Wizard.

5. Make sure your modem appears in the Select a modem box. If not, drop down the list to select it.
6. Click the Configure button. The properties for your modem appear, with the General tab selected.
7. You can adjust your modem's properties in the General and Connection tabs. I won't go through all this stuff now, but if your modem was on the Windows 95 list when you installed it, the default settings should be fine. If it wasn't on the list, please consult your modem manual and set it for the best throughput for your access provider's baud rate. For now, move on to the Options tab, as shown in Figure 1-34.
8. Assuming that you'll be using your modem to dial the call to your access provider rather than dialing manually, leave everything in this tab unchecked, with two exceptions: you *should* check Bring up terminal window after dialing and Display modem status.

   You need to bring up the terminal window after dialing in order to complete the process of logging on to your Internet access provider.

   Displaying modem status will make it much easier to troubleshoot connection problems.

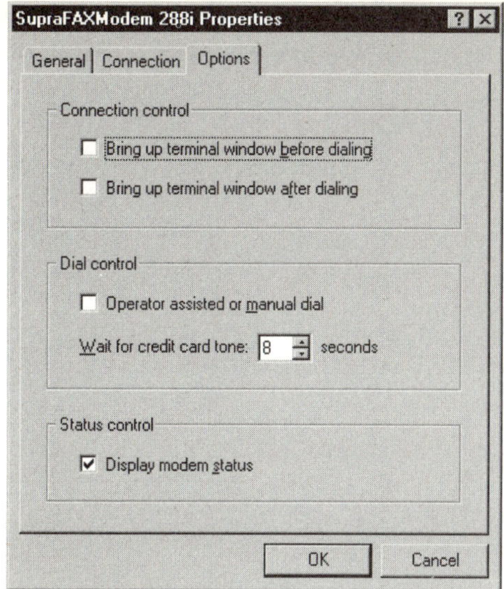

Figure 1-34: The Options tab.

9. Click OK to return to the Make New Connection Wizard, then click Next. The phone number page appears, as shown in Figure 1-35.
10. Type in the correct information, then click Next.
11. Follow any further instructions that appear, and complete the configuration by clicking the Finish button.

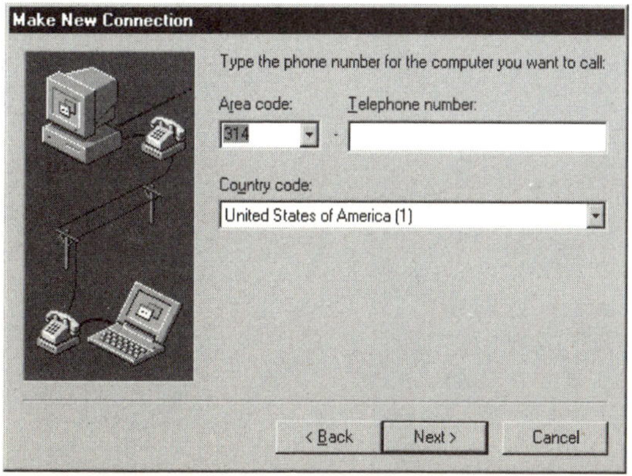

Figure 1-35: The Make New Connection Wizard phone number information.

Configuring Your New Dial-Up Connection

OK, now for a few finishing touches. You have to configure your new connection to work properly with the Internet settings given to you by your access provider.

In the Dial-Up Networking folder, which is still open on your desktop, there is now an icon for your particular access provider. For instance, in my case the icon is labeled Computerland, as shown in Figure 1-36.

Figure 1-36: The Dial-Up Networking folder with a new connection.

To configure the properties for this new connection:

1. Click the icon with the secondary (usually the right) mouse button, then choose Properties from the pop-up menu. The connection's properties pop up, with the General tab selected as shown in Figure 1-37.

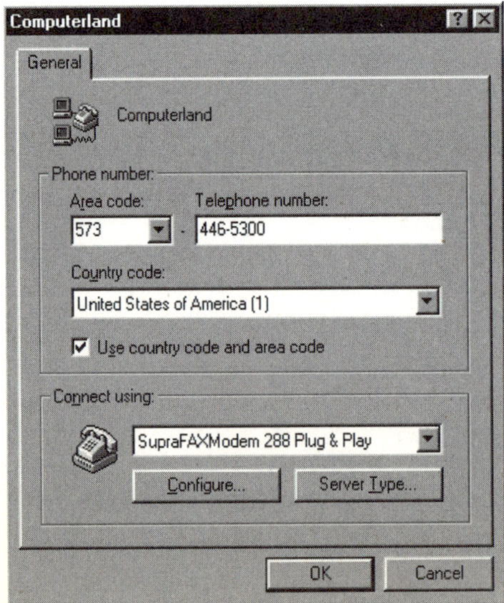

Figure 1-37: The General tab.

2. Click the Server Type button. The Server Types dialog box appears. You should complete it so that it looks something like Figure 1-38.
   Select your server type from the Dial-Up Server drop-down list:
   - For PPP, choose PPP: Windows 95, Windows NT 3.5, Internet.
   - For SLIP, choose SLIP: UNIX Connection.
   - For CSLIP (or SLIP that supports IP header compression) choose CSLIP: UNIX Connection with IP Header Compression.

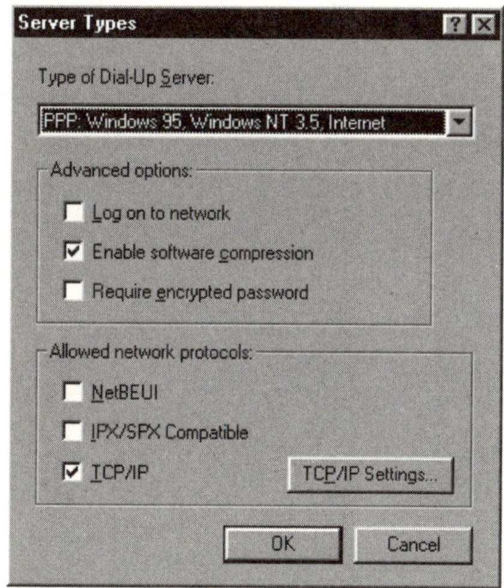

Figure 1-38: The Server Types dialog box.

   - In the Advanced options section, only Enable software compression should be checked. If you have problems with communications later, ask your access provider if this option should be turned off.
   - In the Allowed network protocols section, only TCP/IP should be checked.
3. Click the TCP/IP Settings button. The TCP/IP Settings dialog box for this connection appears.
4. If your access provider dynamically assigns you an IP address each time you dial in, click the Server assigned IP address radio button. Otherwise, click the Specify an IP address radio button and type in the IP address assigned to you by your access provider.

5. Unless you've been given different instructions, click the Specify name server addresses radio button and type in the DNS address or addresses assigned to you by your access provider.

   You can ignore the two WINS fields.

6. Unless you've received specific instructions to the contrary from your access provider, you should check the bottom two check boxes, Use IP header compression and Use default gateway on remote network.

   If your access provider has assigned you specific IP and DNS addresses, your completed page should look something like Figure 1-39.

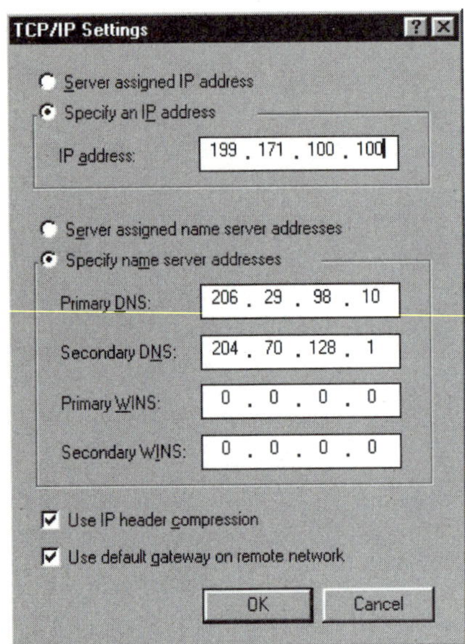

Figure 1-39: Completed TCP/IP settings for fixed IP and DNS addresses.

If your access provider assigns you an IP address dynamically each time you call in, your completed page should look something like Figure 1-40.

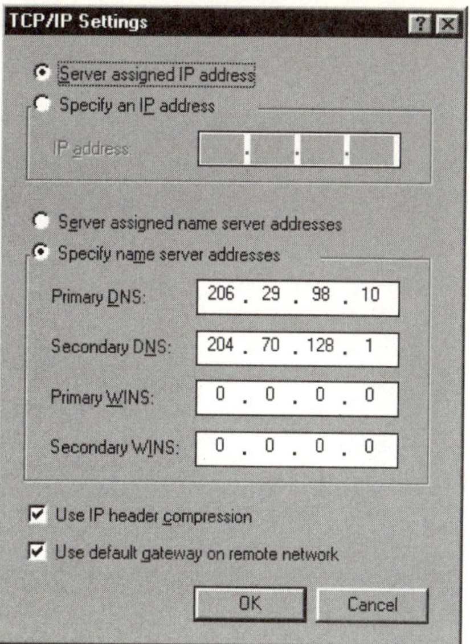

Figure 1-40: Completed TCP/IP settings for dynamically assigned IP addresses.

7. Click OK to return to the Server Types page, then OK again to return to the General tab.

There's one more step: you have to tell Dial-Up Networking to pop up a terminal window after you connect with your access provider. The terminal window allows you to interact with the host at the other end of the link, entering your name and password so that you can log on.

Here's how to set your new connection so that it pops up a terminal window when you connect:

1. Still in the General tab, click the Configure button. The connection properties dialog box appears, as shown in Figure 1-41.
2. Click the Options tab. A new dialog box appears.
3. Check the "Bring up terminal window after dialing" check box.
4. Click OK, then OK again to save your new connection properties.

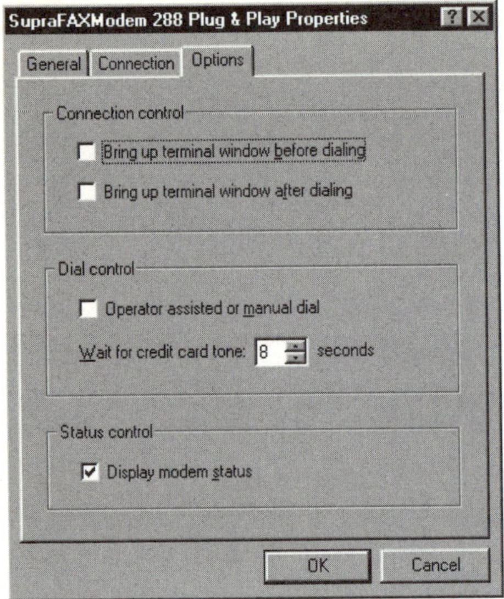

Figure 1-41: More properties for your new connection.

Congratulations! You've created and configured a new PPP or SLIP connection to the Internet. To get connected, just follow the instructions in the following section, "Getting On & Off the Net."

TIP

To get on and off the Net, you'll be accessing your new connection icon on a regular basis. You can simplify this process by creating a shortcut on your desktop. Simply press the Ctrl key and use your mouse to drag a copy of the icon from the Dial-Up Networking folder out to the desktop.

Getting On & Off the Net

This is the fun part. Now that you've gone through this admittedly tedious setup process, the Internet is only a few clicks away.

To log on to the Internet using your access provider:

1. Double-click the icon for your access provider in the Dial-Up Networking folder or on your desktop. The Connect To dialog box appears, as shown in Figure 1-42.

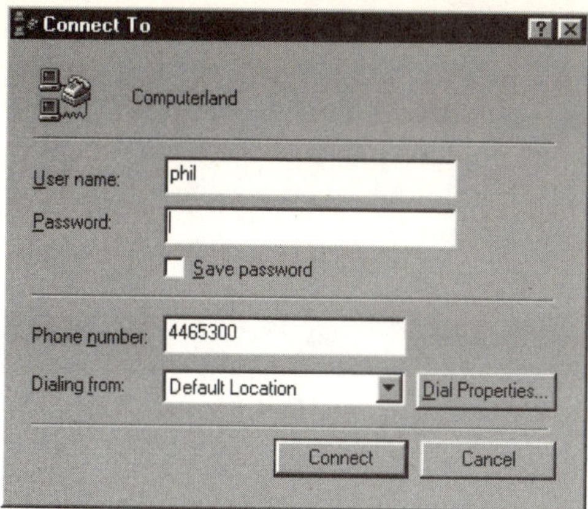

Figure 1-42: The Connect To dialog box.

2. Fill in the User name and Password fields for your Internet access account.

   Even though you'll type these in again after you establish your connection, you may need to do it here as well. This is because the information in these fields is used by some systems for a special kind of user authentication. In the case of some access providers, however, filling in your user ID and password in these fields won't do you any good. If you want, try connecting without filling in these fields and see if you can log on successfully.

   If you're calling from a different location than usual, you may want to reconfigure the Dial Properties by clicking the Dial Properties button.

3. Click Connect. The Connecting message box appears, and once your modem connection is established, the Post-Dial Terminal Screen pops up, as shown in Figure 1-43.

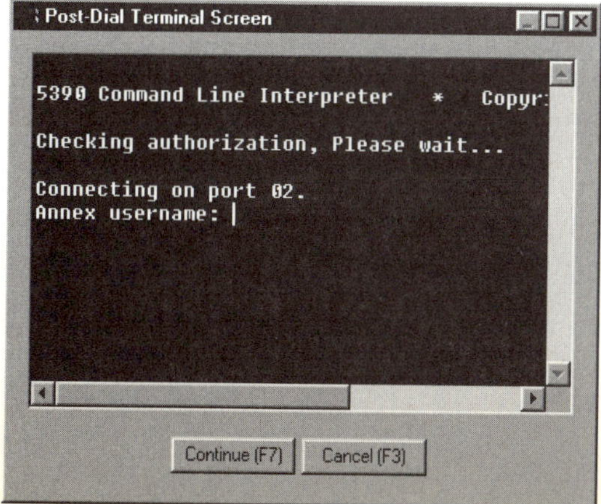

Figure 1-43: The Post-Dial Terminal Screen.

4. When prompted by the host system, type in your user ID, password, and any other information that is required. You may need detailed information from your access provider to get this right. If the host system assigns you an IP address at this point or presents you with other important information, be sure to jot it down! When you've completed the process, click the Continue button or press F7.

Logging On—The Hard Way & the Easy Way

Each time you call your Internet access provider, you need to enter a user ID and password before you're actually connected to the Net. There may be other prompts as well. In order to complete this login process, Windows 95 can be configured to bring up a terminal window that lets you interact with the host computer. If you do not do this, you probably won't be able to establish your link.

Wouldn't it be nice if the software took care of this for you, sending your user ID and password to the host computer as well as responding to other prompts at the appropriate times? Well, Windows 95 *can* do this—but not right out of the box. You have to add the *scripting tool* that's only on the CD version of Windows 95 (it installs along with the SLIP software). This is the way it works: you write a short text file (the script) telling the scripting facility what to do. Your script includes commands that tell the software what prompts to wait for, how to respond to the prompts, how long to pause at certain points, and so forth. When you call your access provider, the script starts running, and *presto!*—you're online without ever typing a thing.

Unfortunately, it's beyond the scope of this book to show you how to use the Windows 95 scripting facility, but if you want more information—OK, here comes a blatant authorial plug—take a look at my book *Internet Guide for Windows 95*, which covers this topic in detail. You might also be able to get a pre-written script file from your access provider.

If you are connecting to a system that dynamically assigns you a different IP address every time you log in, another dialog box may pop up asking you to verify or enter your IP address. Enter the IP address that you just jotted down and click OK to continue with the connection process.

After a few seconds, the Connected message box appears, as shown in Figure 1-44. You're on the Net, and you can now use Netscape Navigator 3.0 or just about *any* Windows Internet client programs for e-mail, Web-browsing, Telnet, or FTP.

Figure 1-44: The Connected message box.

As you might guess, breaking your Internet connection is even easier than establishing it. Look at the Connected message box in Figure 1-44. Let's see if you can figure out how to disconnect. Yep, you got it!

TIP

If you've installed Microsoft's Internet Startup Kit, or the Internet Jumpstart Kit on Microsoft Plus!, then by default, Dial-Up Networking runs automatically whenever you attempt to use Netscape Navigator 3.0 and are not already connected to the Net. This feature is called AutoDial, *and it means you don't ever really need to double-click the dial-up icon for your access provider in order to connect. In addition, your link to the Internet is broken automatically after 20 minutes of idle time. If you leave your machine in the middle of a long FTP file transfer, for instance, the transfer will be completed and then you will automatically be disconnected from the Net after 20 minutes.*

If you don't like AutoDial or want to change some of its settings, double-click the Internet icon in Control Panel and make your changes in the AutoDial tab.

Setting Up Your Macintosh for a SLIP or PPP Connection

Unless you are already using Mac System 7.5, which includes Apple's Open Transport, you will need a TCP/IP Open Transport layer. What is a TCP/IP layer? When you type a message into an e-mail program, for instance, it has to be formatted for transmission over the Net; in addition, it has to have an address attached so that it gets to the right destination. Conversely, incoming messages must have the addressing information stripped off and have to be reconstituted into something you can read. This process of packaging and unpackaging Internet information is the task of the Transmission Control Protocol/Internet Protocol (TCP/IP) layer.

If you're directly connected to the Internet via a LAN (AppleTalk or Ethernet), that's all you'll need. But to establish an active account with a SLIP or PPP service provider, you also need software that dials an access number and packages TCP/IP packets so that they can be sent out via modem. Fortunately, most TCP/IP software packages also include a dialer and SLIP or PPP features.

MacPPP is a Macintosh implementation of PPP, the Point-to-Point communications protocol which allows you to use TCP/IP applications over asynchronous serial lines. This means you can use Telnet, FTP, Gopher, and Wide Area Information Servers (WAIS) client servers, and other services directly from your Macintosh over conventional voice-grade telephone lines. FreePPP is the "official" successor to the earlier MacPPP which was developed at, and is copyrighted by, the Merit Network, Inc. and the University of Michigan. (These products are shareware, and are therefore readily available.) MacPPP requires MacTCP 1.1 or higher, Macintosh systems 6.0.5 or higher, and a Hayes-compatible modem for dial-in connections. FreePPP currently requires Color QuickDraw, which limits its use to 68020 or higher processors, and also requires System 7.1 or later Macintosh system software.

To use PPP on an earlier Macintosh, you'll need three packages: MacTCP, which is Apple's control panel device that provides a standard network interface for TCP/IP applications; MacPPP or a similar package; and software that supports MacTCP. You must also be dialing into a terminal server which supports PPP. If you have System 7.5, make certain you install 7.5.3 Update 2.0, which includes the latest version (as of this writing) of Open Transport 1.1. According to the developers, Netscape Navigator 3.0 will not work reliably with versions of Open Transport earlier than 1.1!

Let's assume that you've obtained the software we discussed earlier, and you'd like to get a few tips about getting it installed and connected to the Net. Let's start from the beginning, keeping in mind that individual steps may vary depending upon your specific hardware and software configuration:

1. Make sure you have obtained stable versions of MacTCP or Open Transport 1.1 (earlier releases of Open Transport are not stable with Netscape Navigator 3.0), and MacPPP 2.1.4 SD or FreePPP 1.0.5. Use a clean copy of MacTCP. MacTCP Updater 2.0.6 will patch a clean copy from your unused master diskettes, updating version 2.0.4 to 2.0.6. MacTCP Updater is free to licensed owners of MacTCP.

2. If you've already been using a version of MacTCP, go to your System folder and drag the MacTCP DNR file to the trash. Also, find MacTCP Prep and PPP Preferences in the Preferences folder, and drag them both to the trash. These files will be recreated for you automatically.

3. Drag your new PPP icon to the Extensions folder, and the ConfigPPP icon to the Control Panels folder, both of which should be in your System folder. Open the MacTCP control panel from the Apple menu, and configure it to use PPP by selecting the PPP icon and clicking on the More button. Select Server in the Obtain Address section of the dialog box, mark C in the Class box of the IP Address (leave the rest alone), then complete the Domain Name Server Information. The first domain name server should be your access provider's host, with its IP address. Mark this one as the default position. Click on the OK button and restart your Mac.
4. If you're using Open Transport 1.1, configure your system with FreePPP. Open the TCP/IP Control Panel and select PPP as the interface to use. Turn on the button marked Manually, and type in 0.0.0.0 for the IP Address assuming you will be assigned this number dynamically by your server. Subnet Mask and IP Router information will be filled in by the server. Then complete the Domain Name Server information. Click on the OK button and restart your Mac.

Now let's move on to configuring MacPPP or FreePPP so we can connect to the outside world! The following steps assume you are working with FreePPP, the more recent of the two shareware applications.

1. Make sure you have PPP in your Extensions folder. From the Control Panels folder, open Config PPP. Set Port Name to Modem Port, set Idle Timeout (minutes) to None, Set Echo Interval (seconds) to Off, check the Hangup on Close and Quiet Mode boxes. Make sure Terminal Window is *not* checked.
2. Choose the New button, and type in the name of your server. Click OK, then click Config. Set Port Speed to 57,600 for Global Village Teleport and US Robotics 28.8 bps modems. Set other 28.8 baud modems to 38,400 and 14.4 baud modems to 19,200. Flow Control should probably be set to CTS only. Select Tone Dial, type in the access telephone number assigned you by your provider, and set the modem initialization string to whatever your modem manufacturer recommends. Modem connect timeout should be set at 90 seconds. Next, click on Connect Script and enter a login script.

3. Wait Timeout should be set for 30 or 40 seconds. Your login script should look similar to this:

(*)	Out	( )	Wait		[X]
( )	Out	(*)	Wait	gin:	[ ]
(*)	Out	( )	Wait	[your username]	[X]
( )	Out	(*)	Wait	word:	[ ]
(*)	Out	( )	Wait	[your password]	[X]
(*)	Out	( )	Wait		[ ]
(*)	Out	( )	Wait		[ ]
(*)	Out	( )	Wait		[ ]

4. Click on OK, and then on Authentication. If you enter your username and password here, you may let your Macintosh automatically connect you to your server whenever Netscape Navigator 3.0 launches. You may want, on the other hand, to leave these items blank, in which case you will need to enter your username and password each time. This is a security decision you have to make, depending upon whether it is likely or not that others may have indiscriminate access to your system. (I have set my system on "automatic pilot" because I work at home. Others might not be as comfortable as I am with this approach.)
5. Now go to the Control Panels, open Config PPP, make sure you have selected the correct PPP server, and click on Open. At this point, the Open button should be darkened and the words PPP DOWN should be displayed in the upper-left corner of the Config PPP dialog box. If not, make sure that all your fax extensions are turned off, that there is no other program using your modem, and the modem is not set at a speed higher than its capability.
6. Click on the darkened Open button. The modem will dial out and make a connection. You may see various intervening messages on the screen, indicating what progress is being made. These messages will vary depending upon your access provider's creativity and ingenuity; Macintosh users are accustomed to seeing smiling faces. Therefore, once the connection has been made, the two faces in the upper-left corner of the dialog box will be smiling. So will you! To disconnect, be sure to click on Close.
7. Test your connection with something simple, that is, if you can wait to launch Netscape Navigator 3.0.

For more information about connecting your Mac to the Internet, see the Netscape Press online companion at http://www.netscapepress.com/. Once you have finished installing and configuring MacTCP and MacPPP on your system, your dial-in sessions will be handled automatically. You will simply click on the Open button on MacPPP's Config PPP Control Panel (Netscape Navigator 3.0 will do this for you) and your modem will dial and connect automatically.

Installing Netscape Navigator 3.0

If you have already installed Netscape Navigator 3.0 as a part of your ISP installation, you can skip this section. Or if you want to install a copy of the software you have downloaded from the Internet, make sure to carefully follow the instructions included with the program. Remember, Readme files are our friends.

After all that Windows 95 and Macintosh configuration, this is going to be a breeze. Let's get right down to business:

1. Insert the CD at the back of this book into your CD-ROM drive.
2. Select Run from the Windows 95 Start menu or the Windows 3.1x File menu. In the Run dialog box that appears, type **D:\LAUNCHME**, where **D:** is the drive name of your CD-ROM. For instance, if your CD-ROM drive is E, type **E:\LAUNCHME**.

   If you are using Windows 95 and have Auto Start enabled, the main window may appear automatically when you put the CD in; in that case you do not need to follow step 2 above.

   After a few seconds, the *Book* screen appears. There are several buttons along the left side of the window. Most of these offer you more information about Netscape Press as well as other titles by Ventana. You should take some time to browse this information, but for now:
3. Click the Software button.

In case the CD has changed slightly since this book went to press, you should follow any instructions that appear for installing Netscape Navigator 3.0. The next few steps, however, describe the general process:

1. If you are using Windows 95 or Windows NT, use your mouse to select the Windows 95 version of the program. If you are using Windows 3.1, make sure to select the Windows 3.1 version.

TIP

If you are using Windows 95 or Windows NT but want to continue accessing the Internet with a 16-bit TCP/IP stack such as Trumpet, you must *install the Windows 3.1 version of Netscape Navigator 3.0. The Windows 95 version will only work with a 32-bit TCP/IP stack.*

2. Once you have selected the proper version, be sure to read any Readme files. Again, follow the on-screen instructions for installing the program. Move your mouse cursor over the correct setup or installation file in either the Windows 95 or Windows 3.1 folder, depending on your system. A separate window displays information about the file.
3. Once you have chosen the proper installation file, simply click the Launch Installer button to begin the process. After a few moments an Install Wizard appears.
4. Read the Welcome message and then click Next. The Choose Destination Location dialog box appears, as shown in Figure 1-45.

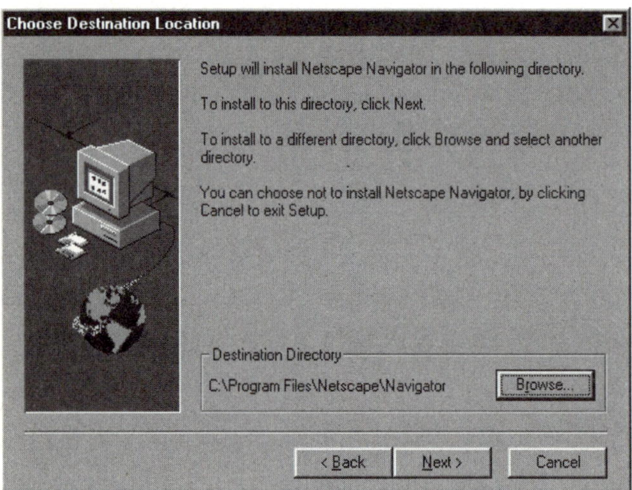

Figure 1-45: The Choose Destination Location dialog box.

5. If you want to change the drive or directory where Netscape Navigator 3.0 is stored, click the Browse button and choose a new destination directory. In most cases, you should leave this dialog box as it is and simply click Next. A new dialog box appears asking you if you want to install CoolTalk. If you do, check the Yes checkbox and click Next.

TIP

CoolTalk is a pretty amazing new Netscape Navigator feature that lets you use your Internet or intranet connection like a phone line, actually talking to other users by means of your computer's microphone and sound card. It also allows for chat (typing messages back and forth) and collaborative work via a special electronic "white board." It requires at least a 486 machine and 8MB of RAM. To use its phone features, you also need a sound card and microphone. If you have the proper hardware, I highly recommend installing this option.

6. Once you click Next, a new setup window appears, as shown in Figure 1-46.

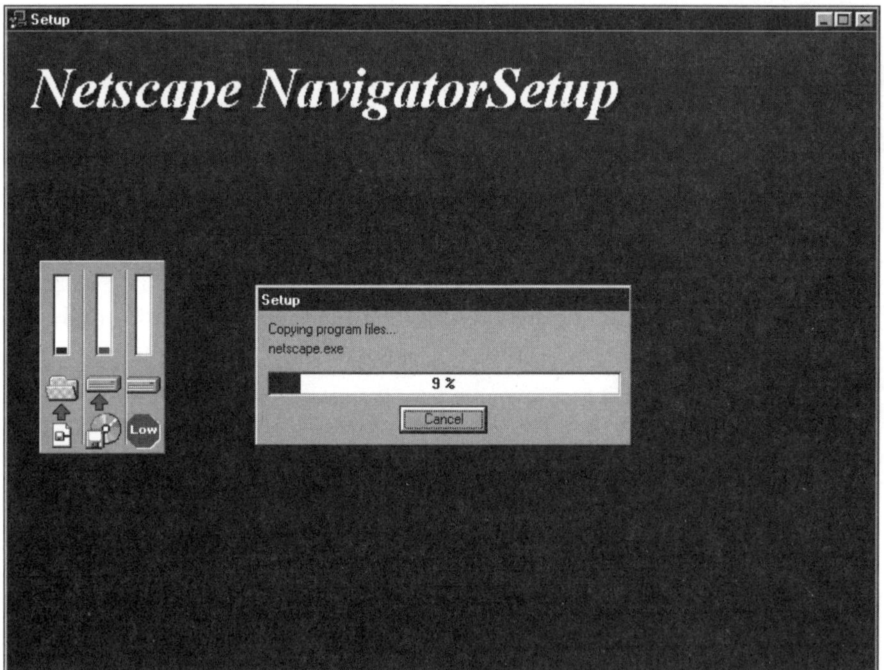

Figure 1-46: The Netscape Navigator Setup window.

This window could use a little explaining. First of all, the Setup progress bar right in the middle indicates the install program's progress as it copies files to the destination directory. On the left side of the window, another control gives you more detailed information about when the program is extracting files, when it is copying them from the CD-ROM, and how much space you have on your drive.

CoolTalk Watchdog

Toward the end of the installation process you will be asked if you want to install CoolTalk Watchdog. And since that's not a question you get asked every day, you might not know how to answer. Here's the deal:

You already know a little about CoolTalk itself. The CoolTalk Watchdog is a special supplemental program that sits around and waits for a call to come in from some other CoolTalk user. At that point it wakes up and barks loudly. No, not really. It simply launches CoolTalk so that you can establish communications with the remote user. With the low-memory Watchdog program installed, you don't have to have CoolTalk running at all times just in case a call comes in.

If you specify you want CoolTalk Watchdog installed, the Netscape Navigator 3.0 installation program places a shortcut to Watchdog in your Startup folder. That means that as long as Windows is running, Watchdog is running. Obviously it doesn't make much sense to have CoolTalk Watchdog sitting around waiting if you don't have a permanent connection to the Net or to an intranet, so if you're a SLIP/PPP user you may not want to bother with this.

Once the program files have been installed, a dialog box pops up, asking if you want to connect to the Netscape Setup site to continue.

To register your copy of Navigator, click Yes. After filling out a short questionnaire, you'll receive your registration number. But for this to work, a few things have to be in order:

- You must currently be connected to the Internet via a direct connection or a SLIP or PPP connection to your access provider.
- Or, your Internet access software must be configured so that it dials your access provider automatically when you launch an Internet program. (Remember the discussion of AutoDial back in the section on Windows 95 setup?)

If you are not currently connected to the Internet and you do not have an automatic dialing feature installed, then you must click No in this dialog box. (Don't worry, you won't be missing much!)

Assuming you click Yes, you're on your own for a while. All you have to do is follow the instructions that appear. If you can't figure out how to move around at all in the program, you might skim the first few pages of Chapter 3, "A Quick Look Around." And if you get completely disoriented, don't worry: just click the Home button and join the rest of the class in the section called "Configuring Netscape Navigator 3.0."

TIP

By going through the Netscape online registration process, you will automatically receive what is known as a digital ID *or* digital certificate. *This is a unique software key that Netscape Navigator 3.0 can use to identify you to secure Web servers. A digital ID will enable an online bank, for instance, to verify that you are really you—or at least that they're dealing with somebody who's sitting at your machine!*

Whether you click Yes or No, another dialog box appears asking you if you want to read the Readme file. Demographic studies have shown that only intelligent people buy my books, so I'm not going to remind you how important it is to read the Readme file right away. I won't even bother telling you that Readme files often contain crucial, last-minute information, information that can mean the difference between pleasant, trouble-free navigating and late-night wrestling matches with the software.

Once you're done reading the Readme file, one last information box pops up letting you know the setup process is complete. Simply click OK and the installation program exits. There is now a new Navigator folder or program group on your desktop. It contains Netscape Navigator 3.0 itself as well as CoolTalk and a Readme file, as shown in Figure 1-47.

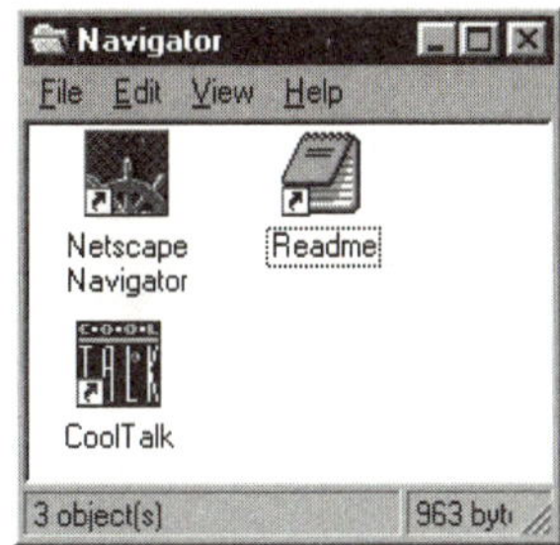

Figure 1-47: The Navigator folder.

TIP

If you are using Windows 95 or Windows NT 4.0, the Setup program also creates Navigator and CoolTalk shortcuts right on the desktop.

Okay, on to configuring Netscape Navigator 3.0. Even if you worked through Netscape's own online setup instructions, you should still read the next section to check your configuration and gain a better understanding of some of the options.

Configuring Netscape Navigator 3.0

Once it's installed, Netscape Navigator 3.0 needs very little configuration. Most of the default options will work just fine for you, and there are only a few dialog boxes where you have to enter specific information in order to activate a particular feature. For instance, you have to enter your e-mail address in order for e-mail to work.

Most of the configuration options are covered in detail in the appropriate chapters of this book, but for now let's take a quick look around in case you want to start customizing the program on your own. To look at the configuration options:

1. Make sure you are connected to the Internet, either directly or through a SLIP or PPP connection with your access provider. If you are using SLIP or PPP and are not currently connected, double-click the Dial-Up Connection icon for your access provider.

   If you have AutoDial turned on, you can skip this step. Windows 95 will attempt to connect to your access provider after you launch the program.

   If you are using Windows 3.1 rather than Windows 95, or if you are using Windows 95's built-in networking, follow the instructions that came with your TCP/IP software for accessing the Internet.

2. Double-click the Netscape Navigator 3.0 icon to launch the program. The main window appears, and the Netscape home page starts loading, as shown in Figure 1-48.

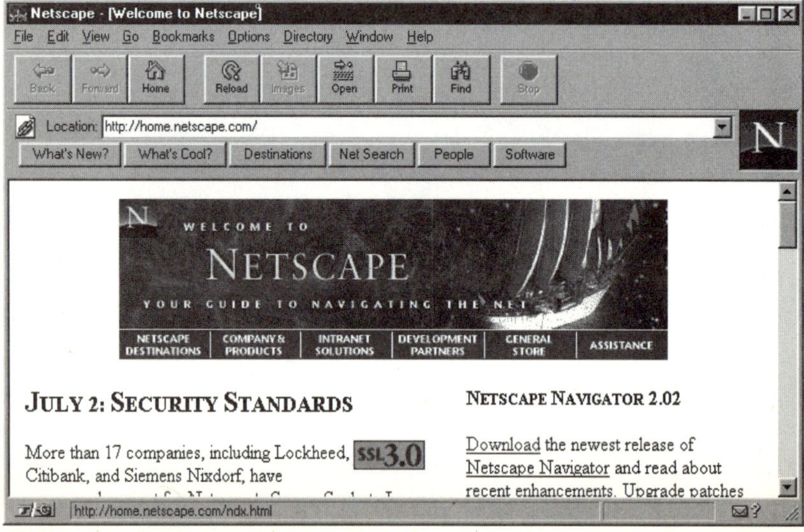

Figure 1-48: The Netscape home page.

That colorful Netscape page probably makes you eager to start exploring right away, but hold on—that's coming up in Chapter 3, "A Quick Look Around."

3. Click the Options menu. The menu drops down, as shown in Figure 1-49.

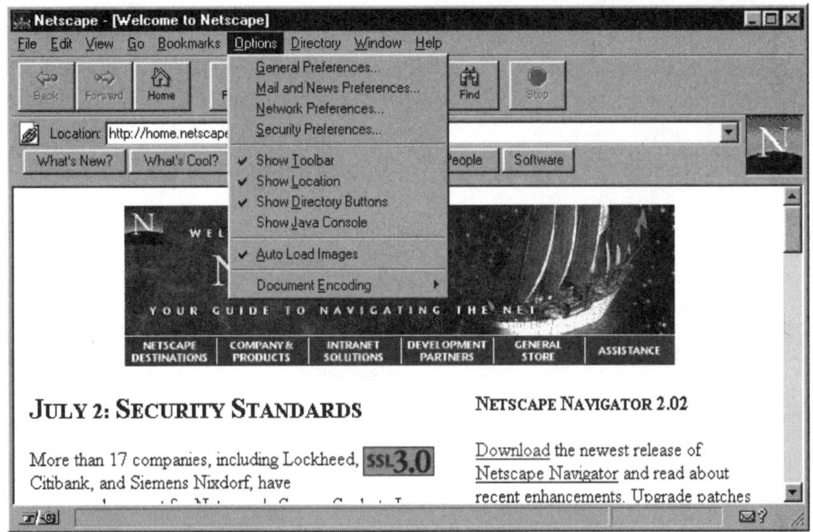

Figure 1-49: The Options menu.

Adjusting Navigator's Look & Feel

In the second section of the Options menu are several "checkmark" items, or toggles. When these items are checked, they are active; when unchecked, they are inactive. Most of them have to do with user interface objects that are displayed in the main Netscape Navigator 3.0 window. Later on, when you get more familiar with the program, you may not need all of the "window dressing." You can play around with these items to see what works best for the way you use the program. But for now leave them alone, or set them back to the default settings after trying them out. That way your screen will look pretty much like the illustrations in this book.

In the top section of the Options menu there are four items representing different areas of Netscape Navigator 3.0 that can be customized: General Preferences, Mail and News Preferences, Network Preferences, and Security Preferences. The Mail and News settings are covered in Chapters 4, "Netscape Mail," and 5, "Newsgroups," respectively. We won't bother looking at those options right now, but let's glance at the General Preferences options so you get a sense of what kind of customization is possible in Netscape Navigator 3.0.

General Preferences

To access the General Preferences, select General Preferences from the Options menu, shown earlier in Figure 1-49. The Preferences dialog box appears, with the Appearance tab selected as shown in Figure 1-50. If that tab isn't selected, click it now.

Now we'll go very quickly through each of the tabs, pointing out where you can get more information on each one.

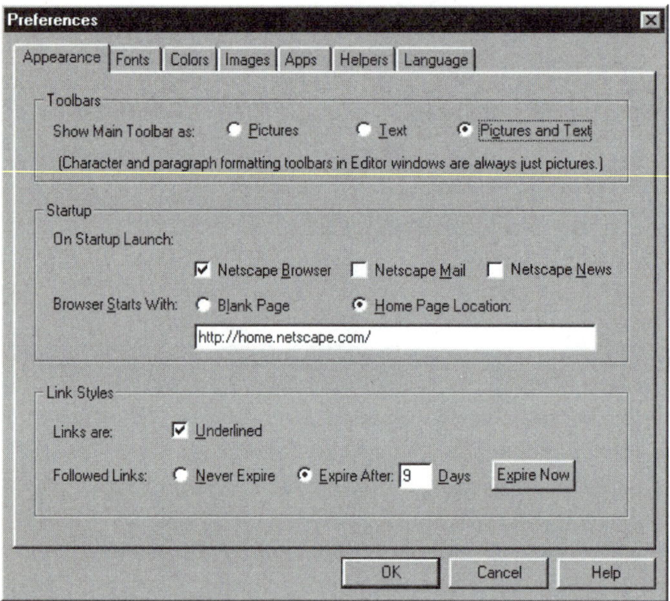

Figure 1-50: The Appearance tab.

Appearance

In the Appearance tab you can make several choices that determine how Netscape Navigator 3.0 will look on your screen:

- You can choose whether the toolbar buttons will be displayed as Pictures, Text, or Pictures and Text. The default is Pictures and Text, but you can change this to one of the other options if you find the text annoying, or the pictures too busy.

- You can choose to have Netscape Navigator 3.0 start with the Mail or News window displayed instead of the usual browser window. This may be useful if you use Navigator principally for e-mail or Usenet news rather than Web browsing (see Chapter 4, "Netscape Mail," and Chapter 5, "Newsgroups").
- You can choose which Web document, if any, Netscape Navigator 3.0 displays when you launch the program. The default is the Netscape home page, located at the Netscape site. In Chapter 3, "A Quick Look Around," we'll talk about why you might want to change this.
- As you'll learn later, Web documents contain links to other documents. You have to be able to recognize these links, and Netscape Navigator 3.0 lets you choose whether or not they should be underlined so that you recognize them more easily.
- Once you've clicked on a link to access a new document, or a new section of the current document, the link changes color to indicate that you've used it. The Appearance tab lets you choose how long the link will stay this new color. More about this in Chapter 3, "A Quick Look Around."

Fonts

The Fonts tab lets you associate incoming data with particular display fonts. In the United States, just about all the Web information you receive will be in the ISO-Latin-1 character set, and this character set will be displayed using the default Times New Roman and Courier New fonts. However, you can change these fonts if you want.

Colors

The Colors tab lets you change the default colors for text and links that are displayed in Netscape Navigator 3.0. In addition, it lets you specify a new background color, or even a .GIF file for the display background. You can also decide here whether or not you want Netscape Navigator 3.0 always to use these colors rather than responding to the special color requests in Web documents.

Images

The Images tab, shown in Figure 1-51, lets you specify how images are displayed. In most cases you should leave these settings alone, but on fast network connections you might want to click the While Loading radio button to display images a little quicker. More about these settings in Chapter 8, "Graphics, Sound & Video."

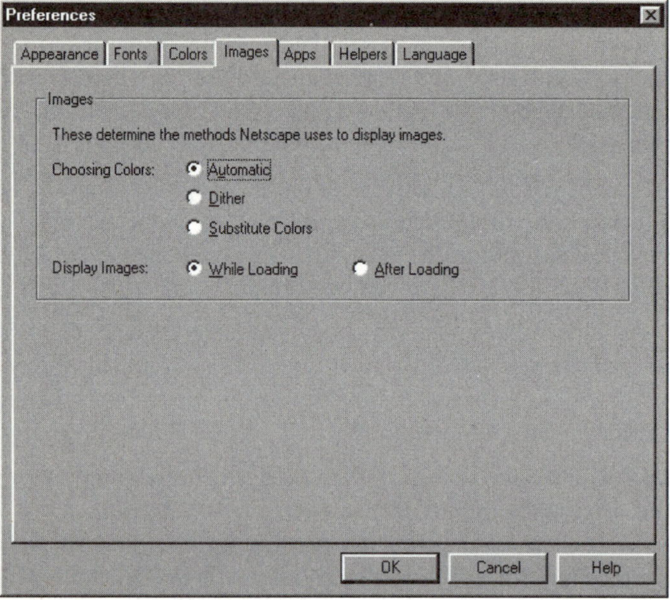

Figure 1-51: The Images tab.

Apps

To access Telnet resources, Netscape Navigator 3.0 can launch a separate application anywhere on your hard drive. This allows you the maximum flexibility in connecting to sites via Telnet or TN3270 (please see Chapter 7, "Gopher & Telnet," if you don't know what I'm talking about). The Apps tab lets you choose what applications to use. In addition, it lets you specify an external text viewer or editor to look at the source HTML code of Web documents you view, and you can even choose the work directory Netscape Navigator 3.0 uses to store temporary files.

Helpers

Helper applications are separate programs on your system that handle particular tasks for Netscape Navigator 3.0. For instance, a helper application might play a sound that's included in a Web document, or display a video clip. When Netscape Navigator 3.0 encounters particular kinds of files that are part of Web documents, it launches the appropriate helper applications. You will read lots more about helper applications and this tab in Chapters 7, 8, and 9.

Language

In the Language tab you can specify which languages you want Navigator 3.0 to accept from a Web server. Let's say you access a site that includes versions of the lyrics to "Louie, Louie" in Chinese, Dutch, and Swedish. You could view the Chinese lyrics if you've specified Chinese in the Accept List of this tab. As for the "User define" field, that's where some of us have added Klingon.

Cache Settings

Okay, bear with me for a few minutes, we're going to get a little bit technical. It won't hurt too much, and it's for your own good. (Do you ever *really* believe it when people tell you that?) If you're not too worried about performance right now, you can just skip the rest of this chapter and come back here later. But if you want to make sure Netscape Navigator 3.0 is operating as efficiently as possible—and this can be important when you're paying for Internet access on an hourly basis—read on.

A *cache* (pronounced "cash") is a reserve area on your computer that houses information downloaded from the Internet as you navigate. You can think of it as a temporary holding area that Netscape Navigator 3.0 uses to store data between the time it is downloaded and the time it is displayed. If your cache is large enough, it can store entire Web pages and even graphics. That way, when you return to a previously visited site, Netscape Navigator 3.0 doesn't have to download the information all over again; it can simply grab it from the cache.

There are actually two caches, a memory cache and a hard disk cache. The memory cache holds text and graphics only as long as you run Netscape Navigator 3.0. The hard disk cache, on the other hand, is persistent: it holds information even after you exit the program. That way you can retrieve large documents quickly, without having to re-download them from the original site on the Net.

TIP

The Netscape Navigator 3.0 Refresh command (available from the View menu) redisplays the current document using information stored in the cache. The Reload button, on the other hand, actually goes back to the original document, checks to see if it has changed since the last time you accessed it, and then reloads it from the Internet if there are any changes. So if you think that a document may have changed since the last time you visited it during the current session, you should use the Reload button to view any updates.

There are advantages and disadvantages in setting high cache sizes for both types of caches. Even though memory caches are much quicker than disk caches, devoting more RAM to this type of cache can slow down your computer's overall performance. On the other hand, higher disk cache settings eat up your hard disk space.

Follow these steps to change your settings for cache sizes:

1. Select Network Preferences from the Netscape Navigator 3.0 Options menu. Click the Cache tab, shown in Figure 1-52.

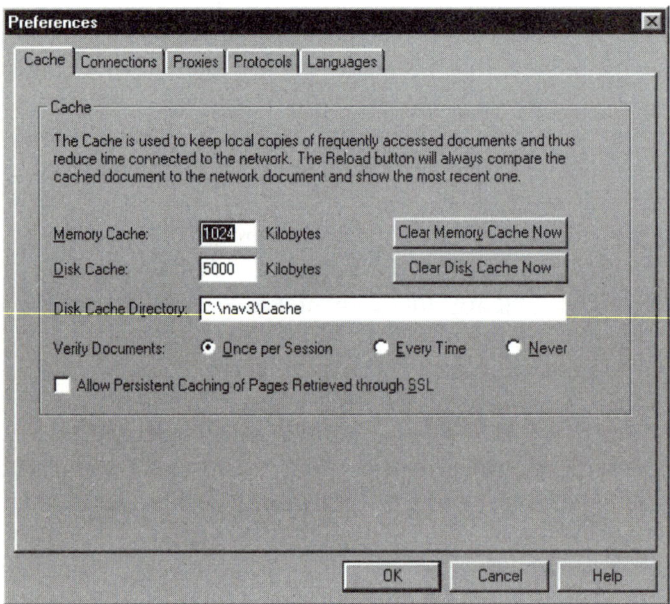

Figure 1-52: The Cache tab.

2. You can set the size of the memory cache in the Memory Cache field. The default setting is 1024K of RAM (about 1MB of memory). Unless you have a large amount of memory on your system, such as 16MB or more, you may want to keep this setting where it is. Otherwise, you can try setting it at 1200K to see if your browsing speeds increase.

3. Set the amount of hard disk space that you want to reserve for a disk cache. This value is entered in the Disk Cache field; its default is set to 5000K (5MB) of hard disk space. On most newer computers that come with hard disks of 450MB or more, you should have no problem reserving 5MB or even 10MB for this cache.

TIP

Experiment with both the memory cache and hard disk cache sizes to determine the best settings for your system. If you tend to use Netscape Navigator 3.0 without other applications running at the same time, such as a word processor or spreadsheet, you can set the memory cache much higher to make Netscape Navigator 3.0 run quicker. If you generally run Netscape Navigator 3.0 with other applications that need large amounts of memory, keep the memory cache low, around 600K. This ensures that each application has ample RAM to run properly.

4. You can change the directory or folder in which Netscape Navigator 3.0 stores the cached items to disk by entering the name in the Disk Cache Directory field. By default, Netscape Navigator 3.0 creates a directory called CACHE in the Netscape Navigator 3.0 folder. Unless you have specific reasons for changing it, this location should be fine.
5. To clear the current content from your disk or memory caches, click Clear Memory Cache Now or Clear Disk Cache Now. When you click either of these buttons, a confirmation box pops up, asking if you are sure you want to clear the selected cache. Click OK to confirm that you do; click Cancel if you change your mind.

Why Would I Want to Clear a Cache?

Depending on how much navigating you do or how often you visit a site, you may want to periodically clear a cache setting. Having a cache decreases the time it takes to access sites that you've recently visited, but it does increase the strain on your local computer. When your memory cache is set to a high value, the amount of memory devoted to Netscape Navigator 3.0 cannot be used by other resources. This slows down your machine when you run these other applications. Also, you may want to clear the memory cache if you've been online for several hours and you feel your machine responding sluggishly to Netscape Navigator 3.0. After you clear the cache, you should notice an improvement in your PC's performance.

6. Click one of the radio buttons in the Verify Documents section. If a document stored in the cache has been revised, you'll want to see the revision instead of the old document. These buttons specify how Netscape Navigator 3.0 checks the Web for document revisions:
   - **Once per Session.** Checks for page revisions only once during the time you start and quit Netscape Navigator 3.0. This is the default setting.
   - **Every Time.** Checks for changes each time you request a Web document rather than relying on data stored in the cache. Because Netscape Navigator 3.0 is constantly checking the cached item against the Web page, you encounter a little performance degradation when you use this option.
   - **Never.** Performs no verifications; a page available in cache is always brought from cache. Not a good selection if you want to see the latest—and greatest—offerings at a particular Web site.
7. You can ignore the "Allow Persistent Caching of Pages Retrieved through SSL" option.
8. Click OK to return to the main Netscape Navigator 3.0 window.

Setting Network Connections

One way to speed up a connection to a site is to increase the number of connections to a specific server (a server is the computer that houses the Web page). With more than one connection to a server, Netscape Navigator 3.0 can bring in a page's text and multiple image files simultaneously. You can set this by clicking the Connections tab after selecting Network Preferences from the Options menu. By specifying a larger number of connections in the Number of Connections field (4 is the default), you are specifying more simultaneous connections. However, doing so can slow down the speed of each individual connection.

The other setting in this tab is the Network Buffer Size value. You can set the amount of data that your computer receives per transmission. The default is 32K. Larger values may speed things up, but they may also allow so much data through that your computer becomes saturated. This means it may slow down instead of speeding up. Unless you really know what you are doing, you should leave this setting as it is.

When you're done looking through the Network Preferences tabs, simply click the Cancel button to return to the main Netscape Navigator 3.0 window. Now you can either exit the program or get busy exploring the Net. I know which I'd do!

Moving On

By now you know how to get on and off the Internet, and you have Netscape Navigator 3.0 installed on your computer. Netscape Navigator 3.0 is so easy to use that I'd be surprised if you have any trouble at all cruising around and discovering exciting new resources on the Net.

In the next chapter, you'll learn all the basics of using Netscape Navigator 3.0 effectively, and subsequent chapters will show you how to take advantage of some of the program's most powerful features. Before you know it, you'll be a seasoned Net explorer, cruising from newsgroups to file archives to hypermedia Web sites with a few easy clicks of the mouse.

The Net & the Web

Internet. World Wide Web. Just about everywhere you go these days you overhear somebody using these words. And not just the words themselves, but dozens of phrases derived from them. If you paid attention to the mass media hype, you'd think that most people spend a significant portion of their time "cruising the Net," or "checking out Web sites," or even "surfing cyberspace" (now *there's* a mixed metaphor to make your old English professor cringe).

As with most new technologies, jargon precedes popular understanding. New terminology makes it possible to explore new ideas, but it also exacerbates the epidemic of Geek Answer Syndrome. There is no shortage of people who will blab on authoritatively but incorrectly about anything to do with information technology, flashing their vocabularies like bright plumage. Well now you can tell them to take a walk, because in the next few minutes we'll make sure that you *really* understand what the Net is, what the Web is, and how you can use these exciting new resources. By the time you've finished this chapter you won't be a cybergeek, but you'll be able to answer these questions and probably more:

- Just what *is* the Internet? How did it start? How did it evolve?
- What kinds of services and information are available on the Net?
- How does Internet addressing work?
- What is the World Wide Web? How is it related to the Net?

- What is hypertext? How about hypermedia?
- How does Netscape Navigator give you access to the Web and the rest of the Net?
- Are there any general guidelines for using the Internet?

Enterprise Netscaping

This book concentrates on using Netscape Navigator 3.0 to cruise around the Internet, but there are other ways you can harness its power. For instance, if your office is on a local area network (LAN), you can use Netscape Navigator 3.0 to share multimedia information among employees. You might want to create a colorful tutorial for coworkers, or your personnel department might want to enliven the company expense regulations with songs and animation. Everybody connected to the network could then view these multimedia files using Netscape Navigator 3.0. In addition, you could use Netscape Navigator 3.0 as a front end for accessing *any* kind of files, not just multimedia ones. You can even use Netscape Navigator 3.0 for your company e-mail. Throughout this book I'll include occasional sidebars that point out interesting uses for Netscape Navigator 3.0 on enterprise-wide *intranets*. In essence, an intranet is an internal Web site that can't be accessed from the outside world, but can be reached from within the organization.

What Is the Internet?

It's really a lot simpler than you'd guess. A network is a collection of computers connected together so they can share information, and the Internet is a network of networks. It lets individuals on one network share information with users on another network that may be thousands of miles away. The shared information can take many forms. For instance, you can use the Internet to send e-mail messages, or to download files, or to view video clips, or to listen to music. You can receive the same quality of news reporting you'd find on any TV network. You can even use the Net for banking and shopping. It's a lot like the phone system, except that instead of just talking, you can exchange all kinds of information.

The physical Internet looks like a vast net of wires. A few high-speed "backbone" cables branch out into other cables, which in turn radiate outward into finer strands. Most of the developed areas of the world have already been wired, so by routing your information or requests through this vast system, you can reach other Internet users all over the world. Fortunately, the routing happens automatically, just as it does with telephone calls, so you don't need to know *how* data gets from your computer to a computer in Timbuktu.

And the system is democratic. Anyone can use it. You don't even need to have your own network in order to connect—you can communicate using the current infrastructure by plugging into somebody else's network. Maybe you're already doing this. If you have a Serial Line Internet Protocol (SLIP) or Point-to-Point Protocol (PPP) account (see Chapter 1, "Getting Started"), you simply connect via modem and phone line to your access provider's network site (known as a "point of presence"). The actual transmission of data is free, but you'll probably need to pay the access provider for the time you spend accessing its equipment.

There are hundreds of thousands of users sitting at their PCs right now, gathering information from far-flung reaches of the globe. Pretty soon the Internet will be accepted as a simple fact of modern life, and people will forget how it originated.

Origins of the Internet

I'm not going to cover the Internet's history with any depth. There are other books, even a couple of mine, that cover the topic in more detail. But it may be useful for you to have a little background. If you really don't care about the history, just skip this section. On the other hand, if you want to be the hit of the next propeller-head party you attend, memorize the following four paragraphs:

As with many technological advances, the Internet began as a military research project. It was the early 1970s, a time full of menace to civilization as we knew it: muscle cars, leisure suits, wide ties, platform shoes, and the threat of nuclear war. The U.S. Defense Department implemented a network, called ARPAnet, that was designed so that even if part of its physical structure were destroyed, information could still be sent to any remaining destination.

In the early 1980s, LANs at a variety of research institutions started hooking into ARPAnet. They were able to do this by using the same underlying technology that ARPAnet used to transfer data and make sure it got to the right place.

Then in the late 1980s, the National Science Foundation (NSF) established five supercomputer centers and connected them via its own network, NSFnet. Based on the same technology as ARPAnet, the sites were physically linked by special phone lines. Since the phone companies charged by the mile for these lines, it was very expensive to gather information from one of these centers. The NSF decided to create several regional networks with dozens of connected sites; any data could be passed along the line from one node to another, saving on the costly line charges.

The rest of the Internet's history is one of expansion. As new educational institutions and government agencies developed their own networks and joined NSFnet, the original wiring quickly became overloaded. Much faster lines were put in, faster computers were installed, and what is now known as the Internet opened its virtual doors to most of the academic and government community. Universities from other nations, not to mention foreign governments, started joining the Net. In the early 1990s, commercial organizations began to jump on board, and it is now common for companies to promote and sell all sorts of products and services over the Net.

The latest trend on the Internet is the rapid growth of personal information, with individuals making available all sorts of things they'd like to share with the world. I can almost guarantee you that somebody you know has a poem out on the Net, and that another friend has provided humanity with a picture of a favorite pet cat. And of course you can access all of this stuff with Netscape Navigator 3.0. Andy Warhol predicted a time when everyone in the world would enjoy 15 minutes of fame. That hasn't quite happened, but we are fast approaching a time when everybody can enjoy 15 *kilobytes* of fame.

What Is Out There

What services does the Internet actually provide the average user right now? Let's take a slightly deeper look at a few that can have a real impact on your life.

Electronic Mail

Thanks to the Internet, you can send messages to just about anybody who has a computer and a network connection or a modem. If the individual you want to contact is not directly on the Net, you can use Netscape Navigator 3.0 to send a message to him or her on one of the popular online services such as CompuServe or America Online.

There are a number of advantages to sending messages via e-mail instead of the U.S. Postal Service (known affectionately as "snail mail" by e-mail advocates). First of all, there's the speed. It may take only seconds for your message to reach somebody on the other side of the world. The recipient can read your text immediately on the screen, respond to it right away, save it for later, print it out, or quickly forward it to somebody else. You can create electronic mailing lists for sending notices to hundreds or even thousands of people at once. Messages you receive can be organized into convenient electronic folders and saved for as long as you want without taking up any office space. And with e-mail, it's possible to verify very quickly that your message has indeed arrived at its destination. Because of these advantages, and several others that you'll learn about in Chapter 4, "Netscape Mail," e-mail has become my principal means of communicating with the world. I receive several dozen e-mail messages a day and send about as many. In several months I generate more messages than all the old-fashioned paper letters I've written in my life!

Netscape Navigator 3.0 includes full-featured e-mail support, and Figure 2-1 shows what its main Mail window looks like.

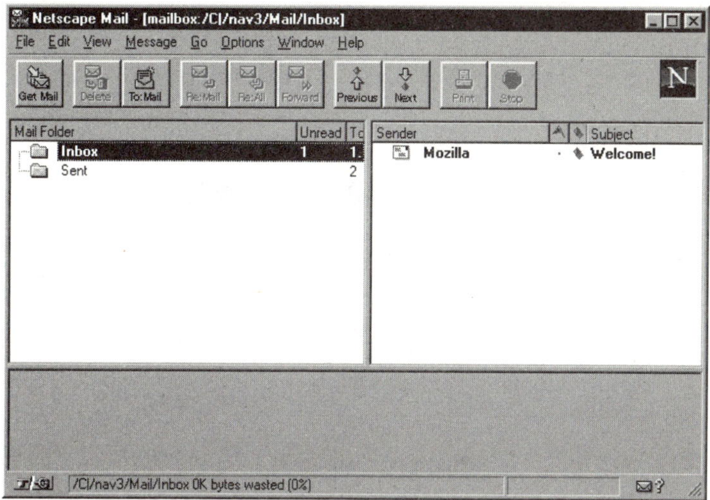

Figure 2-1: E-mail in Netscape Navigator 3.0.

Research

Locating specific information used to be a tedious and time-consuming process. Remember digging through library card catalogs and then wandering through dusty stacks of books, only to discover that what you needed wasn't even at that library? Now finding references to topics can be as simple as typing in a keyword and clicking a button—from the privacy of your own home! The Internet includes entire libraries of specialized information, and thousands of these are accessible, free of charge, to the general public.

The Internet also supports a variety of research techniques and styles. Suppose you're trying to come up with a topic for a speech you have to deliver. At first you might want to browse a variety of materials to refine your subject area. This process is much like going to an area in a library and starting to pull books off the shelf, except that on the Internet you can leap from library to library, following associative links or trains of thought. Once you've determined the exact subject of your speech, you may need to track down some very specific information, such as statistics to back up a particular point. (Statistics always make it sound like you know what you're talking about, don't they?) Once again there are Internet services that will help you; powerful search tools that will scurry around the Net and quickly find your needle in the information haystack. Netscape Navigator 3.0 gives you access to these tools through the Net Search feature on the Netscape home page, shown in Figure 2-2. If that isn't easy enough, a number of programs have recently appeared on the market that will automatically connect to these popular search engines, research the topic you've specified, and allow you to jump right to relevant Web pages and resources.

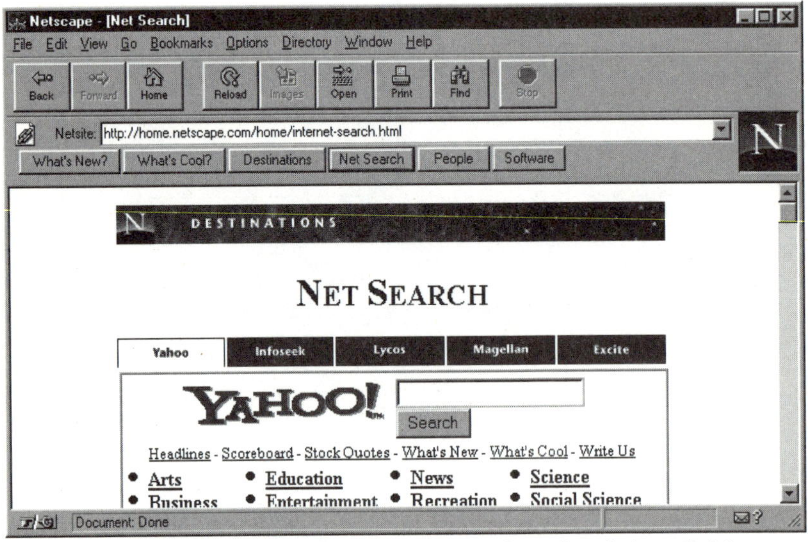

Figure 2-2: Net Search gives you access to a variety of search tools from the Netscape home page.

Under the Hood: TCP/IP

You can probably get through life just fine without understanding the technical underpinnings of the Net. But if you like the nuts and bolts stuff, boy have I got a sidebar for you!

TCP/IP really means "the TCP/IP protocol suite." It is a group of protocols that allows data to be transmitted correctly from one machine to another over the Net. And what exactly is a protocol? It's simply a set of standardized conventions for communication. In the human world, a typical protocol is saying "Your Honor" when you talk to a judge. In the world of data communications, a protocol might require that a sending machine include a special string of characters before and after every chunk of data so that the receiving machine can determine where that data begins and ends.

The TCP part of TCP/IP stands for *Transmission Control Protocol.* It divides any information you send into manageable blocks; conversely, it reconstructs received blocks into a stream of information. TCP does not require that all the blocks be received in the right sequence, since it attaches sequence numbers for reassembly. TCP also includes error checking; if blocks are missing or garbled, it requests that they be resent. When you run Internet applications, you remain blissfully unaware of all of this activity, since the TCP software layer "sits below" the application software. Information is passed from the application software to TCP without any human intervention; at the other end, reassembled information is passed *from* TCP to the appropriate software program.

The IP part of TCP/IP stands for *Internet Protocol.* The Internet Protocol is the real workhorse of the Internet. When you send something over the Internet, TCP passes its packets on to IP. This is roughly like dropping a letter at the post office, because IP repackages the data and makes sure that all of it gets delivered from point to point on the Internet on its way to the final destination: the specified IP or domain name address. Conversely, when IP receives packets, it "delivers" them up to TCP. There are other low-level Internet protocols, but these are the two most important ones, the basis of most Internet communication.

News & Information

This is the age of information, and success in many fields depends on getting the latest news as quickly as possible. The Internet provides numerous sources for specialized, up-to-date information. You may want to subscribe to an electronic mailing list, for instance, that keeps you posted on the latest developments in nanotechnology; you may want to get stock prices more current than those you can read in your local newspaper; or you may want to participate in a Usenet newsgroup where specialists in some arcane area of knowledge keep you abreast of what you need to know. Because of its scope and speed, the Internet is by far the most efficient way to make sure you maintain expert status in your little corner of the information universe. Netscape Navigator 3.0 gets you the information you need.

Figure 2-3 shows you what a list of Usenet newsgroups looks like from Netscape Navigator 3.0.

You can also keep up to date on the latest national and world events. There are a number of well-known and well-regarded Web sites maintained by news networks, like CNN Interactive.

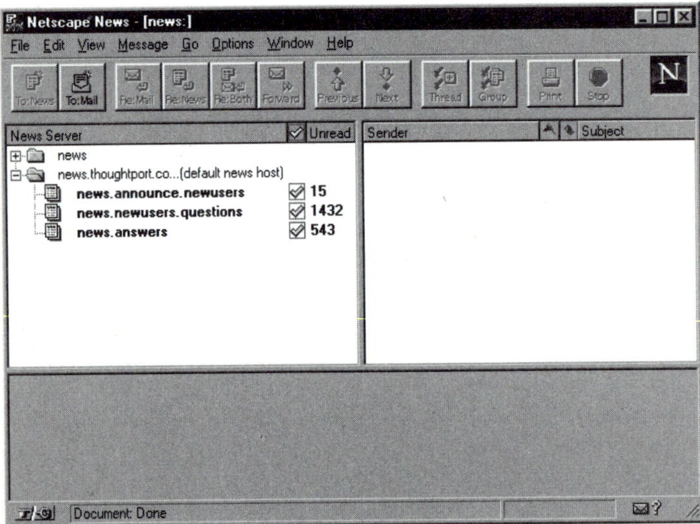

Figure 2-3: A few Usenet newsgroups.

Software

One of the most astounding features of the Internet is the availability of thousands and thousands of software programs that you can download at no charge. In fact, until recently you couldn't even buy commercial Internet client programs for PCs that were anywhere near as good as the freeware and shareware available on the Net. (For more information about freeware and shareware, see Chapter 6, "Getting Files via FTP.") That situation is starting to change, but there still are times when you need a program dedicated to a very specific task, such as playing a new kind of sound or video file.

Many of the sites that allow you to download programs are large, and most do not include descriptions of the files. Fortunately, Netscape Navigator 3.0 helps you locate and download exactly what you need.

Additionally, most hardware manufacturers now distribute software drivers and upgrades through their Web sites, so you no longer need to connect to a bulletin board system (BBS) long-distance to download the latest support software.

Figure 2-4 shows you some of the directories of files available at Netscape's own FTP site.

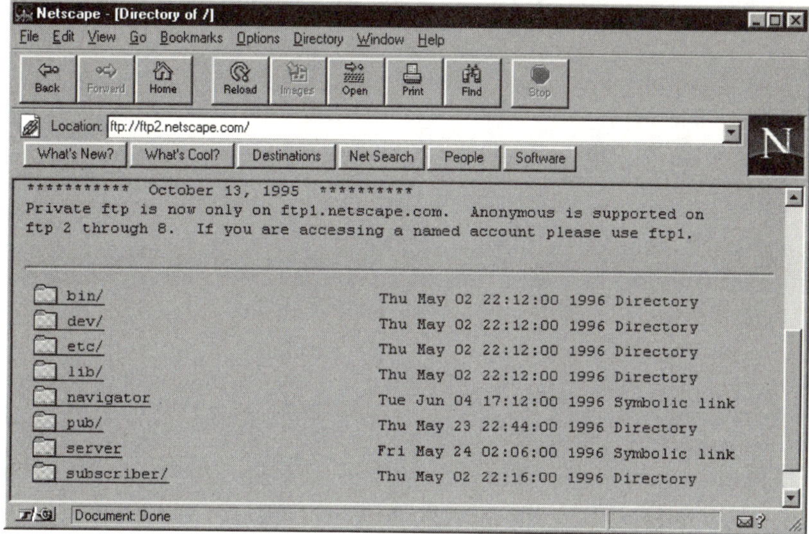

Figure 2-4: The Netscape FTP site.

Promotion, Shopping & Online Transactions

For years the Internet was a commerce-free zone. It was funded and monitored by dedicated bureaucrats and academicians who instituted strict usage policies restricting anything that smelled vaguely of money. Well, all that's changed. Now there are vast areas of cyberspace that look less like research libraries than like your local mall, and most major corporations maintain Web sites where they promote their products and services.

Figure 2-5 shows Open Market's Commercial Sites Index, a vast directory of commercial services and products (http://www.directory.net).

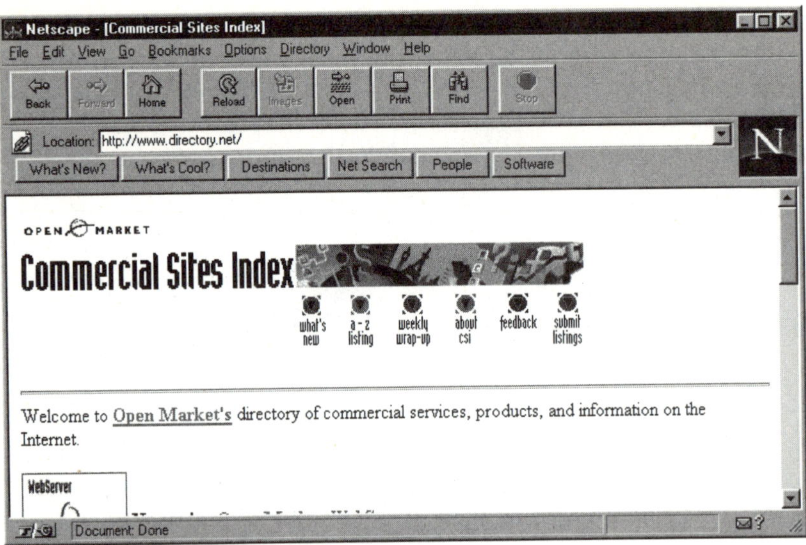

Figure 2-5: Open Market's Commercial Sites Index.

Recreation

Planning a vacation? The Internet can provide current travel information on just about any area of the globe. Considering taking up a new sport? Want to find out about the latest foreign movies? The Internet can point you to the resources you need.

But the Internet not only supplies information *about* recreational activities, it also provides its own diversions and amusements. If you like interactive online games, for instance, you might be in danger of staying glued to your keyboard and monitor well into the wee hours. Figure 2-6 shows one of the many games sites available to you via the Web.

And if you're a more cyber-gregarious person than I am, the Internet offers plenty of opportunities for meeting friends and chatting online. Then of course the World Wide Web, which we'll talk about later in this chapter, is full of unclassifiable forms of fun and nonsense, and Netscape Navigator 3.0 brings it all right into your own home.

But before discussing the Web, we need to take a quick look at how information actually gets from one place to another on the Web. A basic understanding of Internet addressing will make it easier for you to find the sites with information you're interested in.

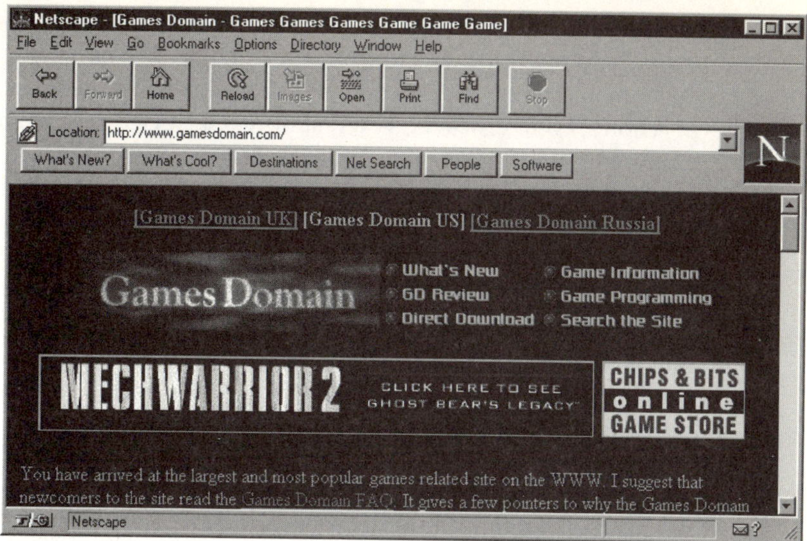

Figure 2-6: The Games Domain site on the World Wide Web.

Internet Addressing

The whole basis of the Internet is that machines are constantly sending messages to other machines. Some of these messages are software commands, some are requests for data, and some include the human-readable data itself. Obviously there has to be a way for information to get to the proper recipient, and so the underlying suite of Internet protocols includes an addressing scheme. At the heart of the addressing scheme is the concept of domains.

Domains & Domain Names

By *domain*, we simply mean where a computer resides. For instance, a specific computer at the University of Missouri is in the *missouri* domain, which in turn is within the top-level *edu* domain, the domain that includes all Internet-connected colleges and universities in the United States. The complete domain name of a machine called *bigcat* at the University of Missouri, for instance, would be *bigcat.missouri.edu*. No other machine anywhere on the Internet has the same domain name. Every name is registered with a special Internet organization to ensure that it is unique.

I have an e-mail account on echonyc.com. To reach my account, all you need to do is add my username to the domain name. My username is pjames, so my full e-mail address is *pjames@echonyc.com*. If you wanted to visit the Web pages at echonyc.com, however, you'd simply tell Netscape Navigator 3.0 to get a document from the Web server machine at that site, www.echonyc.com.

At first these addresses might look impossible to pronounce, but pronunciation conventions have developed. Pjames@echonyc.com is pronounced "p-james at echo-n-y-c dot com," and ftp.vmedia.com is pronounced "f-t-p dot v-media dot com." Of course usernames don't have to be as simple as mine. If your LAN administrator or access provider lets you choose your own name, you might want to be zzzx_12_qwerty@serviceprovider.com. Then again you might not. Keep in mind that people who send you e-mail need to remember your address.

Fortunately, the Internet almost never cares about case-sensitivity in e-mail addresses. You can send a message to pJaMeS@EcHoNyC.cOm, and I will still get it. But most experienced Internet users stick with lowercase when typing addresses—it's just easier. If you use both uppercase and lowercase letters in your addresses, some of the old-timers will chuckle at the newcomer, more often called a "clueless newbie." Even worse, if you use all uppercase, people will tell you to "stop shouting"!

TIP

Even though Internet e-mail addresses are usually not case-sensitive, remember that URLs (Uniform Resource Locator, which I'll explain in a second) for Web pages and FTP directories are!

As I mentioned earlier, the last part of a domain name address is called the top-level domain. There are six standardized domain names corresponding to types of organizations, as shown in Table 2-1.

Domain	Type of Organization
com	Commercial entity
edu	Educational institution
gov	Government agency or department
mil	Military organization
net	Network resource
org	Other type of organization, usually a not-for-profit

Table 2-1: Top-level domains.

In addition, Internet sites outside the United States are identified by a special two-letter, top-level domain name. For instance, a computer in Finland would have a top-level domain name of *fi*, and a computer in Germany would have a top-level domain name of *de* (for Deutschland). As you start cruising around the Net, you will run into these foreign domain names on a daily basis. There is even a two-letter designation for the United States (you guessed it, *us*), but it is rarely used since the six "organization type" names are more descriptive.

IP Addresses

Pretty simple, isn't it? Well, luckily for those of us who make a living explaining such things, it's not *quite* that simple. Domain name addresses are really easy-to-remember translations of the kind of addresses the Internet really uses, numeric *IP addresses*. IP stands for "Internet Protocol." You may have read about IP in the earlier sidebar, "Under the Hood: TCP/IP." For now, it's only important to understand the difference between the two kinds of addresses.

If you're my age, you probably remember when phone numbers always began with the name of the exchange, as in "Murray Hill Seven, Five Five Five Five." You can think of Murray Hill Seven, the exchange, as a top-level domain name. But in fact your telephone didn't really care about the words Murray Hill Seven, it simply transmitted down the line the fact that you had dialed the numbers 647. You can think of 647 as the top-level portion of the IP address. When you use a domain name address to attach to a Web server, for instance, a special Internet service known as a Domain Name Service (DNS) looks up the name and replaces it with an IP number. And as long as you're connected to the Net, you have your own IP address so that remote machines know how to send you the information you request.

IP addresses are structured very much like domain name addresses, but backwards. They consist of four numbers, each less than 256, separated by periods. The rightmost number specifies the actual machine, while those to the left identify the network and subnetwork. When I link to the Net via my PPP account with the access provider ThoughtPort, for instance, my IP address is 199.171.225.100. The "100" part of that address is my actual computer on the ThoughtPort network.

OK, that's enough technical talk for now. Let's move ahead to one of the most fascinating Internet resources available, the World Wide Web.

What Is the World Wide Web?

There is a lot of confusion among the general public about what the Web really is, and especially about how it relates to the Internet as a whole. Let's clarify these issues right now.

The World Wide Web is, quite simply, a global hypermedia document that resides on and stretches across most of the Internet. Whoa! What the !@#$ am I talking about? To understand the Web you really need to know what we mean by hypertext and hypermedia.

Hypertext & Hypermedia

Imagine you are reading this book on your computer screen instead of on the page. As you read along, you notice that some of the words are underlined and may appear in a different color or **font**, just like that. In this example, you try clicking your mouse on the word font. Magically, a new document appears on your screen, explaining what fonts are. This new document also contains words and phrases that you can click on, taking you to yet other documents or to other places in the same document. That's what *hypertext* is all about: the nonlinear presentation of text, letting you jump from idea to idea following your own associative pathways. The clickable words and phrases are known as links, and the activity of moving around through these linked documents is known as *browsing*.

Now imagine that when you click on the **font** link you don't just get a text explaining fonts. Instead, a fancy picture pops up, a colorful depiction of fonts through the ages from Guttenberg to Adobe. Perhaps you're even presented with a video clip complete with a Charlton Heston narration and a corny John Williams score. Congratulations! You've just learned what *hypermedia* is: the nonlinear presentation not just of text, but of a variety of other media including graphics and sound.

Hypermedia on the Net

So what's this got to do with the Internet? Well, this is where it gets interesting. When you click on a link, the document that you get—whether it's text, graphics, sound, or full-motion video—does not have to be on the same machine as the original document. Thanks to a special protocol known as *HyperText Transfer Protocol* (HTTP), the primary protocol for the World Wide Web, you can access documents on any public World Wide Web server on the Internet! The original document might be on your own computer, or on the Netscape site; the video clip about fonts might reside on a machine in Hollywood or

Timbuktu. Now here's the conceptual leap that makes this new technology so exciting: you can think of the collection of all the documents linked together as one big hypermedia document.

Let's go back to our original definition of the Web: a global hypermedia document that resides on and stretches across most of the Internet. Make sense now?

What's So Great About Hypermedia?

Suppose you're reading one of those wonderful but frustrating Russian novels in which 36 major characters are introduced during the first two chapters. If you're anything like me, you'll continually find yourself flipping back and forth trying to keep track of who's who. Was Natasha Galanskaya the one who ran away with the Count against her father's wishes, or was that Natalia Balanchina? Wouldn't it be great if you could just push a button on a character's name and instantaneously be transported to a full description of that character's relevant history? Well, you can't do that in a book or a magazine or even a regular computer document, but the magic of hypermedia makes it possible.

Let's look at another example of how hypermedia can improve the communication process, and even make learning more fun and interesting. Suppose you're a high-school student studying astrophysics. One option is to open your textbooks and review the mathematics of planetary motion in the abstract. Even if you enjoy solving a few motion problems, it's still a fairly boring exercise. But what if your physics lab computer is linked to the Web and takes you to a virtual textbook with animations that show the orbits of the bodies, in full color and motion? Or plays back short lectures on the day's exercises, by the foremost authority in the field? Educators and trainers know the power of multimedia to speed learning and increase students' retention levels. This type of presentation has become popular in education and corporate training environments, as it presents information in an interesting and entertaining format.

When we click on the graphics, video, and sound objects embedded in a compound-document Web page, we are fulfilling prophesies made years ago for a global information system. When you're up and running with Netscape Navigator 3.0, you'll see exactly what all the excitement's about.

Servers & Browsers

The Web utilizes what is sometimes called a *client-server* model. Special machines or software known as World Wide Web servers make the linked hypermedia documents available to the public. Individuals then move around through these documents using software known as Web clients or, more commonly, Web browsers. Obviously a Web browser has to be able to display or "play" a wide variety of hypermedia formats.

Because the World Wide Web uses a standardized protocol (HTTP) for transferring the information across the Internet, and because all Web software adheres to this protocol, any kind of Web browser will work with any kind of Web server. For instance, a site may decide to use one of the server packages developed by Netscape, but any World Wide Web browser will be able to access the information available at that site. Conversely, the browser we are discussing in this book, Netscape Navigator 3.0, can access hypermedia documents on any Web server anywhere in the world.

What's a Home Page?

Once you start exploring the World Wide Web, you'll encounter the term *home page* or *homepage* over and over again, and it won't always be used the same way. Here are some of the things it can mean:

- A home page is the document that's displayed by a Web browser such as Netscape Navigator 3.0 when you first load the program. This document may be located on your local machine or at a remote site. In the case of Netscape Navigator, the default home page is a document located at Netscape's own Web site, but as with most other browsers, you can change this.
- A home page is the top-level document at a particular Web site. For instance, a typical small business's home page would contain a title, a logo, some introductory information, and a bunch of links to more detailed marketing information.
- A home page is a personal Web document created by an individual and made available to the public (Joe Blow's 15 kilobytes of fame). Many access providers now let users copy Web documents to their public Web servers, and the Net sprouts hundreds of new personal home pages every day. You'd be surprised who's out there!
- In some contexts, a home page is simply any hypertext Web document, though I have to admit it bugs me when I hear people use the term this way.

A Quick Dip in Acronym Soup

OK, let's get all of our technical-sounding acronyms out of the way in OSF (one swell foop). There are only two you really need to worry about: HTML and URL. Not only will they give you a better handle on navigating around the Web, but if you pepper your conversation with them, many people will think you are really cool in a geeky sort of way.

HTML

All Web pages that contain text are written in a language called HTML, which stands for *HyperText Markup Language*. HTML is a subset of SGML (Standard Generalized Markup Language), a very generalized system originally designed for typesetting and document page description. HTML is simply ordinary ASCII text with embedded codes (usually referred to as *tags*) that represent instructions for displaying the text or for linking to other Web documents. For example, *<I>italic</I> or <B>bold</B>* in a Web document tells the browser to display the phrase "italic or bold" with the word "italic" in italics and the word "bold" in boldface. It is important to understand that HTML does *not* indicate exactly what the resulting text should look like—that is up to the browser software. On a system that can't display true italic or bold fonts, for instance, the browser might just display the words in a different color. When you create your own Web document, you simply label various text elements rather than specifying exactly what the text will look like. This makes HTML a universal language, ensuring that Web pages are displayable in one way or another on any conceivable machine or operating platform.

Figure 2-7 shows a typical Web page, and Figure 2-8 shows what some of the HTML source code for it looks like.

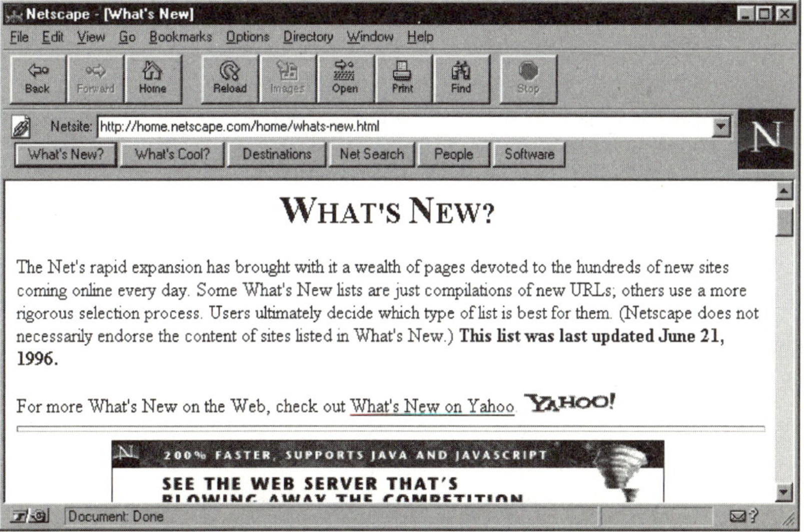

Figure 2-7: A typical HTML document.

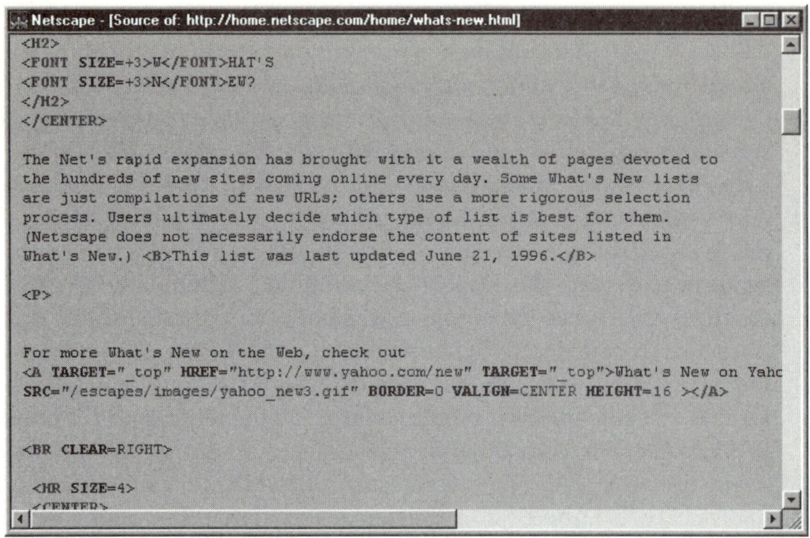

Figure 2-8: The HTML source code for the same page.

TIP

Yes, Netscape Navigator 3.0 not only displays Web documents properly, but it also lets you see the source code for any document it displays! This is especially useful if you're learning how to create your own Web page. Simply select Document Source from the View menu.

HTML is an evolving language. Tim Berners-Lee of the European Particle Physical Laboratory (CERN) in Switzerland, started it all in 1990 by releasing an initial specification to the public. It was pretty basic, supporting only the basic text handling tags. Berners-Lee started an Internet mailing list to solicit suggestions for refining and adding to the language, and in 1992 Dan Connolly released a "level 1" HTML specification. As soon as it was released, work began on a level 2 specification that would contain more advanced text handling capabilities. HTML 2.0, now completed and approved by a standards body known as the Internet Engineering Task Force (IETF), also includes support for interactive forms and image maps. Interactive forms let you enter data on the screen that is then sent to the host site, and image maps let you link to other documents by clicking on "hot spots" within an image. All good browsers now support the HTML 2.0 features, and work continues on new advancements while you're reading.

HTML Filenames

Files that contain HTML tags are known as HTML files, and they always have an extension of either .HTM or .HTML. On UNIX and other systems that support long filenames, the extension is .HTML; on DOS-based systems, it's .HTM. This extension tells the browser it is dealing with a hypertext document rather than some other type of hypermedia document, such as an image or audio file.

What's next? The latest proposed standard is for HTML 3.2, which includes a wide variety of enhancements. Netscape has been at the forefront of the collaborative design process in proposing *and implementing* new features for HTML 3.2. Many of these exciting new extensions are covered later in this book, particularly in Chapter 9, "Power Navigator 3.0."

More History

If you're the kind of person who likes to know all about the origins and evolution of new information technologies, here are some sites to try once you've learned how to use Netscape Navigator 3.0:

- About the World Wide Web (http://www.nmsi.ac.uk/usage/).
- World Wide Web and CERN (http://www1.cern.ch/CERN/WorldWideWeb/WWWandCERN.html).
- The World Wide Web: Origins and Beyond (http://homepage.seas.upenn.edu/~lzeltser/WWW/).

I mentioned before that HTML also includes the format for specifying links to other documents or to other areas of the same document. Here's what one of these links looks like:

```
<a href="http://www.faraway.com/explain-directory/explain.html">Click here
for an explanation</a>
```

Looks a little strange, doesn't it? That's OK. All you really need to know is that when you click the phrase "Click here for an explanation," a new HTML document (the file explain.html, which is located at a remote site) pops up. This will all make more sense when you learn about URLs, and so without further ado....

URL

URL stands for *Uniform Resource Locator*. Back when $10 was worth something, that's what we used to call a bunch of $10 words, but it's really pretty simple. URLs are like signs pointing to hypermedia documents on the Web. They provide the protocol and addressing information that Netscape Navigator 3.0 or another browser uses to connect to the target document. The first part of a URL specifies the type of data or the protocol necessary to retrieve the data, the second part specifies the server where the information is located, and the optional third part specifies the exact path to that data. For instance, the URL http://www.vmedia.com/vvc/index.html tells Netscape Navigator 3.0 to retrieve the file index.html from the vvc directory at www.vmedia.com (Ventana Online's Web server) using the HTTP protocol, the basic support protocol on the Web. (See Chapters 6 and 7 for information about accessing resources available via other major Internet protocols, including FTP and Gopher.)

URLs are used in several different ways. First of all, they are part of the HTML tags that tell your browser to jump to a remote document. In the middle of an HTML file, for instance, the above URL might be used like this:

```
<a href="http://wwwymedia.com/vvc/index.html">Click here to go to the Ventana
Online home page!</a>
```

You can also type URLs directly into Netscape Navigator 3.0 to jump immediately to a remote document. And finally, you can add URLs to Netscape Navigator 3.0 as "bookmarks" for easy access at some later time.

Netscape Navigator 3.0 & the Future of the Web

Remember how I said that any Web browser can access hypermedia documents from anywhere on the Web? If that's true, why would you choose one browser over another, especially since there are a number of shareware and even freeware browsers available?

Well, here's the catch: while any browser can *access* available documents, different software packages vary greatly in their ability to *present* hypermedia information to you. For instance, some browsers are exclusively text-based. If you click on a link to a graphics document, all you'll get is a message saying something like "There is a picture here." But even among browsers that support a wide variety of hypermedia formats, there are still differences. For instance, different browsers support different versions or different features of HTML. Some browsers, for instance, will not let you enter information into interactive forms that may be essential for online shopping, or may not be able to display text in table format. As I mentioned earlier, Netscape Navigator 3.0 is the most popular browser on the Net, and it not only supports the full range of standard HTML features, it also supports a huge number of *proposed* HTML features; formatting options that are very likely to become standards in the next couple of years. With Netscape Navigator 3.0, you can view the future of the Web today.

Web Conferencing

Some of you may be familiar with electronic Bulletin Board Systems (BBSes), which allow users to post public messages in various discussion areas or forums. Others of you may be familiar with CompuServe or America Online, which also have discussion areas for people with similar interests. This format for electronic communications has been around since the mid-1980s, but ironically, one of the newest trends on the Web is to emulate this approach with HTML forms. In other words, you can now use Netscape Navigator 3.0 to log onto what looks something like an old-fashioned BBS and then read and post messages. The Web pages, forms, and special scripts that support this kind of communication are often called *Web conferencing systems*. Web conferencing systems reside on Web servers. Though they are technically accessible using any forms-capable Web browser, they often require users to register before actually reading or posting messages.

To see a Web conferencing system in action, you might want to take a look around Utne Reader's Web "café," which is more like a salon where people discuss culture, politics, and art as well as the usual technical issues. You will have to go through a registration procedure, but it's worth it. The URL is: http://www.utne.com.

Some Pointers on Using the Net

OK, we talked about the Internet a little, then about the World Wide Web. We're going to end this chapter by focusing once more on the Internet as a whole. The Web, after all, is really only one feature—albeit a dazzling one—of the new information landscape. And remember, Netscape Navigator 3.0 is more than a Web browser; it is more like a luxury cruise-mobile for exploring *all* the resources of the Net. And so in this section, I'd like to give you some very general pointers on using the Net effectively and efficiently.

Some people view the Internet as an experiment in grassroots self-governance. There aren't many laws, and there aren't many cops, and the best way to keep it that way is with generosity and common sense. If the Internet is to stay the wide-open magical place it is today, users will have to keep concentrating on the welfare of the community as a whole instead of exploiting it for individual gain. The Net can be seen as an *information environment* in which everything is interconnected, and we should all practice our "Internet ecology."

The online culture has developed its own guidelines, and before actually exploring the Net, it's a good idea to get familiar with some of these mostly unwritten rules of the road. Here are just a few that will make your Internet travels more efficient, more pleasant, and more "ecological." I think these guidelines are so important that I try to include the following subsections in every book I write. (Sure took that Harlequin Romance editor by surprise!)

Avoid Traffic Jams

They call it a superhighway, but sometimes it's more like driving through Bombay. Every day several thousand clueless newbies start exploring the Net. (Don't worry, you're not one of them: you bought this book!) Servers can support only a certain number of clients, and routers start to seem "sludgy" when they're called upon to transfer packets of data for thousands of users. Certain sites are practically impossible to reach, especially those distributing the latest free software or pictures of naked people.

To avoid traffic jams, and to avoid creating them, follow these simple rules of thumb:

- Connect during nonbusiness hours whenever possible. (Since this is a world-wide system, remember to compensate for different time zones!)
- If you're unable to connect with a particular server—for instance, if you get an "unable to connect with host" message when you try to access a Web page—wait a while before trying again. Bombarding the Net with unsuccessful connection attempts only adds to the problem.
- Use what are known as "mirror sites" for downloading files via FTP. Since some of the large anonymous FTP servers are so busy, a number of hosts sprinkled around the Net have been kind enough to "mirror" the exact contents, keeping their file lists completely up-to-date. The original site usually informs you about these mirror sites in its sign-on message. FTPing to a mirror is just like FTPing to the original host, except that you'll be out of the heaviest traffic.
- Find the closest site that has what you need. Don't Telnet to Timbuktu if you can get the same information by FTPing to Peoria. When you access far-flung reaches of the globe, your packets of information must travel point-to-point through dozens of locations.
- Don't create unnecessary message traffic. This is especially important in Usenet newsgroups (see Chapter 5, "Newsgroups"). If you have something to say, by all means say it, but the Net provides a useful venue for practicing eloquent restraint. Don't send the text of your Great American Novel to the whole world, simply tell users where they can find it. And remember that even a short message like "Ha ha ha!" expands to several hundred bytes of control and addressing information, and may require the services of dozens of routers. Sending a message like this may look free to you, but it definitely costs the community as a whole.

- Follow any instructions that are given to you for logging off a particular site. If you don't follow the proper procedures for logging off from a Telnet site, for instance, a connection may be left open, perhaps making it difficult for others to log on.

Understand Acceptable Use

Certain networks on the Internet, including the large backbones, have published standards for information that may be transmitted via their equipment and cabling. When you sign up with an access provider, you are mailed or e-mailed a document that outlines the acceptable-use policies in effect for the networks used by that provider. You must adhere to these strictly! Besides the obvious prohibitions against using the network for trafficking in drugs and bombs, these policies usually make clear what kinds of commercial activities are permitted.

Here's a typical list of prohibitions from an acceptable-use policy statement:

- Users may not transmit any data or programs that cause disruption of service for others.
- Users may not transmit any form of computer worm, Trojan horse, or virus.
- Users must not use the network to violate intellectual property laws by distributing copyrighted or otherwise protected information, documents, or software programs.
- Users may not distribute unsolicited advertising.

But the written policies are really only the beginning of acceptable use. Common sense and respect for others should be your guiding principles when communicating over the Net. The Internet is not a good place for personal attacks and threats, as they frequently escalate into full-blown "flame wars" that waste resources. It's not necessarily a good place for challenging local community ethical standards, either, since various factions are looking for excuses to impose more stringent regulation. Make sure that you post your materials at the appropriate sites.

Respect & Protect Privacy

Privacy is the big hot topic on the Internet today. To what extent should government agencies have access to private Internet communications? Should the content of public sites be regulated? Should there be safeguards against commercial entities adding you to electronic mailing lists? It remains to be seen how these issues will be decided, but it is very clear that the Internet community expects its citizens to respect the privacy of other individuals. Nothing will get you in more trouble than trying to "hack" somebody else's account, trying to take advantage of technological loopholes to access private data, or publishing confidential information.

At the same time, you should realize that in a culture as large as the Internet there are going to be occasional problems with privacy, and you should do what you can to protect yourself and others by keeping your accounts secure:

- Always use good, specific passwords; your spouse's name or the name of a *Star Trek* character just won't cut it.
- Change your passwords often.
- Always inform the appropriate network administrators when you think there may have been a security breach.
- If you're worried about particularly sensitive information, use some form of encryption such as Pretty Good Privacy (PGP), which is available on most large anonymous FTP sites.
- And just in case, remember that there is no such thing as true privacy on the Internet! Don't make any information available on the Net if you wouldn't want it to appear on the front page of *USA Today* or your hometown newspaper. Yes, I learned this lesson the hard way once, but we're not going to talk about that!

Be Willing to Ask for Help

In my experience, the most annoying Internet users are those who "know just enough to be dangerous." They go crashing around the Internet, leaving a mess for others to clean up. Look, the Internet is full of *real* experts; if you don't know how to do something, just ask. You'll be amazed at how helpful and friendly the seasoned Net veterans can be. I've asked some pretty stupid questions on the Internet, but only rarely have I received a snooty response.

Of course, before asking questions of other users, you should look for available resources such as help files or appropriate technical documents. The Netscape site, which appears as soon as you load Netscape Navigator 3.0, is full of useful information. Many Usenet newsgroups even maintain files of frequently asked questions, called FAQs. But if you've exhausted other resources, there's nothing wrong with a plea for help.

Don't Be Afraid to Explore

On the other hand, one of the most valuable ways to learn how to use the Net is simply to explore. As long as you're not trying to do something too tricky or arcane, common sense will usually get you where you want to go. Half the fun of the Internet is wandering around, guided as much by your instincts as by a conscious plan. Certainly you can do no harm by getting out there and seeing the world!

Moving On

What makes Netscape Navigator 3.0 the premier product for accessing the Internet is not its slick interface, or its availability on a variety of platforms, or its solid reliability, or even its early support of forward-looking Web features. What really sets this product apart is that it lets you do *everything you need to do on the Net*. In addition to browsing the Web, you can use Netscape Navigator 3.0 to send and receive e-mail; to read and post Usenet newsgroup messages; to gather files; and to explore a wide range of specialized Internet services. In the following chapters, we'll be exploring all aspects of this versatility using a hands-on approach, and you'll see for yourself that becoming a seasoned Internaut is easy and fun.

But first let's make sure that you understand how to navigate with your new software. The next chapter introduces you to the Navigator interface—by the time you've finished Chapter 3, you'll be ready for the *real* fun!

A Quick Look Around

Now that you've installed Netscape Navigator 3.0, selected a service provider, and configured the program so that it works properly on your system, it's time to take a look around the Net. In this chapter, you'll learn some of the basics of the program and of Internet navigation. You'll learn:

- How to use the various controls in the program.
- How to move around a Web document, and how to get from one document to another.
- How to take advantage of exciting Web resources like Yahoo!, where you can easily search for specific topics and keywords on pages all around the world.
- How to use navigation aids such as the history list, bookmarks, and desktop shortcuts.

Netscape Navigator 3.0 is so simple to use that you can really master the program by trial and error. I taught my daughter how to use it by saying, "When you see some words that are underlined and in another color, click on them. That takes you to other places." After an hour she was whizzing around the Web like a seasoned veteran. Of course, she is 13 years old and learns this kind of stuff a lot faster than those of us who were born before PCs and Nintendo. By the end of this chapter, you may not quite be an adolescent Web-geek, but you'll know how to use the main features of Netscape Navigator 3.0 and how to find what you're looking for quickly and easily. Now let's get going!

The Netscape Navigator 3.0 Window

We'll start by taking a closer look at the Netscape Navigator 3.0 main window:

1. Make sure you are connected to the Internet, either directly or through a SLIP or PPP connection with your access provider. If you are using a SLIP or PPP connection and are not currently connected, double-click the Dial-Up Connection icon for your access provider.

   If you are using Windows 3.1 rather than Windows 95, or if you are using Windows 95 and are not using its built-in networking functionality, follow the instructions that came with your TCP/IP software for accessing the Internet.

2. Double-click the Netscape Navigator 3.0 icon to launch the program. The main window appears, and the Netscape home page starts loading as shown in Figure 3-1.

   - By default, Netscape Navigator 3.0 uses the Netscape home page as your personal home page (your *home page* is the document that loads automatically when you launch the program). Depending on the speed of your Internet connection and how busy the Netscape site is, this might take a few moments. Later in the chapter, you'll learn how you can select a different Web document as your home page in the sidebar "Changing Your Home Page."
   - If you configured Navigator 3.0 so that it requires a password, you will be asked to enter your password when you launch the program.

Let's identify each of the major components of the Netscape Navigator 3.0 window:

- **The Menu bar**. Like any other Windows program, Netscape Navigator 3.0 arranges all of its user-accessible features in a menu bar across the top of the window. Some menu families like File and Edit are familiar and practically self-explanatory, while others are unique to an Internet application. We'll discuss the Bookmarks and Directory menu families in detail later in this chapter, in the "Bookmarks" section and in the "Directory Menu" sidebar.

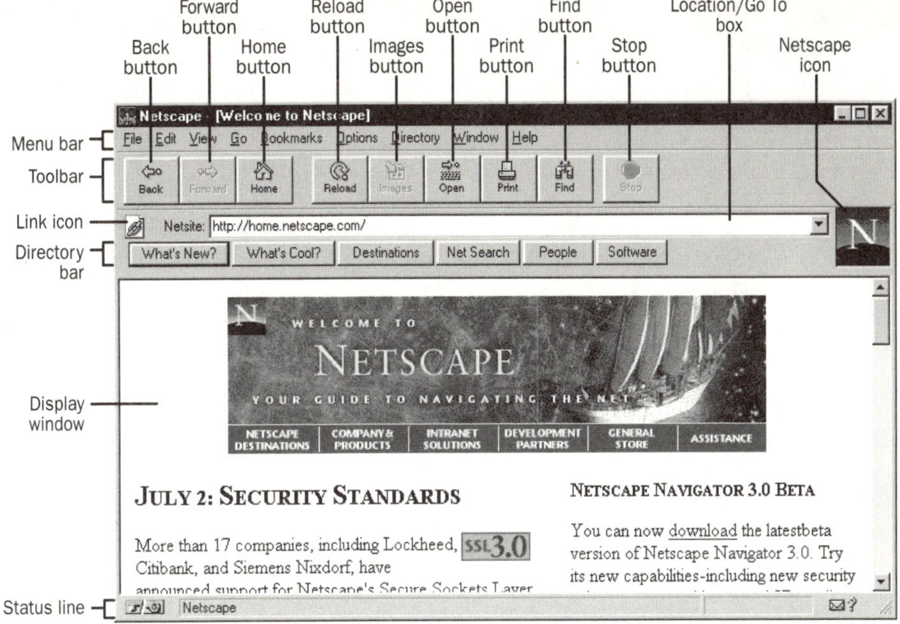

Figure 3-1: The Netscape Navigator 3.0 window with the Netscape home page.

- **The Toolbar**. Again, a toolbar is a familiar feature in most Windows programs. You click each individual button to control a different program function. The toolbar is such an easy way to use the program that you may never resort to the menus. You won't be tested on this since we're going to cover each button more thoroughly later on, but from left to right, the Netscape Navigator 3.0 buttons are:
  - **The Back and Forward buttons**. Pressing these buttons allows you to cycle through the documents you have already viewed. You can revisit these documents in reverse order (relative to the order in which you originally viewed them) by pressing the Back button, and then you can retrace your path using the Forward button.
  - **The Home button**. Pressing this button returns you to your home page.
  - **The Reload button**. Pressing this button reloads the currently displayed document into the Netscape Navigator 3.0 window.
  - **The Images button**. This button is available only if you've turned off the Auto Load Images option on the Options menu. With Auto Load Images off, Web pages are displayed without graphics. Instead, icons appear where the graphics normally would be loaded. When you press this button, Netscape Navigator 3.0 loads the images for the current page.

TIP

If you have a slow Internet connection, surf the Web in text-only mode (which is much, much faster than graphics mode) and load graphics only for those pages with images you'd like to see.

- **The Open button**. Pressing this button pops up a dialog box that lets you type in a URL to open a new document, as shown in Figure 3-2. (If you don't know what I mean by a URL, please refer to Chapter 2, "The Net & the Web.")

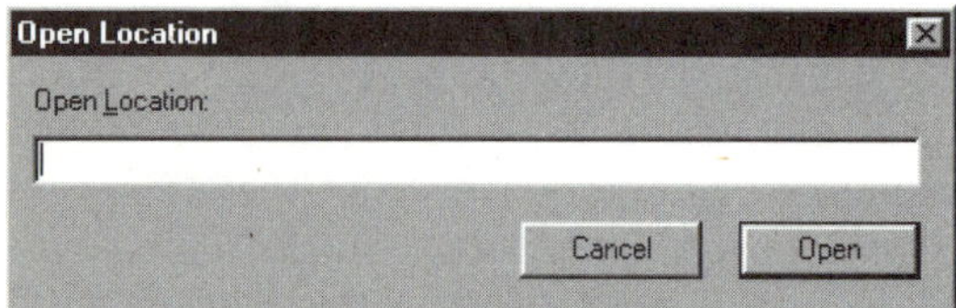

Figure 3-2: The Open Location dialog box.

- **The Print button**. Pressing this button prints the currently displayed document.
- **The Find button**. Pressing this button lets you search for a word or phrase in the currently displayed document.
- **The Stop button**. When this button is red, Netscape Navigator 3.0 is loading a document into the window. Pressing this button stops the document from loading.

That's it for the menu bar and the toolbar. Now let's move on down to some of the other components of the main Netscape Navigator 3.0 window:

- **The Netsite or Location box**. This text box has a label that changes according to how you use it. When Netscape Navigator 3.0 displays a Web document retrieved from a site that uses a Netscape Web server product, such as FastTrack or the Netscape Enterprise Server, the box is labeled Netsite; when it displays information retrieved from a non-Netscape server, the box is labeled Location. If you want to enter a URL manually, you can either type it or paste it directly into this field (the label changes to Go To while you're typing the new URL). Press Enter when you've finished entering the URL, and Netscape Navigator 3.0 jumps to that page.

TIP

*You'll notice an arrow button directly to the right of the Netsite box. You can click this button to display a drop-down list of the sites you've recently visited. Click any site in the list to return to it. (**Note:** This list only shows pages whose URLs you have entered in the Netsite or Open boxes.)*

Entering URLs the Easy Way

You learned in Chapter 2, "The Net & the Web," that a URL, or the address of a particular resource such as a Web page, includes three parts: the protocol used to retrieve the resource (such as HTTP, Gopher, or FTP), the name of the server where the information you want is located, and optionally a directory or file name. For instance, the URL for the Netscape home page is http://home.netscape.com, and the URL for one of its FTP sites is ftp://ftp.netscape.com. Both these examples include a protocol specification and a server name.

Most often you get to a site by clicking on a link within a Web page, but sometimes you need to type the URL itself into the Netsite or Location box. Wouldn't it be nice if you didn't always have to type that "http://" or "ftp://"?

Well, you don't! Netscape Navigator 3.0 has brains. You can leave off the protocol specification and the program will do its best to figure out what kind of resource you had in mind. For instance, if you type in home.netscape.com, Navigator 3.0 knows you really mean http://home.netscape.com. If you type in gopher.well.com, you are automatically transported to gopher://gopher.well.com. And if the URL is http://www.something.com, you can even get by with typing in something.com—Navigator will add the WWW for you. At the rate I type in URLs, after a year I'll be able to take a three-week vacation with the time I've saved.

Throughout this book I'll tell you to type in complete URLs, including the protocol specification. I'm doing that so you get used to the format and to make very clear what kind of resource we're talking about. But after a while you might want to take advantage of this handy shortcut.

- **The Link icon**. The Link icon is a little picture of a chain link just to the left of the Netsite/Location box. This icon is really a shortcut representation of the current URL. If you double-click the Link icon, the current URL is copied to the Windows clipboard; you can then paste it into any Windows application such as a text editor or e-mail program. You can also drag the Link icon onto the Windows 95 desktop to create a shortcut to the URL, and you can drag it into the Bookmarks window to create a new bookmark (see the upcoming section on Bookmarks).

- **The Directory bar**. The directory bar is made up of buttons, much like the toolbar. But the directory buttons display only commands from the Directory menu. For example, clicking the What's New button on the directory bar is the same as selecting the What's New entry from the Directory menu—just a little more convenient. Both actions result in Netscape Navigator 3.0 displaying Netscape's own What's New page, as shown in Figure 3-3.

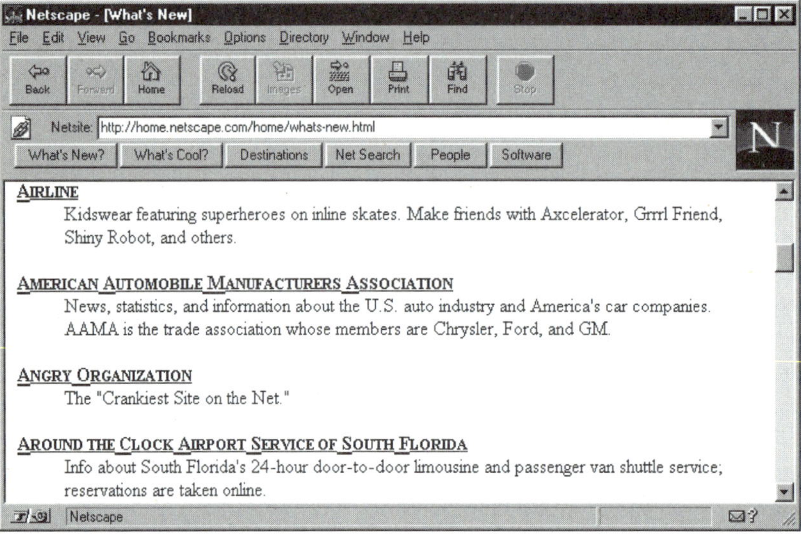

Figure 3-3: The What's New page.

We'll be looking at each of the directory bar buttons more closely later, under "The Directory Buttons," but for now let's continue our overview of the Netscape Navigator 3.0 main window.

- **The Netscape icon**. Although it's not really a control, the Netscape logo at the top right of the Netscape Navigator 3.0 window is very useful nonetheless. When this icon is animated with shooting stars, it indicates that the program is busy retrieving data from a Web site. When the icon is motionless, Navigator has received the entire document and is ready for your next action. ***Bonus:*** Clicking on the Netscape icon while you're connected to the Net will take you directly to Netscape's home page.

- **The Display window**. The display window is the most important area within Netscape Navigator 3.0. This is where Navigator 3.0 displays the formatted text, links, hot spots, form fields, graphics, and other items that make up a Web page. Some of these fields and controls are "static," like a standard paragraph of text, while others are "active" and actually perform a function. Some controls may be immediately obvious, like a button, while others may be hidden. For example, the Netscape page in Figure 3-4 includes a Welcome to Netscape graphic with hot spots. When you click on these hot spots, you are magically teleported to other Web pages, just as if you'd clicked a text link. You'll learn more about these components of a Web page later in this chapter. For now, though, just remember that if your mouse cursor turns into a hand with a pointing finger, you can click there to do something or go somewhere!

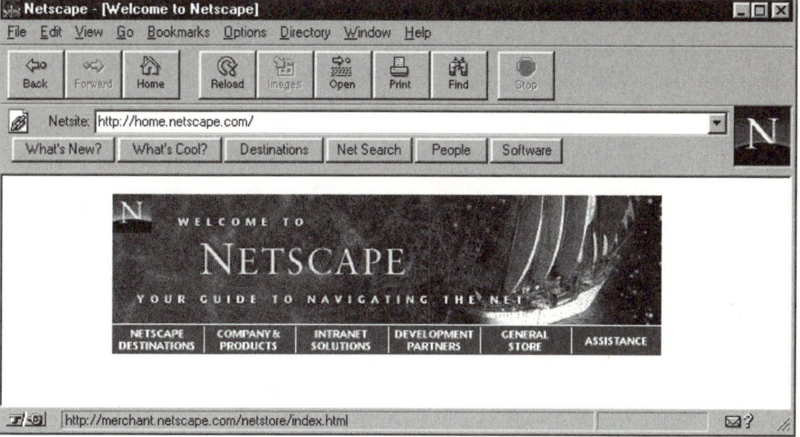

Figure 3-4: A graphic menu with hot spots.

TIP

Netscape Navigator 3.0 includes standard scroll bars along the right and bottom edges of the display window. If you resize the window (or if a Web page is longer than one screen length, which is usually the case), these controls let you scroll the display so that you can view the entire page.

- **The Status line**. Navigator uses the last line of the window to display current status information. For example, if you're currently receiving a picture from a Web site, Netscape Navigator 3.0 fills in the status line with the name of the image file and a status bar that indicates the progress of the transfer. Or if you move your mouse pointer over a link, the status line shows its URL, as you can see in Figure 3-5.

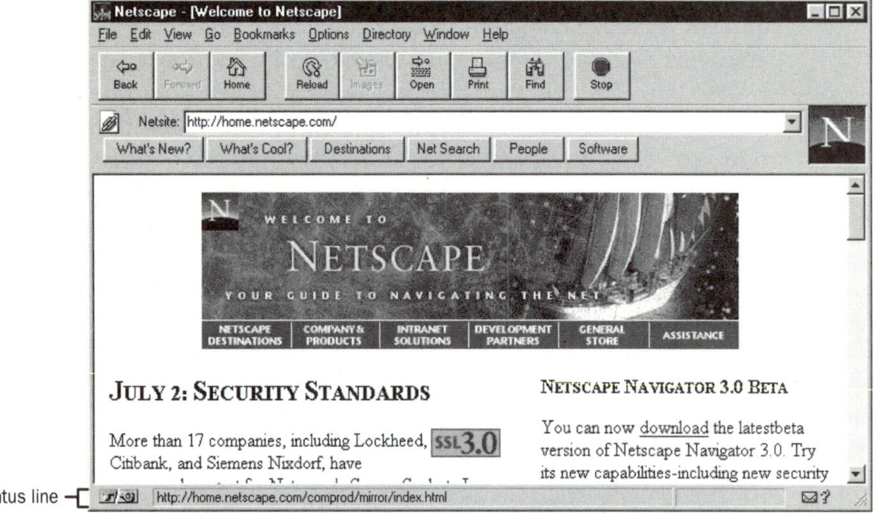

Figure 3-5: The Netscape Navigator 3.0 status line showing the URL of a link.

Note the small icon that looks like a broken key on the left side of the status line. This icon indicates whether or not your current session is using a special secure protocol for financial and business transactions. As you might guess, when the icon is "broken," the session is not secure. (Don't worry—you don't really need heavy-duty security for most of what you'll be doing on the Web.)

In addition, a small envelope icon at the far right of the status line links you to the Netscape Navigator 3.0 mail window. You simply click it to access your e-mail. If the icon has an exclamation point next to it, you have new mail. If it has a question mark next to it, Netscape Navigator 3.0 is configured so that it cannot automatically check your mail server for new messages. You'll learn more about e-mail in Chapter 4, "Netscape Mail."

Local Area URLs

As I mentioned in Chapter 2, "The Net & the Web," you don't even need the Internet to use Netscape Navigator 3.0 effectively. If you're on a local area network (LAN), you can use the program to access documents within your own organization. For instance, employees could call up the latest sales data, or view a fancy multimedia demonstration of a new product or service.

To access a document that is stored locally rather than at a remote site, press Ctrl+O or select Open File from Netscape Navigator 3.0's File menu. A File Open dialog box pops up. Now you can simply choose the document you want. HTML documents appear with the Netscape logo, but you could also choose to view text or graphic files.

You can also access a locally stored document by clicking a link to it within another document. For instance, you may want to construct an intranet home page that contains links to a variety of important files on your LAN. The URL for a locally stored file looks a little different from other URLs, and you should know how to construct one in case you ever need to enter one directly in the Netsite/Location box. A local file URL starts with *file:*. Next, there are *three* forward slashes rather than the usual two, the letter name of the local or network drive, a vertical bar (the pipe symbol...Shift+\), and the path to the file. Got all that? Here's an example, an HTML file called PRODUCT.HTM that's located in the Public directory on the Q drive of your LAN: file:///Q|/Public/PRODUCT.HTM.

Of course Netscape Navigator 3.0 supports all the same media on a LAN as it does on the Net. You can use the program to play sound files, run video clips, and even gather information from other employees using HTML forms (see "Forms on the Web" later in this chapter). And of course a document can contain a mix of links to Internet sites and to local files. This power and flexibility make Netscape Navigator 3.0 an excellent tool for disseminating enterprise-wide information through an intranet.

Links & Hot Spots

Let's continue our discussion of Web navigation with the most common active control found within Web pages: the *link*. A link is a special text string embedded within a document. It tells Netscape Navigator 3.0 to jump to another document or to a different place in the current document. Linked documents may be physically stored at the same site or another site halfway across the world. As I explained in Chapter 2, "The Net & the Web," this is the essence of hypertext.

Links are considered "followed" once you click on them to display the new information. Netscape Navigator 3.0 changes the color of a followed link to indicate that you've used it before. This color coding can help you retrace your steps.

To use a link, simply move your mouse pointer over the link text and click. But how can you be sure you're on a link? It's really simple.

How Can I Tell I'm on a Link?

Netscape Navigator 3.0 provides a number of visual cues to indicate the presence of a link:

- By default, links are underlined and appear in blue, while regular inactive text is not underlined and appears in black. If you return to a page after using one of its links, the link now appears in purple to indicate that you've been there. You can always click the same link again; it does not become inactive once you've clicked it. The change in color is only a helpful reminder.
- As I mentioned earlier, if you rest your mouse cursor on a link, the status line changes to indicate the link's URL. No URL in the status line, no link!
- As I also mentioned earlier, your mouse cursor changes to a pointing hand when it rests on a link.

Figure 3-6 shows a section of Netscape's own online handbook that contains a number of links.

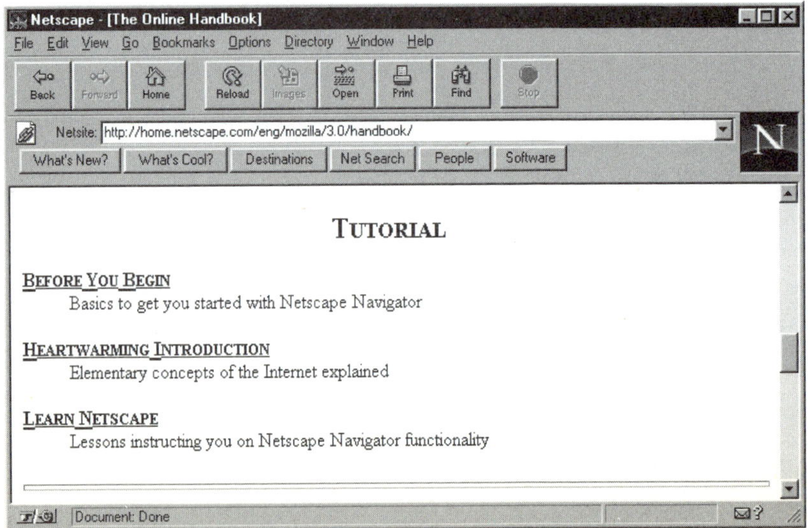

Figure 3-6: Netscape's Online Handbook, showing typical links to more detailed information.

TIP

Often the context of the text containing the link indicates what the link will do. For instance, "download PROGRAM.ZIP now" and "jump to the index" are self-explanatory.

Changing What Links Look Like

You can change the properties of link text from the Options menu. Click the General Preferences item to display the Preferences dialog box. In the Colors tab, you can change the default colors for links you've used and those you haven't tried yet. In the Appearance tab you can specify whether links should be underlined or not. Here you can also set how many days it takes for a followed link to "expire" (expired links are returned to the default color, just as if you had never followed them).

Using Hot Spots

Hot spots are just like links, except they are embedded within graphical information rather than text. Like links, hot spots perform an action when you click them. You might click one to jump to another page, or to view an image or even play a piece of music. Sometimes hot spots are smaller "thumbnail" versions of full-size images that you can download, or they may be beautifully designed arrows pointing to the next in a series of linked documents. Many sites also use hot spots as "menu items" within larger images that serve as menu systems. In the Netscape home page, for instance, you can click on various areas within the same graphic to jump to different documents. Let's give this a try:

1. Make sure you are connected to the Internet, either directly or through a SLIP or PPP connection with your access provider. If you are using a SLIP or PPP connection and are not currently connected, double-click the Dial-Up Networking icon for your access provider.

   If you are using Windows 3.1 rather than Windows 95, or if you are not using Windows 95's built-in networking, follow the instructions that came with your TCP/IP software for accessing the Internet.
2. Double-click the Netscape Navigator 3.0 icon to launch the program. The main window appears, and the Netscape home page starts loading, as shown earlier in Figure 3-1.

3. In the large graphic near the top of the page, click the General Store section. The General Store appears, as shown in Figure 3-7.

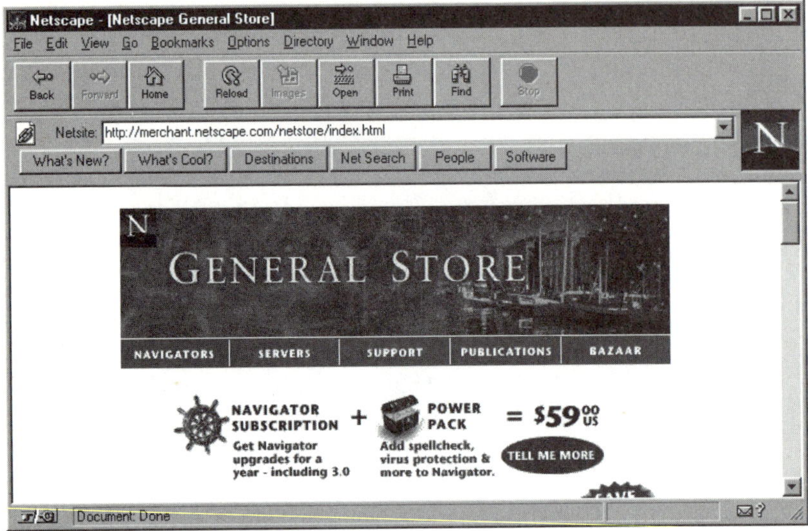

Figure 3-7: The General Store.

Congratulations! You just used a hot spot to get from the Netscape home page to the General Store. Traveling sure is simple in cyberspace.

TIP

Usually clicking a link causes the text and graphics currently displayed in the Navigator window to be replaced with new text and graphics. Sometimes, however, your current window will stay the same and an entire new window opens up to display the new information. The command to open a new window is part of the control information in the HTML file itself.

In this example, it was easy to find the hot spots in the graphic because they included text. But there are other ways to indicate hot spots as well. Sometimes they are displayed with a colored border, or the author of a Web page might refer to a hot spot in a line of text such as "Click the right arrow to move to the next page."

Right-Clicking on Links & Images

Normally you click with your left mouse button on links and hot spots. But by clicking your *right* mouse button instead, you can access a wide range of ways to manipulate these interactive elements.

When you click a link with the right mouse button, a context menu appears that lets you:

- **Open the Link.** This is the same as clicking with the left mouse button.
- **Open in New Window.** This creates a new browser window for the target document.
- **Save Link as.** This lets you save the target HTML file on your hard drive or network drive.
- **Copy Link Location.** This copies the link to the Windows clipboard. It is the same as double-clicking the Link icon, except you do not need to be currently displaying the target document.
- **Add Bookmark.** This lets you add the link to your Bookmarks without actually having to navigate to the target document.
- **Internet Shortcut.** This lets you create a desktop shortcut to the link. It is equivalent to dragging the Link icon out to the desktop, except you do not currently need to be displaying the target document.

  When you click a hot spot or graphic with the right mouse button, you see the following additional items on the context menu that appears:

  - **View Image.** This allows you to view the current image by itself, without the surrounding text or other graphics.
  - **Save Image as.** This lets you save the graphic to your hard drive or a network drive.
  - **Copy Image Location.** This copies the URL of the image to the Windows clipboard.

And if you want, you can even use the context menu to navigate back or forward from the current document or frame instead of using the Back and Forward buttons.

Using the Netscape Navigator 3.0 Toolbar

As I mentioned earlier, the Netscape Navigator 3.0 toolbar is the program's control center. You can use these buttons like the forward and reverse gears of a car, moving back and forth through Web documents. You can also use them to print the contents of any page or to locate a specific word or phrase within the text of a page.

Of course, all these functions are also available from the menu bar, but most Internet surfers find that the graphical nature of the Web lends itself to mouse control, making the toolbar the easiest and most convenient method for harnessing the power of Netscape Navigator 3.0.

In this section, we'll discuss the buttons you'll use the most as we navigate through Netscape's own Web site.

TIP

Note that pages on the Netscape Web site may change from time to time, so the screens and links we use may not agree exactly with what you see on your screen. However, you should still be able to follow the steps in a general fashion.

The Back & Forward Buttons

You've already seen how easy it is to get to a new document by clicking on a link or hot spot. But what if you need to return to a previously viewed page? Perhaps you forgot to download a file, or you suddenly decide to back up and follow a different information trail. This is where the first two buttons on the toolbar come into play. Back and Forward allow you to retrace your steps to a previous page or, if you've already backtracked, to jump forward to the last page you accessed.

To see how this works, follow these steps:

1. Make sure you are connected to the Internet either directly or via your SLIP or PPP access provider. If Netscape Navigator 3.0 is not currently running, launch it by double-clicking its icon.
2. In the Netscape home page, click the hot spot for the General Store.

   If you're already at the General Store because you're a good student who followed the last set of directions, just stay there!

3. Now click the Back button. We're back where we started, at the Netscape home page. Can you guess what the Forward button does? Go ahead and click it now. As you probably guessed, the General Store page pops up once more.
4. Now click a new link or hot spot. It doesn't really matter which one. Once the new document appears, click the Back button twice. Yes, as you probably expected, the Back button can lead sequentially back through all the pages you have visited. And of course Forward works the same way, in reverse.

Multiple Connections

You can display several Web documents at once with Netscape Navigator 3.0. Select New Web Browser from the File menu, or simply press Ctrl+N. Another window appears, and you can use it, like the first window, to navigate to any site. As I mentioned before, some sites automatically open new browser windows to display information, so you may have several windows open already. And why would you want to connect to more than one site at a time?

- If you're researching a specific topic and you've found more than one page with pertinent information or links, it's a good idea to load each page in a separate window if you need to compare them.
- Certain sites may be particularly slow, and opening an additional window allows you to continue exploring while you wait for the display of the first page to finish.
- Extra-large files like .MOV or .AVI animations may take several minutes to download. With a second window, you can continue surfing while you wait; don't forget, however, that the download will have to "share" your connection with the second window, so it will probably not continue at full speed.
- When you first open a new browser window, it "inherits" the history of the original window and displays the oldest page in that history, which is usually the Netscape home page. If you're wondering what I mean by *history*, it will all make sense after the section on "The History List and Bookmarks." Don't worry about it for now—all you need to know is that the new window is just like the old one, and you can use it to get anywhere you want on the Web.

The Home Button

You can click new links and dance around with the Forward and Back buttons as long as you want, but eventually you might get dizzy and long for home. To return to the Netscape home page:

1. Click the Home button.

That's it. (I love throwing in these one-step procedures.)

Why Do I Need a Home Page, Anyway?

You may be asking, "Why do I need a home page, anyway?" There are several reasons:

- A home page helps you stay oriented with a familiar starting point. Imagine what surfing would be like if you started without a home base—or, even worse, jumped to a random page every time you started the program!
- Many seasoned Web surfers set their home pages to their favorite site, especially if the contents of the page change often. This way, you can check your favorite page each time you begin a Netscape Navigator 3.0 session. If you have your own personal Web page, for example, you might set it as your home page.
- Some pages are especially designed to offer as much as possible for new Web surfers, making them ideal launching pads for Web exploration. For example, the Netscape home page offers links to the newest and most popular pages, Web search tools, and a wealth of exciting Internet resources—all from one screen.

As you can see, the Home button returns you directly to whatever home page you've selected with a single click of your mouse. And by the way, changing your home page is easy. To find out how, see the "Changing Your Home Page" sidebar.

Changing Your Home Page

Why change your home page? First, a purely practical reason: if your current home page is particularly busy or it's operated on a slower connection, it may take 30 seconds or so to load the page! Delays like that can get quite tiring after a few sessions, so you'd probably want to select a faster site (or perhaps even use a page you've created on your local hard disk). If you're really interested in saving time, you can even set your home page as "blank," so there's no load time at all.

Additionally, your interests are likely to change. You can save valuable Internet time by constructing a customized home page and including in it the sites you access the most.

To change your home page, follow these steps:

1. Select General Preferences from the Options menu.
2. Select the Appearance tab.
3. Click the Home Page Location radio button and type in the URL of your new home page. Make sure you spell the address correctly! If you've saved or created a page on your local hard drive, you can enter the URL for the file instead of a remote site.
4. Click OK.

The Print Button

Okay, so you've found the Secret to Life's Eternal Mystery on a particular Web page, and you'd like to save it for future reference. You could highlight the text with your mouse and copy the text to the Windows clipboard, but why not print out the whole thing? That way you can keep a hard copy of all of the contents of the page, including the images.

To print the contents of a page, click the Print button. Like most Windows applications, Navigator provides standard options that you can access from within the Print dialog box, and you can change the appearance of printed documents by selecting Page Setup from the File menu.

You can also display a preview image of the output before you print it by selecting the Print Preview option from the File menu. Figure 3-8 shows a print preview of the Netscape home page.

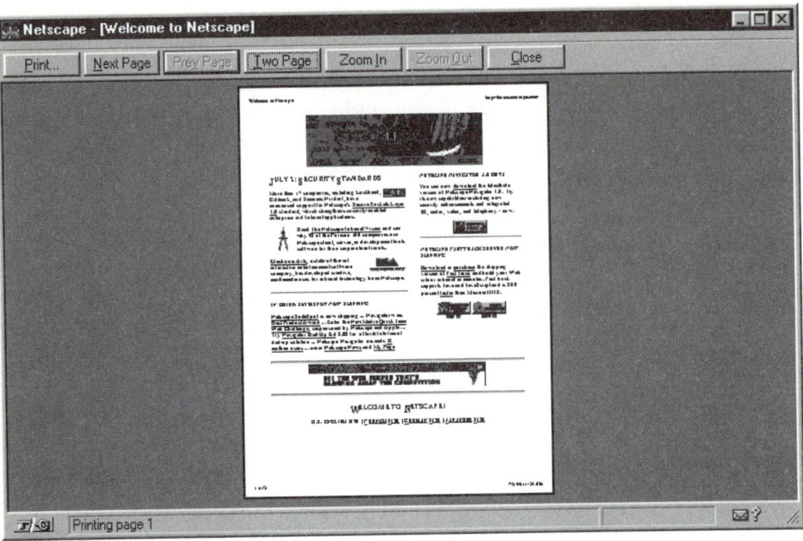

Figure 3-8: Print preview of the Netscape home page.

The Find Button

From time to time you'll encounter huge documents that are crowded with text and links. Scrolling slowly through a mountain of text line by line is one method of locating that link you remember, but Netscape Navigator 3.0 makes it much easier with the Find command.

Let's look for a specific string of text in Netscape's own Handbook.

1. Make sure you are connected to the Internet either directly or via your SLIP or PPP access provider. If Netscape Navigator 3.0 is not currently running, launch it by double-clicking its icon.
2. From the Help menu, select Handbook. Netscape's online Handbook appears, as shown in Figure 3-9.

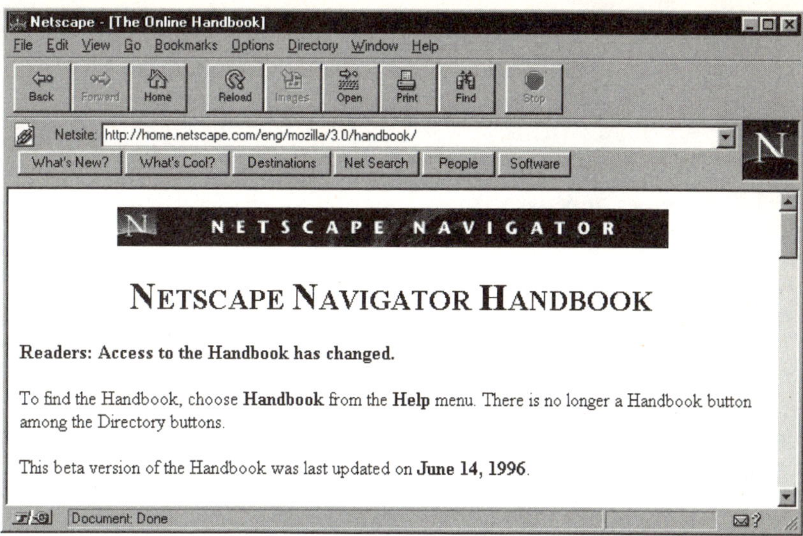

Figure 3-9: The Netscape Navigator Handbook.

3. Click the Find button. Netscape Navigator 3.0 displays the Find dialog box, as shown in Figure 3-10.

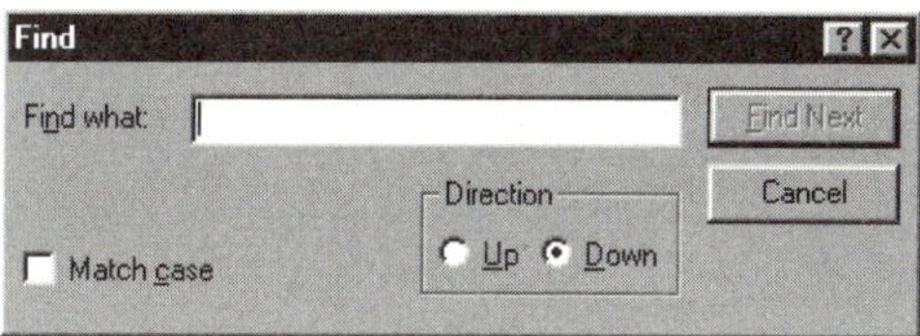

Figure 3-10: The Find dialog box.

4. For the purposes of this tutorial, type the word **Mail** in the Find what field and click the Find Next button. In a flash, Netscape Navigator 3.0 finds a mention of Mail, highlights it, and displays the surrounding section of the document, as shown in Figure 3-11.

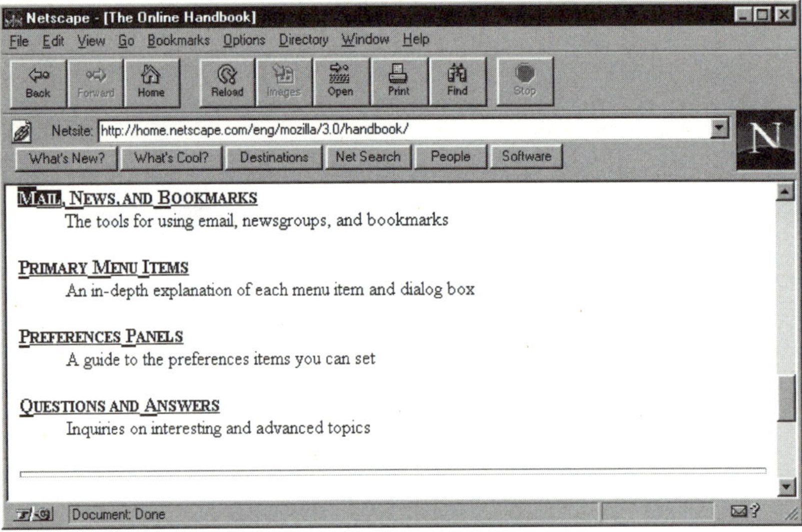

Figure 3-11: The results of a successful Find command.

If you need a case-sensitive search, enable the Match case option; Netscape Navigator 3.0 will display only those instances in which the capitalization matches your entry. You can also specify in which direction the program should search—click the Up radio button to search upward through the document or the Down radio button to move downward. The search begins at the current cursor position.

5. To search for more occurrences of the same string, click the Find Next button again.

The Stop Button

Our final stop on the Netscape Navigator 3.0 toolbar is the Stop button. If you need to abort the transfer of any data to or from Navigator, click this button. You might not need the Stop button often, but when you do it'll make the difference between continuing your session or waiting for what seems like a lifetime for the transfer attempt to finally time out.

Why do some pages seem to take forever to load? Possible reasons for a long wait can include:

- **Heavy usage on the Web site you're calling**. Try calling during low-traffic hours—late at night or early in the morning.

- **Heavy usage on the system that provides your Internet connection**. Check with your access provider to see when the system is being used the least. Remember that the server where a particular page is located may be in another part of the world, so you may have to make allowances for time differences.
- **Extra-large graphics or files you're receiving**. (Remember, you can always keep track of where you are in the transfer process by watching the progress bar that appears in the Navigator status line.)
- **A slow data pipeline**. In plain English, this means that some sites are connected to the Web by leased modem lines or older networks, and these slower connections can be bottlenecks.

TIP

If Navigator is attempting to receive a Web page or a file and the transfer seems "stuck," you can often retrieve the data successfully by aborting the current transfer with the Stop button and immediately trying the same link again.

Here's a good rule of thumb: the best time to surf the Net is when you really should be sleeping. No wonder I'm so tired!

So far we've looked at Web pages that simply present information. But Netscape Navigator 3.0 supports more interactive uses of the Internet as well. In the next section, we'll look at a different kind of Web page, the fill-out form.

Reloading versus Refreshing

I haven't talked much about the Reload button because it's pretty obvious: it simply goes out on the Net and reloads the Web document that's currently displayed.

Well, it's not *quite* that simple. First Navigator checks to see if the page has changed at all, and it only reloads it if it's different from the one stored in its cache from the last time you loaded it. This can be useful if you want the latest information from a site that changes daily, for instance. But since reloading means *reconnecting* with the remote site, it can also be slow, especially when the Net is particularly busy. If you want to redisplay a page in Netscape Navigator 3.0 but don't particularly care if it's the very latest version, you can use the Refresh command that's located in the View menu. This command loads the most recent version of the URL that has been saved to the program's cache.

You can also *force* a reload, in other words make Navigator go out and get a fresh copy of a page even if it hasn't changed. To do this, hold down the Shift key while clicking the Reload button.

Forms on the Web

"Please fill in your name, address, and phone number." You've been doing it your whole life on paper, and now you can do it electronically too.

Forms are scattered all over the Web. Some let you fill in a search word and then find it for you in a collection of documents; some let you buy a CD or new software product; some even engage you in a real-time conversation. Whatever their purpose, World Wide Web forms share a common look and feel when displayed in Netscape Navigator 3.0. Here's an example:

1. Make sure you are connected to the Internet either directly or via your SLIP or PPP access provider. If Netscape Navigator 3.0 is not currently running, launch it by double-clicking its icon.
2. Click the Open button. The Open Location dialog box appears.

   Yes, you could simply type the new URL in the Netsite box. It's a good idea, though, to try the various ways to accomplish a particular task in Netscape Navigator 3.0 so you can see which feels easiest to you.
3. In the Open Location field, type **http://hoohoo.ncsa.uiuc.edu/archie.html** and click Open. The Archie request form appears, as shown in Figure 3-12.

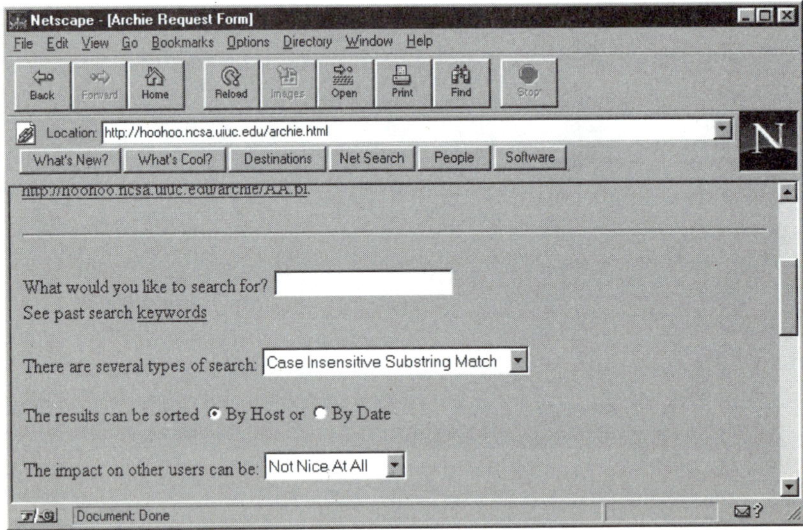

Figure 3-12: The Archie Request Form.

TIP

Remember, you don't need to type in entire URLs. Typing **hoohoo.ncsa.uiuc.edu/archie.html** *will do the trick.*

Archie is an Internet service that's been around much longer than the Web. It is a tool for finding files at FTP sites (see Chapter 6, "Getting Files via FTP"). But until the Web came along and provided convenient fill-out forms like this one, Archie was much more difficult to use.

Take a few minutes to scroll through this page and examine its various form elements. There are boxes you can type text into, drop-down lists, and radio buttons. There is also a Submit button that lets you send your request once you have completed filling in the information. If you want, type something in the What would you like to search for? box and then click the Submit button. Let's say you typed the word **test** and left all the other fields alone. In a few seconds you'd be presented with something like Figure 3-13.

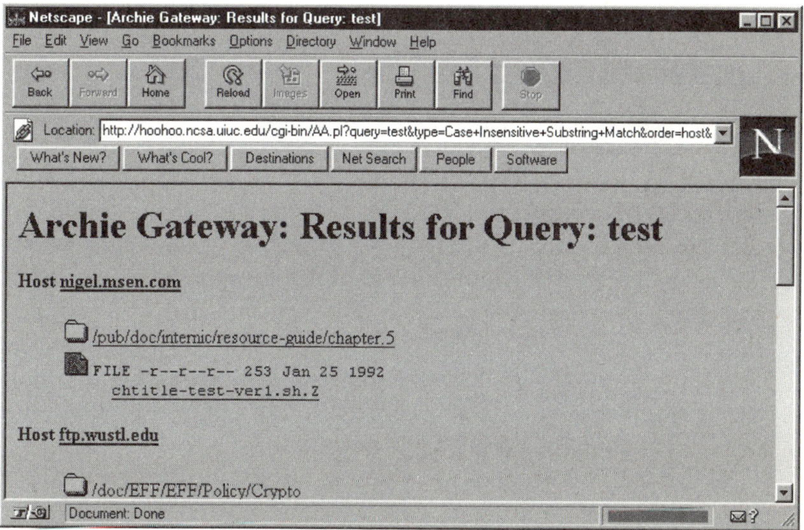

Figure 3-13: The results of an Archie search.

As the commercial uses of the Internet become more prominent, we'll see more and more forms for actual transactions. Already you can buy all kinds of products directly over the Net, and the Web's forms interface makes it easy. By the way, Netscape has been a leader in Internet security, and Netscape Navigator 3.0 indicates when a form is not secure by displaying the following text:

```
Any information you submit is insecure and could be observed by a third
party while in transit. If you are submitting passwords, credit card
numbers, or other information you would like to keep private, it would be
safer for you to cancel the submission.
```

This may sound a bit frightening, but security is typically not a problem with the vast majority of forms you'll fill out online. As a rule, simply take the same precautions as you would if someone were asking similar questions over the telephone. If you feel uncomfortable providing a particular piece of private information, you'll probably want to follow Navigator's recommendation and cancel the form without submitting it.

As more and more companies start collecting data and even selling products via the Internet, online forms may become the bread-and-butter interface on the Web. But fortunately the Web is not all bread and butter; it's champagne and Jell-O, too. Let's take a look at something a bit more fun than forms: *frames*.

Understanding Frames

One of the coolest features of Netscape Navigator 3.0 is its support for frames. Frames are distinct areas within the Netscape Navigator 3.0 display area. Special HTML commands in a Web document tell the program to partition the display. Each frame is a stand-alone environment that recognizes mouse clicks, has its own scroll bars, and can include all the features of any Web page. Each frame has its own distinct URL. In short, each frame is actually a window displaying its own Web page. Netscape Navigator 3.0 can actually "freeze" one of the frames so that it stays onscreen all the time while you interact with the links and hot spots in another frame. You might see logos, advertisements, or tables of contents handled in this fashion.

And not all frames look alike. Using Netscape Navigator 3.0 you might see frames with wide borders, narrow borders, or even no borders at all.

Let's take a look at an example of frames, as shown in Figure 3-14. This figure is the Netscape Web site at http://home.netscape.com/comprod/upgrades/.

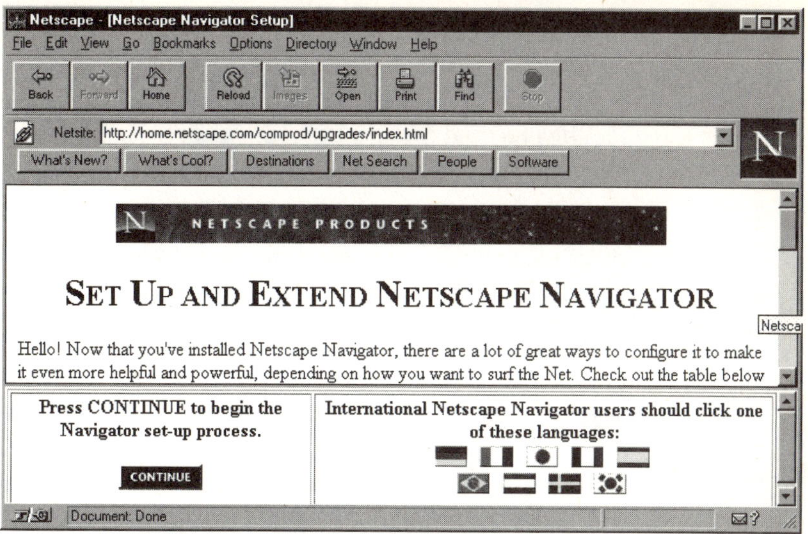

Figure 3-14: An example of a Web page with frames.

TIP

Because each frame is its own entity, make sure you select the appropriate frame (by clicking) when you decide to print something. Only the contents of the selected frame, and not the entire display window, print. In addition, you can reload the contents of individual frames by selecting Reload Frame from the View menu, and you can even e-mail the contents of a frame by selecting Mail Frame from the File menu.

The way developers use frames makes Web sites very flexible and dynamic for the user. At this Netscape site, notice how each of the two frames is used differently. The top frame displays information and instructions, while the bottom frame solicits user input. Also, notice how each frame has its own scroll bars.

Other sites use frames to display different types of elements. One frame, for instance, may contain text, while another contains graphics. As you click and read through the text, the graphics can change or rotate based on the text displayed. Frames are also used with multimedia or 3D objects. One pane may contain instructions or a story about how to navigate a VRML world, while the other contains the actual VRML objects. (What, you don't know what VRML is? Please turn to Chapter 9, "Power Navigator 3.0.")

TIP

You can go back and forward in frames just as you do in the browser window as a whole. To go back to the information previously displayed in a frame, select that frame (by clicking in it) and click the Back button. To go forward, select the frame and click the Forward button.

By now you're well on your way to gathering a wide variety of information from the Web. In the next few sections, we'll look at some ways of organizing all this information.

The History List & Bookmarks

As you travel around the World Wide Web, you'll often find yourself jumping back to the same pages over and over again. From time to time you may also need a specific URL that you visited two or three sessions ago. And you're certain to find a number of Web pages that become your favorites, so you'll want to visit them often.

Netscape Navigator 3.0 provides several methods for keeping track of where you are on the Web—and where you've been. In this section, we'll discuss the two important features that help you maintain your own Web road map: the history list, which keeps track of where you've been in the current session, and bookmarks, which are permanent pointers to your favorite Web pages.

Using the History List

The history list is actually a collection of entries automatically maintained by Netscape Navigator 3.0. Each entry represents a single site you have visited. Each time you load a new Web page, the URL for that site is saved. This makes the history list an excellent tool for jumping among pages while you check references.

There are three ways to access a list of sites you've visited. First, the simplest:

1. After you have viewed several documents using Netscape Navigator 3.0, click the down arrow just to the right of the Netsite/Location box. The history list appears right there, as shown in Figure 3-15. Note that the list is scrollable, with only the most recent 10 pages showing.
2. Click any entry in the list to return to that document.

TIP

The Netsite/Location box history list includes only URLs you've entered in the box itself or visited by using the Open button; it does not include any sites you've visited by clicking on a link. The other methods of accessing your online history, described later in this chapter, show all *the sites you've visited.*

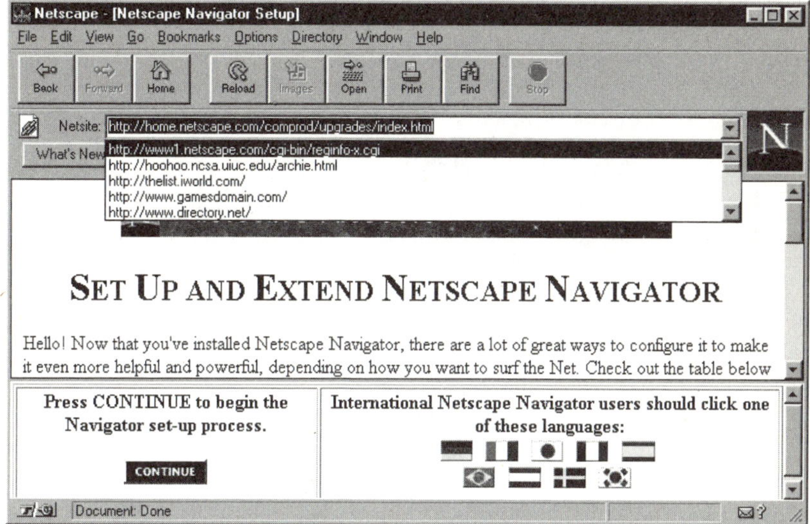

Figure 3-15: The drop-down history list.

You can also return to a previously viewed page right from Netscape Navigator 3.0's Go menu. Simply click Go. You will see the history list at the bottom of the menu, as shown in Figure 3-16. Once again, you can simply select one of the entries to jump to it immediately.

Lastly, you can display the history list within a dialog box, which allows for a neater and more complete presentation of each entry:

1. Select History from the Window menu, or simply press Ctrl+H. Netscape Navigator 3.0 displays the History dialog box, as shown in Figure 3-17.

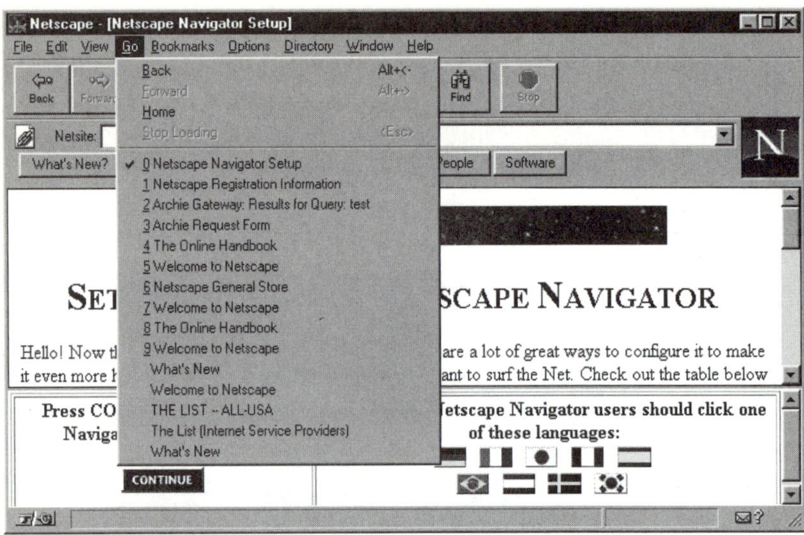
Figure 3-16: The Go menu, showing the history list.

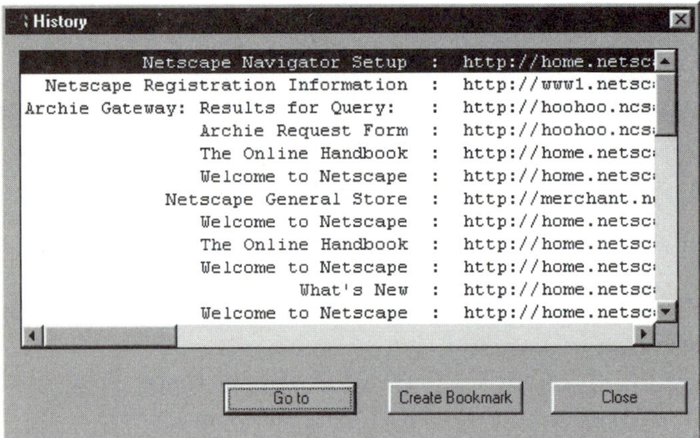
Figure 3-17: The History dialog box.

Notice that each entry appears as a single line, complete with both the page title and its URL address.

2. To jump to a particular page, simply double-click directly on the entry or select it and click the Go To button.

3. To add a history entry to your bookmarks, click the Create Bookmark button. (We'll cover bookmarks in the next section.)
4. To return to the main browser window, click Close.

TIP

Remember, your history list is erased when you finish your session. The Netsite/Location box list is maintained, but again, it contains only URLs you've entered yourself. That's why bookmarks are important.

Bookmarks

Now that you're familiar with the history list, you may be saying to yourself, "Well, that's great for a single session, but what about documents that I want to return to at some later date?" Luckily you don't have to resort to paper and pencil or try to maintain a text file of your favorite sites—Netscape Navigator 3.0 provides you with bookmarks, which are saved permanently in your own "Web page directory." You can also create a simple Web page of your own that includes your favorite sites; we'll discuss this in Chapter 9, "Power Navigator 3.0."

Adding & Using Bookmarks

The two actions you'll perform most often with bookmarks are (1) adding them and (2) using them to jump to a stored URL. To add a bookmark for the document that's currently displayed in Netscape Navigator 3.0:

- Select Add Bookmark from the Bookmarks menu, or simply press Ctrl+D.

Using bookmarks to jump to a document is just as easy:

- Click the Bookmarks menu, then select one of the bookmarks that appears at the bottom (see Figure 3-18). You are immediately teleported to the selected URL.

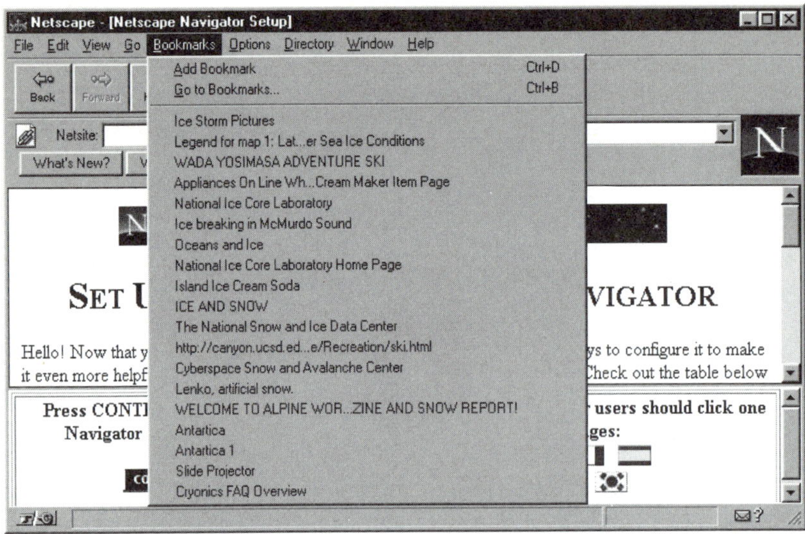

Figure 3-18: The Bookmarks menu, showing a list of bookmarks at the bottom.

As with the history list, Netscape Navigator 3.0 provides a fuller, alternative interface to your bookmarks: the Bookmarks window.

TIP

You can also add a bookmark for a link within a document by right-clicking on the link and then choosing Add Bookmark from the context menu that appears.

The Bookmarks Window

Now that you know how to use bookmarks at the simplest level, let's advance a bit. Just as history entries can be displayed in the History dialog box, you can also display a bookmark list that offers a lot more functionality than the Bookmarks menu. To open the Bookmarks window, select Bookmarks from the Windows menu, or simply press Ctrl+B. The Bookmarks window appears, as shown in Figure 3-19.

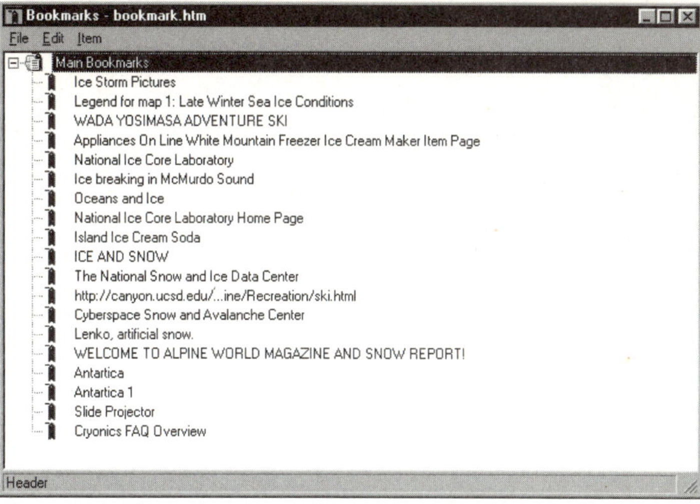

Figure 3-19: The Bookmarks window.

- Depending on what sites you've already added to your bookmarks list, your window may look different from mine.
- If you've already configured the Identity settings in Mail and News Properties, the top-level bookmark folder may include your own name instead of what you see in the illustrations here.

TIP

You can change the name of any bookmark folder, including the top-level one, by right-clicking it and selecting Properties from the context menu that appears. You can also change the name of individual bookmarks this way.

As you can see, Netscape Navigator 3.0 displays the contents of the current bookmark file in a tree format, with entries appearing under the folder icon. The Bookmarks window has its own menu bar, which we'll refer to as we explain the other bookmark functions. But to jump to the document represented by a bookmark entry you don't even need the menu. Simply double-click the entry itself.

TIP

Netscape Navigator 3.0 lets you use more than one bookmark file and also makes it easy to switch between files. From the File menu in the Bookmarks window, you can choose Open to select a new file, or Save As to save the current file under a new name.

Organizing Your Bookmarks

If you're familiar with the Windows drag-and-drop function and the tree structure common in Windows 95 applications like Explorer, you'll have no problem organizing your bookmarks any way you like.

For example, let's say you'd like to categorize your bookmarks by subject matter, with each subject represented by its own folder. For the purposes of this exercise, we'll add a new folder called Computers under the existing Main Bookmarks folder.

First, to create a new bookmark folder:

1. Highlight the existing folder under which the new folder should be created. In this case, the existing folder is Main Bookmarks.
2. Choose Insert Folder from the Item menu. Netscape Navigator 3.0 displays the Bookmark Properties dialog box shown in Figure 3-20.

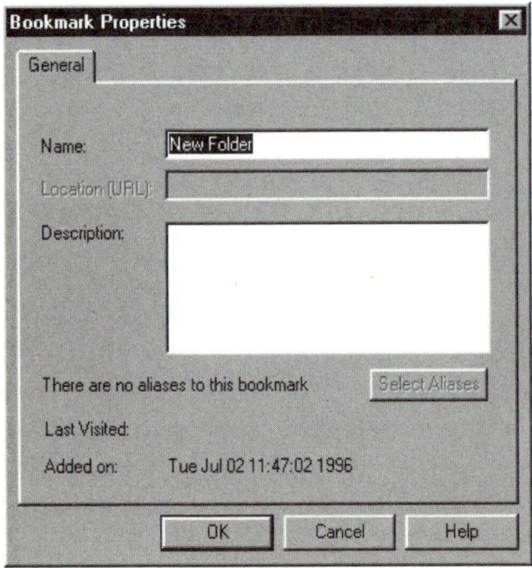

Figure 3-20: The Bookmark Properties dialog box.

3. Type **Computers** in the Name field. If you like, you can add a simple text description that will display when you right-click on the folder and select Properties.
4. Click OK to save the folder.

Now that you've added the Computers folder, you can either create new bookmark entries within it, or move existing entries into it.

To create a new bookmark:

1. Highlight the folder under which the new entry should be created. In this case, we'll click Computers.
2. Select Insert Bookmark from the Item menu. Netscape Navigator 3.0 displays the Bookmark Properties dialog box, shown before in Figure 3-20.
3. Type the name for your new bookmark in the Name field. As an example, let's use **A nifty Computer URL**. If you like, you can add a simple text description that will display when you right-click on the entry and select Properties.
4. Type the URL into the Location (URL) field. Make sure you type the complete address correctly!
5. Click OK to save the entry. Your Bookmarks window should now look something like Figure 3-21.

   A question mark is displayed next to a bookmark created this way until you actually click it and link to the site it represents.

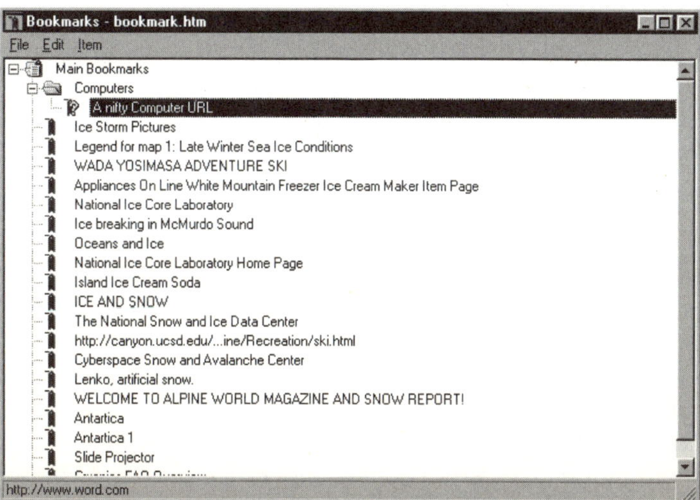

Figure 3-21: The Bookmarks window with new entry.

TIP

Try clicking the right mouse button on an entry within the Bookmarks window. As you can see, the context menu that pops up provides a quick, convenient way to access most of the Bookmarks commands we've been talking about.

It's even easier to move an existing bookmark into a folder. Click and drag the entry icon (which looks like a sheet of paper with the edge folded down) and drop it on top of the desired folder. Notice that your cursor changes appearance to indicate you're dragging the entry to a new spot. The entry will now appear as a sub-branch under the folder.

When you add entries under a folder, Netscape Navigator 3.0 also displays the entries and folder hierarchy as part of the Bookmarks menu. Folders with entries in them appear with arrows on the right side of the menu; when you select the folder, the folder name expands to show the bookmark entries within.

If you'd like to separate your entries or folders on the Bookmarks menu, highlight the name in the Bookmarks window and select Insert Separator from the Bookmarks dialog box Item menu. When you return to the Bookmarks menu, you'll see a line separating that entry or folder from the others on the menu.

TIP

Once you've expanded your entries within several folders, it may be harder to find a particular entry. Of course, you can use the Find command in the Bookmarks window, but it also helps to close folders you're not using. Closing a folder hides all the bookmark entries under it. To close a folder, double-click its icon; to expand it and display the entries it contains, double-click its icon again. You can also single-click the plus or minus icon to the left of the folder icon.

Adding Bookmarks With the Link Icon

One of the most convenient new features in Netscape Navigator 3.0 is the Link icon, located just to the left of the Netsite/Location box. You can use this icon to drag Internet shortcuts to the desktop, to copy URLs to the Windows clipboard, and yes, to add new entries into your bookmarks file.

But you already know how to add bookmarks, you say. Pressing Ctrl+D or selecting Add Bookmark from the Bookmarks menu certainly *does* add a bookmark, but it always puts new bookmarks in the same place. Suppose you want more control over where a bookmark ends up? That's where the Link icon comes in handy.

To add the currently displayed URL to the bookmarks file using the Link icon:

1. Open the Bookmarks window by pressing Ctrl+B.
2. Drag the Link icon into the Bookmarks window. You can drop the URL into any folder that appears in the window.

As you can see, the Link icon helps you stay organized "on the fly." You can start right out by putting bookmarks in the proper folders instead of having to clean up later.

What's an Alias?

You'll notice that the Item menu in the Bookmarks window, as well as the context menu that pops up when you right-click on a particular bookmark, contains a Make Alias command. This command lets you create an alternate bookmark that links to the same URL as the original one. In addition, if you change the original bookmark in any way, the alias changes along with it.

What's the point? Using aliases, you can have the same bookmark in more than one folder. Simply move the aliases you create into whatever folder locations you want. If you simply *copy* the bookmark to a different folder, any changes in the original are not reflected in the copy. Aliases ensure that even multiple instances of the same bookmark remain up-to-date.

Changing Where New Bookmarks Get Added

There is another way to stay organized. You can configure Netscape Navigator 3.0 so that new bookmarks are always placed in a folder you specify. By default, when you press Ctrl+D the new bookmark is added to the end of the top-level bookmark folder. But let's say you want all new bookmarks to go into a subfolder called New. Here's how you do it:

1. In the Bookmarks window, select the folder you want to use for all bookmarks added using Ctrl+D or the Add Bookmark command.
2. With that folder highlighted, select Set to New Bookmarks Folder from the Item menu. A book icon appears on top of the file icon for that folder, as shown in Figure 3-22.

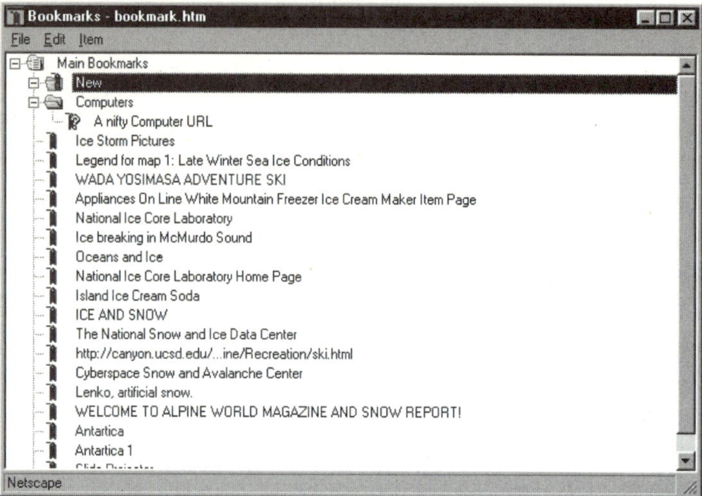

Figure 3-22: The New folder, with icon indicating it is the default New bookmarks folder.

There can be only one New bookmarks folder at a time, at least within the same bookmarks file. If you want to change it, simply select a different folder and repeat step 2. Remember, you can always return the program to its default mode of operation by selecting the top level folder as the default New bookmarks folder.

Customizing the Bookmarks Menu Display

As you collect dozens or even hundreds of Bookmarks, all neatly categorized within their folders, the Bookmarks menu starts looking pretty long. You probably don't need to see all these Bookmarks every time you run the program, so why not limit what's displayed in the menu? Netscape Navigator 3.0 makes this easy:

1. In the Bookmarks window, select the folder that you want to have displayed on the Bookmarks menu.
2. With the folder highlighted, select Set to Bookmark Menu Folder from the Item menu.

Now only the items in that folder will appear in the Bookmarks menu. You can always change back to the program's default display of all bookmarks by selecting the top-level folder and repeating step 2.

Checking for What's New

Let's suppose it's been a week or two since you last surfed the Web (after all, there is more to life than the Internet), and you'd like to catch up on any changes to your favorite bookmarked Web sites. Unfortunately, you have dozens of sites, and not enough time to check all of them for updated information.

Netscape Navigator 3.0's advanced What's New? feature takes all the hassle out of keeping up-to-date with some or all of the sites you've added to your bookmark files. To check for updated Web pages in a bookmark file, follow these steps:

1. If you want to scan a selected group of sites, highlight them with your mouse.
2. Choose What's New? from the File menu. Netscape Navigator 3.0 displays the What's New? dialog box shown in Figure 3-23.

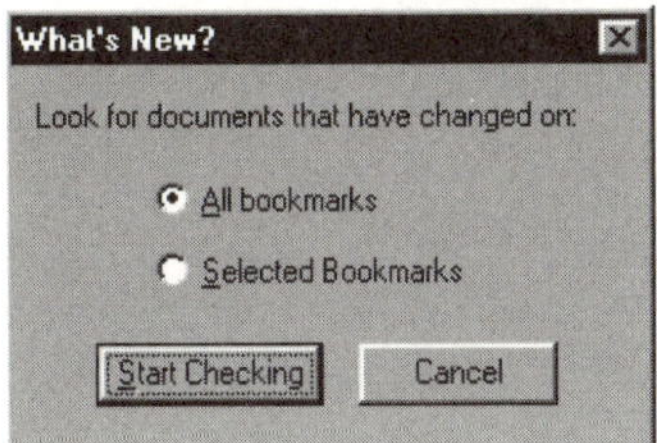

Figure 3-23: The What's New? dialog box.

3. To check all documents for updated information, choose All bookmarks. To check only the sites currently selected in the Bookmarks window, click on Selected Bookmarks.
4. Click Start Checking to begin the scanning process.

Netscape Navigator 3.0 will report the sites where any information has been updated or changed.

Importing & Exporting Bookmarks

As you build your collection of bookmarks, you may want to share your favorite Web sites with others. In fact, many Web surfers keep a "favorite sites" file or "hotlist" in HTML format that they can share with others through Internet mail. Netscape Navigator 3.0 makes it simple to import a bookmark file (bring new entries from some other HTML file into your bookmark file) or export your entries (create an HTML hotlist that others can use).

Remember, an HTML file is simply a text document that contains links to other Web documents. HTML documents are standardized so that all Web browsers can interpret them correctly. That's why importing and exporting allow you to trade files with any Web user, whether or not they have Netscape Navigator 3.0.

From the Netscape Navigator 3.0 window, follow these steps to *import* a bookmark file:

1. Select Go to Bookmarks from the Bookmarks menu. The Bookmarks window appears, as shown earlier in Figure 3-19.
2. From the Bookmarks window's File menu, select Import. Netscape Navigator 3.0 displays a standard Windows or Windows 95 Import bookmarks file dialog, as shown in Figure 3-24.

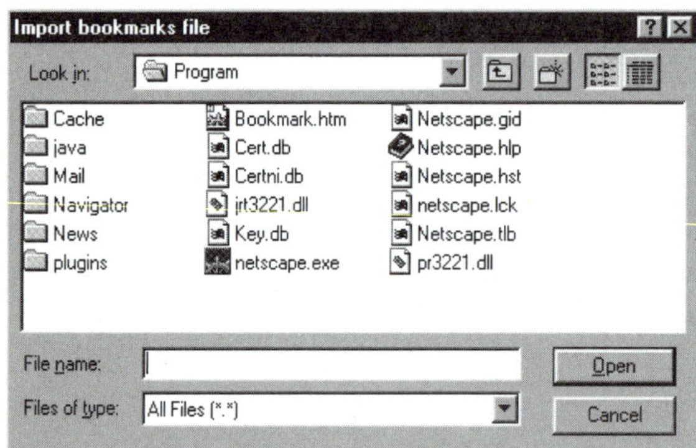

Figure 3-24: The Import bookmarks file dialog box.

3. Navigate to the directory where the HTML file is stored and then double-click it.

From the Navigator display window, follow these steps to *export* a bookmark file:

1. Select Go to Bookmarks from the Bookmarks menu. The Bookmarks window appears, as shown earlier in Figure 3-19.
2. Select the bookmark file you want to export.

3. From the Bookmarks window's File menu, select the Save As command. Netscape Navigator 3.0 displays the standard Windows or Windows 95 Save bookmarks file dialog box, as shown in Figure 3-25.
4. Save the file in any location and under any name you want. Make sure the file type is set to HTML Files.

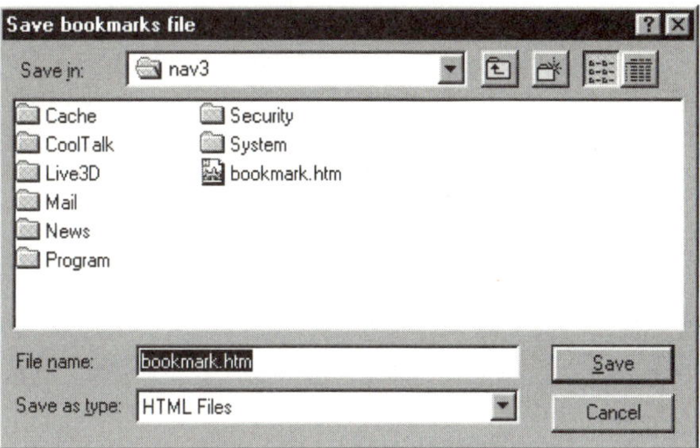

Figure 3-25: The Save bookmarks file dialog box.

Netscape Navigator 3.0 Shortcuts for Windows 95

If you're running Netscape Navigator 3.0 under Windows 95, you can create iconized desktop shortcuts that will make connecting to your favorite Web page as easy as a click of your mouse!

There are several ways to create shortcuts:

- If you click and drag a link, the pointer will change to indicate that the link can now be dropped onto your desktop. A highlighted link is shown in Figure 3-26, while the new desktop shortcut should look something like Figure 3-27.
- You can click your right mouse button on a link and then select Internet Shortcut from the context menu that pops up.

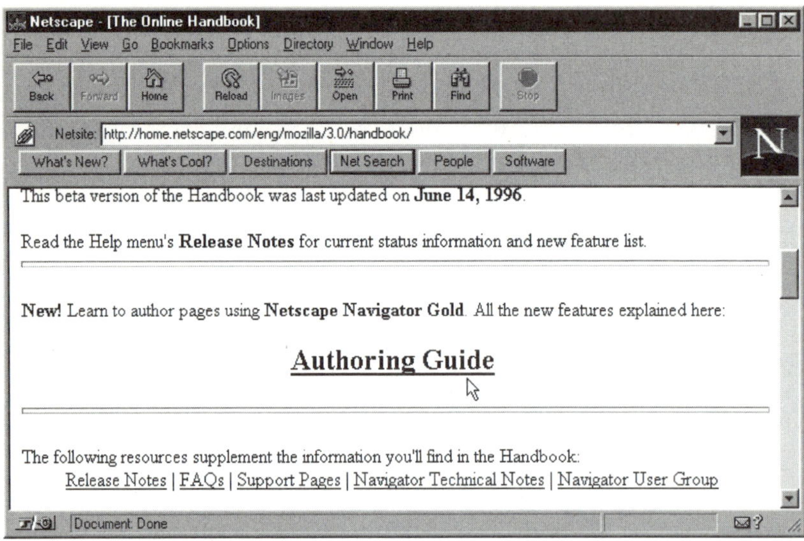

Figure 3-26: A highlighted link, soon to become a desktop shortcut.

Figure 3-27: A Netscape shortcut icon on the desktop.

- You can drag the Link icon (just to the left of the Netsite/Location box) out onto the desktop. This creates a shortcut to the current URL.

Once you've created a desktop shortcut, all you have to do is click on it to access the site. Netscape Navigator 3.0 doesn't even have to be running—clicking the shortcut will automatically launch it with the correct URL.

Now that you're familiar with some of the program's main features, let's take a quick look at the information Netscape makes available to you with a single mouse click.

The Directory Buttons

Already you know how to use many of Netscape Navigator 3.0's main features, and you're probably pretty used to leaping from link to link across the vast stretches of the Internet. One of the great things about Netscape Navigator 3.0 is that it not only provides the tools for getting places, it actually has some of the best Web links built right in. The Directory buttons serve as quick and easy shortcuts to some of the most important Internet resources. We'll also pop in on one of the most popular and well-known sites on the Web: the Yahoo! Web page search site.

The What's New? Button

Let's face it: the World Wide Web is an immense world within cyberspace, and it's getting bigger every day. Even the mass-market magazines are listing Web sites these days, and your Net-surfing friends will certainly send you their share of cool URLs.

But where do you go for the very latest sites? Wouldn't it be nice to check a single page for the "best of the newest" sites that have recently opened?

That's the idea behind the first button on the Directory bar, What's New? This button brings up a page that acts as a doorway to the latest sites on the Web, and it's one of the most popular starting points for owners of Netscape Navigator 3.0. In this section, let's check the What's New? page and jump to a new site. Follow these steps:

1. Make sure you are connected to the Internet either directly or via your SLIP or PPP access provider. If Netscape Navigator 3.0 is not currently running, launch it by double-clicking its icon.
2. Click the What's New? button on the Directory bar. Netscape's What's New? page appears, as shown in Figure 3-28.

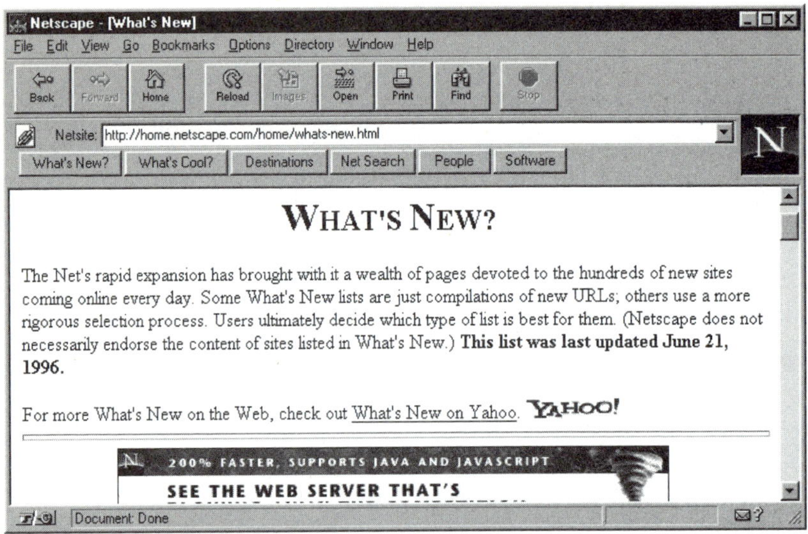

Figure 3-28: The What's New? page.

TIP

You can click the Directory buttons no matter where you are on the Net. You don't have to be displaying documents from the Netscape site for these buttons to work.

3. Scroll down until you see the links to new sites, along with their descriptions. To jump to one of these new pages, simply click its link.
4. To return to the What's New? page, simply click the What's New? button again.

The What's Cool? Button

The What's Cool? button has a similar function to the What's New button. It brings up a page full of links to documents that may not be brand new, but which:

- Are especially well designed or colorful.
- Have unique resources, like extensive image libraries or databases.
- Offer animation or unusual Web applications.
- Have proven particularly popular with Web surfers.

Figure 3-29 shows what was on the What's Cool? page when this book went to press.

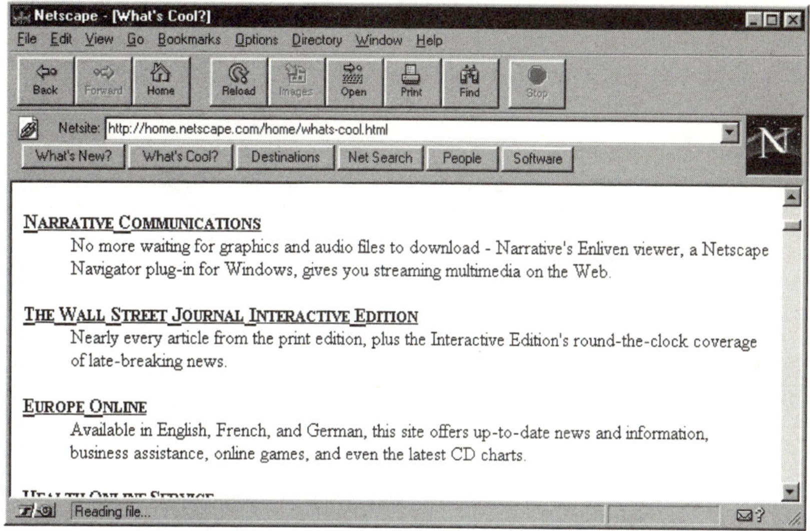

Figure 3-29: The What's Cool? page.

The Destinations Button

As you start exploring the Web, it may become helpful to have a home base, a site that contains links to all sorts of resources organized by category or area of interest. There are many such sites on the Internet, but Netscape provides one of the best in its Netscape Guide by Yahoo!. This is a nicely designed launchpad into the farther reaches of the Net, and we'll take a close look at it in the section called "Exploring the Netscape Guide."

To reach the Netscape Guide, click the Destinations button. Once the page appears, just start clicking. You'll be amazed at what you can find.

The Net Search Button

As we mentioned earlier, the sheer size of the World Wide Web makes it extremely difficult to locate a particular piece of information or a specific Web page by simply fishing for the right URL. Large launchpad pages like Netscape Destinations help, but sometimes you need to find something very specific. For this reason, topical search engines have been around for as long as the Web itself.

Search engines usually look through an index of documents for a query string that you specify. Some search tools also allow you to add logical operators like "either," "and," and "or" so that you can perform more sophisticated searches.

Netscape Navigator 3.0 provides you with links to all the search engines you're likely to need. Clicking the Net Search button brings up the Net Search page, shown in Figure 3-30.

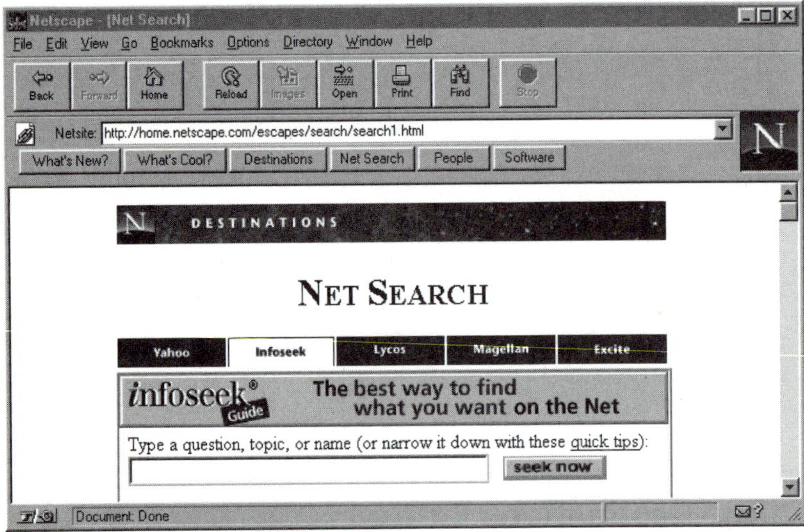

Figure 3-30: The Net Search page.

You can access a variety of search engines such as Infoseek, Lycos, Magellan, Excite, and Yahoo! directly from this page. Simply press the appropriate button near the top of the page.

Let's search for a specific topic using Infoseek:

1. Click the Infoseek button.
2. Enter the string **batman** in the search field and then click the seek now button. Infoseek returns the search results shown in Figure 3-31.

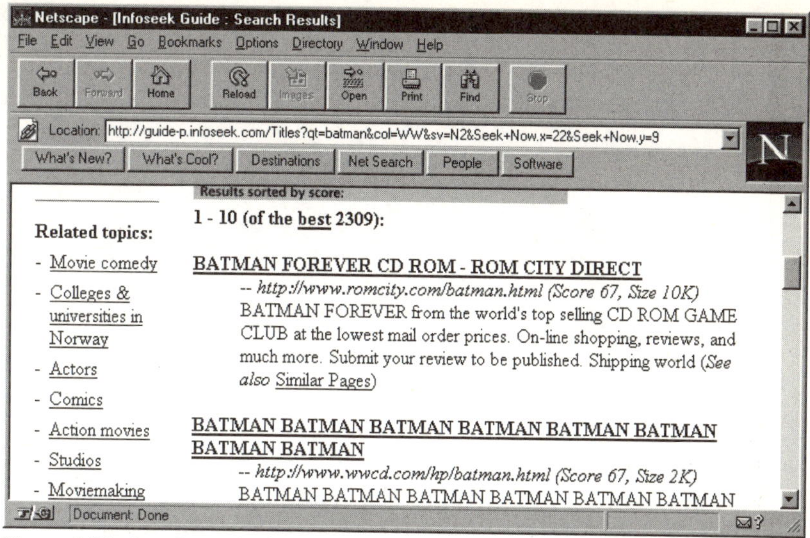

Figure 3-31: Search results from an Infoseek query.

3. To jump directly to one of the pages, simply click on the corresponding link.

A Net search is not guaranteed to locate every site on a particular topic, but if you're hunting for reference material or just surfing because you're interested in the subject, you'll find more than enough sites to keep you busy.

Searching the Easy Way

You don't always need to click the Net Search button to initiate a search. If you type something in the Netsite/Location box that *doesn't* look like a valid URL or part of one—i.e., if it contains two or more words—Navigator 3.0 assumes you're trying to initiate a search. For instance, if you type **netscapepress.com** into the box and press Enter, Navigator will try to connect you to Netscape's home page. But if you type **batman robin** instead, Navigator will automatically use the default search engine to search for occurrences of the words batman and robin throughout the Web! Is this program smart or what? Figures 3-32 and 3-33 show just how easy it can be to find a needle in a Webstack.

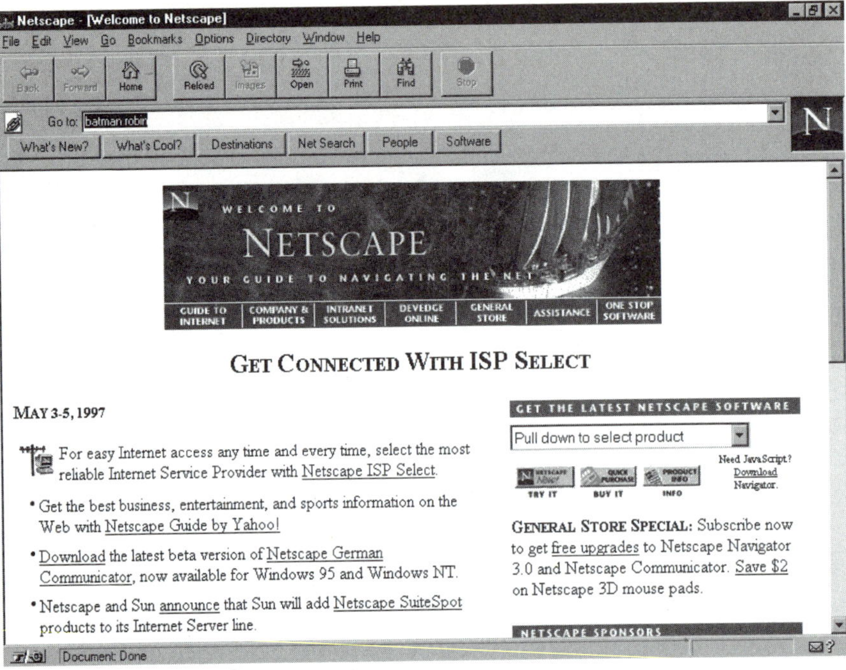

Figure 3-32: Searching the easy way.

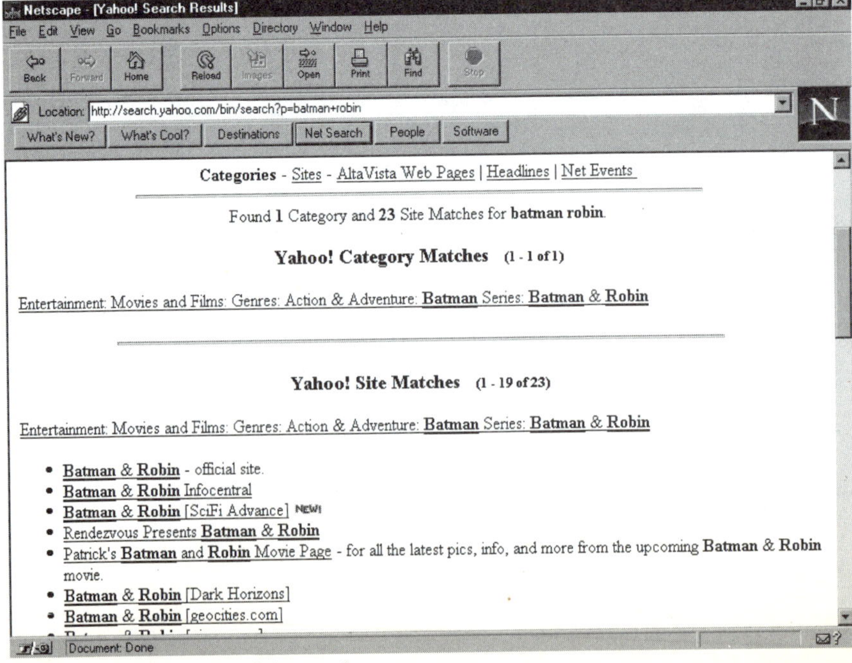

Figure 3-33: The results of the search.

The People Button

The Web is not just pages, it's also *people*. Behind every great URL there's a living, breathing human being, or at least a Cro-Magnon with some minor technical savvy.

How do you find people on the Net? There are a number of "Internet phone books," specialized listings, and search facilities available to anyone with a Web browser. Netscape's People button gives you access to several of these. If you're looking for your long-lost Aunt Prudence and you know she likes to surf the Net, this is the place to start. And Netscape is committed to adding new directories and search tools to the page as they become available.

Figure 3-34 shows the "white pages" resources that are available through the People button.

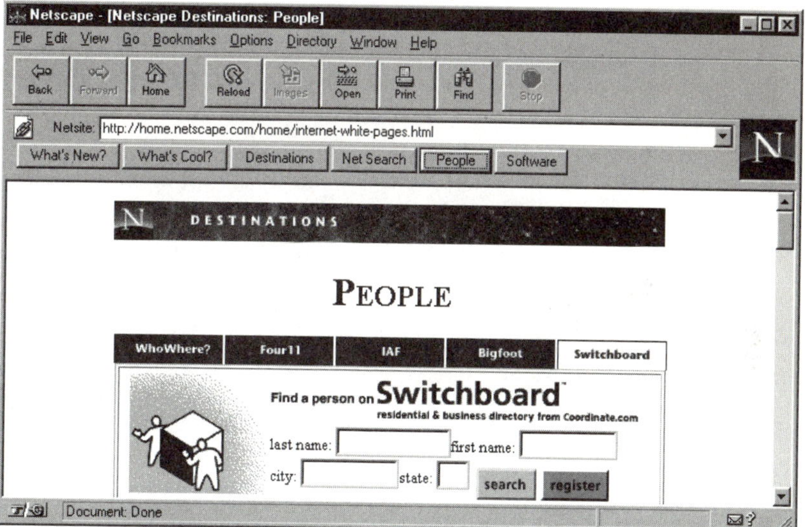

Figure 3-34: The People page.

The Software Button

Finally, let's take a look at the last Directory button. Click the Software button to display the Netscape Navigator Upgrade page, which contains all the details on purchasing and upgrading Netscape software. The Upgrade page provides information on the Netscape Navigator Subscription Program and the latest-released versions of Navigator for different computers. Of course, you'll also find a number of convenient links for downloading demonstration software.

Just think of the Software button as your Netscape software catalog, complete with the option to purchase products online.

Exploring the Netscape Guide

For a taste of the limitless expanse of information available on the Web today, there's no better place to begin with than the Netscape Guide, developed by Yahoo. Yahoo started as a hobby project by Stanford University students David Filo and Jerry Yang in April 1994. Since then, Yahoo has mushroomed into a profitable business that's become a career, but Filo and Yang still offer their original service free of charge to everyone, and their own site has become the home page for uncounted Web surfers. Their latest creative venture is this collaboration with Netscape on the Netscape Guide.

What are we waiting for? Let's start exploring! To access the Netscape Guide, make sure you are connected to the Net and then just click the Destinations button. You can also navigate to the URL **http://guide.netscape.com/guide**. The main Netscape Guide page appears, as shown in Figure 3-35.

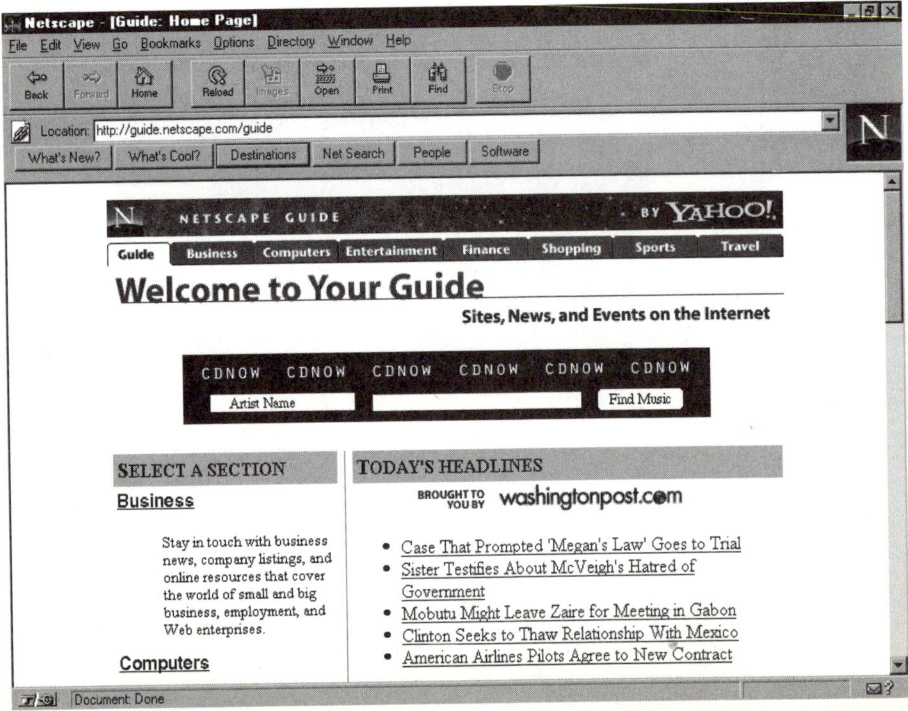

Figure 3-35: The Netscape Guide page.

You can see that the Guide is divided into several broad sections, accessible by clicking the tabs across the top of the page. For instance, if you click the Business tab, you are taken to a page that includes several more subcategories such as Employment, Small Business, and Web Business. But Netscape Guide is much more than a simple hotlist of links. If you scroll down the top Business page, you'll discover daily news headlines related to business, a listing of Web events, an economic calendar, and even a facility for tracking FedEx letters and packages!

But the most interesting feature of the Netscape Guide is that you can customize it to display the information you're most interested in. To do this, simply click the Customize This Page link in any one of the categories.

The Directory Menu

The Netscape Navigator 3.0 Directory menu contains all of the same commands available using the Directory buttons, but it also offers a couple of other resources of interest to new users:

- **Netscape Galleria.** The Netscape Galleria is a collection of links to Web servers running Netscape's server software, including the Commerce Server package for secure online financial transactions. Some of these sites are commercial; others focus on educational and scientific content. If you're interested in running a Web server, this page offers a great chance to sample what other individuals and companies have done.
- **About the Internet.** This menu item is provided for those who would like additional information about the Internet itself. The links on this page jump to other pages that provide both basic concepts and technical details on every aspect of the Internet and the World Wide Web, including the history of the Internet and current demographic statistics.

Moving On

In this chapter, you learned the basics of surfing the World Wide Web, as well as how to operate the major features of Netscape Navigator 3.0. You now know how to search for a particular site, as well as where you can find the newest and coolest pages on the Web.

In the next chapter, we get serious about Netscape Mail. You'll learn how to compose electronic mail to others, read mail they've sent to you, and reply to mail messages. We'll discuss features that Netscape Navigator 3.0 provides for electronic mail power users as well, including mailing lists and message forwarding.

Netscape Mail

Netscape isn't content with just making the world's best Web browser. In Netscape Navigator 3.0, Netscape has created a multipurpose software product that can do much more than just display Web documents.

The most basic of all Internet tools is electronic mail, or e-mail. E-mail is the most widely used software tool of any kind, and Netscape Navigator 3.0 provides a separate interface just to handle this messaging service. In this chapter, we'll show you how to use the Netscape Mail window to send, receive, read, and store e-mail. This window, shown in Figure 4-1, is accessed by selecting Netscape Mail from Navigator's Window menu.

TIP

If you're already using Microsoft Exchange for e-mail in Windows 95, you can integrate it with Netscape Navigator 3.0. See the sidebar "Using Netscape Navigator 3.0 With Microsoft Exchange" toward the end of this chapter.

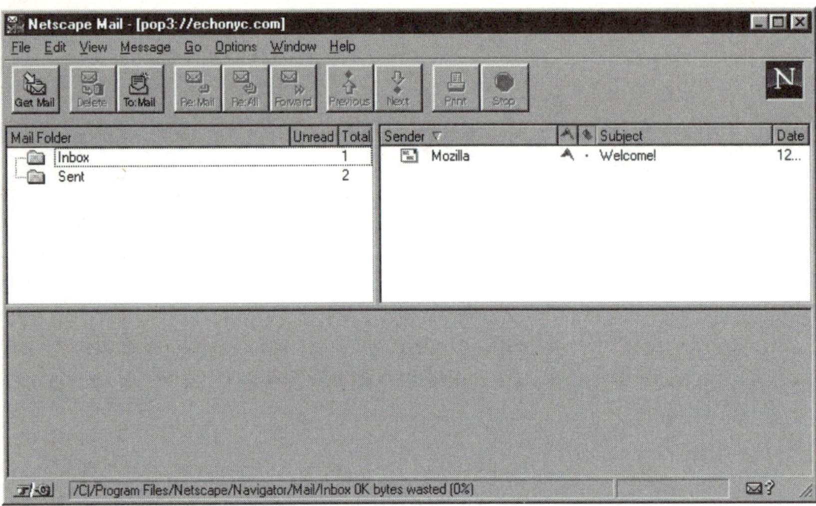

Figure 4-1: The Netscape Mail window.

Before we get into that, however, let's begin with a few words about e-mail itself.

What Is E-mail & How Does it Work?

E-mail, as you probably know, is the electronic messaging service of the Net. When you send a message to a friend via e-mail, that message travels from your machine over the Internet until it arrives at your friend's machine, or to a special electronic post office on a machine he or she can access. The message is then kept there until your friend retrieves it and reads it.

How does the Internet know how to get a piece of e-mail from your machine to your friend's post office account? It works just about like regular old-fashioned snail mail: all the necessary delivery information is contained in your friend's e-mail address.

When you write a piece of e-mail, it's essential to get the address right. No friendly Mr. Postman is going to figure out that you really meant the house down the block from the address you indicated. Every character counts. If there is a mistake in the address you enter—even one wrong letter—the mail will simply be returned to you as undeliverable.

The standard form for an Internet address is *user@domain*. This address is in two parts, separated by an @ sign (press Shift+2 on your keyboard). The part before the @ is the username, and the part after the @ is the domain name—the name of the machine where that user has an e-mail account. It is important that e-mail addresses not have any spaces in them.

Usernames are how users are identified by their Internet access providers. For instance, the username part of Count Dracula's e-mail address, dracula@transylvania.com, is *dracula*. Domain names are the names of the machines themselves. The domain name in the address, *transylvania.com*, identifies the name of a machine, transylvania. The *.com* at the end of the domain name means that this is a commercial service. There are also *.gov* services, which are governmental institutions; *.edu* services, which are at educational institutions; and so on. We touched on some of this in Chapter 2, "The Net & the Web." Sometimes addresses will end with information about a country or network instead of a type of service. For example, addresses ending in .ca are in Canada, and addresses ending in .uk are in the United Kingdom.

What Is My E-mail Address?

Your e-mail address is your identity in the online world; you were probably given your e-mail address by the people who provide you with Internet access. If you are on an office network, your Internet e-mail address may be your network login name followed by an @ sign and the domain name of your company. Then again, it may not—you really need to check with your network administrator.

If you get on the Net using a SLIP or PPP account, you can usually figure out your e-mail address. If your login name is *frank* and your Internet access provider is *graveyard.com*, then your e-mail address is probably frank@graveyard.com. If this isn't correct, then you will have to call your access provider to figure out what your address is.

TIP

If your Internet access provider doesn't give you an e-mail account and free Web page space, you should seriously consider switching access providers!

Exchanging Messages With Online Services

What if you have friends who are not connected directly to the Internet via a network or a SLIP or PPP account, but are users of some online service such as America Online (AOL) or CompuServe? Can you exchange e-mail messages with them?

Sure! Users of CompuServe, MCI Mail, AT&T Mail, Prodigy, or AOL can send you e-mail using your regular Internet address. Typically, the procedure is no more complex than sending a message to another user of the service. You can also send e-mail to a user on any of these services, using Netscape Navigator 3.0 in the same way you would when communicating with another individual on the Net. The only difference is the addressing. If an online service user gives you his or her ID, you have to know how to turn it into a valid Internet address so that any message you send can be delivered. The method for translating addresses varies from service to service.

CompuServe

User IDs on CompuServe take the form of two numbers separated by a comma, as in 71234,5678. To send e-mail to a CompuServe subscriber, you address it to that ID number at (@) the domain compuserve.com. The only trick is that the comma between the two numbers must be replaced by a period. Thus the Internet e-mail address for the user whose ID is 71234,5678 would be:

```
71234.5678@compuserve.com
```

That's all there is to it; you send the message just like any other e-mail.

MCI Mail

MCI Mail users really have three IDs: a number; a "handle," or abbreviated name; and a normal full name. For instance, the user Jake Barns might have the following set of IDs:

```
123-4567
jbarns
Jake Barns
```

To send e-mail to Jake, you could use any of the following Internet e-mail addresses:

```
1234567@mcimail.com
jbarns@mcimail.com
jake_barns@mcimail.com
```

Please note that in the user number, you drop the hyphen, and in the full name you have to add an underscore (_) character between the first and last names.

America Online

All you need to know is the AOL user's "screen name"; you then just add the at sign (@) and the domain aol.com. A valid Internet e-mail address for an AOL user might be, for instance:

```
aoluser@aol.com
```

Note that even if the AOL user has a space in his or her AOL name—John Doe, for instance—you can ignore that space and simply address your e-mail to johndoe@aol.com.

Prodigy

This is just like America Online. You send e-mail to a particular user ID at prodigy.com. Here's an example:

```
abc123@prodigy.com
```

AT&T Mail

As with AOL and Prodigy, each AT&T Mail user has a unique username. To address a message, you simply append @attmail.com to the username. A valid address might be as follows:

```
msmuffet@attmail.com
```

Configuring Netscape Navigator 3.0 Mail

Now that you know about e-mail addresses, you are ready to configure the Netscape Navigator 3.0 Mail window for your personal use. Let's start by configuring what the window looks like.

TIP

If you're eager to start communicating with the world and don't want to slog through all the setup options right now, just skip ahead to the Servers and Identity tabs. Those are the only ones that absolutely must be filled out in order for Netscape Mail to work properly. You can always come back and modify the settings in the other tabs later.

The Appearance Tab

1. With Netscape Navigator 3.0 loaded, select Mail and News Preferences from the Options menu. The Preferences dialog box appears, with the Appearance tab selected as shown in Figure 4-2.

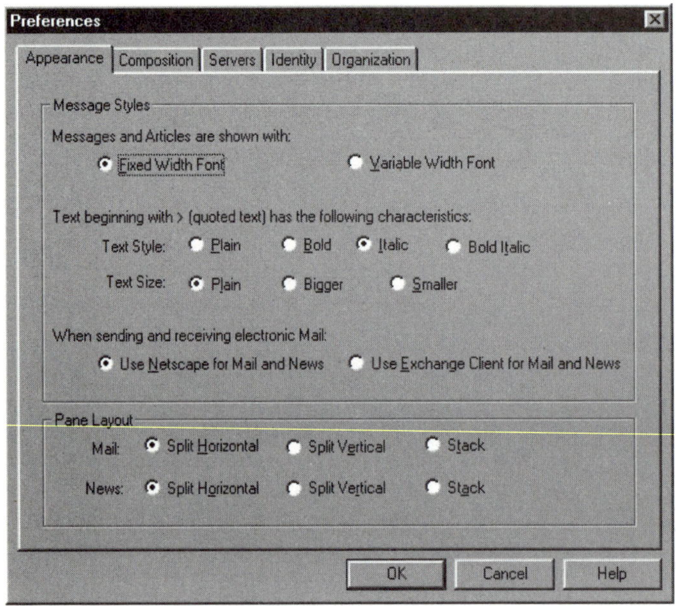

Figure 4-2: The Appearance tab.

If the Appearance tab isn't automatically selected when you choose Mail and News Preferences from the Options menu, select it now.

2. Select whether you want messages to be displayed in a fixed-width font or a variable-width font by clicking the respective option button. You might want to try it both ways. (***Note:*** You can select the font itself using the Display properties dialog in the Windows Control Panel.)
3. Select how you want *quoted text* to appear by selecting a style and a size option button.

What Is Quoted Text?

One of the great advantages of e-mail over snail mail is that without any retyping you can include the text of previous messages you have received. For instance, in responding to a message you may wish to include sections of the original text as part of your reply, or you may want to forward the message to another recipient. Using text you've received is called *quoting*.

The Internet convention for quoted text is to precede each quoted line with the greater than symbol (>). You will sometimes see messages in which somebody includes quoted text that has already been quoted by somebody else—in that case each line is preceded by two greater than symbols. In Netscape Mail, you can make quoted text stand out even more by selecting among the font options in the Appearance tab.

One important note on quoted text that is preceded by the > character: the lines are sent "as is," without wrapping at 72 columns like other text you enter into the Message Composition window. This is because it is essential that each line always begins with the special character. The lines of quoted text may *appear* to be wrapped in your window if you've resized the window, but when your recipient gets the quoted text it will look right.

4. If you are using Windows 95 or Windows NT 4.0 or greater, the next option lets you choose Microsoft Exchange as your e-mail client when sending and receiving messages through Navigator 3.0. For now leave this option set to "Use Netscape for Mail and News."

5. In the Pane Layout section of the Appearance tab, select how you want your Mail and News windows to look. The default, shown in Figure 4-1, is Split Horizontal. In this layout, the pane that contains the contents of a selected e-mail message is below the two other panes, one which lists your e-mail folders and another which lists the messages within that folder.

   If you want to align the message content pane to the right of the two split panes, choose **Split Vertical**.

   If you want to stack all three panes on top of each other, with the content pane at the bottom, select **Stack**.

TIP

In most cases the default window layout is the most convenient. You can always change it later, after you've become more familiar with the various e-mail features.

The Composition Tab

This tab lets you set various options such as an e-mail address or a file to copy all your outgoing messages to. This can be useful if you want to save a paper trail (or rather a byte trail) of your correspondence. There are two other options in the Composition tab that might need some explaining:

- **Send and Post.** This option lets you choose between two standard protocols for attaching files to your mail messages. Please refer to the sidebar, "Making Sure Your Attached Files Arrive Safely."
- **Automatically quote original message when replying**. If this is checked, Netscape Mail automatically includes the original message as part of your reply to that message. Each line of the quoted message is preceded by the greater than symbol (>).

Now the two most important tabs, the ones where you tell Netscape Mail who you are and how to actually send and retrieve your messages.

The Servers Tab

In the Servers tab, there are two pieces of information Netscape Navigator 3.0 needs: your SMTP (*Simple Mail Transport Protocol*—aren't you glad you asked?) address, and your POP3 (*Post Office Protocol*) address. These are the network addresses the program uses to send and receive your e-mail. If you don't know what these addresses are for your Internet access provider, you still might be able to figure them out. If your access provider is **provider.com**, for instance, try **mail.provider.com** for both the SMTP and POP3 addresses. If that doesn't work, give them a call.

SMTP & POP3

Like all Internet programs, Netscape Navigator 3.0 relies on established protocols to send and receive data. As explained earlier in this book, protocols are simply conventions that allow one piece of software to exchange data with another. For instance, a client program might expect a particular kind of acknowledgment after it sends a packet of data. Both sender and receiver need to play by the same rules, or the transfer of information won't be successful.

Internet mail programs use SMTP (Simple Mail Transport Protocol) to *send* messages. The client, Netscape Navigator 3.0, first establishes a connection with the remote SMTP server, the machine that acts as host for the recipient's e-mail account. Once the link is established, Netscape Navigator 3.0 sends the recipient's name. If the server can accept mail for that user, it responds with an OK. If there are several intended recipients, this negotiation continues for each of them. Finally, Netscape Navigator 3.0 sends the actual body of the e-mail message.

To *retrieve* messages from your e-mail server, Netscape Navigator 3.0 uses a very different protocol, called POP3 (Post Office Protocol, version 3). I won't go into the details of POP3 because they're somewhat complex, but it's important to make sure that your e-mail account is on a server that supports this protocol (most do).

OK, let's do this:

1. Enter the domain name for your Internet access provider in the Outgoing Mail (SMTP) Server field. Count Dracula would enter **transylvania.com**.
2. Now enter the domain name for your Internet access provider in the Incoming Mail (POP3) Server field. Once again, Count Dracula would enter **transylvania.com**, as shown in Figure 4-3.
3. Enter your username in the POP3 User Name field. Count Dracula would enter **dracula**, as shown in Figure 4-3.

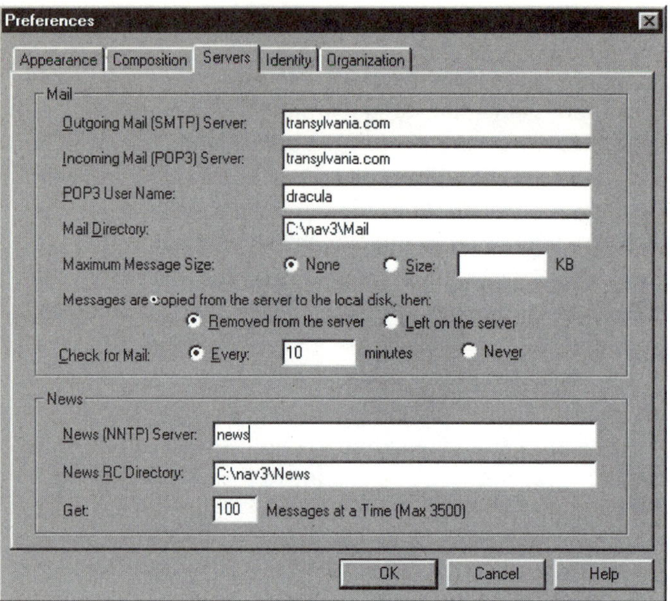

Figure 4-3: Configuring the Servers tab.

4. Unless you have very strong feelings about how your hard drive should be organized, leave the Mail Directory field alone. The default location should be fine for storing mail files; however, you should always make sure this drive has several megabytes of space available, since your mail files will grow with time.
5. Unless you want to limit the size of messages you receive, leave the None radio button selected in the Maximum Message Size area. If you decide to limit the size, the value you enter is the maximum number of lines.
6. Select the Removed from the server radio button if you want all messages deleted from your post office account when you retrieve your mail. If you want your messages to remain on the server so that you can download them again later, select the Left on the server radio button.

   If you decide to leave retrieved messages on your post office server, you may receive the same messages over and over when Netscape Navigator 3.0 gets new mail.
7. In the Check for Mail area, tell Netscape Navigator 3.0 how often you want the program to log on to your post office server to collect any new messages.

   If you click the Never radio button, you will have to click the Get Mail button in the Netscape Mail window every time you want to check for messages.

You can ignore the News options, which I cover in the next chapter. For now, move on to the Identity tab.

The Identity Tab

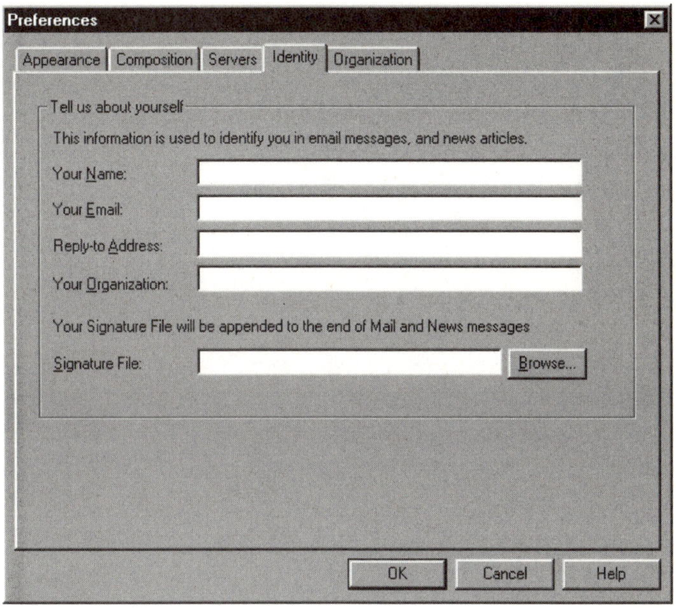

Figure 4-4: The Identity tab.

This is where you enter the information that will appear on all your outgoing mail. To configure your identity preferences:

1. Type your name into the Your Name field. Dracula would enter **Count Dracula**.
2. Type your e-mail address into the Your E-mail field. Dracula would enter **dracula@transylvania.com**.
3. Optionally, enter an alternate e-mail address in the Reply-to Address field. This is the address others will use when replying to your messages. It isn't likely you'll need to do this. You would only use Reply-to Address if, for instance, you wanted to send mail out from Netscape Navigator 3.0 using a commercial access provider, but you wanted to get replies on another account, such as an account you have through school.

4. Optionally, enter the name of an organization or affiliation in the Your Organization field. This simply adds an identifying tag to your mail. Think of it as a kind of electronic letterhead, there if you want it but not really necessary.
5. Optionally, create a signature file for yourself and specify where to find it in the Signature File field.

What's a Signature File?

A signature file is simply a file that gets tacked on to the end of every piece of mail, so if Dracula always wants to add a closing line like

Count Dracula, Moderator, Bloodsuckers Anonymous Mailing List

he would simply create a text file called something like SIG.TXT with a text editor such as Notepad, save it on his hard drive, and use the Browse button to tell Netscape Navigator 3.0 where to find it. Like Your Organization, a signature file (often called a ".sig" on the Net) can be used to include more information in your mail, but isn't necessary. If you do include a signature file, make sure it is short (no more than four lines long) and pertinent (long and/or pointless .sig files tend to attract flames for wasting bandwidth). Also, avoid high-bit ASCII characters, which display as garbage on other machines.

Your completed Identity tab will look something like Figure 4-5.

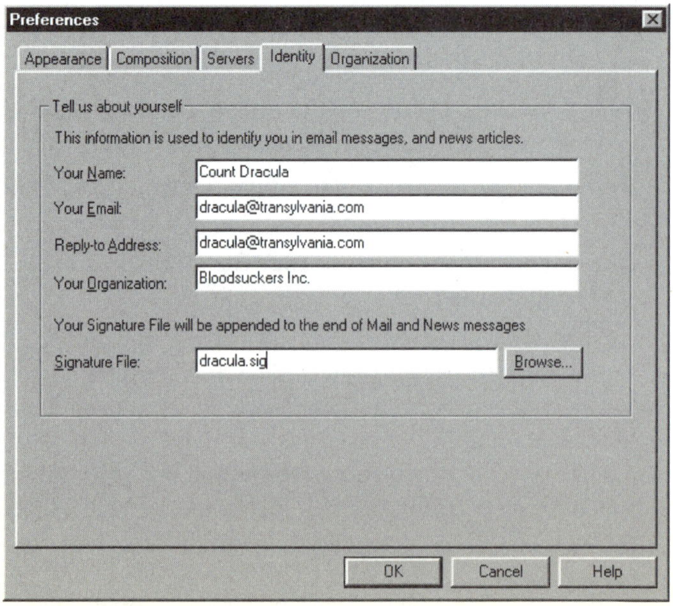

Figure 4-5: A configured Identity tab.

One more tab to go!

The Organization Tab

The Organization tab offers several options:

- **The Password option**. When you open the Netscape Mail window, a dialog box asks you for your password for your POP3 server. You can avoid this message by checking the Remember Mail Password check box.
- **Threading options**. You can choose whether or not to *thread* e-mail messages. Threading is simply a means of organizing messages whereby all replies (and replies to replies) are kept together with the original message, creating a sort of automatic "file" of the related correspondence. Threading is almost essential for Usenet News (see the next chapter), but it can be pretty convenient for regular e-mail as well.
- **Sorting options**. In the Organization tab you can choose whether to sort your incoming e-mail messages by the date you received them, by who sent them, or by subject. The default is to sort them by date received.

Click OK to leave the Preferences dialog box and save your changes. Now it's time to try out the basic mail operations: sending and receiving a message.

TIP

You can change the fonts Netscape Navigator 3.0 uses to display messages by selecting the Appearance tab from the Preferences dialog box. If you don't like the default fonts, you might want to experiment a bit.

Sending & Receiving E-mail

Once you have configured your preferences, you are ready to send yourself a message. That might seem at first like an odd thing to do, but it's the best way to try out both sending and receiving e-mail. Let's get started.

Sending an E-mail Message

While you are still in Netscape Navigator 3.0 and connected to the Internet, select New Mail Message from the File menu or simply press Ctrl+M. If you are already in the Netscape Mail window, click the To:Mail button. Whichever method you use, the Message Composition window appears, as shown in Figure 4-6.

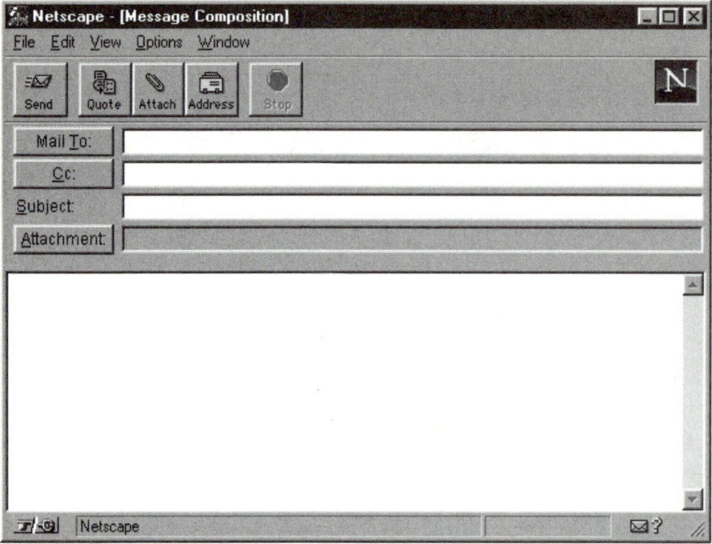

Figure 4-6: The Message Composition window.

As you can see, this window is divided into two parts. The top part contains the header information about the message, the text that will appear at the very beginning of the message when it is received. The bottom part is the pane where you type in your actual message.

Each of the headers in the top pane has a specific function:

- **Mail To.** The Mail To field is where you enter the e-mail address of your recipient. If you want to send the same piece of mail to more than one person, just enter all their addresses in the Mail To field, separating each address with a comma.
- **CC.** The cc field works like carbon copies in the old-fashioned world of paper and typewriter—a copy of your message is sent to everyone listed on the cc: line. Typically, the message is sent to these recipients for their information, and they don't need to reply. Note that the designated recipient or recipients of the mail will see who has been cc'ed.

TIP

Click the Mail To, CC, or Address button to select addresses from your Address Book. You can read about setting up your Address Book later, in the section called, unsurprisingly, "The Address Book."

- **Subject.** The Subject header is whatever you want it to be—it tells the recipient what your letter is about. Try to keep your Subject lines, which are optional, short and informative.
- **Attachment.** Netscape Navigator 3.0 allows you to attach other files stored on your computer to your mail, so that when you send the mail, a copy of that file travels along with the mail. You can also send URLs, links to files that aren't even on your machine but that will appear in your recipient's Mail window! We'll talk more about this in the section "Attaching Files to Messages."

There are other header lines you can add to your e-mail—Reply To, Newsgroups, Followups To, From, and Bcc lines—which you add by selecting them under View in the menu (or, if you want to see everything, just select Show All).

- **Reply To.** The Reply To line is where you can put the e-mail address of another account where you want responses sent.
- **Bcc.** Bcc, for *Blind,* is used when you want to send a copy of a letter to someone but do not want that person's name to appear in the cc line. The recipient or recipients of the mail who are listed on the Mail To and CC lines will not know who has been Bcc'ed.
- **Newsgroups.** In this field, you can list the names of any Usenet newsgroups you'd like your epistle posted to. Select Newsgroups from the View menu. You will learn more about Usenet newsgroups in Chapter 5, "Newsgroups."
- **Followups To.** This field is also for use with Usenet newsgroups. For more information, please see "Replying to an Article" in Chapter 5.

Some of the addressing fields, like Mail To, CC, and Bcc, have buttons next to them. Clicking these buttons will open your Address Book and allow you to select your recipients by mouse clicks. We'll talk more about the Address Book in just a bit.

To write a test letter to yourself, you really only need to fill in a couple of these fields:

1. Fill in the Mail To field with your own e-mail address.
2. Fill in the Subject field with a subject like **Letter from me**.
3. Write yourself a message in the pane below the headers, just as you would type new text into a word processor document. In the end, you should have a message that looks something like the one in Figure 4-7.

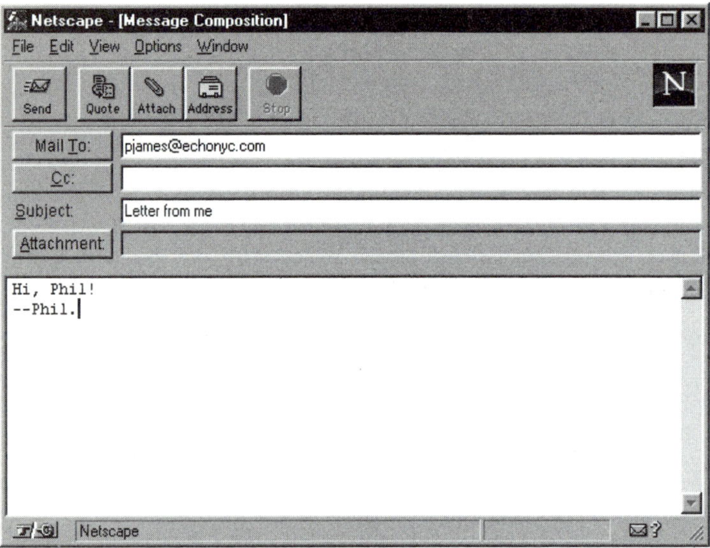

Figure 4-7: A test letter to yourself.

TIP

As you write, your lines wrap when you reach the right edge of the editing area. But when your recipient receives your message, the lines are not wrapped the same way you see them in the Message Composition window. Instead, they always wrap at 72 characters. This assures that even if you work in a very large or very small window, your messages will always be the same width and look right to your recipients. If you don't like this and instead want your messages to appear to your recipients exactly as they appear to you while you're writing them, uncheck Wrap Long Lines from the View menu of the Message Composition window.

Once you have the Mail To and Subject fields filled out and you've entered some text in the text pane, you are ready to actually send your message.

1. Make sure you are connected to the Internet, either directly or through a SLIP or PPP connection with your access provider. If you are using SLIP or PPP and are not currently connected, double-click the Dial-Up Networking icon for your access provider.
2. While you are still in the Message Composition window, click the Send button in the toolbar.

If everything is set correctly, Netscape Navigator 3.0 will contact your Internet access provider and send the message. If it can't send the message properly, make sure that your Internet connection is really open, and check the name of the SMTP and POP servers in the Servers tab, shown earlier in Figure 4-3. If all of this is correct and you still can't send a message, you may need to contact your Internet access provider to make sure you have the right names for the machines handling the mail on your system.

Netscape Navigator 3.0 is also configured to save a copy of your outgoing messages in a folder called "Send." If you don't want a copy of these messages, you can delete them, which you will learn how to do later in this chapter under "Organizing Your Mail Folders."

MAILTO: Tags

Besides calling up the Message Composition window, Netscape Navigator 3.0 offers another way to send mail. Web pages can include special HTML tags called MAILTO: tags. They look just like ordinary links, although often they appear in italics. When you click one of these, Netscape Navigator 3.0 pops up the Message Composition window, allowing you to send a message to the recipient indicated in the Mail To tag.

MAILTO: tags provide a convenient way to solicit feedback or comments in a Web document.

Retrieving E-mail

Now that you have sent yourself a message, you can go ahead and retrieve it from your post office server:

1. You should still be connected to the Internet. Back in the Netscape Navigator 3.0 main window, click the small envelope icon at the bottom right corner. You will immediately be asked for a password.

   You will not be asked for a password if you checked the Remember Mail Password check box in the Organization tab of Mail and News Preferences.

TIP

The mail icon at the bottom right of the Navigator 3.0 window is the easiest way to access Netscape Mail. Simply click it. If there is a question mark next to the mail icon, that means that Navigator 3.0 cannot automatically check your mail server for new messages—probably because you've told it not *to check for new messages in the Server tab under Mail and News Preferences. If there is an exclamation point next to the icon, it means there are new messages for you.*

2. In the Password Entry dialog box, enter your e-mail password. If you're connecting to the Internet via SLIP or PPP, this is probably the same password you use to connect to your Internet access provider.

   Once you enter your password, Netscape Navigator 3.0 logs you in to your post office account to retrieve your mail.

   If you have configured Netscape Navigator 3.0 so that it does not retrieve mail automatically, you need to click the Get Mail button in order to get your waiting message.

If this is the first mail message you have sent, your test message is the only one that will be retrieved (if you don't see your test message in the mail window, press the Get Mail button to check once more). But if you are already using the e-mail address you filled in earlier in Preferences, Netscape Navigator 3.0 will get the rest of your e-mail stored at that address as well.

TIP

Once Netscape Navigator 3.0 retrieves any e-mail from your post office server, it puts an exclamation point next to the envelope icon in the main browser window. That way you know immediately when new mail has arrived, even if you are not in the Netscape Mail window.

Let's assume that the test message was the first piece of e-mail you have ever received—other than the Welcome message from Netscape's "Mozilla." Once Netscape Navigator 3.0 retrieves the new message, your mail window will look like the one in Figure 4-8.

As you can see, this window is divided into three panes—Folders in the upper left, Messages in the upper right, and the main reading window below. Each of these panes has information sorted in columns. In the Folders pane, you will see an Inbox, where incoming mail is stored, with a list of Unread and Total messages. (If the test message is the only mail you have, both Unread and Total will read "1.")

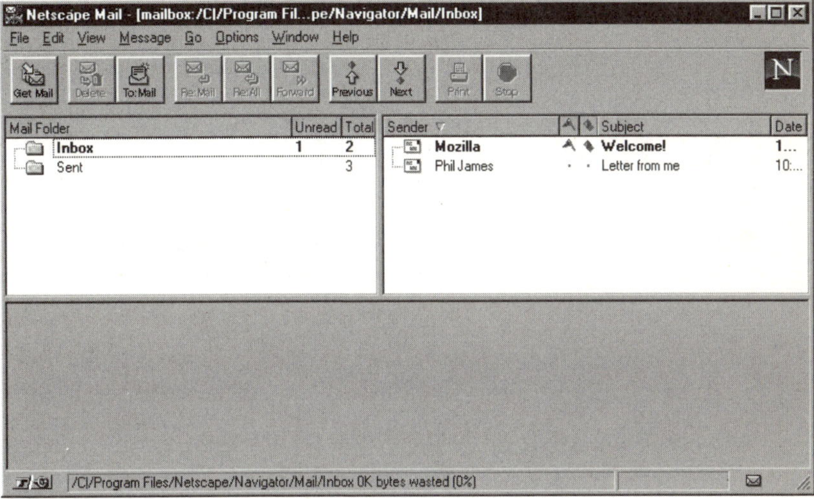

Figure 4-8: Mail window after retrieving new e-mail message.

TIP

You can change the layout of the three panes in the Netscape Mail window. See the section on the Appearance tab above.

Now click on the Sent folder. The Messages pane now displays information about the message you sent, as shown in Figure 4-9.

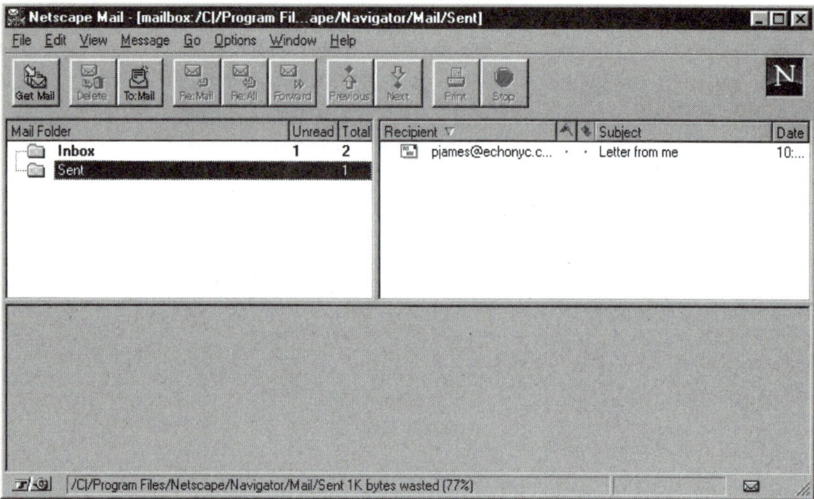

Figure 4-9: Information about sent mail in the Messages pane.

You can move from folder to folder simply by clicking like this. For now, return to the Inbox folder. The Messages pane shows you several things:

- The Subject line of the incoming mail.
- Whether you have marked the messages (a method of flagging important mail). Marked messages are indicated with a red flag.
- Whether you have read the message yet. Unread messages are flagged with a green diamond that may look like a dot if your eyes are like mine.
- The Sender line.
- The date of the message.

The width of each of these columns is adjustable. To change the size of the columns:

1. Position your mouse over the border of the column until it displays a pair of arrows pointing left and right.
2. Now click and drag the border of the column to the left or right, depending on which column you want to widen.

TIP

You can even switch the order of any of the columns in the Message and Folder panes. Simply drag the header button (the button at the top of the column with the word Sender, Subject, Date, etc. on it) right or left to its new location. For instance, you might want to drag the Date column to the far left in the Message window.

The borders between the panes operate exactly the same way, and you will probably want to shrink the size of the Folders pane to the left so that you can have more room to expand the From and Subject headers of your e-mail in the Messages pane, as shown in Figure 4-10.

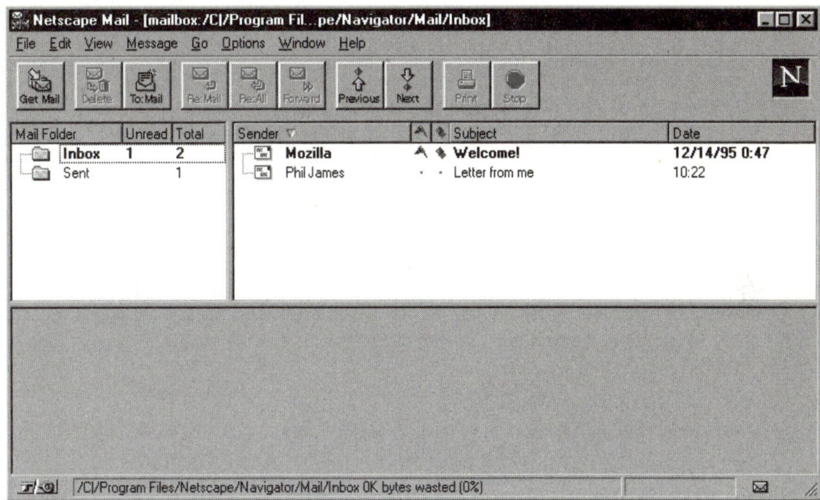

Figure 4-10: A window configured to give more room to the Messages pane, where information about the mail (like Sender and Subject) is displayed.

TIP

To flag a message you've received, simply select it and click the dot in the flag column. You might want to flag messages that really need to be answered, thus differentiating them from those that are merely informational. Once you have replied to a message, you can unflag it by clicking in the flag column again.

Now let's actually read the test message:

1. If your Inbox folder is not currently open, open it by clicking it in the Folders pane. The headers of your messages appear in the Messages pane.
2. Click the Subject line of the mail you want to read. The message itself is now displayed in the lower window for reading, as in Figure 4-11.

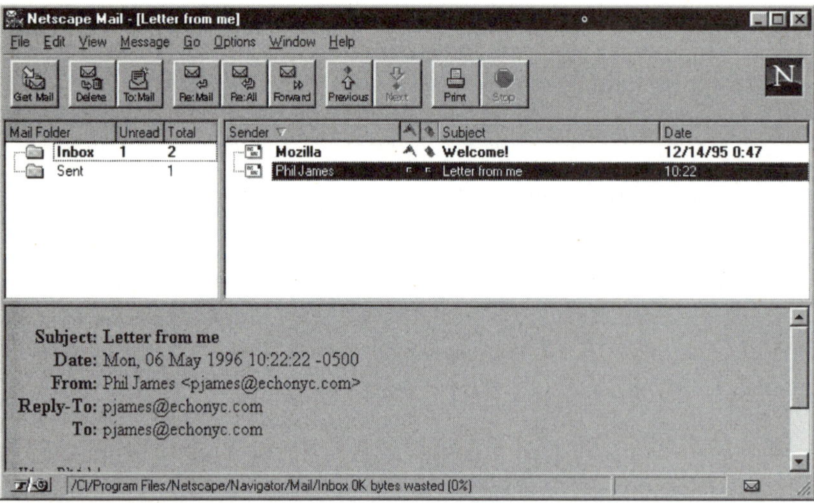

Figure 4-11: New mail opened in the mail window.

Since you've been nice enough to send yourself a message, maybe you should be polite and send yourself a reply. Replying to e-mail is the last of the basic messaging functions.

Replying to E-mail

Replying to a piece of e-mail differs from sending new mail in several important ways. First of all, when you reply, Netscape Navigator 3.0 fills in the Mail To field automatically, since the intended recipient is simply the sender of the original message. The program also fills in the Subject field with "Re:" and the subject of the mail you are replying to.

There is another important difference: the program lets you use a special quote feature to include the text of the e-mail you are responding to right in the body of your reply.

Let's try it:

1. In the Mail window, select a received message and click the Re:Mail button.
2. When the Message Composition window opens, the text of the letter to which you are replying appears in the bottom pane. You will notice that every line begins with a ">"—this is the Internet standard for indicating quoted material.

   The text of the original message does *not* appear in your reply if you unchecked "Automatically quote original message when replying" in the Composition tab of Mail and News Preferences.

At this point, you can add whatever text you like below the quoted text. You can also add other people to the Mail To or CC fields if you like. If the message you have quoted is long, or if you want to respond to only one or two sentences of a letter, it is considered polite to delete the portions not relevant to your reply, although it is bad etiquette to delete or alter quoted text without indicating removals by inserting **[...]** or **(snip)** or some other indication that you edited the quoted material.

Following these steps for replying to your test message, you should end up with a New Message Composition window like the one shown in Figure 4-12.

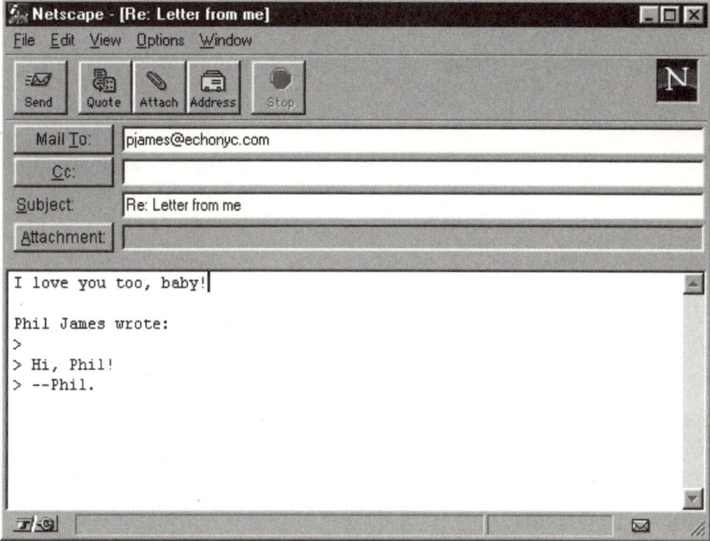

Figure 4-12: A reply including quote of the original message.

Once you've completed your reply, sending it is just like sending a new message: simply click the Send button. The status line will display messages telling you about the status of your message transmission.

Reply to All & Forward

There are two other ways to reply to a letter—Re:All and Forward. The ordinary Re:Mail function just grabs the e-mail addresses of everyone on the From field, but it ignores everyone in the CC field. Re:All will send your reply out to everyone in both the From and CC fields. This is a good way to have a kind of group conversation via e-mail, since Re:All allows you to address the same group of people the sender of the letter addressed originally.

To select the Re:All option when you are reading a message, simply click the Re:All button on the toolbar.

E-mail Etiquette

- Keep in mind that e-mail can be saved, and you can find that what you write in haste can come back to haunt you. Every piece of e-mail is potentially permanent, so before you say something in e-mail, make sure you really mean it because you may see it again later.
- Don't assume that the person getting your mail can always understand what you meant when you wrote it. E-mail can be very impersonal. We instinctively understand the difference between a bill, a business letter, and a post card when they arrive in our mail box, but all e-mail looks the same. Without this context, it is easy to misinterpret and to be misinterpreted, so write carefully. If someone has written a message that upsets you, don't rule out the possibility that he or she didn't mean it the way you took it.
- Don't send abusive mail. This advice seems obvious, but the line can sometimes be hard to draw. What seems like a straightforward comment to you may be read as an insult by someone else. There is one Golden Rule: if someone complains about mail you are sending them, stop.
- Reread your message before you send it. It is so easy to dash off a thoughtless message; the only defense is to reread everything you write before sending it. That goes double if you are angry when writing, in which case it is best to save the message and reread it later before deciding whether or not to send it. Once you send a message, there is no way to retract it.

You use Forward when you want to send a letter along to someone other than the people listed in the From or CC fields. Forward is similar to Re:Mail, with a couple of differences. The Subject line is filled in with the subject line of the letter labeled Fwd instead of Re (with the entire field enclosed in square brackets), and the Mail To field is not filled in. To select the Forward button when you are reading a message, simply click the Forward button in the toolbar.

The message being forwarded is automatically included as an attachment to the mail rather than as text in your actual message. Clicking the Quote button will include the text of the forwarded letter, bracketed by >'s, but if you use this feature to annotate the forwarded letter, remember to delete the attachment so that you don't send two copies of the same letter.

The Address Book

Now that you know how to send and retrieve e-mail messages, you're ready to start communicating with anybody who has an Internet e-mail address. Chances are that you already know dozens or even hundreds of individuals and businesses with e-mail accounts, but how do you remember all these addresses?

E-mail addresses are a little easier than phone numbers because they often include part of a name or some other meaningful information, but as the Net grows and names get used up, e-mail addresses will become more and more devoid of any real-world significance. I suspect that some day they'll be like license plates, and you'll have to pay extra for a meaningful one!

Of course, you can jot e-mail addresses in a paper address book, but that's pretty old-fashioned for a Net geek like you. Fortunately, Netscape Navigator 3.0 provides an electronic address book for storing frequently used e-mail addresses.

The Address Book has two options—it allows you to enter single addresses and groups of addresses. To use the Address Book:

1. Select Address book from the Netscape Navigator 3.0's Window menu. A window like the one in Figure 4-13 pops up.

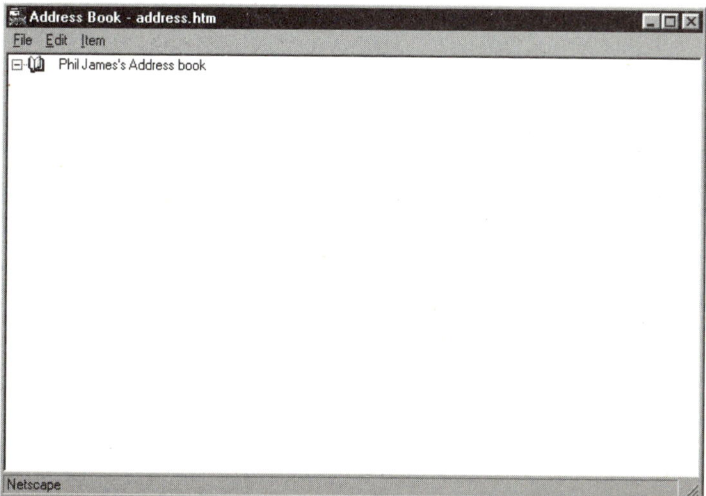

Figure 4-13: The Address Book.

As in other hierarchical tree displays, clicking the plus sign to the left of an item expands it to show all the entries it contains. Clicking the minus sign closes, or collapses, the item. In the Address Book window, an open book icon indicates an expanded mail folder, while a closed book indicates a collapsed folder.

2. To add a new user, select Add User from the Item menu. A dialog box like the one in Figure 4-14 appears.

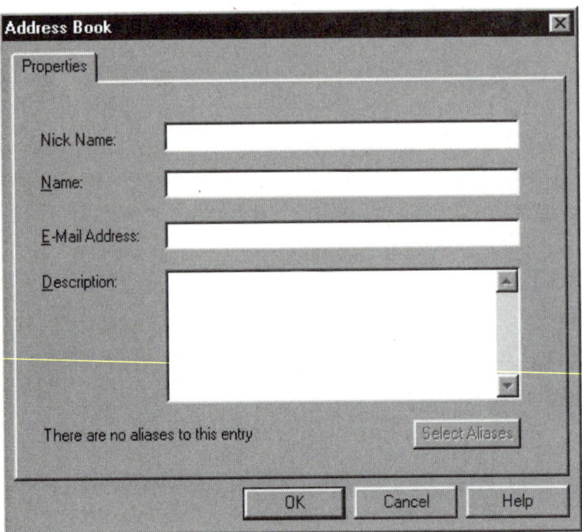

Figure 4-14: Add User dialog box.

3. Fill in the Nick Name field. It doesn't matter what you enter as long as it's easy for you to remember and to associate with this entry. The nickname is your way of remembering who the recipient is.
4. Fill in the Name field with an actual name.
5. Fill in the E-Mail Address field with a complete e-mail address for the new entry.
6. Optionally, fill in the Description field. This field is just for your reference.
7. Click OK. You are returned to the Address Book window, and the new entry appears under your top-level folder, with a little "person" icon next to it.

Let's say you entered your own address in the Address Book with the nickname **me**. Now, when you go to write a new piece of mail, you only need to type **me** in the Mail To field; Netscape Navigator 3.0 will fill in the real information automatically. This means that you can reduce e-mail addresses to a few easy-to-remember keystrokes. Why type in **president@whitehouse.gov** when you can simply enter **bill**? (After all, you're on a first-name basis, right?)

You can also add lists of recipients to the Address Book. That way, a single nickname can represent as many addresses as you want. For instance, you could create an Address Book entry called Executives that lets you automatically send the same message to both Bill and Al. To create a list:

1. In the Address Book window, select Add List from the Item menu. A dialog box like the one in Figure 4-15 appears.

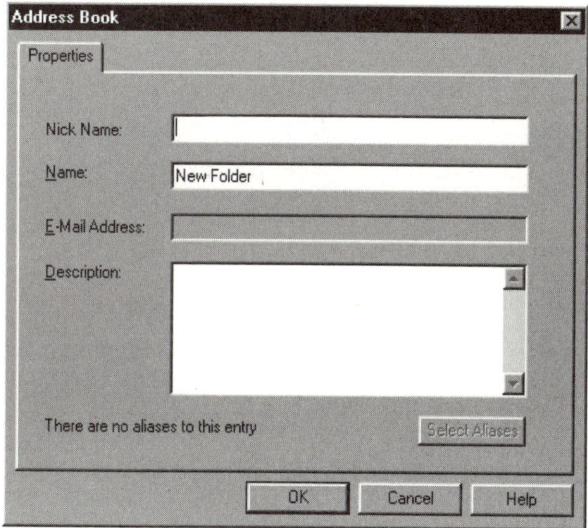

Figure 4-15: Add List dialog box.

2. Fill in the Nick Name field with an easy-to-type nickname.
3. Fill in the Name field with the name of your list, for instance, Executives.
4. Optionally, fill in the Description field. This field is just for your reference.
5. Click OK.
6. Back in the Address Book window, drag the names of people you want included into the new list from the main address book. You will get a new folder in your address book with all these names in it, like the one shown in Figure 4-16.

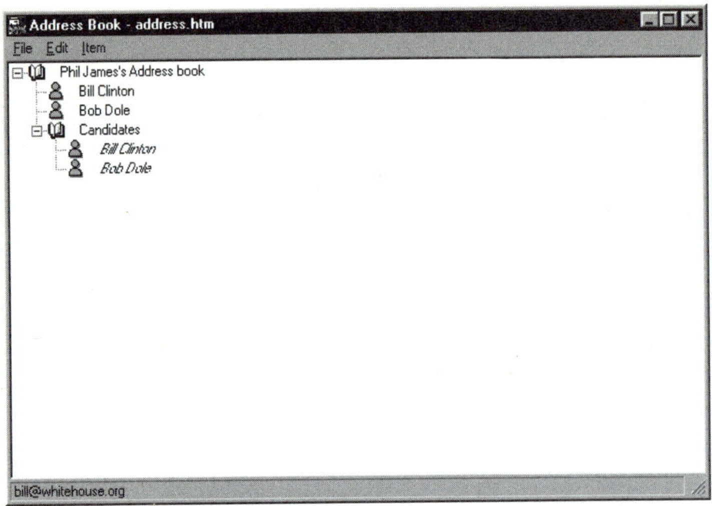

Figure 4-16: A new folder (address list) in the Address Book window.

TIP

You can also add entries to a list by selecting the folder and then clicking Add User in the Item menu.

Multimedia Mail

Netscape Navigator 3.0 is really a multimedia program, and as you might guess, it can handle more than just plain text in e-mail. It can also display HTML formatting and GIF or JPEG images in the e-mail window, just as it can in the main Web browser window. You can see this in the piece of welcome mail included by Netscape in every browser, part of which is shown in Figure 4-17.

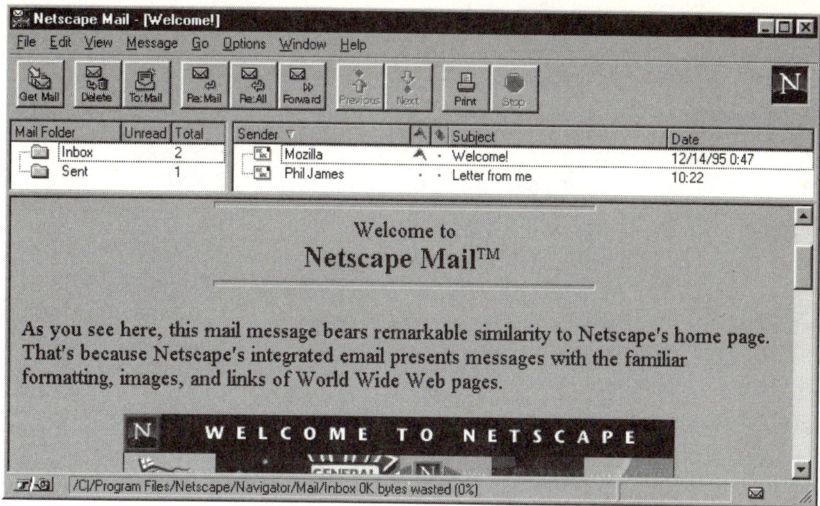

Figure 4-17: An e-mail message with HTML formatting and a GIF image.

When you send someone a piece of mail with HTML tags in it, Netscape Navigator 3.0 interprets these tags just as it would if they were in a Web page. This is how the message in Figure 4-17 is able to have text in boldface and italics. Although a course in HTML is beyond the scope of this chapter, if you know HTML and you are sending mail to someone else who uses Netscape, you can format the text, include inline images, and even add links to your mail. In fact, Netscape Navigator 3.0 is so good at handling HTML that if someone mentions a URL in a piece of mail, the program will recognize it as a URL and turn it into a link automatically! Just click on it, and you are transported to the site mentioned in the message.

In addition, when you send someone a GIF or JPEG image via e-mail, Netscape Navigator 3.0 opens it directly in the mail window, displaying the image for the recipient. This means you can now mail images directly to other Netscape Navigator 3.0 users. All of this allows you to create truly multimedia mail.

Finding People on the Net

Suppose you want to find somebody's e-mail address. You can just go to the Internet "phone book" and look it up, right? Unfortunately the answer is, "No, not yet."

The Internet's greatest advantage as a communications tool is that it is decentralized, which allows small organizations and even individuals to take care of setting up their own Internet connection with little need to consult a central authority. The greatest disadvantage of this method is that it is, well, a little too decentralized to allow for anything like a net-wide "phone book." Instead there are several partial systems for looking people up, many of them good, but none of them perfect. Netscape in its wisdom has provided a page of specialized services for finding people, accessible simply by clicking the People button in the browser window. Figure 4-18 shows what it looks like:

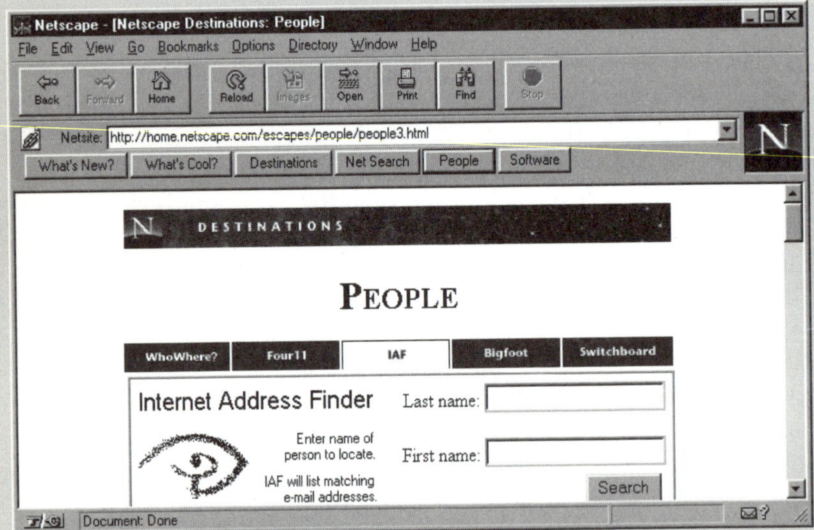

Figure 4-18: Netscape's People page with Internet Address Finder selected.

To select a particular search tool, simply click the appropriate button such as WhoWhere?, Four11, IAF, Bigfoot, or Switchboard. The services offered on this page may change from time to time.

Attaching Files to Messages

Besides including HTML tags and inline images in messages, you can also include entire HTML files or attach any kind of file, whether it's text or binary. There are no restrictions on the type of material you can include with your message. You can send spreadsheets, graphics, sounds, word processor files, programs, you name it. You can even attach files that are not on your own computer by sending the URLs for the files as attachments to your message!

To attach a file to an e-mail message:

1. Follow all the steps outlined earlier for creating a new e-mail message.
2. Before sending the message, click the Attachment button in the Message Composition window. The Attachments dialog box appears, as shown in Figure 4-19.

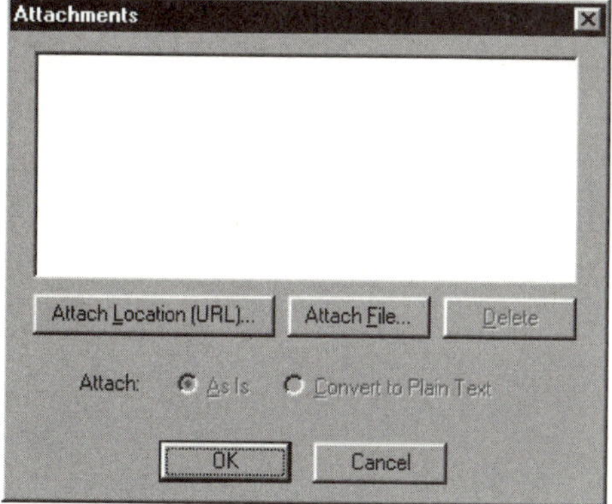

Figure 4-19: The Attachments dialog box.

3. Click either the Attach File button or the Attach Location (URL) button to send a file with your message or to include a link to a file that is on a remote computer.

   Any kind of file can be attached to your mail. But if you are sending an HTML file, you can choose to send it as is (with its HTML formatting) or as plain text, without any special formatting. Select either the As Is or the Convert to Plain Text radio button.
4. Once you have selected a file or typed in a URL, click OK to return to the Attachments dialog box.

Tip

You can add as many files as you want to the attachment list before you close it.

5. Click OK to attach the file(s) and return to the Message Composition window.
6. Send the message, including any attachment, by clicking the Send button.

Making Sure Your Attached Files Arrive Safely

Internet e-mail is a system designed primarily for exchanging text messages, and attached files require special handling by Internet software. Netscape Navigator 3.0's default settings will work fine in most cases, but if somebody complains that a binary file you attached to a message was corrupt or wouldn't run, here's what to do:

1. Select Mail and News Preferences from the Options menu in the main window.
2. Select the Composition tab.
3. Click the MIME Compliant (Quoted Printable) radio button.

This makes Netscape Navigator 3.0 use an alternate method of encoding when it sends attached binary files.

Dealing With Attached Files You Receive

Not only does Netscape Navigator 3.0 let you attach all kinds of files to e-mail messages, but it also includes special options for dealing with attached files that you receive. For instance, as I mentioned before, when you receive an image file, it is automatically displayed as an image.

But Netscape Navigator 3.0 cannot automatically handle every type of file you might receive. Obviously there are thousands of different file formats, and new ones come along every day. Although Netscape Navigator 3.0 can't possibly know about all these different file types, it includes a facility for using special *helper applications* to handle them. For example, if you receive a Microsoft Word document attached to an e-mail message, Netscape Navigator 3.0 will automatically launch Word, if it's available on your system.

If you're an advanced user, you can customize the way Netscape Navigator 3.0 associates particular types of files with different helper applications, but that topic is beyond the scope of this chapter. For a full discussion of helper applications, turn to the section "Helper Applications" in Chapter 6, "Getting Files via FTP." All of the information there applies to e-mail as well as FTP.

Organizing Your Mail Folders

Once you start receiving lots of e-mail, your Inbox folder can get pretty crowded. Luckily, Netscape Navigator 3.0 lets you create new folders besides the Inbox. It also lets you move messages around from folder to folder. Maybe you want to distinguish between personal mail and business correspondence. You can create new folders called "Friends" and "Business" to help you keep them separate.

To create a new folder:

1. In the Netscape Mail window, select the New Folder option from the File menu. The Netscape User Prompt dialog box appears, as shown in Figure 4-20.

Figure 4-20: Netscape User Prompt dialog box.

2. Enter a name such as **Friends** in the dialog box and press Enter. The folder you just created will appear in the Folders pane alongside the Inbox folder, as shown in Figure 4-21.

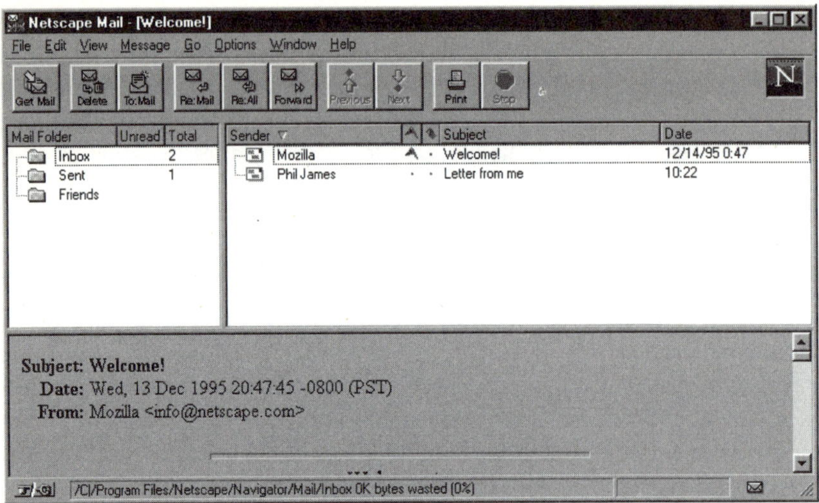

Figure 4-21: A new folder in the Folders pane.

Once you have created a new folder, you can move mail into it to organize your e-mail in the same way you organize files on your desktop into folders. There are several ways to move e-mail around:

- You can move a piece of mail into a folder by dragging and dropping the letter icon from the Messages pane into the folder icon in the Folders pane.
- You can use Move under Messages to move a selected letter or letters to another folder.
- You can use Copy to copy selected mail while leaving a copy where it is as well.

What about removing e-mail you don't want to keep around any more? That's even easier!

1. Select one or more pieces of mail by clicking them.
2. Click the Delete button on the toolbar.

When you do this, a folder called Trash is created in the Folders pane. The Trash folder allows you to remove messages without making them unrecoverable. There are two ways to empty the Trash folder so that the e-mail in it is truly deleted.

1. Click the Trash folder in the Folders pane. You should now see a list of messages to be trashed.
2. Select all the messages you want to delete.
3. Click Delete on the toolbar.

TIP

If you don't need to look at the mail in the Trash folder before deleting it, select Empty Trash Folder from the File menu. Now it's really *gone.*

Sorting E-mail Messages Within Folders

Folders provide a convenient way to sort mail into broad categories, but you still need ways to sort different pieces of mail within a folder. The Messages pane provides several ways to do this:

- By default, mail in a folder is sorted in chronological order, with the earliest mail at the top of the folder and the latest mail at the bottom. To sort alphabetically by subject, click on the Subject bar at the top of the Messages pane, as shown in Figure 4-22. Note that the program ignores any "Re:"s when sorting by subject.

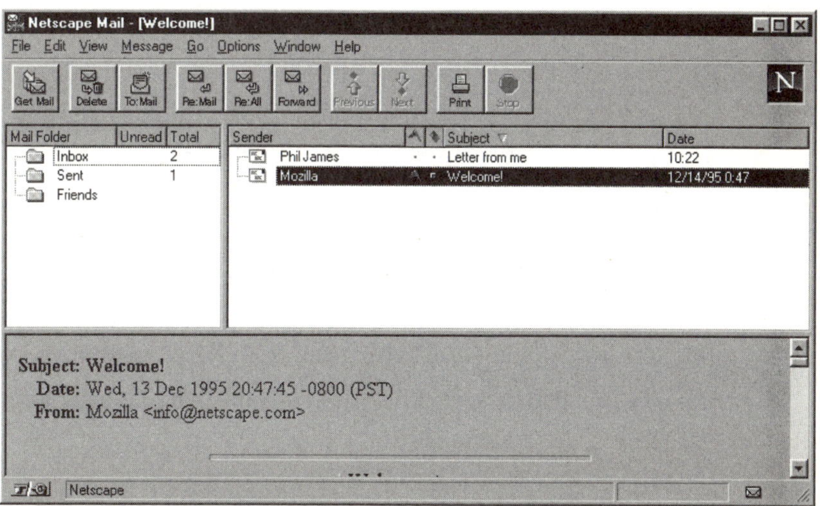

Figure 4-22: Mail sorted by subject.

- You can also sort by sender name, as shown in Figure 4-23. To do this, simply click the Sender bar.

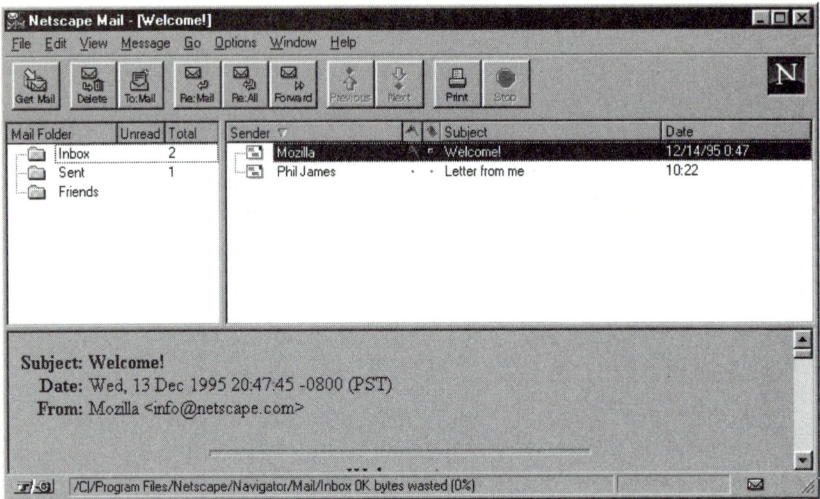

Figure 4-23: Mail sorted by sender.

TIP

Clicking Sender sorts your messages in alphabetical order by the first character in the From line, whether it is a first name or a last name. This can make your message list confusing.

- You can reverse any of these sorting tools by selecting Ascending in the Sort menu under View. This makes date sorting run from most recent to earliest, and alphabetical sorting run from Z to A, as shown in Figure 4-24.

Messages can also be sorted by Subject, Date, Sender, or by thread (shared subject field).

- Selecting Thread Messages from the Sort menu (under the View menu) selects all messages in the same folder that are grouped together by a shared Subject line, such as an original letter and a number of replies to it.

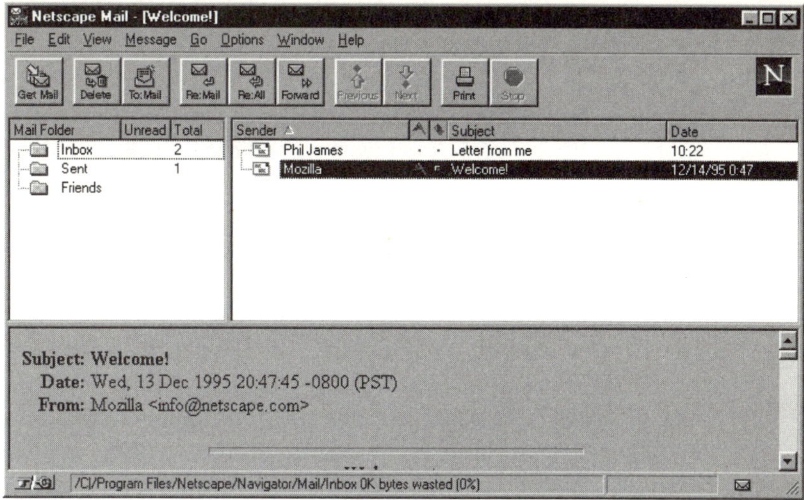

Figure 4-24: Mail sorted by name in reverse order.

Changing the Default Sorting Options

There are two mail sorting options that you can access by selecting Mail and News Preferences from the Options menu and then choosing the Organization tab. You can sort your mail by *threading*, which means that all messages with a shared subject line will be grouped together automatically. You can also change the default sorting Netscape Navigator 3.0 provides when you open the Mail window. As you've seen, sorting by date is the default, but you can change the default to sorting by subject or by name.

Mailing Lists

Internet e-mail is not just for exchanging private messages. It can also be used for gigantic group conversations among Internet users via an Internet service known as *mailing lists*.

A mailing list is simply a list of the e-mail addresses of everyone who wants to send and receive mail about a certain topic. There are mailing lists for discussing bonsai trees, rap music, adoption, cars, computer software, folk dancing, and on and on. There are thousands of lists, with new ones being created every week.

Adding your e-mail address to a mailing list is a way of joining these conversations. This is called *subscribing*, and removing your e-mail address from such a list is called *unsubscribing*. Once you've subscribed to a list, any mail you send to the list address gets sent back out to all the other e-mail addresses included on the list, and any mail from any of the other subscribers also gets sent to you.

When you subscribe to a mailing list, you immediately begin receiving mail from the other subscribers. If, after reading what other people on the list are talking about for a few days, you have something to add, you send mail back to the list address, and everyone else on the list sees your message.

So how do you find out what mailing lists are out there, and how to subscribe to them? The closest thing the Net has to an official list is Stephanie da Silva's list of *Publicly Accessible Mailing Lists*, originally created by Chuq Von Rospach. This list is an impressive compendium of mailing lists with a name, a short description, and information on how to subscribe for each one. The list itself is currently arranged alphabetically and stored on a machine at MIT.

How do you retrieve this list of lists? Simple; you use Netscape Mail:

1. From the main Netscape Navigator 3.0 window, select New Mail Message from the File menu (or simply press Ctrl+N). The Message Composition window appears.
2. Enter **mail-server@rtfm.mit.edu** in the Mail To field.
3. Enter **Mailing Lists** in the Subject field. (Do this for your own information. The MIT mail-server doesn't care what's in the Subject field.) You must enter something in the subject field, however, in order to complete your message for transmission.
4. Type only one line in the body of the message:

   ```
   send pub/usenet/news.answers/mail/mailing-lists/part01
   ```

   Your completed message should look like the one in Figure 4-25.

This message instructs the MIT mail server, a kind of electronic file clerk, to send you Part 1 of the list. The list is large, and Part 1 is only the beginning!

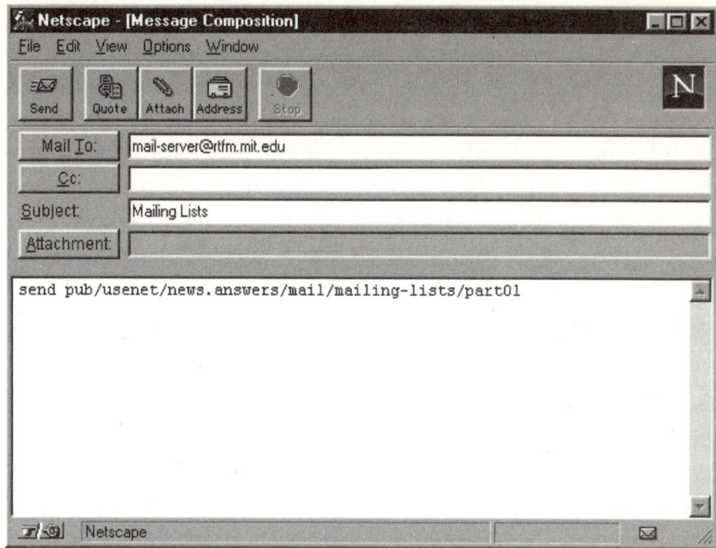

Figure 4-25: Mail ready to go to the MIT mail server.

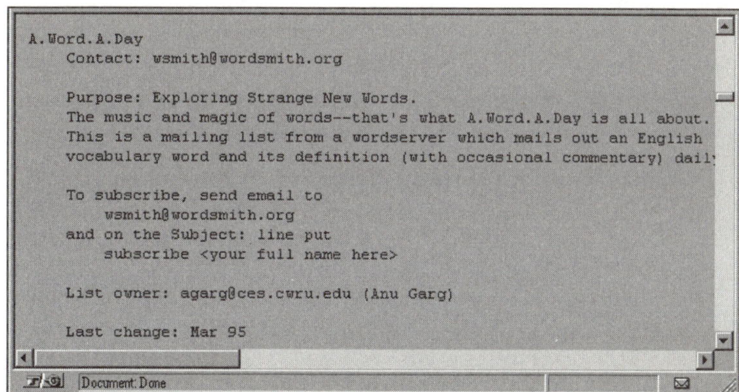

Figure 4-26: A sample mailing list entry from Part 1 of the list of Publicly Accessible Mailing Lists.

If you want to see more of the list, send another piece of mail to mail-server@rtfm.mit.edu with just this line:

```
send pub/usenet/news.answers/mail/mailing-lists/part*
```

You need to replace the asterisk shown above with the number for the part of the list you're interested in. To get Part 7, for instance, the last part of the message should be "part07."

Using Mailing Lists

There are a few differences between sending and receiving mail from a mailing list and sending and receiving personal mail, because mailing lists are a public forum. When you send a message to a mailing list, you don't even know how many people are reading it, much less who all of them are. This changes the way people read and write e-mail. Mailing lists are famous for long-running, voluminous, and often quite heated exchanges of e-mail, and because they are public forums, there are different rules of conduct there.

Mailing List Etiquette

- **Read before you write.** This is Rule #1. Before you send e-mail to a mailing list, remember that you are writing for a particular audience, and make sure that what you have to say is relevant. The rule of thumb when dealing with mailing lists is to read what other people are saying for about a week before sending any mail yourself, to make sure that any questions or comments you might have are pertinent. (Reading a list without posting is called *lurking.*)
- **Don't waste people's time.** This advice seems self-evident, but you will often see people posting mail that adds nothing to the discussion. Don't jump into a conversation just to tell everyone you agree with what someone else has said. If you are quoting another person's message, only quote what is relevant to your point. Nothing wastes people's time more than scrolling through screen after screen of a message they have already read once, only to read "I think you are completely correct" at the end.
- **Use private e-mail when appropriate.** When you read something posted to a mailing list, you have a choice between replying to the writer in private or sending your reply to the entire list. If you merely want to say you agree, or ask where you can get a copy of something mentioned in the post, send e-mail to the writer instead of to the list.
- **Use the Subject line carefully.** As with private e-mail, the Subject line is the first thing anyone sees in mail from you, and it tells people whether they are interested in what you have to say. Use the Subject line to describe, as succinctly as possible, the contents of your mail.
- **If you are no longer interested in a particular mailing list, use the proper procedure for unsubscribing.** When you signed up for the list, you were probably sent a message that included thorough instructions. Now's the time to follow them! In most cases, you send your *unsubscribe* command to an address that's different from the one where you send regular messages. The whole world really doesn't care to know that you've decided to quit the list.

One of the main differences between mailing list mail and personal mail is that when you want to reply to a message, you have a choice between replying only to the author of the article or sending the reply out to the whole list. If you have something to add to the debate, you should send your mail to the list, but if you just want to say that you agree with what someone has said, send it to the author only. The best way to tell what's appropriate is to read what other people are posting to the list to see what kinds of things are being discussed in public.

When replying to something you have read on a mailing list, make sure to examine the Mail To field of your outgoing mail. Different mailing lists handle the return address differently. On some lists, when you use the Reply function, the Mail To field is set up assuming that you want to send mail out to the whole mailing list, while on others it is set up assuming that you want to reply only to the author of the original post. If you want to reply to the whole group, you would select Reply to All.

TIP

Checking the Mail To line of your mail before you reply will prevent you from sending mail you meant to be private to everyone on the list or from sending mail you meant to be public only to one other person.

One concept that you will sometimes hear discussed on mailing lists is the *signal-to-noise ratio*. This is an engineering term that has been pressed into service to describe the percentage of messages sent to any given mailing list that are useful or interesting. Lists where there is generally an engaged and articulate discussion going on are said to have a high signal-to-noise ratio, while lists where the subscribers are posting messages needlessly are said to have a low signal-to-noise ratio. Good mailing list etiquette helps create a high signal-to-noise ratio.

Using Netscape Navigator 3.0 With Microsoft Exchange

This chapter has shown you how to use Netscape Navigator 3.0's excellent e-mail features to send messages to anyone on the Net. But what if you're already using Microsoft Exchange, the e-mail client that comes with Windows 95? You might already have spent hours configuring it to behave just the way you want, and why should you go through that process all over again?

No problem! Simply select Mail and News Preferences from the Options menu and then go to the Appearance tab. At the bottom of the tab, you can select the Use Exchange Client for Mail and News radio button. You'll never see the Netscape Mail window again.

But how does this work? Well, suppose you are viewing a Web document that has a Mail To link in it. When you click the link, you will now see Exchange instead of Netscape Navigator 3.0's Message Composition window. And even if you select New Mail Message from Netscape Navigator 3.0's File menu, you'll find yourself in Exchange.

Moving On

In this chapter, you've learned about using Netscape Navigator 3.0 to exchange e-mail with other Internet users, and you've worked with some of the program's powerful messaging features. In the next chapter, you'll learn another way to communicate with others on the Net: Usenet News. Like e-mail, News is a way of sending and receiving messages, but where mail is usually private, News provides a public forum. Netscape Navigator 3.0 also includes a separate interface, similar to the Netscape Mail window, just for handling News.

Newsgroups

The first time I heard the terms "network news" and "newsgroups," I expected they referred to some Internet version of Tom Brokaw and Dan Rather, or maybe a digital CNN. In fact, these terms refer to a special messaging system that is more akin to a public bulletin board at the local library or the grocery store.

It turns out that Netscape Navigator 3.0 is not only the best World Wide Web browser around, but is also a top-notch news reader: a program that enables you to access and participate in newsgroups. After reading this chapter, you'll be able to read and respond to newsgroup articles and begin your own discussions. This chapter introduces you to Usenet (the "official" name for network news and newsgroups) and explains how to use Netscape Navigator 3.0 to get all the "news" that is fit to "print"—as well as some that might make Tom and Dan and maybe even Ted Turner blush!

Introduction to Usenet

Before we look at how to use Netscape as a news reader, let's take a quick look at Usenet itself.

What Is It & How Does It Work?

Usenet (also known as Netnews) was originally developed for UNIX systems in 1979. It has become a worldwide network of thousands of Usenet sites, known as *news hosts* or *news servers*, running many operating systems (such as UNIX, MS-DOS, and Windows NT) on various types of computers. Millions of people share messages electronically over these Usenet sites. The messages are sent from news server to news server using UNIX-to-UNIX Copy Protocol (UUCP).

People post their Usenet messages or articles to categories known as *newsgroups* instead of to individuals (as would be the case with e-mail). A newsgroup is a great place to exchange ideas, ask questions, or discuss opinions and experiences. It's the place to learn what both your neighbor next door and someone in Moscow you've never met think about almost any subject imaginable. Everyone who subscribes to a newsgroup can read and respond to the articles posted there. Popular newsgroup categories include computers (of course), business, biology, recreation, science, social issues, miscellaneous, and alternative discussions.

Individual discussions posted to a particular newsgroup are known as *threads*. I post a message. You post a response. Someone else responds to your response. And so it goes. Generally speaking, all threads posted to a particular newsgroup share a common theme: music, cars, sports, pinball machines, electronics, bizarre sexual practices, and so on.

Most newsgroups are *unmoderated*, which means subscribers may post directly to the newsgroup. In *moderated* newsgroups, on the other hand, a moderator screens the messages and posts only messages deemed of interest to other subscribers.

Usenet servers don't have to be connected to the Internet; many are not. But because thousands of Usenet sites do have access to the Internet, the Internet has become the most commonly used electronic postal route for network news. The total number of distinct newsgroups on the Internet is in the thousands and growing daily. Consequently, millions of people who may have started using the Internet to gain access to the World Wide Web or to the Internet's electronic mail find that they can participate in Usenet newsgroups as well, provided they have the right client software. News servers on the Internet use Network News Transfer Protocol (NNTP) to communicate with client software. Luckily for you, Netscape Navigator 3.0 knows NNTP.

Before you can use Netscape Navigator 3.0 to access newsgroups, you must do two things:

- **Obtain access to a news server**. Generally speaking, most Internet service providers (ISPs) run news servers. If you haven't already done so, ask your ISP for the name of the news server to which you have access (the name will be something like *news.myisp.com*). Later in this chapter (in the "Configuring Netscape News" section), you'll learn how to configure Netscape Navigator 3.0 to access this news server.
- **Subscribe to one or more newsgroups**. Subscribing to a newsgroup is nothing more than adding it to the list of newsgroups you want your news reader software (Netscape Navigator 3.0 in this case) to check each time you go online. Follow the procedures described in this chapter (in the "Subscribing to & Unsubscribing From Newsgroups" section) to subscribe to newsgroups.

How Many Newsgroups Can I Get?

How many angels can dance on the head of a pin? Nobody knows, and the same is true regarding the total number of newsgroups available at any time via the Internet. To impose some order on the basically anarchic structure of Usenet, newsgroups have a fairly strict hierarchical naming convention. Newsgroup names look similar to Internet addresses, and are a series of words or abbreviations separated by dots: rec.arts.movies.reviews.

The first word in the name denotes the major category to which the newsgroup belongs. A few of the major, hierarchical categories of Usenet newsgroups are:

- **alt.** *Alternative* newsgroups contain articles that are often very interesting, but can be on the controversial side, if not downright disgusting. Reader beware! This major category alone accounts for thousands of Usenet newsgroups.
- **comp.** *Computer* newsgroups discuss computer-related issues.
- **misc.** The *miscellaneous* newsgroups category (as you no doubt have guessed) is a catchall category for discussions that don't fit into one of the other categories.
- **news.** The *news* category is for newsgroups discussing Usenet network news itself. These newsgroups are a great source of information about Usenet.

- **rec.** *Recreation* newsgroups discuss recreation, sports, and the arts.
- **sci.** *Science* newsgroups cover scientific topics.
- **soc.** *Social* newsgroups focus on issues of perceived social importance.
- **talk.** If you like good arguments, *talk* newsgroups are the place for you.

Newsgroups in these categories are usually distributed worldwide. Originally, Usenet consisted only of the newsgroups comp, news, rec, sci, soc, talk, and misc. All other newsgroups were referred to as *alternative* newsgroups. The term Usenet is now more commonly used to refer to the collection of all newsgroups.

Other major categories that may be distributed throughout the world include bionet (biology newsgroups), biz (business newsgroups), and vmsnet (discussions about the VMS computer operating system). Many other topical major categories are usually distributed around the world as well. Geographical, organizational, and commercial newsgroups are usually distributed only within their area of interest.

Newsgroups in the *bit* major category are actually an alternative distribution method for Bitnet LISTSERV mailing lists. Conversely, many newsgroups also distribute articles via mailing lists to users who don't have access to a news server. In effect, the pertinent messages are mailed to the user's electronic mail box, enabling the user to get network news via a simple dial-up Internet e-mail account.

Because of the sheer volume of Usenet traffic, and due to the timely nature of much newsgroup content, most newsgroups put a limit on the number of days an article will be available for reading. Past the time limit, an article is said to have expired and is removed from the newsgroup. The time limit varies from newsgroup to newsgroup, but many long-standing newsgroups keep archives of expired articles.

Do you have access to all the newsgroups on the Internet? Maybe, maybe not, depending on your news server. Later in this chapter, we'll see how to get a list of all the newsgroups available through your server.

The best way to gain an understanding of Usenet news is to browse through several newsgroups, reading the messages but not responding. This practice is affectionately known as *lurking*. In this case, lurking for a while makes a lot of sense. Before you know it, you'll feel compelled to jump in there and participate in the conversation.

Configuring Netscape News

Even though you're probably eager to try your hand at network news, there's still a little bit of housekeeping we need to take care of. Before Netscape Navigator 3.0 can access news, you have to give it the name of your news server. While you're at it, you may also want to configure the way news is displayed.

Specifying Your Network News Server

Because Usenet is a network of news servers, you need access to one or more of these servers in order to participate in network news. The server uses the NNTP protocol to communicate with Netscape Navigator 3.0's news reader. The server keeps track of which articles have been posted to which newsgroups. Netscape Navigator 3.0 keeps track of the newsgroups in which you are interested as well as the articles you have read.

To specify a news server:

1. Double-click the Netscape Navigator 3.0 icon to launch the program. The main window appears. If you are connected to the Internet, the Netscape home page starts loading as shown in Figure 5-1.

   You don't need to be online to configure Netscape News. If you're not connected to the Internet, simply click the Stop button in the main Netscape window so that the program will stop trying to load the Netscape home page.

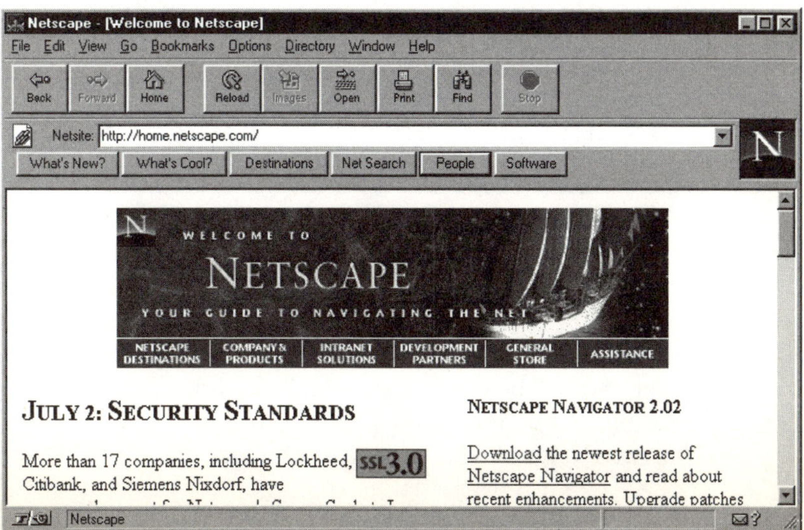

Figure 5-1: The main Netscape Browser window displaying the Netscape home page.

TIP

By default, Netscape Navigator 3.0 starts in the Browser window and attempts to load the Netscape home page. This behavior can be changed to (1) start in either Netscape Mail or Netscape News and (2) load a blank page rather than the home page. To display the screen where you can make these changes, select General Preferences from the Options menu and click the Appearance tab.

2. In the Netscape Navigator 3.0 main window, choose Mail and News Preferences from the Options menu. Netscape displays the Preferences dialog box, as shown in Figure 5-2. The tab last accessed will be displayed.

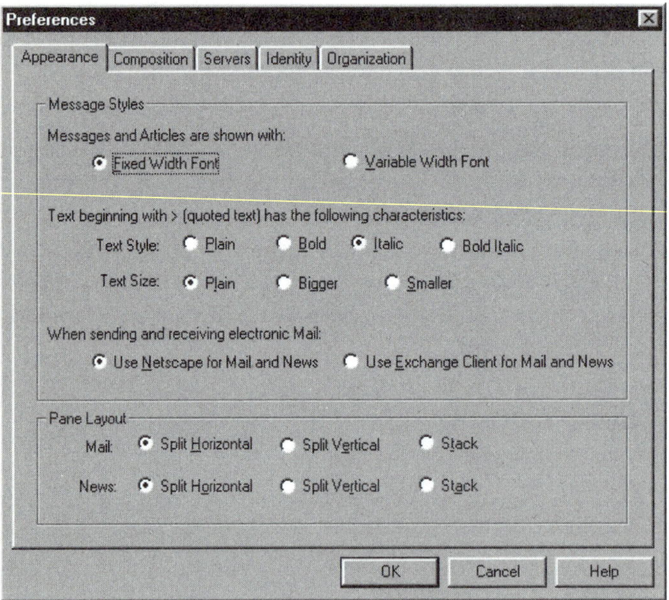

Figure 5-2: The Preferences dialog box with the Appearance tab selected.

3. Click the Servers tab, as shown in Figure 5-3.
4. In the text box labeled News (NNTP) Server, type the name of the news server you will be using. If you don't know this address, obtain it from your ISP or from your system administrator (if you are configuring Netscape News on your computer at work).

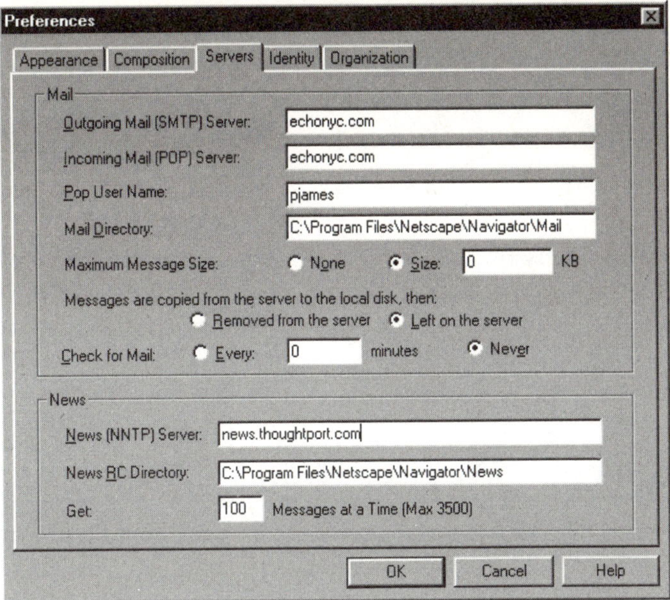

Figure 5-3: The Preferences dialog box with the Servers tab selected.

5. As we mentioned earlier, your news reader software keeps track of your favorite newsgroups as well as the articles you've already read. Most news reader programs store this information using a standard format in a file known as a NEWS.RC file. If you are an experienced Internet user, you may already have been using another news reader to get your network news. To avoid the hassle of re-subscribing to your favorite newsgroups, just point Netscape Navigator 3.0 to the NEWS.RC file generated by your previous news reader. Type the full path of the directory containing NEWS.RC in the News RC Directory text box. If you've never used a news reader, just accept the default setting. Netscape Navigator 3.0 will create a new *newsrc* file and automatically subscribe you to three newsgroups that contain articles of particular interest to new Usenet users. As you subscribe to newsgroups, Netscape Navigator 3.0 stores this information in NEWS.RC.
6. In the Get field, type in the maximum number of new messages you want to receive at a time. Tip: 100 is plenty!
7. If you are interested in configuring other Netscape News characteristics, such as font width, proceed to the next section in this chapter. Otherwise, you are finished specifying a news server. Click the OK button in the Preferences dialog box to confirm any changes you made and return to the main Netscape Navigator 3.0 window.

TIP

Although most people have access to only one news server, you may have access to multiple news servers. To open a news server other than the one listed in the Servers tab of the Preferences dialog box, choose Open News Host from the News window's File menu and specify the server's name.

You are now ready to take a look at network news. You might want to skim through the sections that describe how to configure Netscape News, but you probably don't need to change the default settings. Then proceed to the "Subscribing to & Unsubscribing From Newsgroups" section to try out your first newsgroup.

Configuring the Way Your News Is Displayed

One of the most obvious improvements in personal computers over the past 10 years has been the advent of *graphical user interfaces* (GUIs) such as Windows. A hallmark of GUIs is the capability to display text in multiple typefaces (fonts). Later versions of Windows and all versions of the Mac operating system are capable of displaying fonts in which each character has a unique width (*variable width,* also known as *proportional spacing*), rather than all characters having the same width (*fixed width,* also known as *monospacing*). You are used to seeing proportional spacing in most printed material, such as books, magazines, and newspapers.

Netscape Navigator 3.0 gives you the option of displaying newsgroup messages in either variable-width or fixed-width spacing. Usenet was developed several years before the IBM PC was introduced and almost 10 years before proportional spacing was introduced to PC users in Windows. If you are a purist and would prefer to view newsgroup articles in their "natural" state—fixed-width spacing—you have that option with Navigator.

Since news articles are often a continuation of an ongoing discussion (that is, another article in the same thread), articles often include quoted portions of earlier articles in the same discussion. News reader programs typically denote quoted sections of text by placing an angle bracket (>) at the left margin. Netscape Navigator 3.0 enables you to control the font style and size of these quoted sections as well.

Since electronic mail messages and network news messages are closely related in purpose, Netscape's Mail window and News window are very similar. When you configure the appearance of your network news, you are also configuring the appearance of your e-mail.

To set how Netscape Navigator 3.0 displays news and e-mail:

1. Select Mail and News Preferences from the Options menu. Click the Appearance tab.
2. If you want text displayed in a fixed-width font (the default option), click the Fixed Width Font option button. If you prefer variable-width spacing, click the Variable Width Font option button. (***Note:*** You can select the font itself using the Display properties dialog in the Windows Control Panel.)
3. Choose from among the following options to determine how Netscape News will display quoted text in e-mail messages and news articles:
   - Plain
   - **Bold**
   - *Italic*
   - ***Bold Italic***
4. Select one of the following options to determine the size of quoted text:
   - Plain
   - Bigger
   - Smaller

Using the Microsoft Exchange Mail & News Clients

Windows 95 includes an Internet mail client called Exchange that can be set up to provide a universal inbox for all your electronic correspondence. If you would prefer to use Microsoft Exchange, rather than Netscape Navigator 3.0, as your mail client and news reader, choose the Use Exchange Client for Mail and News option on the Appearance tab of the Preferences dialog box. Refer to your Windows 95 documentation for instructions on setting up and configuring Exchange as your Internet mail and news client.

5. In the Pane Layout section of the Appearance tab, select how you want your News window to look. The default is Split Horizontal. In this layout, the pane that contains the contents of a selected article is below the two other panes, one which lists your subscribed newsgroups and another which lists the messages within that folder.
   - If you want to align the message content pane to the right of the two split panes, choose **Split Vertical**.
   - If you want to stack all three panes on top of each other, with the content pane at the bottom, select **Stack**.

TIP

In most cases the default window layout is the most convenient. You can always change it later, after you've become more familiar with the various News features.

6. Click OK to save your changes.

Storing News

As you have learned, e-mail messages and network news articles are closely related. Navigator's facilities for the two types of messages are nearly identical. However, one significant difference between e-mail and news is the location where incoming messages are stored. While you have the option to store e-mail messages on the server or on your local hard disk, incoming news articles always reside on the server. The news reader displays them to your screen during an online session, but doesn't keep a copy on your hard disk. If you like, you can save an article using the Save As option from the File menu, but Navigator does not do so automatically.

Even though Netscape Navigator 3.0 doesn't automatically keep a copy of news articles that you have read, you may want to have Netscape Navigator 3.0 automatically save a copy of all articles that you post to a newsgroup. You can choose to e-mail a copy to yourself, to add the article to a running text file, or both.

To change how Navigator handles copies of outgoing news articles:

1. Choose Mail and News Preferences from the Options menu. Netscape Navigator 3.0 displays the Preferences dialog box.
2. Click the Composition tab to display the dialog shown in Figure 5-4.
3. To have a copy of each outgoing news article sent to a particular e-mail address, type the address in the News Messages text box.

4. To have the contents of each outgoing article copied to a specific text file stored on your computer, type the full path and name of the file in the News File text box. Each news article you send will be added to the end of the file.
5. Click the OK button to save your changes and return to the Netscape window.

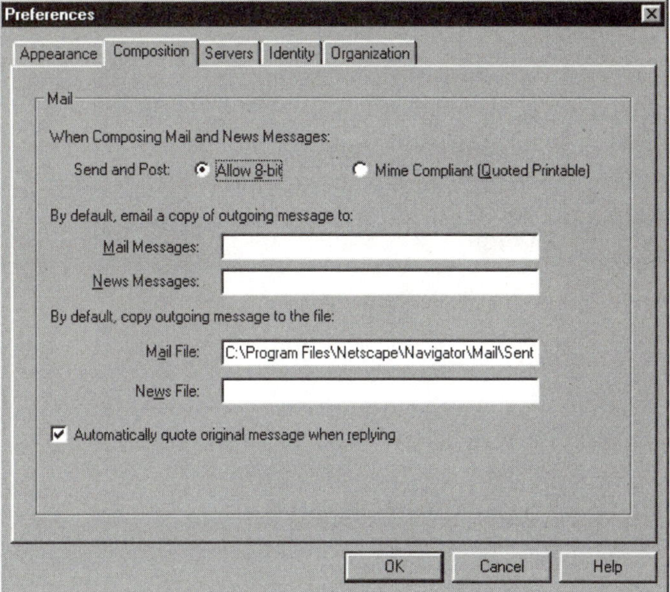

Figure 5-4: The Preferences dialog box with the Composition tab selected.

Configuring Threading & Sorting

As you may recall, a series of news articles on the same topic is called a thread. Usually the articles in a thread make sense only if they are read together in chronological order. Netscape Navigator 3.0 makes it very easy to see the relationship between related articles and to follow the thread of the discussion. But this threading feature is an option, and in order to use it, you must first turn it on.

Netscape Navigator 3.0 also enables you to choose how you want messages sorted: by date, by subject, or by sender. You can configure the threading feature and the sort order from the same configuration window.

To activate the newsgroup threading feature and select a sorting order:

1. Choose Mail and News Preferences from the Options menu. Netscape displays the Preferences dialog box.
2. Click the Organization tab to display the dialog shown in Figure 5-5.

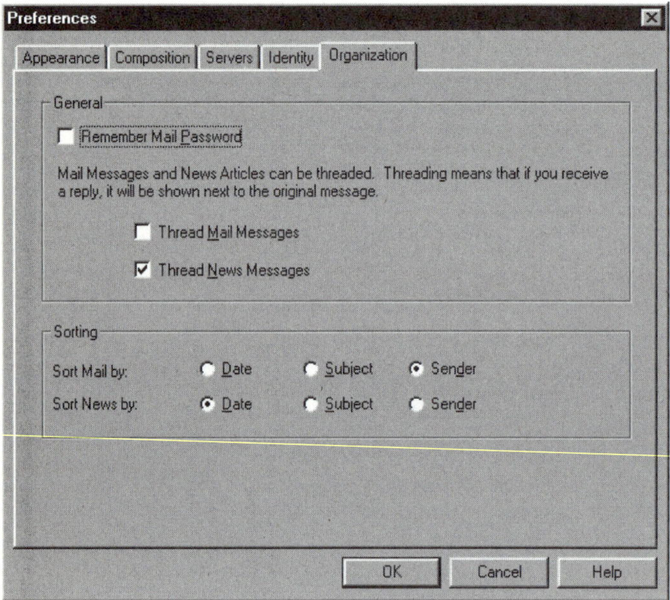

Figure 5-5: The Preferences dialog box with the Organization tab selected.

3. Click the Thread News Messages check box to have articles in the same thread listed together, in chronological order. If you don't activate this option, Netscape Navigator 3.0's news reader will list newsgroup articles in the order received.

   As an alternative way to toggle the threading feature, select the Sort option from the View menu and then choose Thread Messages.
4. You can also specify how articles will be sorted by choosing the Date, Subject, or Sender option button. If you have chosen the Thread News Messages check box, you probably should sort messages by subject, at least for starters. You can change the sort order later if you like. If you choose to sort articles by date, by sender, or by message number, you will still see the articles in each thread grouped together on the screen, but the order in which the threads appear (as well as the order of the articles within each thread) will be by date, sender, or message number, as you specified.
5. Click the OK button to save the changes you have made and return to the Netscape window.

Arranging the Newsgroup List, Message Heading & Message Panes

You can also configure the arrangement of Netscape Navigator 3.0's News window. Before we do that, however, let's go online so that we'll have something to look at as we arrange the parts of the window:

1. Make sure you are connected to the Internet, either directly or through a SLIP or PPP connection with your access provider. If you are using a SLIP or PPP connection and are not currently connected, click the Dial-Up Networking icon for your access provider (or if you are not using the Windows 95 Internet software, click the icon you use to connect to your Internet Service Provider).

   If you are using Windows 3.1 rather than Windows 95, or if you are not using Windows 95's built-in networking, follow the instructions that came with your TCP/IP software for accessing the Internet.

2. If Netscape Navigator 3.0 isn't already running, click the Netscape Navigator 3.0 icon to launch the program. The main Netscape (browser) window appears, and the Netscape home page starts loading.

3. Select Netscape News from the Window menu to display the main News window, shown in Figure 5-6.

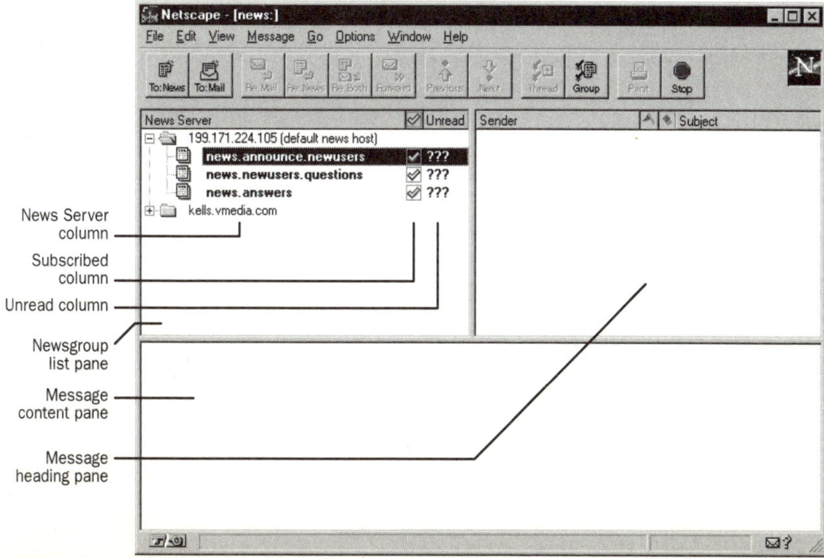

Figure 5-6: The main News window.

The main News window is divided into three panels: the *newsgroup list pane* in the upper left portion of the window; the *message heading pane* at upper right; and the *message content pane* across the bottom. This screen is almost identical to the Mail window that you learned about in Chapter 4, "Netscape Mail." You can control the size of each pane by placing the mouse pointer on a panel border and dragging the pointer in the appropriate direction.

TIP

Remember, you can change the layout of these three panes in the Appearance tab of Mail and News Preferences.

Arranging the Newsgroup List Pane

Obviously, the *newsgroup list pane* lists newsgroups. The first time you use Netscape News, the program lists your news server in the News Server column of the newsgroup list pane and lists three newsgroups intended to provide helpful information to new users of Usenet network news: *news.announce.newusers*, *news.newusers*, and *news.answers*. (If, during configuration, you specified the location of your NEWS.RC file, Netscape News also lists the newsgroups to which you're subscribed.)

The newsgroup list pane has four columns:

- **News Server**. This column lists one or more news servers. By default, it lists the news server you specified when you configured Netscape News. If you know of other news servers to which you have access, you can add them to this list in the Newsgroup window by selecting Open News Host from the File menu and typing the news server's name in the dialog that opens. Each available news server is denoted by a folder icon at the left margin of the Newsgroup list pane.
- **Subscribed**. The Subscribed column (the one with the checkmark at the top) contains an icon that resembles a checkmark if you are subscribed to a newsgroup.
- **Unread**. This column contains a number in each row that indicates the number of articles in the respective newsgroup that you have yet to read.
- **Total**. This column indicates the total number of articles in the newsgroup.

You can control the width of each column by placing the mouse pointer on the right or left border of the column heading and dragging it in the appropriate direction.

TIP

You can even switch the order of any of the columns in the newsgroup and message panes. Simply drag the header button right or left to its new location. For instance, you might want to drag the Total column to the far left in the newsgroup list pane.

Arranging the Message Heading Pane

So that we can examine the message headings and message panes of the window, let's display a message from the *news.announce.newusers* newsgroup:

1. In the newsgroup list pane, click the *news.announce.newusers* newsgroup icon. In the message heading pane, Netscape News displays a message heading for each article currently found in this newsgroup. Figure 5-7 shows several message headings.

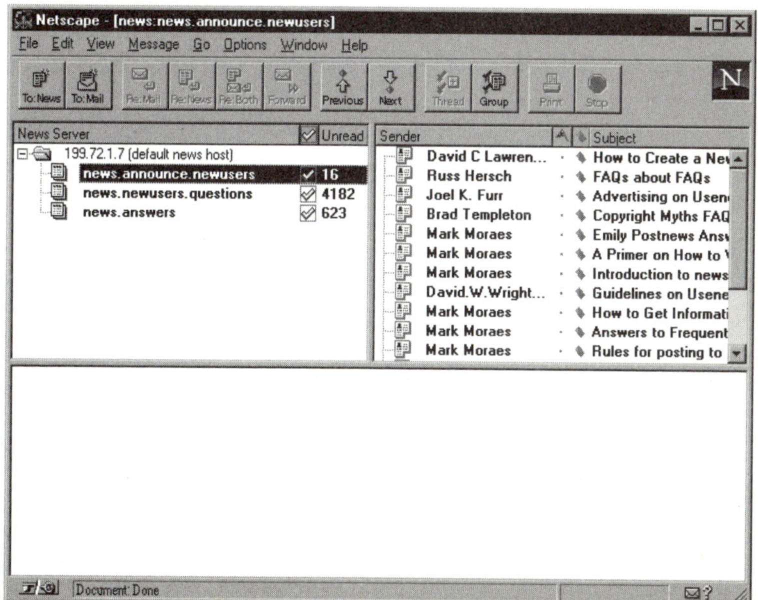

Figure 5-7: The News window with the news.announce.newusers newsgroup selected.

2. In the message heading pane, click one of the messages. Netscape News displays the selected article in the message content pane.

The message heading pane provides information about each article that may be helpful when you're trying to determine which article to read. This information is displayed in five columns:

- **Sender**. This column lists the name of the individual who posted the article to the newsgroup.
- **Flagged**. The flagged column contains a flag icon if you have *flagged* the article using the Flag Message option in the message pane. This feature is discussed in "Flagging Articles to Be Read Later" later in this chapter.
- **Read**. The Read column contains a green diamond if you haven't yet read the article.
- **Subject**. This column lists the subject of the article. The subject of each article was assigned by the article's author.
- **Date**. This column lists the date and time the article was posted to the newsgroup.

You can control the width of each column by placing the mouse pointer on the right or left border of the column heading and dragging the border in the appropriate direction.

You have learned already that you can establish a default sort order for articles in the message heading pane. You can also instantly sort the list again using either of two methods:

- Choose Sort from the View menu and click by Date, by Subject, by Sender, or by Message Number; or
- In the message heading pane, click the Sender, Subject, or Date column heading.

Navigator puts a downward pointer in the column heading of the column by which articles are currently sorted.

By default, the message headings are sorted in descending order. To sort in ascending order, choose Sort from the View menu and click the Ascending option. To toggle off this option, returning to descending order, repeat the same step.

Arranging the Message Content Pane

The message content pane displays *header* information at the top of each article. By default, the message content pane lists the article's Subject, Date, From, Organization, Newsgroups, and References header information (see Figure 5-8).

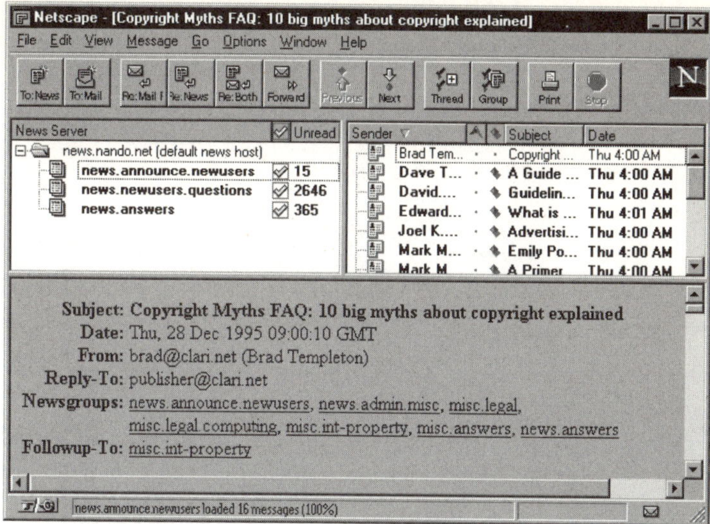

Figure 5-8: The News window with an article from the news.announce.newusers newsgroup selected.

To display additional header information, select the Show All Headers option on the Options menu (see Figure 5-9).

You can control the size of the message content pane by placing the mouse pointer on one of its borders and dragging the border in the appropriate direction.

Determining Which Newsgroups & Articles Will Display

Since there are literally thousands of newsgroups and hundreds of thousands of news articles, there obviously must be ways for you to filter newsgroups and news articles and list a select few for your consideration. We have already discussed briefly the concept of subscribing to newsgroups, and we'll cover the procedure of subscribing to newsgroups in one of the next sections in this chapter. Netscape Navigator 3.0's Options menu also provides several other ways to help you keep the volume of news articles listed on your screen to a manageable level.

Use the following options on the News window's Options menu (shown in Figure 5-9) to control which newsgroups and articles (messages) are listed on your screen (note that tick marks indicate menu options that are currently active).

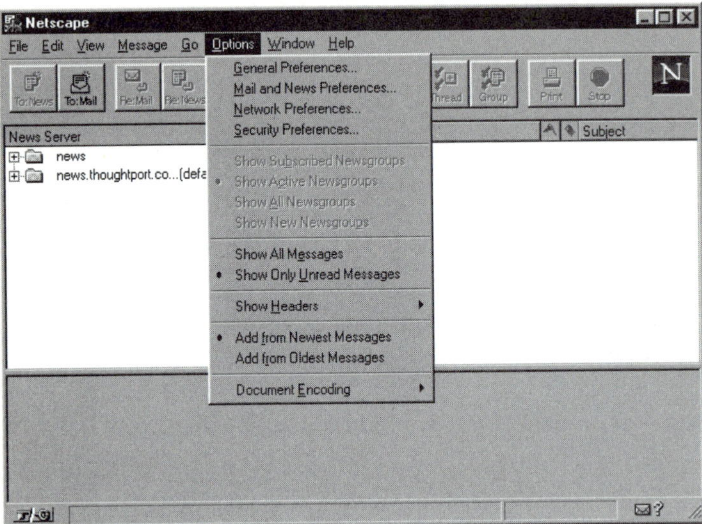

Figure 5-9: The News window's Options menu.

- **Show Subscribed Newsgroups**. This option causes Netscape News to list only newsgroups to which you have subscribed. With this option checked, Netscape News lists all subscribed newsgroups, even if they contain no unread articles.
- **Show Active Newsgroups**. This option lists only subscribed newsgroups that contain articles you have yet to read. This option is active by default.
- **Show All Newsgroups**. This option lists all the newsgroups currently available through your news server. We'll try this option out later in the chapter so that you can subscribe to a few more newsgroups. Be aware, however, that choosing this option causes Netscape Navigator 3.0 to download to your disk a file that may take a few minutes to retrieve.
- **Show New Newsgroups**. Choose this option when you want to list all newsgroups available through your news server that have been added since you last connected to the server.
- **Show All Messages**. This option causes Netscape News to list the message headings of all messages found in the selected newsgroup.
- **Show Only Unread Messages**. This option, active by default, lists in the message heading pane only unread messages from the selected newsgroup.

- **Show Headers**. This option lets you choose how much or how little information you want to appear at the beginning of each article. You can select Brief to show minimal information, or All to show very complete header information. The default, unsurprisingly, is Normal. For more information about headers see the section called "Reading an Article."
- **Add From Newest Messages.** This option, active by default, tells Netscape News to display the newest message headings from the current newsgroup first.
- **Add From Oldest Messages.** This option causes the oldest message headings to be listed first.

TIP

You can change the language Navigator 3.0 expects articles to be in, by selecting Document Encoding from the Options menu and then clicking a new language. This will let you properly display articles that use other character sets.

Subscribing to & Unsubscribing From Newsgroups

The concept of subscribing to network newsgroups is a bit of a misnomer. You don't really subscribe to newsgroups as you might subscribe to a magazine. If your news server has access to a particular newsgroup, then so do you. In the Usenet context, subscribing to a newsgroup simply involves instructing your news reader—Netscape News, in this case—to list articles from that newsgroup in the News window.

Default Newsgroups

The first time you use Netscape News, the program lists your news server in the News Server column of the newsgroup list pane and lists three newsgroups: *news.announce.newusers*, *news.newusers.questions*, and *news.answers* (see Figure 5-10), assuming of course that these newsgroups are available through your news server. These newsgroups are specifically intended to provide helpful information to new users of Usenet network news. (***Note:*** If, during configuration, you specified the location of your NEWS.RC file, Netscape News lists the newsgroups to which you're subscribed.)

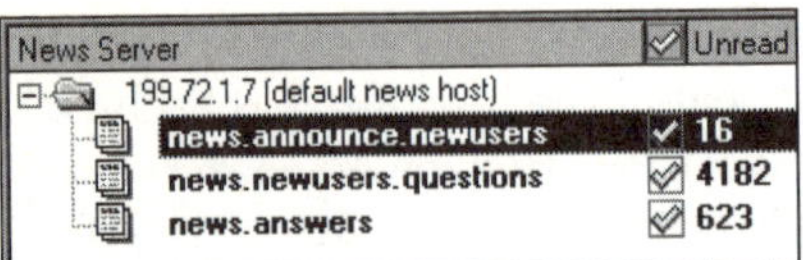

Figure 5-10: The default newsgroups in the newsgroup list pane of the News window.

Notice that a checkmark in a newsgroup's Subscribed column indicates that you're subscribed to that newsgroup.

Getting a List of All Newsgroups

Before you can subscribe to a newsgroup, you have to instruct Netscape News to display a list of all newsgroups available through your news server. To do so:

1. Make sure you are connected to the Internet, either directly or through a SLIP or PPP connection with your access provider. If you are using a SLIP or PPP connection and are not currently connected, click the Dial-Up Networking icon for your access provider (or if you are not using the Windows 95 Internet software, click the icon you use to connect to your ISP).

   If you are using Windows 3.1 rather than Windows 95, follow the instructions that came with your TCP/IP software for accessing the Internet.

2. If Netscape Navigator 3.0 isn't already running, click the Netscape Navigator 3.0 icon to launch the program. The main Netscape (browser) window appears, and the Netscape home page starts loading.

3. Select Netscape News from the Window menu to display the main News window.

4. Select Show All Newsgroups from the Options menu. Netscape News displays a message box, shown in Figure 5-11, informing you that it may take a few minutes to save the list of all newsgroups.

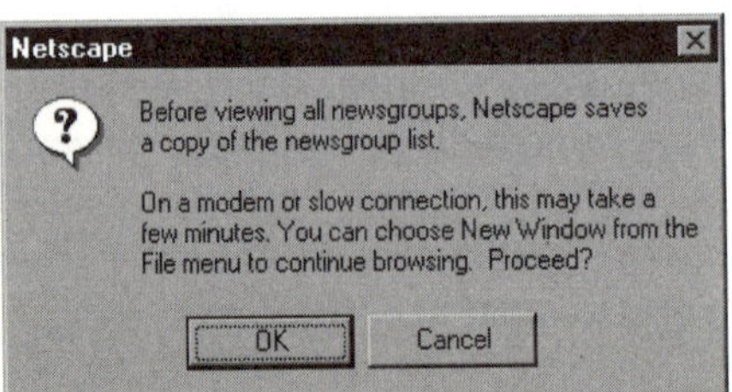

Figure 5-11: Displaying the newsgroup list may take a few minutes.

5. Click the OK button in the message box to proceed. Netscape Navigator 3.0 then retrieves from your news server a complete list of all newsgroups available via the server and displays this list in the newsgroup list pane of the News window, as shown in Figure 5-12.

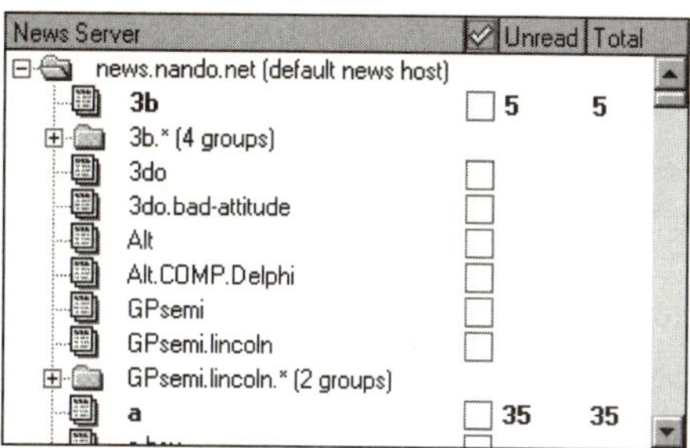

Figure 5-12: The first page of all newsgroups available on the news.nando.net news server.

Notice that Netscape News doesn't immediately show every available newsgroup in the newsgroup list pane. Using a screen design that resembles the Windows 95 Navigator (or Windows 3.1's File Manager), the list groups all newsgroups in folders by category. The first page of the list shown in Figure 5-12, for example, shows two categories of newsgroups: 3b.* and GPsemi.lincoln.*. The plus sign to the left of these folders indicates that each contains newsgroups that are not displayed. The number in parentheses (to the right of the folder's name) tells how many newsgroups there are in the folder.

Many newsgroups no longer contain active articles. When a newsgroup does contain active articles, Netscape News displays its name in a bold font and shows the number of unread articles and the total number of articles in this newsgroup in the Unread and Total columns, respectively.

To see a list of newsgroups in a category, scroll to the category and click the plus sign to the left of the category's folder icon. Netscape News opens the folder and lists the newsgroups in the category. The major category may contain subcategories. In that case, Netscape News groups the subcategories into folders. Figure 5-13, for example, lists newsgroups in the news.* major category. This category contains several subcategories including news.admin.*, news.announce.*, and news.groups.*. Notice that we are already subscribed to the *news.answers* newsgroup.

Figure 5-13: The news. category of newsgroups as listed in the newsgroup list pane of the News window.*

Finding Out About New Newsgroups

If you completed the procedure described in the preceding section, you have discovered just how long it can take to display a complete list of all available newsgroups. Unless you enjoy watching grass grow, you probably don't want to download this list very often. But you probably do want to periodically find out about any new newsgroups that may have formed since the last time you checked. Here's how:

1. Make sure you are connected to the Internet, either directly or through a SLIP or PPP connection with your access provider, and launch Netscape Navigator 3.0. The main Netscape (browser) window appears, and the Netscape home page starts loading.
2. Select Netscape News from the Window menu to display the main News window.
3. Select Show New Newsgroups from the Options menu. Netscape News displays a message box, shown in Figure 5-14, telling you the number of newsgroups that have been added since you last checked. Netscape News adds the new newsgroups to the end of the list of subscribed newsgroups in the newsgroup list pane of the News window.

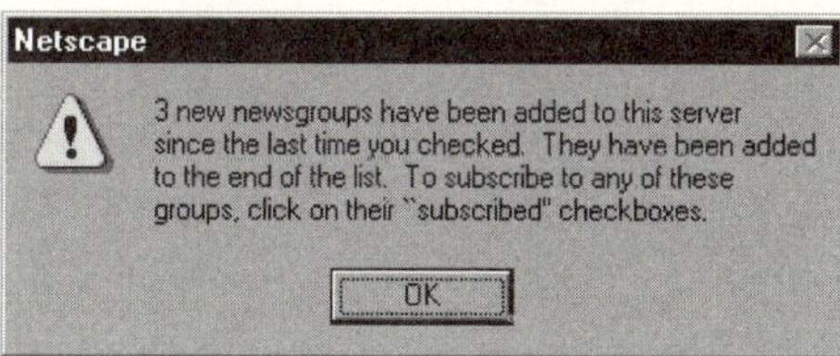

Figure 5-14: A message about new newsgroups.

Subscribing From the List

Once you have displayed a list of available newsgroups, it is very easy to subscribe to one. To subscribe, click the newsgroup's check box in the Subscribed column. Netscape News adds a subscribed (checkmark) icon to the check box.

TIP

If you know the exact name of a newsgroup you want to add, you don't even need to download the entire list of available newsgroups. You can simply select Add Newsgroup from the File menu and type in the name.

Each time you open Netscape News, the program asks your news server to determine whether each of your subscribed newsgroups contains articles you haven't read. By default, Netscape News lists in the newsgroup list pane all subscribed newsgroups that contain unread articles. If you choose the Show Subscribed Newsgroups option from the Options menu, Netscape News will always list all newsgroups to which you have subscribed. (***Note:*** In order to display newsgroups for your server, you may need to click the plus sign to the left of your server's name.)

If you decide later that you're no longer interested in a particular newsgroup, just click the newsgroup's Sub column again to remove the subscribed icon. Netscape News will no longer list this newsgroup in the newsgroup list pane of the News window.

Reading News

Assuming that you have completed the steps described earlier in this chapter to configure Netscape News and to subscribe to newsgroups, you are ready to start reading news.

Choosing a Group

As you know, all network news articles are found in Usenet newsgroups, so before you can read the news, you need to choose a newsgroup. Follow these steps:

1. Make sure you are connected to the Internet, either directly or through a SLIP or PPP connection with your access provider. If you are using a SLIP or PPP connection and are not currently connected, click the Dial-Up Networking icon for your access provider (or if you are not using the Windows 95 Internet software, click the icon you use to connect to your ISP).

   If you are using Windows 3.1 rather than Windows 95, follow the instructions that came with your TCP/IP software for accessing the Internet.

2. If Netscape Navigator 3.0 isn't already running, click the Netscape Navigator 3.0 icon to launch the program. The main Netscape (browser) window appears and the Netscape home page starts loading.

3. Select Netscape News from the Window menu to display the main News window. By default, the News window lists all subscribed newsgroups that contain active articles, as shown in Figure 5-15.

News Server	Unread	Total
news.nando.net (default news host)		
news.announce.newusers	**16**	**16**
news.newusers.questions	**2978**	**2978**
news.answers	**410**	**410**
news.groups	**429**	**429**

Figure 5-15: The active newsgroups in the newsgroups list pane of the News window.

4. Click one of the groups listed in the newsgroup list pane. Netscape News populates the message heading pane with the headings of all active articles in that group. In Figure 5-16, articles from the *news.groups* newsgroup are listed in the message heading pane. (***Note:*** The message heading pane in Figure 5-16 is threaded and sorted by subject.)

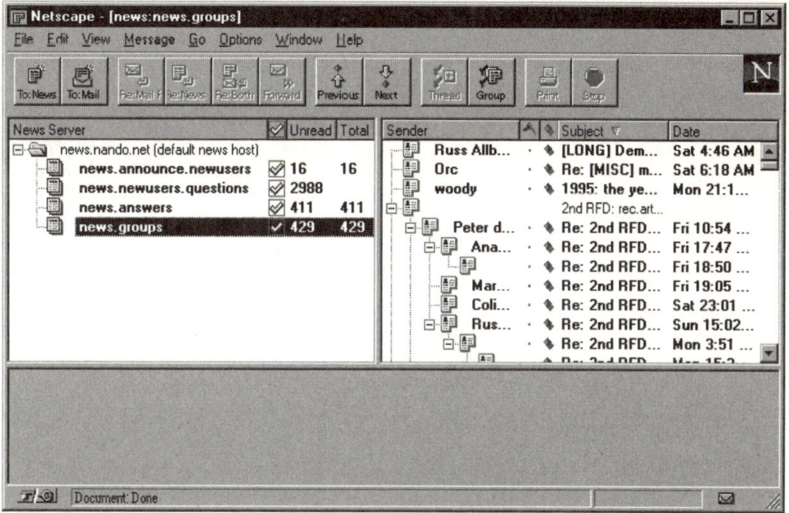

Figure 5-16: The news.groups newsgroup contains 429 unread messages.

Reading an Article

After all the effort you've expended to configure Netscape News, list available newsgroups, and subscribe to newsgroups, actually reading an article is so easy that it's almost a letdown. To display the contents of an article, simply click the article's heading in the message heading pane. Netscape News displays the article's contents in the message pane. The message pane in Figure 5-17 shows the header information of an article from *news.groups*. Use your mouse and the vertical scroll bar or use the cursor keys to scroll the article into view.

TIP

If you don't want to be bothered with all these headers every time you view a message, select Brief from the Show Headers submenu under Options in the Netscape News window. Instead of the usual headers, you'll see a single line that includes the Subject, From, and Date information. If, on the other hand, you want to see even more header information, select All from the same submenu. Some of the supplemental information may be useful in debugging a technical problem or in discovering the true source of a message.

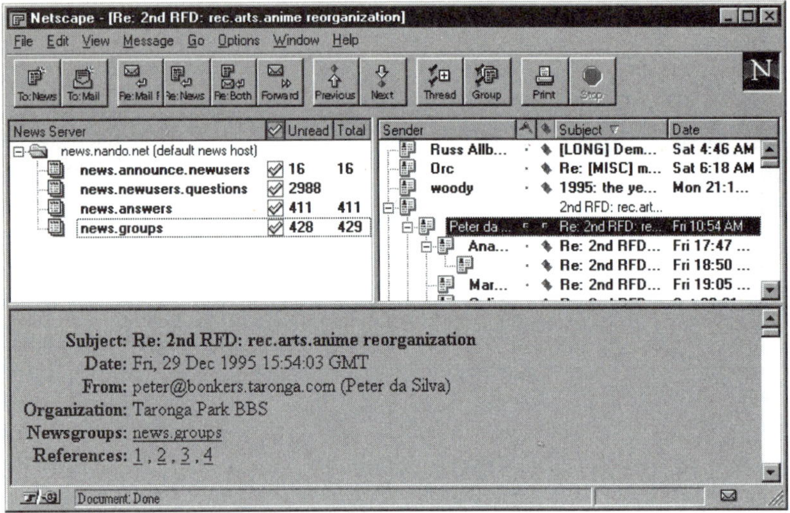

Figure 5-17: An article from the news.groups newsgroup.

By default, Netscape News displays the following article header information at the top of the News window message heading pane:

- **Subject**. Briefly describes the subject matter of the article. All articles in a thread have the same subject.
- **Date**. Gives the date the article was posted to the newsgroup.
- **From**. Provides the return e-mail address of the article's author.
- **Reply To**. Provides an address, specified by the sender, that is used for responding directly to the message.
- **Organization**. Identifies the author's organization (if any).
- **Newsgroups**. Lists hyperlinks to all the newsgroups to which the article was posted. You can go directly to a newsgroup by clicking on the newsgroup name.
- **Followup-To**. Specify the newsgroup to which followup articles should be posted.
- **References**. Identifies as hyperlinks other messages earlier in a thread: the numeral *1* denotes the original message in the thread; the numeral 2 denotes the second message; and so on. You can go directly to the referenced message by clicking on the numeral.

When you display an article, Netscape News removes the diamond from the Read column to indicate that you have read the article. If you want the article to still be marked as *unread*, click the article's Read column to toggle on the diamond.

TIP

You can get another group of messages by selecting Get More Messages from the File menu in the Netscape News window.

Usenet Pictures

One of the more popular pastimes unique to the Internet is the trading of digital pictures of all kinds—pictures of animals, cartoons, heavenly bodies of various sorts, you name it. While digital pictures can be made available on FTP sites or attached to electronic mail, Usenet has become a widely used method of sharing favorite electronic images. Most such files are posted in the newsgroups that have names beginning with *alt.binaries.pictures.*

Many image files on the Internet, including most images displayed on the World Wide Web, are stored as Graphics Interchange Format (GIF) files. The GIF standard was originally designed for use on CompuServe. GIF files can be displayed by Netscape Navigator 3.0 as inline images within a page of text and perhaps other pictures. Or a hyperlink could point to a GIF file that would display in a window by itself when you click the hyperlink.

Because of its high resolution and the relatively high data compression, the Joint Photographic Experts Group (JPEG) file format is the current favorite for storing digital pictures for transmission over the Internet.

If a network news article contains either a GIF file or a JPEG file, Netscape Navigator 3.0 will display the image, along with the rest of the article, in the message content pane.

You can even save the images to disk in a viewable form. Simply right-click on the graphic and select "Save Image as..." from the context menu that appears.

Following a Thread

By choosing to thread newsgroup headings (see the "Configuring Threading & Sorting" section earlier in this chapter), you can quickly read an entire series of related articles from beginning to end. Each subsequent article in a thread is listed, indented, in the message heading pane and just below the article to which it replies. Figure 5-17 shows a series of threaded messages from the *news.groups* newsgroup. To read the next article in the discussion, simply select the next article listed in the message heading pane. To read the preceding message in the thread, display the preceding message in the list.

At times, it may be convenient to maximize the size of the message content pane in order to more easily read news articles. Since the message heading pane wouldn't be visible, Netscape News provides a couple of ways to move from one article to the next and back without displaying the message heading pane. When the threading feature is active, these navigation shortcuts move between articles in the same thread.

To read the next article, as it would appear in the message heading pane, either:

- Click the Next button in the toolbar; or
- Select Next Message from the Go menu.

To read the next unread article, either:

- Click the Next button in the toolbar; or
- Select Next Unread from the Go menu.

To read the preceding message in the message content pane:

- Select Previous Message from the Go menu.

To read the preceding unread article, either:

- Click the Previous button in the toolbar; or,
- Select Previous Unread from the Go menu.

As mentioned in the preceding section, you can also use the References field in the message header to move to previous articles in the current thread. Clicking a reference number displays an earlier article in the thread, but in the main Netscape Navigator 3.0 window (the window normally used to browse the World Wide Web), rather than in the News window. This behavior can be somewhat disorienting since newsgroup articles are normally displayed in the message content pane of the News window.

Flagging Articles to Be Read Later

Often it is convenient to attempt to identify articles of interest from the article headings. As you scroll through the headings list, flag articles that you want to read later by clicking the articles' Mark column. When all the articles you want to read are flagged, you can use the Next Flagged, Previous Flagged, and First Flagged options on the Go menu to move among flagged messages.

Marking Articles Read

A particular newsgroup may contain a thread that you're just not interested in. So that you can avoid seeing the article headers in the future, Netscape Navigator 3.0 lets you "pretend" you've already read them. To mark a thread as already read, simply select the top article in the thread and then click the Thread button.

You can also mark an entire newsgroup as read. Just select that group and click the Group button.

Saving Articles

From time to time as you are perusing the thousands of network news articles available on the Internet, you undoubtedly will want to save an article or two for future reference.

To save an article to a disk file:

1. With the article displayed, hit Ctrl+S or select Save Message(s) As from the File menu. Netscape News displays the Save Message As dialog box.
2. Type a filename for the new file in the File Name text box.
3. Click the OK button. Netscape News saves the file to disk.

TIP

You can save multiple messages at one time by selecting them from the message list and then selecting Save Message(s) As from the File menu.

Printing Articles

Printing a Usenet article is even easier than saving a copy. To print an article:

1. Make sure your printer has paper and other necessary supplies, is turned on, and is properly connected to your computer.
2. Click the Printer button on the toolbar. Netscape News displays the Print dialog box.
3. Make sure the printer settings are correct, and click the OK button. Netscape News sends the article to your printer.

Offensive Material

Unless you've been living on a mountain top in Tibet, you are certainly aware of the Internet's reputation as a place where children can be exposed to offensive material. Most of the offensive material spoken of in the lurid headlines is found on Usenet. Network news is the First Amendment in action, at its best and at its worst. The same network that brings you uplifting information about health, religion, art, and education can also bring you (and your children) explicit sexually oriented conversations and graphic images.

Fortunately, objectionable material tends to be found on a finite list of Internet sites. Several commercial software products are available that enable parents to, in effect, *block* these objectionable Internet sites. The best-known brand of child protection software is SurfWatch. SurfWatch is a subscription-based product, updated monthly, and is available in most major software outlets. Each month, the makers of SurfWatch scour the Internet for new sites that some parents may find objectionable and add these sites to the list of blocked Internet resources. The new blocked list is then encrypted and sent out to parents for installation to their SurfWatch-protected computer. For more information, navigate to the URL http://www.surfwatch.com.

Writing News

You learned earlier in this chapter that lurking on Usenet newsgroups is considered acceptable behavior, but Usenet is fundamentally a collaborative medium of communication, a virtual community of sorts. When you get the urge to become an active member of this community, Netscape News is ready to assist you.

Replying to an Article

The easiest way to begin to participate in newsgroups is to reply to, or follow up on, an existing article. You don't have to worry about how to break the ice or what to type into the various header fields. Just join in the conversation. There are, however, several ways to reply: in public with a posted article; via e-mail directly to the author of the article to which you are replying; or both publicly and via e-mail.

In Public

To reply to a news article publicly with a news article of your own:

1. While connected to the Internet, and with the original article displayed in the News window's message pane, either click the Re:News button in the toolbar (the one with the newspaper-clipping-and-arrow icon on it), or choose Post Reply from the Message menu. Netscape News displays the Compose window.

   For example, suppose you are displaying the article shown in Figure 5-18.

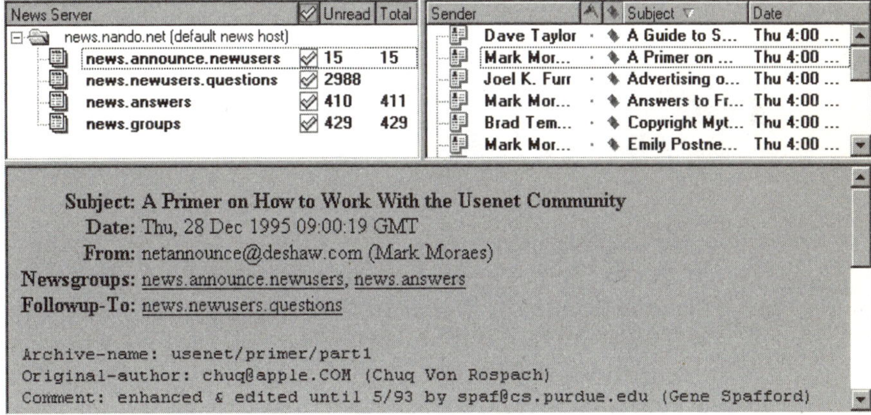

Figure 5-18: The news article to which you are going to reply.

When you click the Re:News button in the toolbar, Netscape News displays the Compose window shown in Figure 5-19. Notice that the Subject and Newsgroups fields in the Compose window are already filled in. Netscape News repeated the subject of the original article and will post your new article to the newsgroup specified by the Followup To field in the original article—the *news.newusers.questions* newsgroup.

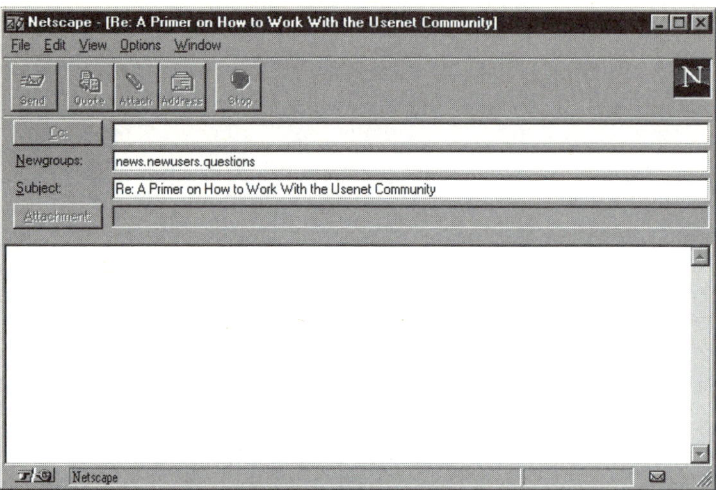

Figure 5-19: The Compose window.

In this example, you see what a Reply window looks like if you have *unchecked* "Automatically quote original message when replying" in the Composition tab of Mail and News Preferences. This may be a more convenient setting unless you often include extensive quotes of articles in your postings.

2. Type your article and either click the Send button on the toolbar or select Send Now from the File menu, or press Ctrl+Enter. Netscape News sends your article to your news server, which takes care of posting the article to the appropriate newsgroup. Netscape News then returns you to the News window.

   For example, after reading the primer shown in the article in Figure 5-19, you might have a question about newsgroups. Type your message in the Compose window and post it to the *news.newusers.questions* newsgroup. You can then check back later in that newsgroup to see if anyone responded to your question.

By default, the Compose window lists the following header fields:

- **CC**. Use this field to address a copy of your message to an e-mail address. If you have filled in an e-mail address in the News Messages field in the Composition tab of the News and Mail Preferences dialog box, that address will appear here.

- **Newsgroups**. By default, this field contains the name of the same newsgroup to which the original article was posted, unless the header of the original article lists a different newsgroup in the Followup To field.
- **Subject**. This field contains the subject of the thread.
- **Attachment**. If you attach a file to your article, the name of the attached file appears here.

You can optionally also display the following header fields by selecting the respective field name from the View menu (or by selecting Show All):

- **From**. By default, this field contains your name and return e-mail address, as entered in the Identity tab of the News and Mail Preferences dialog box.
- **Reply To**. Use this field if you want e-mail replies to your article to be sent to an e-mail address other than your standard From address.
- **Mail To**. Use this field to send the article to an e-mail address.
- **Mail BCC**. Use this field to e-mail a blind copy. This field will not appear in the header of the message actually transmitted to the other recipients of the article/message.
- **Followup To**. Use this field to specify the newsgroup to which followup articles should be posted. If you leave this field blank, followups will be posted to the newsgroup to which your article is posted.

Via E-mail to the Author

If you would rather not post a followup to an article publicly—because what you have to say may not be of general interest, because your comments are of a personal nature, because you are shy, or for whatever reason—you can send an e-mail message instead to the author of the article.

To reply via e-mail:

1. While connected to the Internet, and with the original article displayed in the News window's message content pane, either click the Re:Mail button in the toolbar (the one with the icon of an envelope and an arrow), or choose Mail Reply from the Message menu (or press Ctrl+R). Netscape News displays the Compose window.
2. Type your message and either click the Send button on the toolbar or select Send Now from the File menu, or press Ctrl+Enter. Netscape News sends your message as e-mail to the author of the article to which you are replying. Netscape News then returns you to the News window.

TIP

You can add an author's e-mail address to your address book by selecting Add to Address Book from the Message menu. For more information on the Address Book, see Chapter 4, "Netscape Mail."

Both in Public & to the Author

Occasionally, you may want to post an article in reply to an existing article and also send a copy to the article's author. To do so:

1. While connected to the Internet, and with the original article displayed in the News window's message content pane, either click the Re:Both button in the toolbar (the one with the icons of both a newspaper *and* an envelope with an arrow), or choose Post and Mail Reply from the Message menu. Netscape News displays the Compose window.
2. Type your article and either click the Send button on the toolbar or select Send Now from the File menu, or press Ctrl+Enter. Netscape News sends your article to your news server, which takes care of posting the article to the appropriate newsgroup. Netscape News also sends your message as e-mail to the author of the article to which you are replying. Netscape News then returns you to the News window.

TIP

Just as with regular e-mail, you can also forward newsgroup posts to other recipients. Simply click the Forward button in the Netscape News window.

Posting a New Article

Starting your own thread in a newsgroup is really just as easy as replying to an existing article. You just have to come up with the subject line.

To post a new article:

1. While connected to the Internet, and while browsing in the newsgroup to which you want to post your article, either click the To:News button in the toolbar, or choose New News Message from the File menu. Netscape News displays the Compose window.
2. Netscape News automatically enters the name of the current newsgroup into the Newsgroups field. You can change the newsgroup and/or add other newsgroups as destinations for the article.

3. Type a subject for your article in the subject line. Try to be concise, but make your subject line descriptive. Remember that everyone else browsing the newsgroup will decide whether or not to read your article based on the subject line.
4. Type your article and either click the Send button on the toolbar or select Send Now from the File menu (or press Ctrl+Enter). Netscape News sends your article to your news server, which takes care of posting the article to the appropriate newsgroup.

Including Attachments in Your Articles

You too can distribute GIF and JPEG pictures via network news! It's easy to attach graphics or other binary files to articles you post. With Netscape Navigator 3.0 you can even attach files that are not on your own computer by sending the URLs for the files as attachments to your message.

To attach a file to a newsgroup article:

1. Follow all the steps outlined earlier for creating a new article.
2. Before sending it, click the Attachment button in the Message Composition window. The Attachments dialog box appears.
3. Click either the Attach File button or the Attach Location (URL) button to send a file with your message or to include a link to a file that is on a remote computer.

   Any kind of file can be attached to your mail. But if you are sending an HTML file, you can choose to send it as is (with its HTML formatting) or as plain text, without any special formatting. Select either the As Is or the Convert to Plain Text radio button.
4. Once you have selected a file or typed in a URL, click OK to return to the Attachment dialog box.
5. Click OK to attach the file and return to the Message Composition window.
6. Send the message, including any attachment, by clicking the Send button.

Usenet Etiquette

Even though your contact with Usenet is through your computer, the Usenet itself is really a VERY LARGE community of people. Always keep that fact in mind when you are reading and posting articles. Following is a summary of the article "A Primer on How to Work With the Usenet Community Newsgroups," which is periodically posted to the *news.announce.newusers* newsgroup. I highly recommend you read the full article as well.

"Never forget that the person on the other side is human. Don't blame system admins (short for administrators) for their users' behavior. Never assume that a person is speaking for their organization. Be careful what you say about others. Be brief. Your postings reflect upon you; be proud of them. Use descriptive titles [subjects]. Think about your audience. Be careful with humor and sarcasm. Only post a message once. Summarize what you are following up. Use mail, don't post a followup. Read all followups and don't repeat what has already been said. Double-check followup newsgroups and distributions. Be careful about copyrights and licenses. Cite appropriate references. When summarizing, summarize. Mark or rotate answers or spoilers. Spelling flames (i.e., criticism about misspellings) are considered harmful. Don't overdo signatures. Limit line length and avoid control characters. Please do not use Usenet as a resource for homework assignments. Please do not use Usenet as an advertising medium. Avoid posting to multiple newsgroups."

Moving On

After reading this chapter and trying your hand at network news, you should now feel like a full citizen of Usenet. You have learned how to subscribe to newsgroups and are now able to read and respond to newsgroup articles and begin your own discussions. Move on next to Chapter 6, "Getting Files via FTP," to learn how easy it is to use FTP (File Transfer Protocol) to find and download from the Internet *tons* of useful software.

Getting Files via FTP

I hope that by now you have found a few ways that Netscape Navigator 3.0 can simplify and enrich your life. Through its many easy-to-use features, you can access the Internet for sending and receiving e-mail; for viewing a wide variety of information, available from educational and government institutions as well as businesses and individuals; for reading the subject-specific information contained in newsgroups; and perhaps simply for relaxing and having some fun. But we haven't even touched on one of the oldest "classic" wonders of the Internet: the huge libraries of files that are available for you to download (or copy to your computer) free of charge. The way you actually get these files is via a protocol known as FTP.

What Is FTP?

FTP is one of the simplest and most obvious acronyms you'll come across on the Net: it stands for File Transfer Protocol. That sounds pretty generic, but every implementation of FTP follows the same very specific rules for sending and receiving data. The file must be broken up into pieces at one end and reassembled properly at the other; the data has to be checked for errors and stamped with the correct filename and date; and the FTP software has to enable users to navigate through the host system's directories to find the right file.

Throughout the Internet are scattered thousands of servers that provide files to users via FTP, and they all do their job in much the same way. Many of these sites are known as *anonymous* FTP sites, which means they allow any

Internet user to log on specifically for the purpose of retrieving files. You don't need to be a registered user on the system. Typically, when logging in to anonymous sites, you specify *anonymous* as your username and your e-mail address as the password (see the sidebar, "Your Anonymous Password"). Netscape Navigator 3.0 takes care of the login process automatically; you don't even see any prompts from the remote system.

Are there FTP sites that are not anonymous? Sure! Many corporations, for instance, maintain non-anonymous FTP sites so that employees can trade work-related files while on the road. Of course, you need an account and a real password to access files on those FTP servers. But in this chapter, we'll be dealing primarily with anonymous sites.

Your Anonymous Password

Even when you log onto an anonymous FTP site, it's considered good form to identify yourself by using your e-mail address as your password. By default Netscape Navigator 3.0 does not do this, but I suggest you configure the program so that it minds its Netiquette.

To configure Navigator 3.0 so that it sends your e-mail address as your password when you log onto anonymous FTP sites, select Network Preferences from the Options menu and then click the Protocols tab. Simply check the check box at the bottom of the tab and click OK.

Of course Netscape Navigator 3.0 needs to *know* your e-mail address before it can use it. If you followed the instructions in Chapter 4, "Netscape Mail," you're all set. But if for some reason you decided not to use Netscape Mail, you can still enter your e-mail address into the program. From the Options menu, select Mail and News Preferences. Then go to the Identity tab, fill in the informational fields, and click OK. Now Navigator's FTP feature can send your e-mail address to anonymous FTP sites.

What's Out There?

So what kinds of files are available at these anonymous FTP sites? You name it! There are:

- Fully functional software programs, including spreadsheets, text editors, modem programs, databases, and a dazzling variety of utilities.
- Updates and patches to most major retail software programs.

- Electronic texts ranging from Shakespeare's complete works to David Letterman's latest Top Ten list.
- Thousands of images, sounds, video clips, and animations.
- Technical reports, journals, electronic magazines, news summaries, and archives of user messages.
- Books and tutorials like this one that will help you get started with just about any software task.

Figure 6-1 shows some of the directories at a well-known FTP site, the University of North Carolina SunSITE.

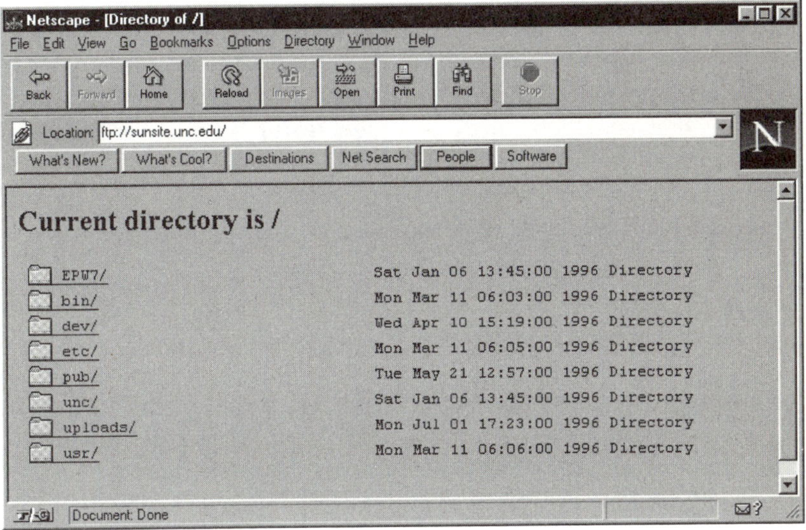

Figure 6-1: Some of the directories of files at SunSITE.

"And I can do whatever I want with all this stuff?" I hear you asking. Well, yes and no. To understand why I'm waffling on this question, you need to understand that there are three broad categories of files on the Internet, and each of these categories has different rules and guidelines for usage.

Public Domain

Public domain files are files that have no copyright, and there are no restrictions whatever on their usage. For instance, you can do whatever you want with Shakespeare's *Hamlet* or *A Winter's Tale*. Modern texts are sometimes released into the public domain as well, by authors who care more about wide distribution than about collecting any royalties or other fees. Many political polemics, for instance, are public domain.

But what about software? Sure, there's lots of public domain software on the Net. This has often been created by altruistic developers as a resource for the good of the community. The old adage "you get what you pay for" doesn't always hold true on the Net. For instance, until recently some of the very best Internet client software was public domain. Of course, there are developers who release unfinished or buggy programs into the public domain to collect feedback, as part of their development process or simply because they don't want to go through the process of refining their work. But programs like these are usually clearly marked, and in some situations they can provide a cost-effective way of dealing with very specific software tasks. And some public domain software is a true group effort: perhaps a programmer started a project years ago, and then somebody downloaded it and worked with it a bit more, then somebody else added new features, and so on. Since there are no restrictions on the redistribution or modification of public domain software, a program may evolve over the course of many years, forged as much by public scrutiny and feedback as by the work of any single designer.

Freeware

Freeware files are copyrighted, but there are no charges for using them. Let's say you write a program that you are very proud of, but you want to make sure anybody can use it for free. You place it on the Internet with a copyright notice and perhaps a text file explaining any restrictions on its use. For instance, you may want to make sure the software is always distributed in its original form, unmodified and bearing your name as the sole author. You may want to make it clear that nobody else may sell the software, but may only distribute it freely as you have.

Many people misunderstand freeware, confusing it with public domain files. They are very different: freeware is free, but you have to play by the rules.

What About Viruses?

In spite of all the hype it gets, the Net is no utopia—it is more like a microcosm. Just as there is a slight chance you could get mugged on your way to the corner store, there is a slight chance that you will someday download a file that "crashes your hard drive" or otherwise messes with your system, causing you that peculiarly modern form of grief known as "restoring everything from backups." (That's assuming you bothered to keep an up-to-date backup as everyone told you to!)

How common are viruses? Certainly much less than sensationalistic mass-media stories would have you believe, but there are some out there. The best defense, of course, is making sure that at any given moment you could restore everything you need from backup tape or disks. If this is not the case at your house, I'd suggest you put this book down and get busy backing up files.

There are other precautions you can take as well. Virus-checking programs such as McAfee Associates's ViruSCAN are available at most major FTP sites, and there are a number of excellent commercial products as well, such as Norton Anti-Virus. It's a good idea to check your entire system once in a while using one of these programs. If you do discover a problem, delete all infected files from your hard drive, or follow any instructions that came with your antivirus software. You will also probably need to completely restore your hard drive from backup.

Many of these programs also provide constant security through background operation; they run constantly on your PC "behind the scenes," checking every file and disk as you load them. Although this is somewhat of a drain on your system's resources, it can catch a virus in the act before it can do any damage to your computer!

Yes, this can be a serious inconvenience. But in the interest of alleviating some of the techno-paranoia that flares up whenever the newsweeklies don't have a juicy enough scandal, let's debunk a few myths:

- Except in very rare cases, you cannot get viruses from text files or from most data files such as word processor documents. Generally speaking, something has to be *run* on your computer to infect it.
- Most viruses do not destroy hardware; they only mess up your software so badly that it seems as though your hardware is faulty. Getting rid of all infected software and then completely restoring your system from backup will usually solve the problem. There are programs that are specifically designed to format hard drives or destroy data, but they're not viruses; they're called *trojan horses*, and they're simply programs that pretend to do something useful while they destroy. Luckily, trojan horses are even more rare than viruses!

➡

- In order to infect a disk, you must load it on an infected PC.
- You won't catch any viruses by hanging around in particular Usenet newsgroups, though it can sometimes feel like you're coming down with something nasty!

For more information about viruses, here are a couple of Web sites to check out:

- The Frequently Asked Questions (FAQ) file for the VIRUS-L/comp.virus mailing list (http://www.cis.ohio-state.edu/hypertext/faq/usenet/computer-virus-faq/faq.html).This FAQ contains a lot of basic information about viruses, including common symptoms and how to proceed if your system is infected.
- Virus Information (http://csrc.ncsl.nist.gov/virus/). This page contains a comprehensive set of links to additional virus-oriented sites, as well as reviews of antivirus software.

Shareware

Shareware is a great marketing innovation that came into being almost concurrently with PCs. Shareware files or programs are distributed on a trial basis: you can download them and use them for free, but only for a short evaluation period. If you like the resource and want to keep using it, you must pay a fee (usually small) to the author or delete it from your machine. Generally it is OK to make copies for your friends to evaluate, but you, of course, can't charge.

Shareware files and programs are copyrighted. You must not copy them except as specifically allowed by the author, and you must abide by any restrictions detailed in the license or accompanying documentation. There has been plenty of litigation over misuse of shareware materials!

The advantages of shareware for the user are obvious: you get to try something out without spending a penny. But there are advantages for shareware authors as well. Distribution costs are kept to a minimum, and there are no middlemen to eat profits. The author also enjoys a direct relationship with the customer and often refines the product based on individual feedback rather than distributors' charts and graphs.

How to Know What You're Getting

FTP sites are really just directories full of files, much like the directories on your own computer. The FTP protocol itself includes no provisions for describing the files or providing additional information, although it does let you view file details such as size, time, and date. So how do you know what all the files in an FTP directory really are? There are two ways:

- Many of the larger FTP sites have Web "front ends." In other words, you initially access them via a Web document that explains a little about the site and what it contains. When you're ready to download a file, you click on a link that fires up the actual FTP protocol, showing you lists of files and directories or going right ahead and transferring the file you want. Figure 6-2 shows an example of a Web front end to an FTP site, on the Netscape server itself.

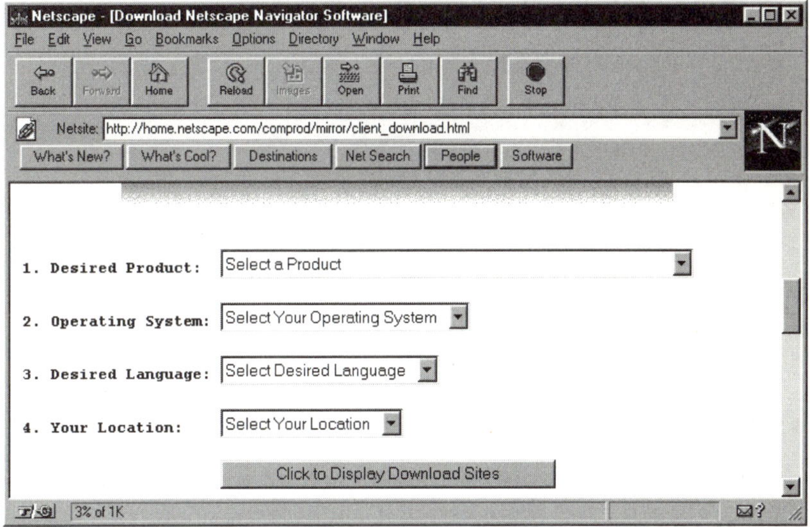

Figure 6-2: Web front end to the Netscape FTP server.

- Most well-established FTP sites include informational files that describe the rest of the available files. These informational files are often named README or INDEX (sometimes in lowercase), or sometimes they have names that begin with a dot, as in .INDEX. You may also encounter informational files called something like WELCOME.TXT.

TIP

By default, Netscape Navigator 3.0 displays text files at FTP sites rather than automatically saving them to your hard drive. But what if you want to save a text file after viewing it? No problem. Just press Ctrl+S or select Save As from the File menu.

Now let's click the WELCOME.TXT file link at Ventana's own FTP site to view its contents, shown in Figure 6-3.

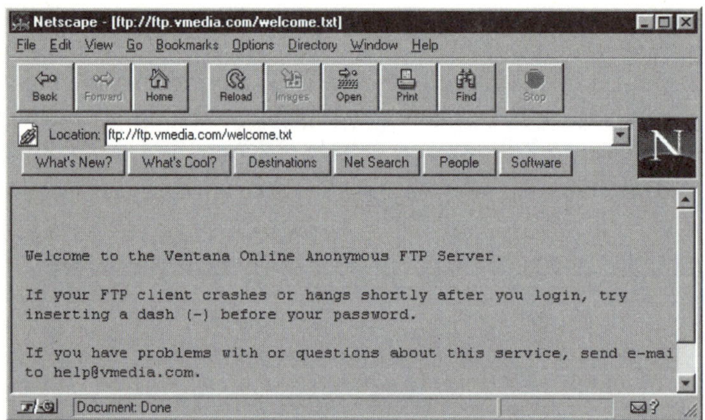

Figure 6-3: The contents of Ventana's WELCOME.TXT file.

As you can see, the WELCOME.TXT file contains important information about the system itself.

Common Filename Extensions

Knowing a person's last name won't necessarily tell you anything about the person, but the few characters that compose the extension to a filename are packed with information. For instance, if a file ends with .TXT, you can be pretty sure it's an ASCII text file, readable on virtually any system by using a simple text viewing program. But not all extensions are so obvious, so I've compiled a table of some of the most common ones you'll come across. Table 6-1 is by no means complete, but it's a good reference to keep handy as you start exploring FTP sites.

Extension	Type of File
.TXT	Simple text file, readable using Notepad, WordPad, or even the DOS type command.
.ASC	Probably a simple ASCII text file as well.
.DOC	May be a text file or a Microsoft Word document.
.EXE	An executable file (DOS or Windows program) that can be run from the command line or from the Windows Run command (or by double-clicking the file's icon in Windows 95). Often it is a self-extracting archive file; when you run it, it is decompressed into several files.
.ZIP	An archive file that has been compressed using the PKZIP compression program. You can use PKUNZIP or WinZip to extract the separate files that are part of the archive (see "Understanding Compression" later in this chapter).
.HQX	A file that has been archived using the BinHex compression program; you must use BinHex to decompress it. This compression standard is more common in the Macintosh world, and chances are good that an .HQX file is really intended for Mac use.
.SIT	A compressed, or "stuffed," Macintosh file. Probably not useful on your PC, although if you need one of these files, several good PC unstuffers are available on the Net.
.ARJ	Another type of compressed file. Several compression and decompression programs such as WinZip and DRAG AND ZIP can handle these files.
.LHA	See note on .ARJ above.
.ARC	See note on .ARJ above. One of the oldest compression schemes around today.
.ZOO	See note on .ARJ above.
.Z	A file compressed using the UNIX Zip. You can use the program GZIP, or a general-purpose utility such as WinZip or DRAG AND ZIP, to decompress it.
.GZ	A file compressed using the GNU Zip program for UNIX. See note on .Z above.
.TAR	An archive file that has been compressed using the UNIX tar facility. It may be decompressed using a PC version of tar or a general-purpose utility such as WinZip or DRAG AND ZIP.

Table 6-1: Common filename extensions on FTP sites.

Understanding Compression

You no doubt noticed that many of the notes in Table 6-1 refer to compression. When you look at the staggering number of files on the Internet (or, if you have Windows 95, at the staggering number of files on your hard drive!), it is clear that it's important to shrink files so that they are as small as you can possibly make them. And of course the smaller the file, the quicker it travels from one machine on the Internet to another, reducing overall transfer time and network traffic. But what exactly is file compression?

Think about the number 20,000,000,000,000,000,000,000. Now imagine trying to read this number to another person so that he or she can write it down. You *could* say "two zero zero zero zero zero zero zero zero zero zero zero zero zero zero zero zero zero zero zero zero zero zero," but that's the stupid way to do it. If you want to maintain your friend's respect, you'll probably say "two followed by 22 zeros." You have effectively compressed the information into fewer words, and your friend can decompress it by actually writing out the 22 zeros.

There are 256 different characters that can appear in a computer file in any order, or just half that number in the case of ASCII text files. In some files, there are no repeated characters and no repeated patterns of characters, but most are full of repetitions even if the repetitions are accidental. This means that most files can be compressed. Think of a database, for instance, in which there are lots of spaces that fill out fixed-length fields. It's easy to see how you can compress a file like this by indicating the space character and the number of times it should be repeated.

Of course, I'm oversimplifying. Compression techniques have become very sophisticated and use a variety of subtle approaches, or *algorithms*, that go far beyond merely tallying repeated characters. Some try to maximize the amount of saved disk space; others try to speed up the process of compressing and decompressing files. Most try for some sort of balance between these two aspects of the process.

You have to decompress most compressed files before they can be used; compressed files are good only for transferring and storing the information. The exceptions to this are compressed graphics and sound files, which you can view or listen to directly, without running any decompression software. In this case, Netscape Navigator 3.0 (or some other viewing program) is automatically decompressing the file for you.

Smaller + Smaller = Bigger

As you travel around to different FTP sites, you'll notice that graphics files such as GIFs are never "zipped up" into archives; they're always left just as they are, with their original extension. Why?

Well, GIF files are *already* compressed. The graphics standard includes an algorithm for storing these files in as few bytes as possible. Images are obvious candidates for compression, since so many pixels are repeated. Think of the background, for instance, or large patches of color. If a graphics file contained position and color information for each individual pixel that appeared onscreen, it would be gigantic!

OK, so a GIF file is already compressed. But couldn't you make it even smaller by compressing it again? Nope. Curiously, by running a GIF file through a compression program such as PKZIP or WinZip, you actually make it *bigger*!

Kind of strange, huh? Well think about it: assuming that GIF compression is pretty tight (which it is), you're only going to eke out a few more bytes of space savings. But this added compression actually costs more space than it saves, for PKZIP has to add to the file the information about how to decompress it. In other words, it has to announce "this file has been compressed using PKZIP version *x*" as well as a bunch of other technical information. For this same reason, it may not always be worth compressing small files that are known to contain lots of nonrepeating information.

Clearly, you really need a compression program to deal with all the files you collect from the Net. In the next section, you'll kill two birds with one virtual stone: you'll learn how to use Netscape Navigator 3.0's FTP features as you download a copy of WinZip 6, one of the best compression/decompression programs available.

Downloading Your First File

In this example, you'll access a Web page that serves as a front end for an FTP site. You will be able to download the WinZip 6 file simply by clicking a link on the Web page, without wading through the actual directories on the FTP server itself. Later in the chapter, you'll see how Netscape Navigator 3.0 displays this more "raw" FTP information.

To download WinZip 6 using Netscape Navigator 3.0's built-in FTP:

1. Make sure you are connected to the Internet, either directly or through a SLIP or PPP connection with your access provider. If you are using a SLIP or PPP connection and are not currently connected, double-click the Dial-Up Networking icon for your access provider.

   If you are using Windows 3.1 rather than Windows 95, follow the instructions that came with your TCP/IP software for accessing the Internet.

2. Double-click the Netscape Navigator 3.0 icon to launch the program. The main window appears, and the Netscape home page starts loading as shown in Figure 6-4.

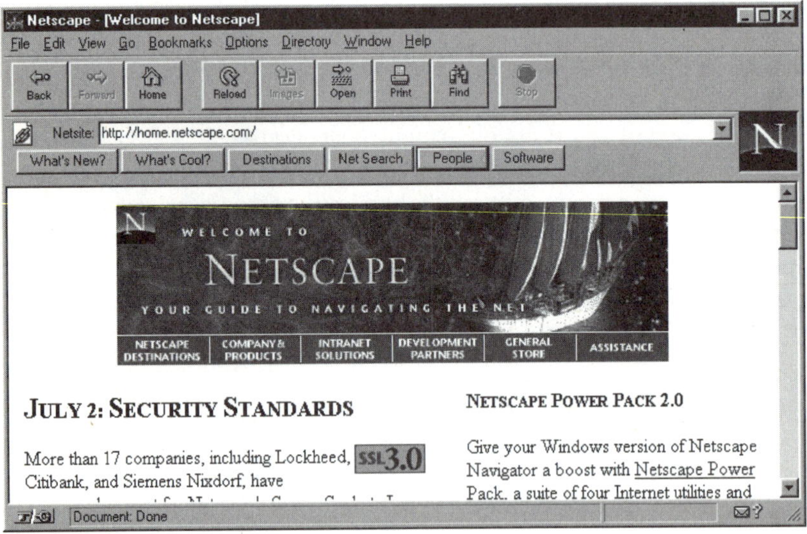

Figure 6-4: The Netscape home page.

3. Click your mouse inside the Location field at the top of the window to select the URL http://home.netscape.com/.

TIP

Remember, you don't always have to type in entire URLs; in many cases you can leave off the two slashes and everything that comes before them. If you simply type in ***home.netscape.com****, Navigator 3.0 is smart enough to figure out that you mean a Web site and will automatically use the HTTP protocol. Similarly, if you type in* ***ftp.vmedia.com****, Navigator knows you are trying to connect to an FTP site and will use FTP.*

4. Replace this URL with the one for the WinZip home page by typing **http://www.winzip.com/**. Once you have typed in the new URL, press Enter. Netscape Navigator 3.0 retrieves the WinZip home page, as shown in Figure 6-5.

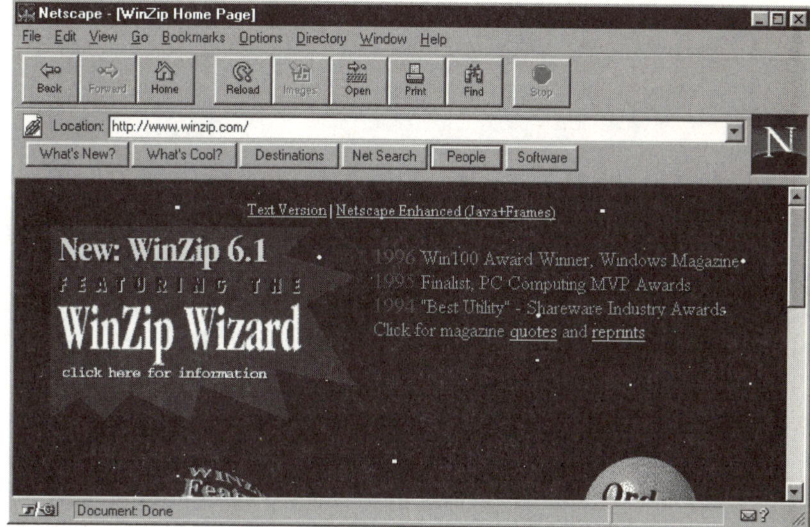

Figure 6-5: The WinZip home page.

5. You might want to take some time to look around the WinZip home page. When you are ready, scroll down the page and click the Download Evaluation Version link. The WinZip:Download Page appears, as shown in Figure 6-6.

TIP

You can save FTP sites as bookmarks just like any Web document. Select Add Bookmark from the Bookmarks menu, or simply press Ctrl+D. This is convenient if you don't have time to download a long file immediately, but want to be able to find it easily later on.

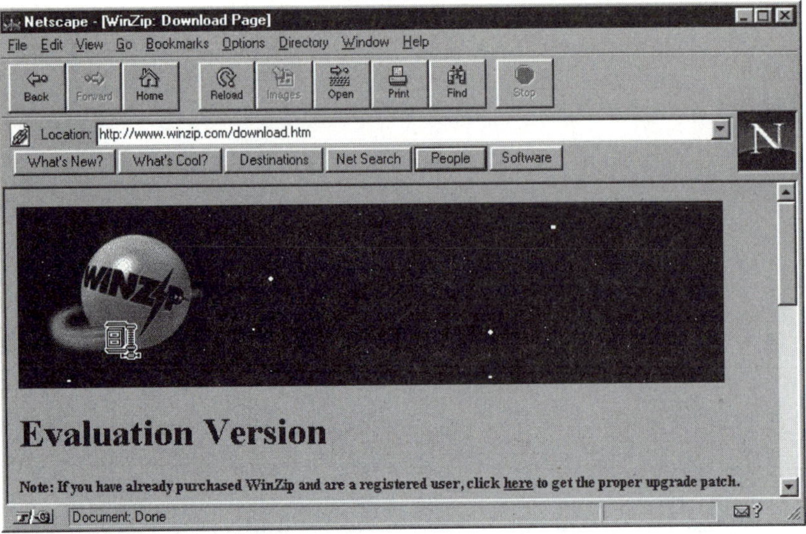

Figure 6-6: The Download WinZip page.

6. Now place your cursor over the top link on the page (don't click just yet). Notice that the status line indicates the URL pointed to by the link, ftp://204.213.250.17/winzip/winzip95.exe. The *ftp* at the beginning of the URL tells Netscape Navigator 3.0 to use the FTP protocol to connect with the site 204.213.250.17, switch to the *winzip* directory, and download the file *winzip95.exe*.
7. Click one of the top two links, depending on whether you are using Windows 95 or Windows 3.1. After Netscape Navigator 3.0 has made contact with the remote FTP site, a typical Windows Save As dialog box appears.
8. Choose a location (such as your \TEMP directory) for the file, and then click the Save button. The Saving Location dialog box appears, showing you the progress of the file transfer. Once Netscape Navigator 3.0 has finished downloading the file, the Saving Location dialog box disappears.

Unknown File Types

Sometimes when you attempt to download a file you may get a message like the one in Figure 6-7 below:

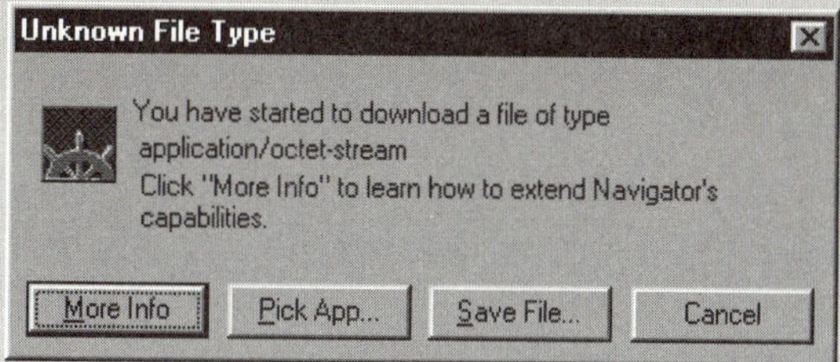

Figure 6-7: The Unknown File Type dialog box.

This simply means that no special action or helper application (viewer) has been configured for this kind of file, and you can choose what to do with it. Netscape Navigator 3.0 can, for instance, automatically run a file like this as soon as it has been received, or it can save it to disk automatically, without popping up the dialog box. To learn how to make these configuration changes, see "Helper Applications" later in this chapter or click on the More Info button to view a tutorial document at Netscape's own Web site.

Tip: You can click the Pick App button to configure an application to run once the file has been downloaded. For instance, if you are downloading a Microsoft Word document, you might want to run Word right away. Again, for more information on helper applications, see the "Helper Applications" section later in this chapter, or click the More Info button.

Congratulations! You've just downloaded your first file via FTP, and you now have an important tool for dealing with files you will download in the future. To install WinZip 6, simply run the executable file that you saved on your hard drive. You can run it from the DOS command line or using the Windows Run command. Be sure to read any informational files included with the program, and please remember that WinZip 6 is shareware: if you continue to use it, you must register it. The WinZip package contains complete information on how to do this.

TIP

Once an FTP transfer has started, you can go back to browsing in the browser window. The file will keep downloading as you work. You can even start another FTP transfer and download several files at once.

Now let's visit an anonymous FTP site the more traditional way, without relying on a Web page as the front end.

FTP Traffic Jams

FTP sites are among the busiest resources on the Net. They may not get as many users as the most popular Web pages, but because of the way FTP works, there is a built-in traffic problem.

When you access a Web page, you quickly download the document and are off. Click a link on the page, and you bop back to the site, or to a different site. You flit from site to site, never staying longer than it takes to get the requested information. But with FTP, you remain logged in to the server while cruising and perusing directories at your own pace, and of course you remain logged in as you download files. The Web is like a fast-food joint, or like the old-fashioned automats where you walked around grabbing the dishes you wanted; FTP is like a real restaurant, with its share of customers who just never seem to stop eating!

Because of this inherent traffic problem, you might sometimes get a message telling you that too many users are already logged on when you connect with an FTP site. Sometimes, however, you will simply be unable to connect at all, and Netscape Navigator 3.0 will just seem to be spinning its wheels. The solution to either of these problems is simple: try again later. In fact, try again *much* later, at a time when there are likely to be fewer info-junkies cruising the Net (3 A.M. works pretty well).

You say you like to sleep at night? Fortunately there is another solution. For many of the larger public FTP servers, there are also *mirror sites*, FTP servers that contain the exact same files and directory structure but may experience less traffic. These mirror sites are kept in sync with the original: anything you can get at the original you can get at its mirror, and you can be sure that you're downloading the same version. Often the "sorry, we're too busy" message you get when trying to log on to an FTP server includes a list of mirror sites.

Navigating FTP Sites

For this tutorial, we'll look at the very large anonymous Oak site at Oakland University in Rochester, Minnesota. Primarily a mirror of the Simtel collection of files, this site houses thousands of programs of interest to the Internet community, from casual Net surfers to seasoned experts. I use Oakland as an example because it is fairly typical of some of the large public FTP sites scattered around the Net—and because you usually don't run into too much of a traffic jam trying to get on.

1. Make sure you are connected to the Internet either directly or via your SLIP or PPP access provider. If Netscape Navigator 3.0 is not currently running, launch it by double-clicking its icon.
2. In the Location box at the top of the window, select the currently displayed URL and replace it with **ftp://oak.oakland.edu/**. Press Enter. After a few moments, the top-level directory at the Oak site appears, as shown in Figure 6-8.

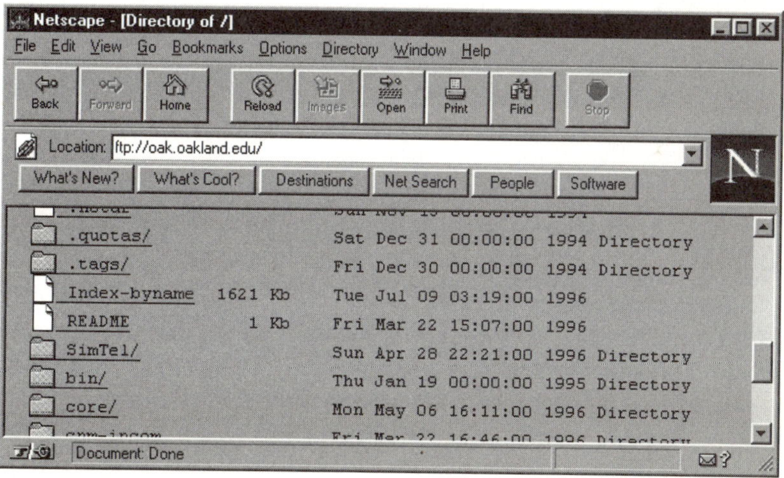

Figure 6-8: The top-level directory at Oak.

3. If there is any information at the top of the page, read it. Then scroll down. You can now see a list of several subdirectories of this top-level directory. Notice that Netscape Navigator 3.0 indicates directories with a Folder icon.

4. Most of the good stuff on Oak is under the /pub directory, so let's go there. (Pub directories often contain files that are useful to the general public.) Scroll down and click the /pub link. The /pub directory appears, as shown in Figure 6-9.

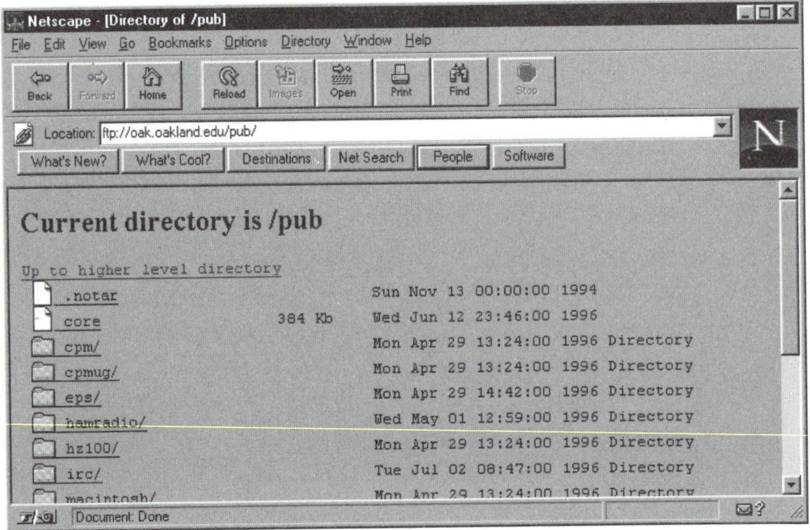

Figure 6-9: The /pub directory.

TIP

*If you know where you want to go on an FTP server, you can include the directory right in the URL. For instance, you could enter **ftp://oak.oakland.edu/pub/** right in the Location box in Netscape Navigator 3.0. And if you know what file you want to retrieve, you can even include the filename in the URL!*

From here you can cruise around on your own for a while—Netscape Navigator 3.0 makes it so easy that you don't need me to hold your virtual hand anymore. If you're interested in ham radio files, click the link to the hamradio/ directory; if you're a Macintosh person, click macintosh/. You can always back up a level using the Back button, or you can return to any level you've already seen via the Go menu.

Some of the most useful files on Oak are the Windows 95 utilities contained in the pub/simtelnet/win95/util/ directory. You already know that you can get there by clicking your way down, level by level. But since you already know how to navigate this way, let's accelerate the process by taking a shortcut:

1. In the Location box near the top of the Netscape Navigator 3.0 window, edit the currently displayed URL so that it reads **ftp://oak.oakland.edu/pub/simtelnet/win95/util/**.

   A long URL like this is an excellent candidate for a bookmark. I, for one, don't want to type it again!

2. Press Enter. Netscape Navigator 3.0 automatically takes you to the correct directory, as shown in Figure 6-10.

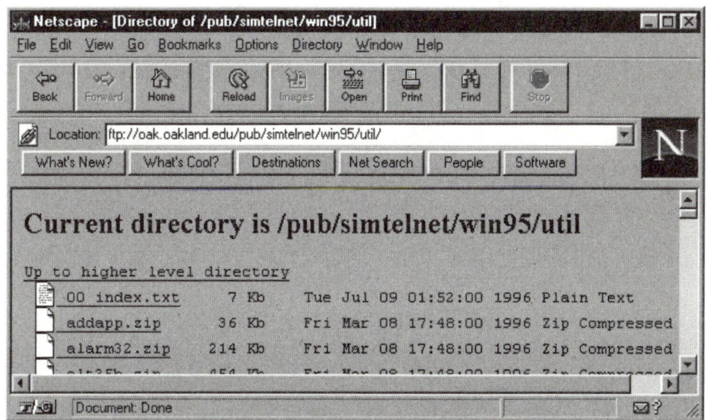

Figure 6-10: The ftp://oak.oakland.edu/pub/simtelnet/win95/util/ directory at Oak.

Notice the 00_index.txt file at the top of the directory list. You should read this file for capsule descriptions of all the files in this directory.

Now take a few moments to scroll down the list of files. Notice that Netscape Navigator 3.0 labels each one with a special blank file icon. This means that Netscape doesn't recognize the .ZIP extension, and when you click on a filename the program will pop up the Unknown File Type dialog box mentioned above. If you want, though, you can have WinZip automatically extract .ZIP files. See "Helper Applications" later in this chapter.

What Are Symbolic Links?

As you look around FTP sites, you'll notice that in any given directory there are files, subdirectories, and something called "symbolic links." What exactly are they?

A symbolic link is really just a nickname or, more exactly, a pointer to another directory or file. Imagine you are the administrator of an FTP site, and you just put a brand new evaluation version of Netscape Navigator in the directory */pub/pc/windows/win95/www/apps/netscape*. That's buried pretty far down in the directory structure, and people are going to take quite a while navigating down to that level. In addition, if they type in the entire URL, they are likely to make mistakes, taking even more time and further adding to the traffic problem. You want to make sure that users get to the new Netscape file quickly and efficiently. What to do? Create a symbolic link in the top-level directory, and call it, for instance, new_netscape. When a user clicks new_netscape, he or she is automatically transported to the directory where the file *really* lives.

The administrators of FTP sites can create symbolic links to directories or to files. If you click a link that's associated with a directory, you "teleport" to that directory; if you click a link to a file, Netscape Navigator 3.0 views the file or begins the download process. Symbolic links make it quicker, and much more pleasant, to navigate FTP sites that have complex directory structures.

Searching for Files

FTP is great if you know what you're looking for and where to find it. But what if all you know is that you need a particular kind of program, let's say, and you have no idea where to start looking? Or what if you can only remember part of the name of a file you want? Fortunately, the Net offers a wide variety of services for locating files in the FTP haystack. One of the old standbys, and still one of the most useful tools on the Net, is a service known as Archie.

Archie

Archie is an Internet service that lets you search indexes of most of the files available at anonymous FTP sites. These indexes are maintained on special Archie servers located around the world. To use Archie effectively, you need to know part of a file's name, or at least be able to make a reasonable guess about what characters might be in its name. For instance, let's say you want to find

WinZip 6 but don't remember the exact name of its self-extracting archive file. Archie lets you specify a string of characters that appears anywhere in the name. It would be safe to guess that the string "winzip6" appears somewhere in the file name, so you can use that as your Archie search criterion and find the correct file even if its name is "latestwinzip600z.exe."

For advanced users interested in specifying very precise search parameters, Archie even supports the full set of regular expressions that let you search for all kinds of patterns within filenames. For instance, you could look for a file that begins with a lowercase letter, followed by any number of digits, followed by the string "zsa-zsa," followed by a number greater than five, followed by an extension of either .TAR or .SH, followed by another extension of... Well, you get the idea. It is beyond the scope of this book to provide a tutorial on regular expressions, but I like to think of them as wildcards on steroids. If you want more information, why not use some of the Internet search tools you've learned about so far?

OK, let's give Archie a try:

1. Make sure you are connected to the Internet either directly or via your SLIP or PPP access provider. If Netscape Navigator 3.0 is not currently running, launch it by double-clicking its icon.
2. In the Location box at the top of the Netscape Navigator 3.0 window, replace the currently displayed URL with **http://www-ns.rutgers.edu/htbin/archie** and press Enter. In a few moments, the Rutgers University Archie Request Form page appears, as shown in Figure 6-11.

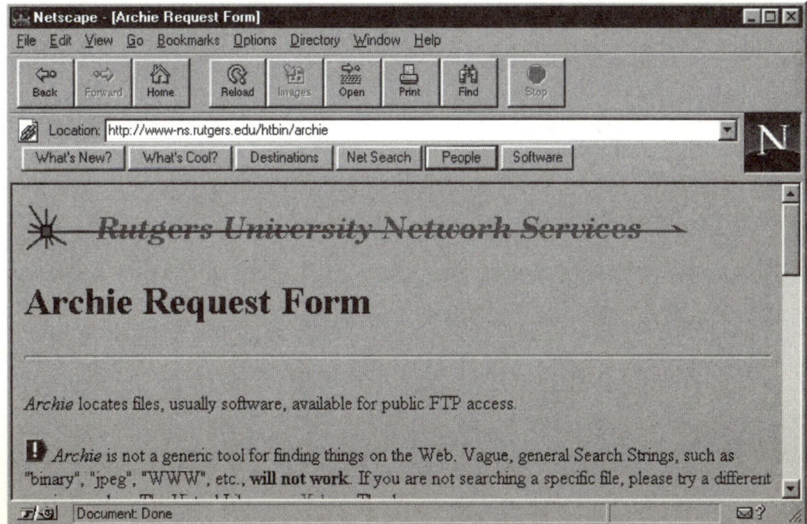

Figure 6-11: The Archie Request Form page.

3. Scroll down the page until you get to the search form itself. Fill it out as follows:
   - In the Search by section, click the top radio button, Looking for Search Term in File Names (Ignore UPPER/lowercase).
   - In the Search Term box, type **winzip6**.
   - Leave the other settings alone.

   Your completed search form should look like Figure 6-12.
4. Now click the Start Search button. In a few moments, the Archie Search Results page appears, as shown in Figure 6-13, providing you with links to a few different FTP sites where you can get WinZip 6.

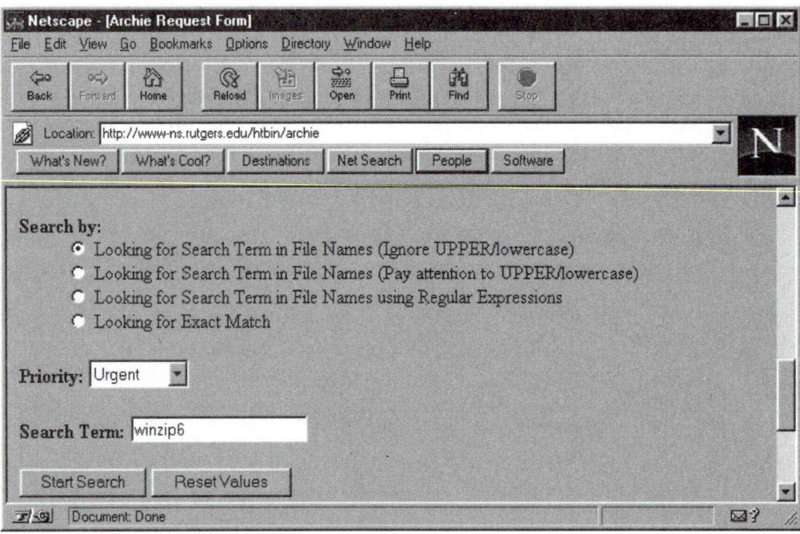

Figure 6-12: The completed search request.

As you can see, Archie is great if you know something—*anything*—about the name of the file you are looking for. But what if you're looking for a particular *kind* of file—a mortgage calculator, for instance—that could have any name at all? Luckily, the Internet provides search utilities for this situation as well. One of the best is the c | net shareware page.

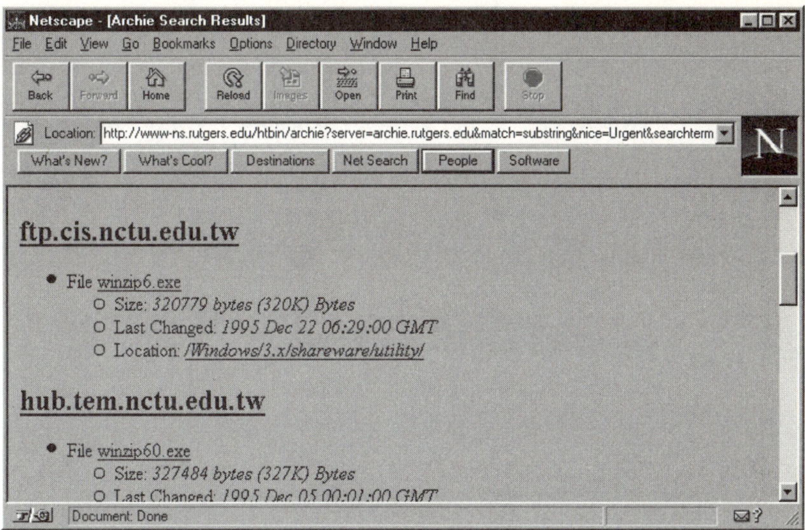

Figure 6-13: The Archie Search Results page.

The c|net Shareware Page

To get to the c|net Shareware Page:

1. Make sure you are connected to the Internet either directly or via your SLIP or PPP access provider. If Netscape Navigator 3.0 is not currently running, launch it by double-clicking its icon.
2. In the Location box at the top of the Netscape Navigator 3.0 window, replace the currently displayed URL with **http://www.shareware.com/** and press Enter. In a few moments, the shareware.com page appears, as shown in Figure 6-14.

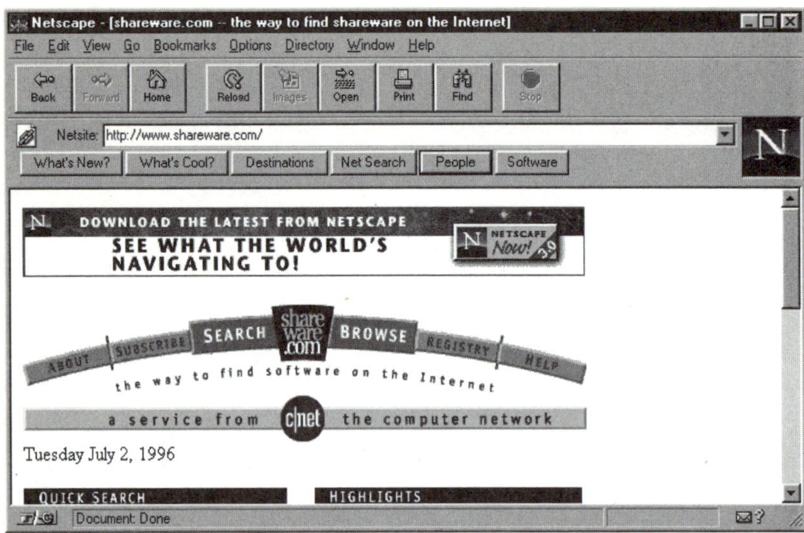

Figure 6-14: The shareware.com page.

3. After reading the introductory information on this page, scroll down to the search form.
4. Since we are interested in mortgage calculators for Windows, leave the drop-down list of file categories set to MS-Windows (all). In the search word box, type **mortgage**. Your completed search form should look like Figure 6-15.

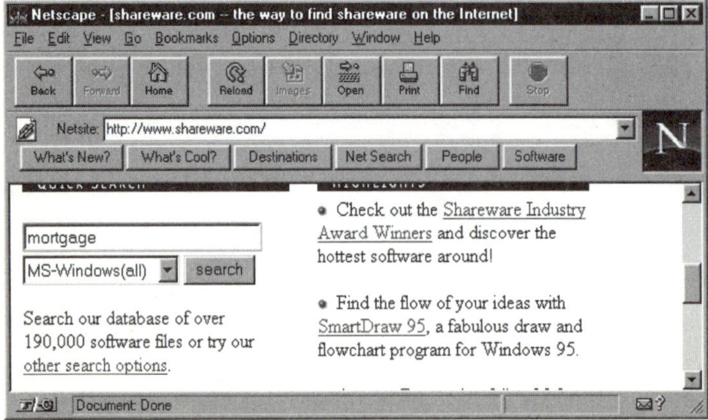

Figure 6-15: Completed search form.

5. Click the search button. In a few moments, the Search Results page appears as shown in Figure 6-16, with links to several different mortgage programs for Windows. You can click any one of these to retrieve the file from its FTP site.

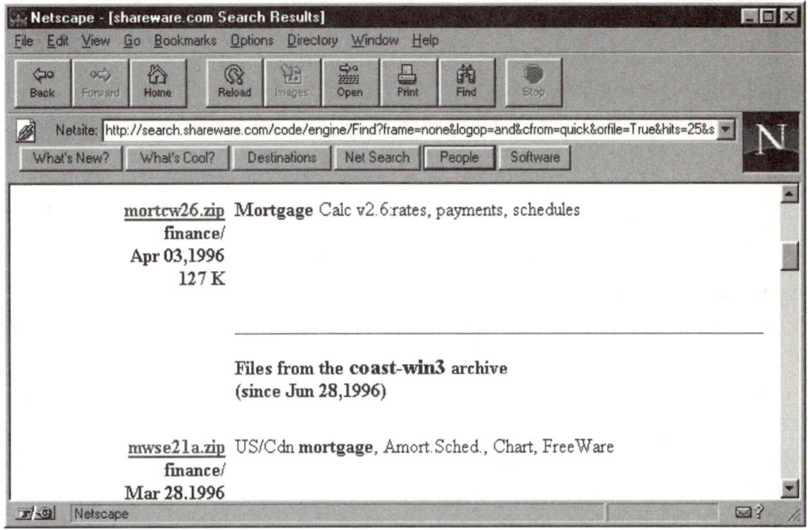

Figure 6-16: The search results.

The shareware.com page provides such a powerful search tool that you'll probably want to add it to your Bookmarks Directory.

Non-Anonymous FTP

Grabbing files from anonymous FTP sites may be the most entertaining use of Netscape Communicator's built-in FTP facility, but there are other practical applications as well. For instance, when I finish writing this chapter, I will FTP it to Netscape Press, where my editor will massage the text and then place it back on the FTP server so I can look over her changes. To do this, I have to log onto an FTP site, which requires that I enter a login name and a password.

Here's how to log onto a non-anonymous FTP site to exchange files:

In Navigator's Netsite/Location box, enter the URL for the site you want to connect to via FTP, but include your login name as part of the URL. (For instance, when I want to log onto the WELL for the purposes of anonymous FTP, I type **ftp://pjames@well.com** and hit Enter. Immediately a dialog box appears asking me for my login password.) Once you enter your password, your home directory appears—or the directory you've been given access to by the system administrator. You navigate around the site just as you would navigate around a public (anonymous) FTP site, and the procedure for downloading files is identical. To send a file, select File Upload from Navigator's File menu. Using the Upload File dialog box that appears, choose a file from your local system to upload.

You can even include your password as part of the URL for a non-anonymous FTP connection. Simply type a colon after your login name, and then your password for the account. Using the example we looked at earlier, I would enter **ftp://pjames:mypassword@well.com**. There is a slight security problem with this method, however—your password ends up in Navigator's history list.

Using Web Tools to Find Files

While there are other specialized tools for finding files on FTP sites, you may not actually need them. The World Wide Web is becoming more and more prominent as a front end for FTP servers. This means that you can find many files without specialized FTP search services; you simply use the same search engines you use for locating other types of information on the Web itself. The best of these utilities are available by clicking the Netscape Navigator 3.0 Net Search button. While an Infoseek search, for instance, may not get you directly to a particular file, it will probably take you to a Web page with a link to the file you're interested in. And of course, you can find lots of files by browsing through the dozens of categories that appear when you click the Destinations button.

As I mentioned earlier, Netscape Navigator 3.0 does more than just go out and retrieve files for you—it can actually help you start working with them right away. In the next section, you'll learn how to take advantage of this powerful feature.

What Are RFCs?

Just when you thought we were done with acronyms!

RFC stands for Request for Comment, and that's exactly what it is: a document put out on a public FTP site so that other Net users can read it and comment on the content. But an RFC contains very specialized information, technical information about the Internet itself. In fact, many of the Internet standards that have developed over the years are the result of this RFC process.

Most RFC files are slow, tedious reading, and nobody's turned them into a musical yet. But they are invaluable to anybody wanting to learn more about the Net, and a few of them are even fun. (Well, if you're a geek like me.) RFC 1208, for example, is a large glossary of networking terminology, and RFC 1325 has lots of tips for new Internet users.

How do you know what the different RFC files cover? Here are two URLs:

- ftp://isi.edu/in-notes/rfc-retrieval.txt
- ftp://isi.edu/in-notes/rfc-index.txt

The first file provides instructions on locating and downloading RFCs, and the second contains short descriptions of all the RFCs that currently exist.

Helper Applications

You've already seen that when you click on a text file at an FTP site, Netscape Navigator 3.0 automatically displays the contents rather than simply downloading the file to your hard drive. But that's only a small example of the automation that's possible. To understand how all of this works, let's take a look at the Helpers tab under General Preferences.

1. Select General Preferences from the Netscape Navigator 3.0 Options menu. The Preferences dialog box pops up with the Appearance tab selected, as shown in Figure 6-17.

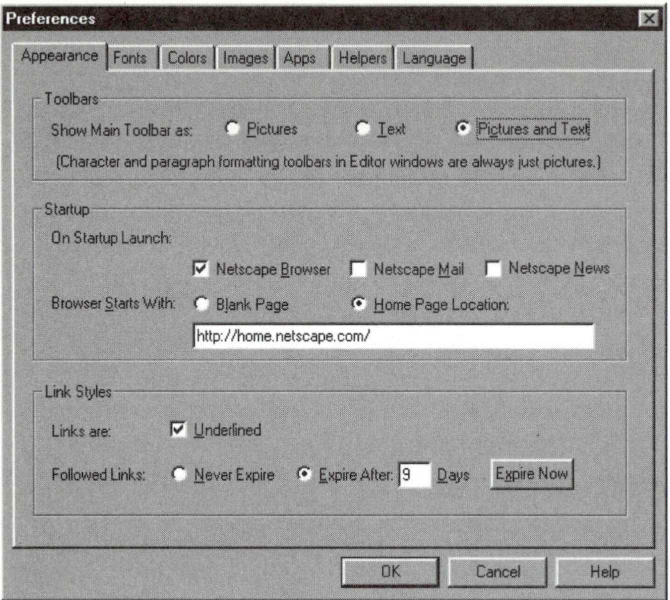

Figure 6-17: The Preferences dialog box.

2. Select the Helpers tab, as shown in Figure 6-18.

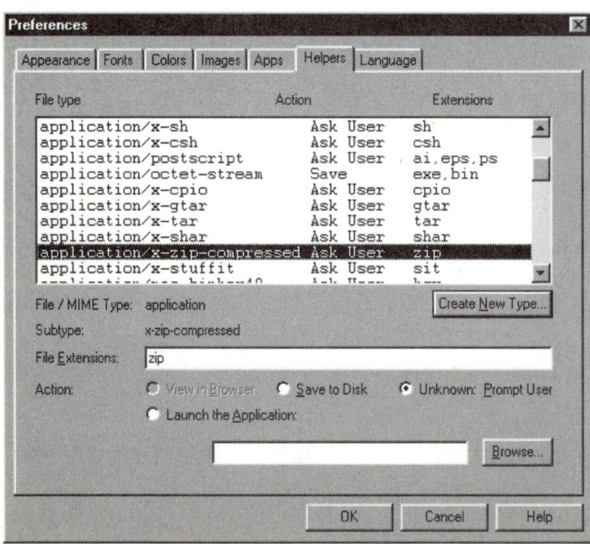

Figure 6-18: The Helpers tab, with settings for the application/x-zip-compressed file type.

TIP

You can also select a helper application by clicking the Pick App button in the Unknown File Type dialog box that appears when you download a file (see Figure 6-7).

This looks like a fairly complicated dialog box at first, but once you understand the concepts, it's really pretty simple. The large scrolling list includes the names of different kinds of files you might encounter as you cruise the Net with Netscape Navigator 3.0. These file types are listed using a naming standard known as Multipurpose Internet Mail Extensions (MIME). In MIME nomenclature, for instance, files with an .EXE or .BIN extension are classified as applications, with a subtype designation of octet-stream. If you scroll down the list, you'll see many different types of files, some familiar and some unfamiliar. Usually the MIME designations make sense, as in the case of Graphics Interchange Format (GIF) files, which are classified as images with a subtype of gif.

Here's where it gets interesting. For each type of file it encounters on the Internet, Netscape Navigator 3.0 has a default action that's listed in the Action column of the list. For image/gif files, for example, you can see that the default action is Browser. This means that GIF graphics will be displayed automatically by Netscape Navigator 3.0 itself, right within the browser window. And for application/octet-stream files, the default is Ask User: when you click on a link to an .EXE or .BIN file, you will be asked what you want to do with the file, as shown earlier in Figure 6-7.

TIP

Settings in the Helpers tab also affect the way attached files are handled in Netscape Mail (see Chapter 4, "Netscape Mail").

But suppose you don't like Netscape Navigator 3.0's default action for a particular file type. Fortunately, it's very easy to change. In this example, we'll change the default action for PKZIP compressed files so that they are automatically saved to disk, without any "What do you want to do with this file?" dialog box popping up.

1. If you are not already in the Helpers tab, select General Preferences from the Netscape Navigator 3.0 Options menu. Click the Helpers tab.
2. Scroll down the list of file types until you find application/x-zip-compressed. Select this entry by clicking on it. The specific settings for the application/x-zip-compressed file type appear, as shown in Figure 6-19.

   Notice that the Action column indicates Ask User for this file type.
3. In the Action section near the bottom of the dialog box, click the Save to Disk radio button. Now the word *Save* appears in the Action column.

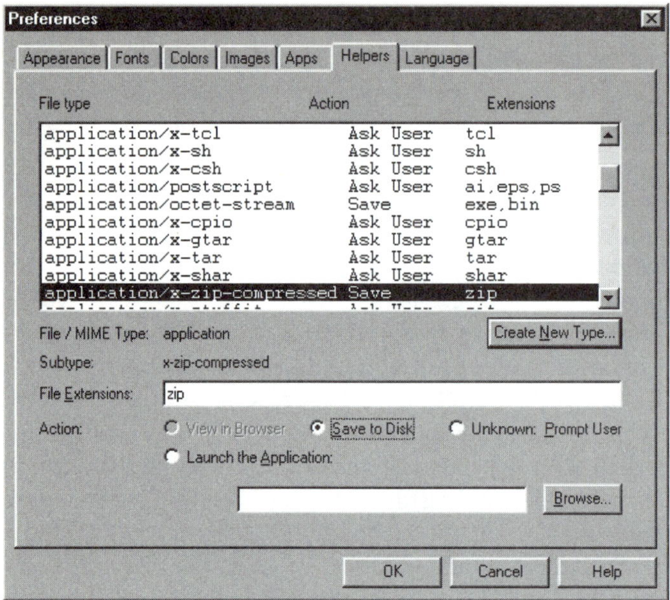

Figure 6-19: A new action for the application/x-zip-compressed file type.

4. Click OK to return to the main Netscape Navigator 3.0 window.

That's all there is to it! Now when you click on a link to a ZIP file, it will be saved to disk automatically.

TIP

Instead of selecting Save to Disk for ZIP files, you may want to select Launch the Application and enter the name of a decompression program such as PKUNZIP or WINZIP. That way, ZIP files will be decompressed automatically.

Let's take a closer look at the other possible actions that you can associate with a file type:

- **View in Browser**. Netscape Navigator 3.0 can display several kinds of image and document files: ASCII text, Joint Photographic Experts Group (JPEG) and GIF graphics, and of course, HTML pages. Typically you'd leave these file types associated with the View in Browser action because it is the simplest and quickest way to view the information, but in some cases you may want Netscape Navigator 3.0 to launch a separate viewing or editing program as soon as the file is retrieved.

- **Save to Disk**. This is obviously the most convenient option for binary files retrieved via FTP, but it can be useful in other situations as well. There are times, for instance, when I need to collect a lot of information directly from text files, but I don't want to view them right away. I temporarily set the Save to Disk option for text files, collecting them on my hard drive so I can view them later.
- **Unknown: Prompt User**. When Netscape Navigator 3.0 encounters a file type that is associated with this action, it pops up the dialog box shown earlier in Figure 6-7. This option is useful for file types you might want to treat differently at different times. In the case of sound files, for instance, you might sometimes want to hear them right away, while at other times you might prefer to save them to disk.
- **Launch the Application**. This is the most interesting and powerful action you can associate with a file type, and one of the most important features of Netscape Navigator 3.0. We are really talking about two different actions here:
    - If you select this radio button *without* filling in the box just below it, Netscape Navigator 3.0 simply launches the associated file as an application. For instance, if you associate all .EXE files with the Launch the Application action, they will run as soon as they are retrieved (this is pretty dangerous—I wouldn't recommend it!).
    - If you select the radio button and enter the name of another helper application in the box, Netscape Navigator 3.0 will run the helper application as a viewer for the associated file. The word *viewer* in this context is traditional but pretty misleading: the helper application might play the associated file rather than display it (in the case of a sound file) or even let you edit it (in the case of a Word document.) Take a look at the example in Figure 6-20, in which CoolTalk files are associated with the CoolTalk application that comes with Netscape Navigator 3.0.

      This means that whenever you click on an .ICE link, Netscape Navigator 3.0 automatically launches CoolTalk with the indicated file. Notice that Navigator 3.0 places the icon for the application next to its name.

TIP

Use the Browse button to find helper applications on your hard drive.

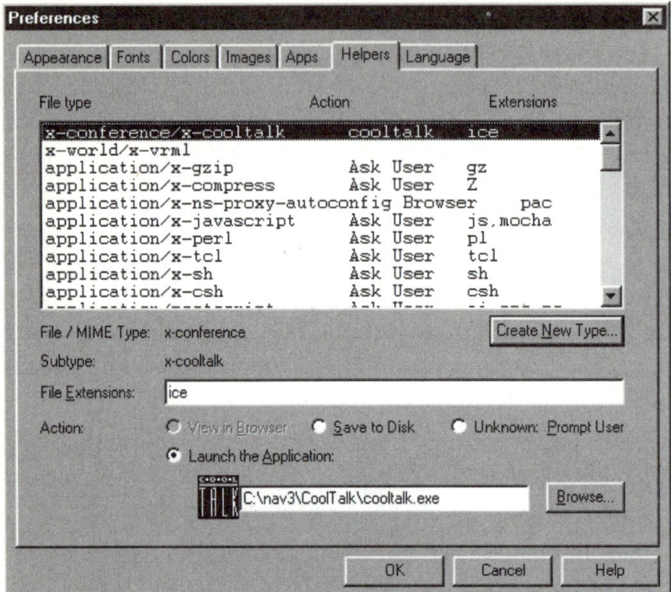

Figure 6-20: CoolTalk files associated with cooltalk.exe.

Adding New Extensions

If you want to get really fancy, Netscape Navigator 3.0 even lets you add new extensions for particular file types. For instance, you might want to add the extension .ASC to the text/plain file type, since some systems use this extension to designate ASCII text files.

To make the change:

1. If you are not already in the Helpers tab, select General Preferences from the Netscape Navigator 3.0 Options menu. Click the Helpers tab.
2. Scroll down the list of file types until you find text/plain. Select this entry by clicking on it. The specific settings for the text/plain file type appear.
3. After the word *text* in the File Extensions box, type **,asc**. The tab should now look like Figure 6-21.

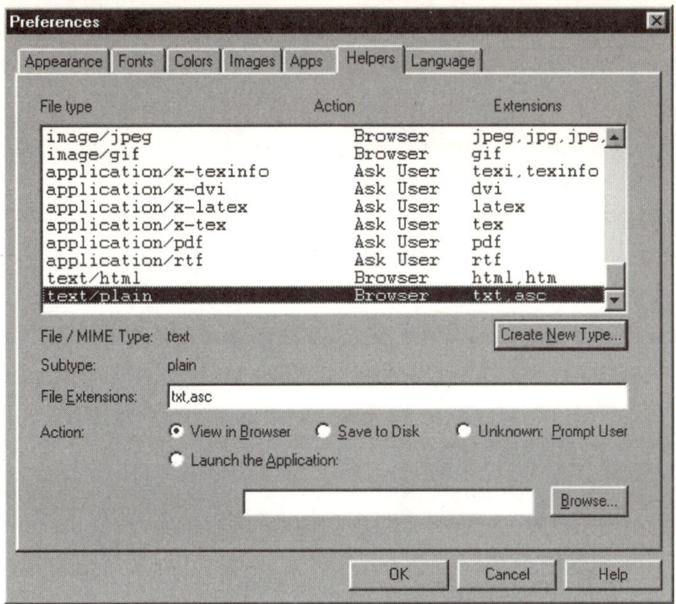

Figure 6-21: Text/plain file type with new extension.

4. Click OK to return to the main Netscape Navigator 3.0 window. If you want to save your changes for future sessions, make sure to select Save Options from the Options menu.

TIP

When adding a new extension, make sure it's not one that is commonly associated with any other file type. For instance, some text files have the extension .DOC, but you should not *add .DOC as an extension to the text/plain file type, because it is more commonly used to indicate MS-Word documents. If you do not heed my warning, you may start seeing blenderized* purée de Word *in your text viewer!*

Adding New File Types

Now if you want to get *really* fancy, you can even add new file types and subtypes to Netscape Navigator 3.0's default list. However, this is truly a propellerhead option: you should not even be thinking about it except to add a new standardized MIME type, and unless you really know what you're doing. Assuming you have the proper geek credentials, though, it's pretty easy:

1. If you are not already in the Helpers tab, select General Preferences from the Netscape Navigator 3.0 Options menu. Click the Helpers tab.
2. Click the Create New Type button. The Configure New Mime Type dialog box pops up, as shown in Figure 6-22.

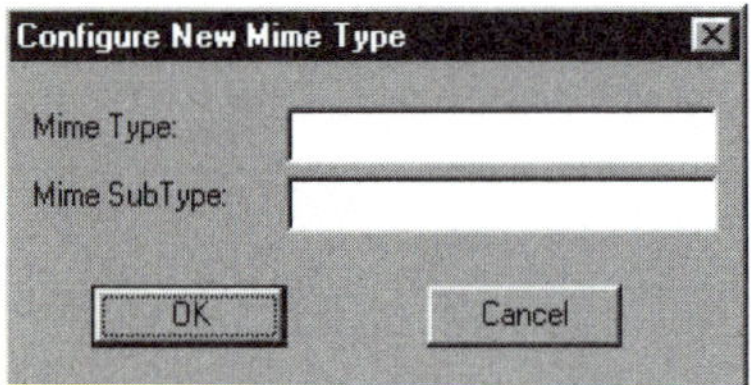

Figure 6-22: The Configure New Mime Type dialog box.

3. Enter the new MIME type and subtype in the appropriate fields and click OK.

Netscape Navigator 3.0's Helpers facility lets you deal efficiently with just about any file on any Internet FTP site. And if you want to further automate Netscape Navigator 3.0 with new viewers, sound players, editors, or any kind of helper application, guess how you get these programs? By FTP, of course!

Moving On

In this chapter, you've learned the basics of navigating FTP sites and downloading files. You've also learned some strategies for finding files on the Net by name or by subject area, and you've seen how Netscape Navigator 3.0 can be customized to help you deal with your new files more efficiently. Now all you need is a bigger hard drive!

You already have most of the Web basics down, and you could easily take off at this point and start exploring on your own. But before you do that, I'd like to show you two more extremely powerful tools that are old mainstays when it comes to exploring the Net. They are Gopher and Telnet.

Gopher & Telnet

There is no question that the World Wide Web is one of the most exciting services available on the Net. It plunges you into an electronic world full of bright images and sounds, and it lets you jump around from link to link, blazing new information trails. Its hypermedia browsing facilities provide a whole new approach to research, an approach that's very different from the plodding linear methods we grew up with. Some say that hypermedia browsing more closely models the way our minds really work, encouraging us to integrate knowledge by associative leaps rather than by carefully planned logical stitching.

Some research tasks, however, call for a more traditional approach to the great volume of data available on the Net; there are also some wonderful repositories of knowledge that have not yet been "Webified." Fortunately, Netscape Navigator 3.0 supports some of the older Internet services that are still very useful tools. The most important of these are Gopher and Telnet.

What Is Gopher?

What if you don't know exactly what you're looking for on the Net and want to refine your search carefully as you explore? What if you want to delve deeply into a particular area of interest, for instance, constitutional law? Typical Web sites may not help you, for often the links to other information are as arbitrary and whimsical as the imagination of the page's author.

Gopher servers, on the other hand, serve up information in tidy hierarchical menus and submenus, sticking to a subject and presenting it in top-down, outline format. Using World Wide Web documents, you leap rapidly from peak to peak. Using Gopher, you follow logically related information trails.

How Do They Come Up With These Names?

Most of the Internet services were developed not by commercial software companies, but by individuals in academia, often graduate students. This evolution is reflected in some of the jargon. If the marketing division of a software company had been involved, we'd probably be talking about Super UltraSearch Max Plus instead of Gopher. But the Golden Gopher is the mascot of the University of Minnesota, where this powerful tool was developed, and there were no people in suits calling the shots.

Once you name something "Gopher," you have to extend the metaphor. If you visit many Gopher sites, you'll discover that they are sometimes called Gopher *holes*. And avid Gopher users often talk about *burrowing* to other sites. It's all kind of quaint in this age of "cyber" this and "surf" that.

In addition to extending metaphors, computer people have a compulsive need to mix them, and so it is very common on the Net to talk about *GopherSpace*. (You can put yourself into an altered state trying to visualize that one.) GopherSpace is simply the total collection of hierarchically organized resources available to you via Gopher.

In the old days (before last year), Gopher servers were usually accessed with specialized Gopher client programs, but Netscape Navigator 3.0 makes extra software unnecessary. Netscape Navigator 3.0 can log you on to a Gopher server and then present you with the information so that it looks very much like any Web page. Menu items are colored like other Web links, and clicking on them brings up the appropriate submenus. Let's give it a try using the *WELL Gopher* as an example.

Using Gopher

The WELL is a large information service known for the variety of its online forums and the lively interactions of its users. It also maintains a very interesting Gopher site that's accessible to anyone on the Net. To begin exploring it:

1. Make sure you are connected to the Internet, either directly or through a SLIP or PPP connection with your access provider. If you are using a SLIP or PPP connection and are not currently connected, double-click on the Dial-Up Networking icon for your access provider.

   If you are using Windows 3.1 rather than Windows 95, or if you are using Windows 95 but are not using the Microsoft TCP/IP facility, follow the instructions that came with your TCP/IP software for accessing the Internet.

2. Double-click the Netscape Navigator 3.0 icon to launch the program. The main window appears, and the Netscape home page starts loading, as shown in Figure 7-1.

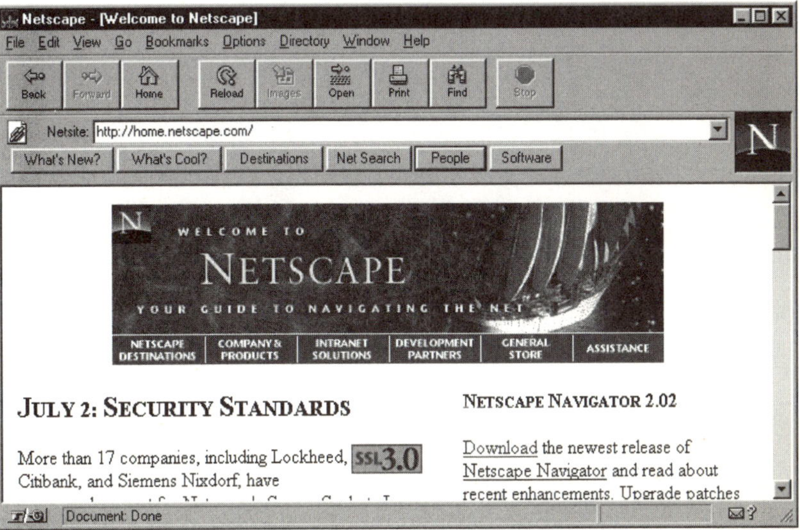

Figure 7-1: The Netscape home page.

3. Click your mouse inside the Netsite field at the top of the window to select the URL http://home.netscape.com/.

4. Replace this URL with the one for the WELL Gopher site by typing **gopher://gopher.well.com/**. Then press Enter. Netscape Navigator 3.0 retrieves the top-level WELL Gopher menu, as shown in Figure 7-2.

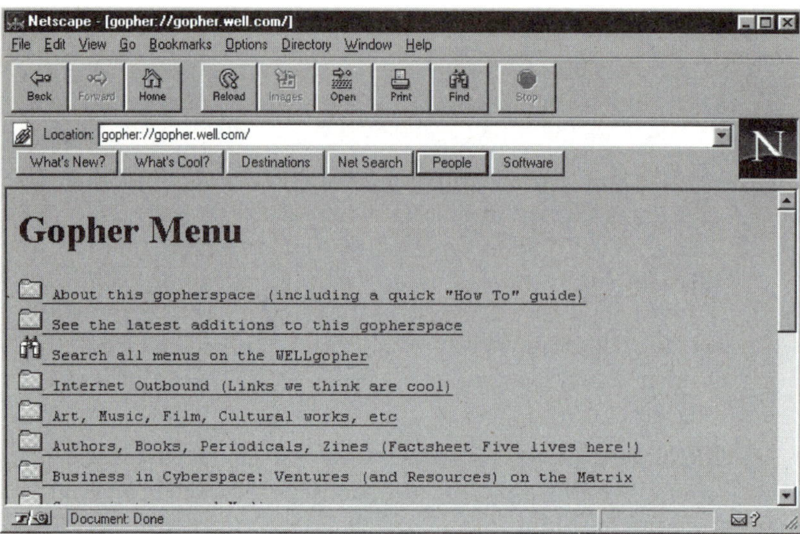

Figure 7-2: The WELL Gopher.

TIP

*Remember that you can type in partial URLs—Netscape Navigator 3.0 is smart enough to figure them out. Instead of typing **gopher://gopher.well.com/**, for instance, you could simply type **gopher.well.com**. Because your abbreviated URL has the word "gopher" in it, Navigator assumes this is a Gopher site.*

Notice that when you connect to a Gopher server, virtually all the text in the Netscape Navigator 3.0 window is composed of links. In the top level of the WELL Gopher, these are links to submenus rather than files, as indicated by the folder icons. The exception is the Search all menus on the WELLgopher item, which brings up a searchable index of the entire Gopher server.

5. Click the top menu item, About this gopherspace. A new submenu appears, as shown in Figure 7-3.

   Notice that most of the links are to actual text files now, as indicated by the icons.

6. Click the top item, What is this place? (The basic story). This time a text file appears, as shown in Figure 7-4.

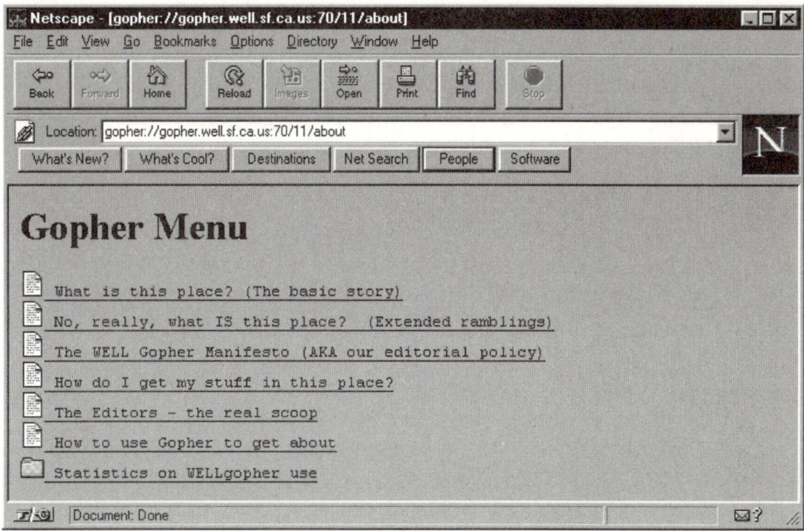

Figure 7-3: The About this gopherspace submenu on the WELL Gopher.

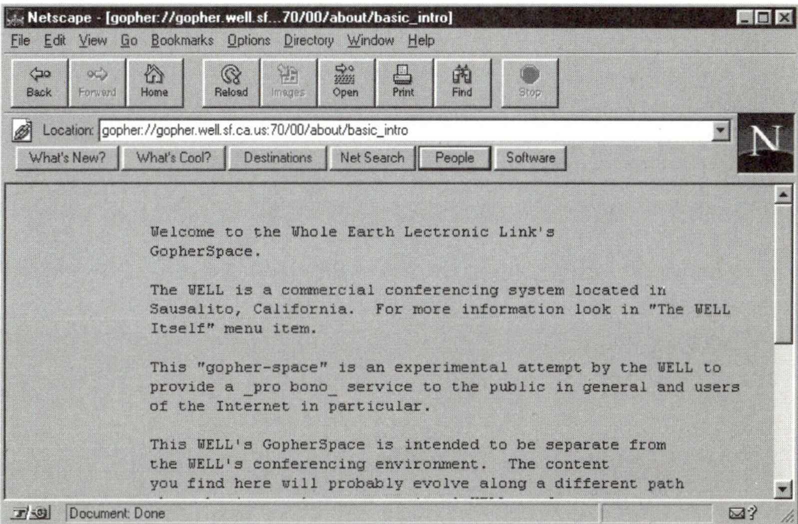

Figure 7-4: The WELL Gopher welcome file.

7. After reading the file, click Netscape Navigator 3.0's Back button to return to the About this gopherspace menu. You might want to read some of the other articles here, such as "How to use Gopher to get about," or the "extended ramblings" version of the "What is this place?" file. (The WELL is famous for its extended ramblings.)
8. When you're done reading, click Back again to return to the top-level WELL Gopher menu. From there you can begin to explore many different areas. Feel free to browse. The WELL Gopher is especially known for its information on media, communications, cyberpunk literature, and music.

TIP

Gopher menus can be saved, printed, copied, or made into bookmarks and shortcuts just like any other kinds of pages. In most cases, you needn't pay attention to whether you're at a Web, Gopher, or File Transfer Protocol (FTP) site. If you can see it in Netscape Navigator 3.0, you can work with it using any of the techniques you learned in Chapter 3, "A Quick Look Around."

Although the hierarchy of all Gopher sites is similar, their content varies greatly. There are Gopher sites that specialize in just about any academic field you can think of, from art to astrophysics. In addition, there are Gopher sites that are just plain fun.

But the great thing about Gopher is that it allows a site to include on its menus links to other sites as well. In other words, you are not restricted to the information available on only that particular server. Gopher is really the precursor of the Web in letting sites link to one another in a vast information net.

As you start burrowing from one site to another, you are actually creating a customized hierarchical pathway for yourself, and you can move backward and forward along it to find the information you need. Let's see how this works.

Stretching GopherSpace

To demonstrate how you can "stretch" GopherSpace, let's use the WELL Gopher site again as a starting point (if the WELL Gopher is already displayed in your Netscape Navigator 3.0 window, skip ahead to step 3 below):

1. Make sure you are connected to the Internet either directly or via your SLIP or PPP access provider. If Netscape Navigator 3.0 is not currently running, launch it by double-clicking its icon.
2. In the Location box at the top of the window, select the currently displayed URL and replace it with **gopher://gopher.well.com/**. Press Enter. After a few moments, the top-level menu at the WELL Gopher site appears, as shown earlier in Figure 7-2.
3. This time, click the Internet Outbound (Links we think are cool) link. The Internet Outbound Gopher menu appears, as shown in Figure 7-5.

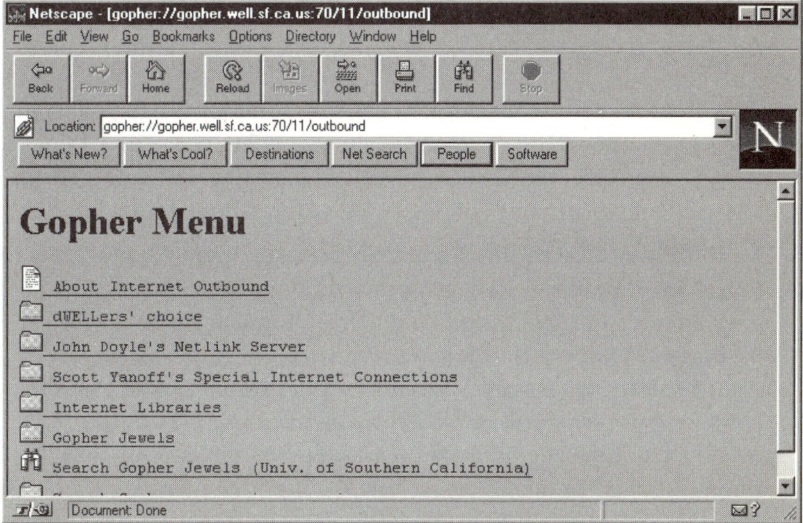

Figure 7-5: The Internet Outbound Gopher menu on the WELL.

4. All of the links on this menu provide useful starting points for Gopher burrowing. For this tutorial, click Scott Yanoff's Special Internet Connections. The Special Internet Connections Gopher menu appears, as shown in Figure 7-6.

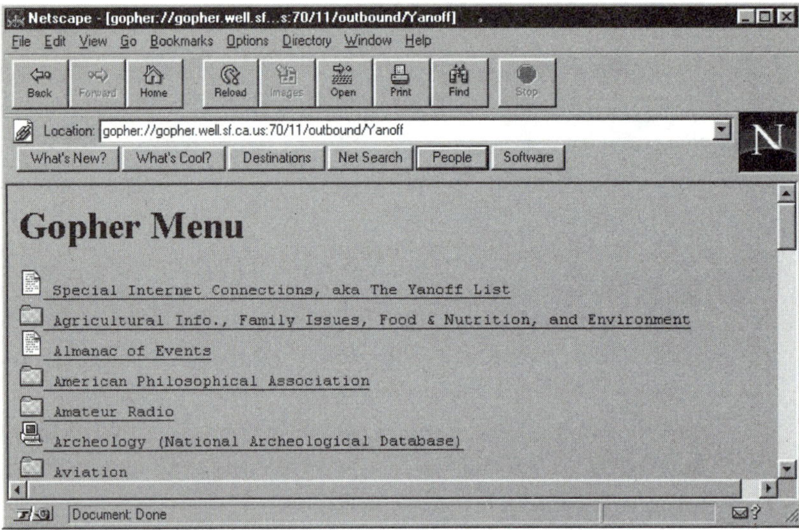

Figure 7-6: The Special Internet Connections Gopher menu.

Notice the icons depicting a computer terminal next to some of the links. This is how Netscape Navigator 3.0 indicates a Telnet connection. If you click on one of these links, Netscape Navigator 3.0 will launch a Telnet session with the host site. (More about Telnet later in this chapter.)

The Yanoff List, as it is sometimes known, offers you a wide variety of new jumping-off points—or digging-down points—for further Gopher burrowing. You should feel free to explore, and you might want to save this menu as a bookmark.

But before you descend into the Gopher tunnels, note that the Location box contains the URL **gopher://gopher.well.sf.ca.us:70/11/outbound/Yanoff**. *WELL* is still part of the site address because you've never really left the WELL; no matter how far or deep you burrow through the menus, *WELL* will still form the initial part of the URL. The URL provides a map of the path you took to get to the target information.

There are many ways to get to The Yanoff List, but you have constructed a tunnel that begins at the WELL and passes through the Internet Outbound menu. What this means is that you have a complete record of your travels, and in saving a particular URL as a bookmark, you are actually saving a map of your entire journey. With this kind of hierarchical structure, there is really no way to get lost.

This is what I mean by stretching GopherSpace. With each new link you click, you are further extending a *customized* information pathway. You can see why Gopher is a useful research tool when you're trying to refine your quest for particular information.

The WELL is only one of many tunnel entrances. In the next section, I'll list some interesting Gopher sites to begin your explorations.

Great Gopher Holes I Have Known

Table 7-1 lists a few of the best-known Gopher sites.

URL	Description
gopher://gopher.uis.itd.	University of Michigan archiveumich.edu/
gopher://ashpool.micro.	University of Minnesota archiveumn.edu/
gopher://wx.atmos.uiuc.edu/	Weather maps
gopher://gopher.eff.org/	Electronic Frontier Foundation archive
gopher://gopher.well.sf.ca.us/	Whole Earth 'Lectronic Link (WELL) archive
gopher://wiretap.spies.com/	The Internet Wiretap
gopher://siggraph.org/	Conference proceedings and materials from the graphics special interest group (SIGGRAPH) of the Association for Computing Machinery
gopher://gopher.cpsr.org:70/ 11/cpsr	Computer Professionals for Social Responsibility archive
gopher://akasha.tic.com/	Sample issues of John Quarterman's Matrix News Internet newsletter, several works from Bruce Sterling
gopher://gopher.echonyc.com	Interesting information about New York City and media

Table 7-1: Some well-known Gopher sites.

Using Gopher to Find People

One of the most important uses of Gopher is to find people. Yes, you can use Netscape Navigator 3.0 to burrow for your long-lost Uncle Waldo—provided he's been spending some of his lost years hanging out on the Net. In fact, Gopher provides the easiest-to-use interface for a wide range of search tools.

To find Waldo, start by going to the URL *gopher://gopher.micro.umn.edu/*. From there, select Phone Books. Many options, including Whois searches, X.500 gateway searches, and phone books at other institutions, will appear. Searching for individuals on the Net requires that you know something about their "Net lifestyle"—where they hang out on the Net, and whether or not they are affiliated with any university or subscribe to Usenet newsgroups—so at this point, you're on your own. You may not find Waldo, but at least you'll have an easy time looking.

Now that you know something about Gopher, let's take a brief look at another faithful old workhorse of the Internet, Telnet.

What Is Telnet?

The World Wide Web is the showroom of the Net. It's where you'll find information in all the latest styles and colors. If you want to show a newbie what the Net is all about, you'll almost certainly start with the Web.

But a fancy new car right off the showroom floor isn't always the best way to travel. Sometimes you need an all-terrain vehicle, a rugged tool that will take you places you can't access using the newer Web protocols. Telnet dates back to the days when the information superhighway was just a two-lane blacktop, and fortunately you can still take advantage of its raw power through Netscape Navigator 3.0.

Using Telnet, you log in to other computers on the Net interactively. Once you log in, the Telnet host presents you with a command line or with text-based menus; you type menu choices or commands. Typical public Telnet sites include library card catalogs, weather information services, and a variety of specialized databases. You can also Telnet to text-based online services such as the WELL or Echo. Even some bulletin board systems have migrated from modem connections to Telnet. And if you have a UNIX account on another computer on the Net, you can use Telnet to log in and run any UNIX program available on the host machine.

MUDs & MOOs

It's great to be able to access vast libraries of esoteric information via the Internet, but at some point we have to step back and take stock again of what computers are really for: playing games!

Some of the most interesting games spawned by modern information technology are MUDs and MOOs. MUDs are *Multiple-User Dimensions*, real-time, interactive role-playing games. MOOs are the object-oriented version, in which users can create their own objects, such as new rooms or features of the landscape. There are also variants of MUDs known as MUCKs, MUSHes, and MUSEs.

What all these games have in common is that several players at a time use the Internet to interact with one another as characters in a fictional world. Some of these text-based virtual worlds are full of magic and dragons, others are more like discussion forums, and some are meeting places for playing out group fantasies. Here are a couple of Web pages to get you started:

- MUDs, MOOs, and Other Virtual Hangouts (http://jefferson.village.virginia.edu/iath/treport/mud.html). Lots of info about MUDs and MOOs, and links to several sites.
- MUDs, MOOs, & MUSHes, "Hip-Waders in the CMC Swamp" (http://www.oise.on.ca/~jnolan/mud.html). Links to information and games.

Also check out the Usenet newsgroups under rec.games.mud. It's important to read the FAQs and whatever other information you can get before trying these games, as each has its own culture and Netiquette.

How does this remote login process work? Telnet is really a *terminal emulation* protocol. That means it makes your PC behave like a terminal that's directly connected to the host computer. What is a terminal? A terminal is a device that can't really do anything on its own, but when it is attached to a computer it provides users with a display screen and a keyboard. In other words, a terminal provides the user interface to a host computer. Normally, terminals are attached to the host by means of cable, but terminal emulation programs allow you to connect remotely using a PC and phone lines. With terminal emulation programs like PROCOMM PLUS and Telix, you dial directly into a host; with Telnet, you connect via the Internet.

Figure 7-7 shows a typical Telnet session. In this example, I am logged in to the Echo online service, and you can clearly see the interactive nature of this kind of connection.

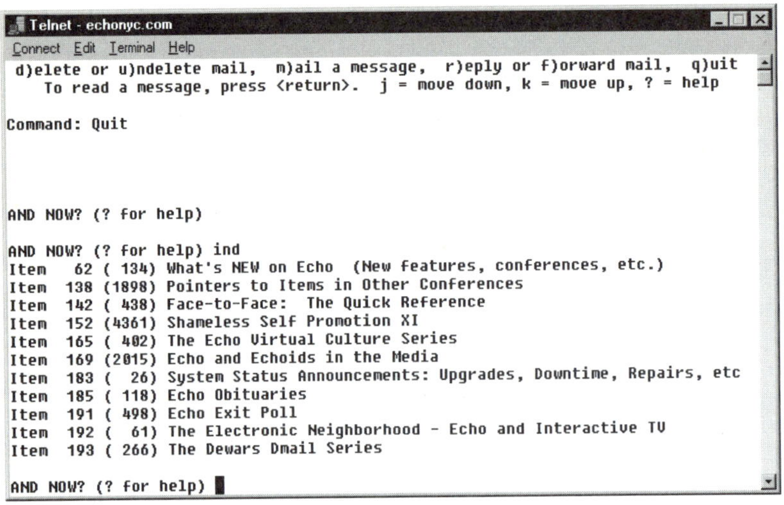

```
Telnet - echonyc.com
Connect Edit Terminal Help
 d)elete or u)ndelete mail,  m)ail a message,  r)eply or f)orward mail,  q)uit
    To read a message, press <return>.  j = move down, k = move up, ? = help

Command: Quit



AND NOW? (? for help)

AND NOW? (? for help) ind
Item   62 ( 134) What's NEW on Echo  (New features, conferences, etc.)
Item  138 (1898) Pointers to Items in Other Conferences
Item  142 ( 438) Face-to-Face:  The Quick Reference
Item  152 (4361) Shameless Self Promotion XI
Item  165 ( 402) The Echo Virtual Culture Series
Item  169 (2015) Echo and Echoids in the Media
Item  183 (  26) System Status Announcements: Upgrades, Downtime, Repairs, etc
Item  185 ( 118) Echo Obituaries
Item  191 ( 498) Echo Exit Poll
Item  192 (  61) The Electronic Neighborhood - Echo and Interactive TV
Item  193 ( 266) The Dewars Dmail Series

AND NOW? (? for help)
```

Figure 7-7: A Telnet session with Echo.

Telnet & Netscape Navigator 3.0

Let's see how observant you are: what's wrong with Figure 7-7?

That's right, it depicts some other software instead of Netscape Navigator 3.0. Instead of the usual toolbar and Netscape logo, you see a much simpler window. Did the author make a mistake? Did the editors miss it?

No. The fact is that Netscape Navigator 3.0 does not actually include built-in Telnet. In fact, Web browsers almost *never* include built-in Telnet. Let me explain.

Terminal emulation programs and Web browsers are two very different kinds of software. Terminal emulation programs concentrate on interpreting ASCII character sequences on the fly, while Web browsers concentrate on displaying multimedia documents.

Since these two functions are not compatible, the authors of most World Wide Web programs have decided to support Telnet by launching an external helper application when necessary. If you click a link that represents the URL for a Telnet connection, Netscape Navigator 3.0 launches your Telnet session by executing a separate program, passing to it the address of the site. As soon as you're finished with the Telnet session, you can return to the Netscape Navigator 3.0 window and to whatever document was last displayed in it. In fact, you don't even have to wait. If you're the kind of person who likes to do several things at once, you can go back and forth between active Telnet sessions and the main Netscape Navigator 3.0 window.

But how does Netscape Navigator 3.0 know what Telnet program to use when you navigate to a Telnet URL? It requires a little bit of setup, but fortunately the setup is very straightforward.

TN3270

Almost all public Telnet sites these days support the standard version of the protocol that uses the VT100 terminal emulation. However, there is a variant of Telnet known as *TN3270.* TN3270 sites require that you use a program that makes your PC act like an IBM 3270 terminal instead of a DEC VT100.

Your regular Telnet program probably does not include TN3270 capabilities. If you plan to connect to TN3270 sites, you'll need to download a special TN3270 program from the Net. Now that you've read Chapter 6, "Getting Files via FTP," and know all about finding files on the Net, this should be no problem at all!

Setting Up Telnet

Way back in Chapter 1, "Getting Started," we took a quick look at the Apps tab, which is where you tell Netscape Navigator 3.0 what program you want to use for Telnetting to remote sites. To get to the Apps tab:

1. In the main Netscape Navigator 3.0 window, select General Preferences from the Options menu. The General Preferences dialog box appears.
2. Click the Apps tab. The Apps tab includes fields where you can specify several supporting applications, including Telnet and TN3270, as shown in Figure 7-8.

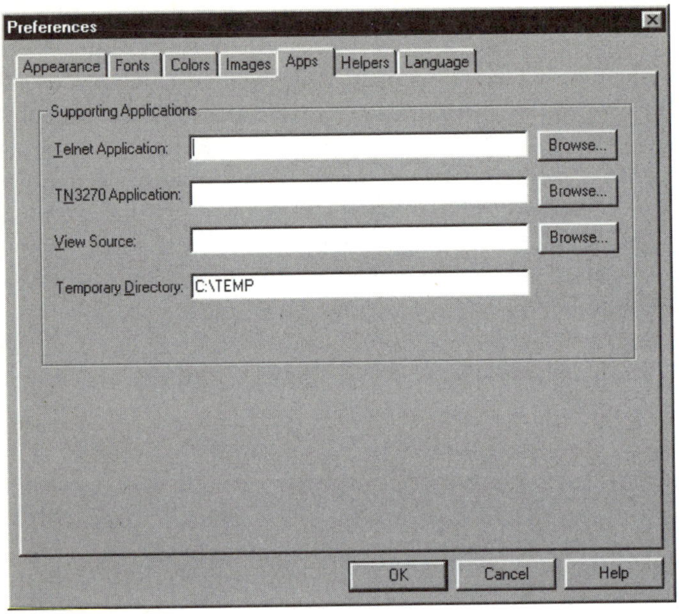

Figure 7-8: The Apps tab.

3. In the Telnet Application field, fill in the name of your Telnet application. Or you can find the appropriate program on your hard drive using the Browse button.

TIP

If you're using Windows 95, you can simply type **telnet** *in the Telnet Application field.*

4. In the same way, complete the TN3270 Application field if you plan to use TN3270.

TIP

While you're in the Apps tab, you might also want to specify an application other than Netscape Navigator 3.0 to view or edit the HTML source of any Web documents displayed in the program. You can also tell Netscape Navigator 3.0 what work directory to use for storing temporary files.

5. Click OK.

That's all there is to it! Now you're ready to start actually using Telnet.

Using Telnet

As with any other Internet service supported by Netscape Navigator 3.0, you can get to a Telnet site by any one of several methods. You can:

- Click a Telnet link in a Web document or at a Gopher site.
- Type a URL in Netscape Navigator 3.0's Location box.
- Select a Telnet link from Bookmarks.
- Double-click a desktop shortcut to a Telnet site.

Any one of these actions will have the same result: Netscape Navigator 3.0 launches your Telnet application, which then logs you in to the site specified in the URL.

Let's give it a try by going back to a Telnet link you may have noticed earlier in a Gopher menu, the National Archeological Database. You may not be the slightest bit interested in archeology, but I have chosen this site because it is very typical of research sites that are publicly accessible via Telnet.

For the sake of this tutorial, I'm assuming you're using the Windows 95 Telnet application. The basic instructions should be close to accurate even if you're using a different program:

1. Make sure you are connected to the Internet either directly or via your SLIP or PPP access provider. If Netscape Navigator 3.0 is not currently running, launch it by double-clicking its icon.
2. In the Location box at the top of the window, select the currently displayed URL and replace it with **gopher://gopher.well.sf.ca.us:70/11/outbound/Yanoff**. Press Enter. (If you've saved the Yanoff menu as a bookmark, you won't have to type in the URL again.)
3. Click the Archeology (National Archeological Database) link. After a few seconds, the Telnet application appears with a login prompt from the remote site, as shown in Figure 7-9.

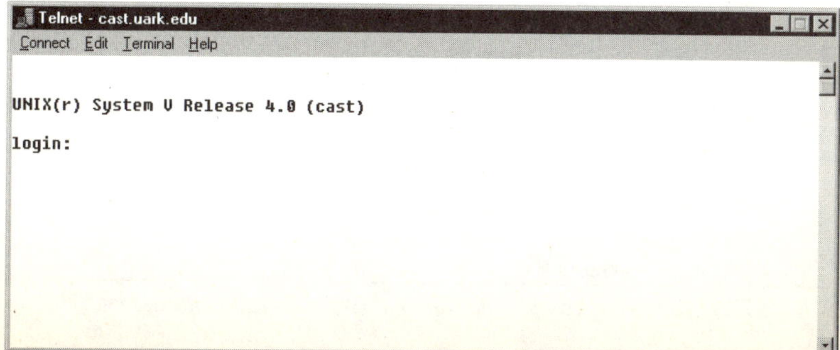

Figure 7-9: Windows 95 Telnet program with login prompt from the National Archeological Database.

In addition, a small message box pops up telling you to log in to this site as "nadb," as shown in Figure 7-10.

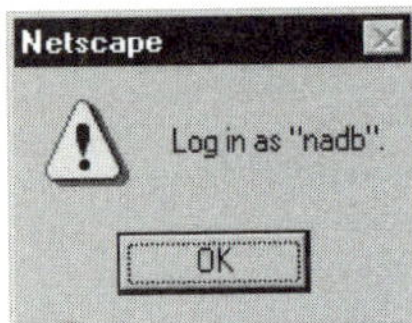

Figure 7-10: Login information message box.

TIP

Not all sites supply you with login instructions like this, but many do. Depending on the exact timing of data received from the remote site, the Telnet window might cover the informational message box so that it is invisible to you. Before experimenting with different logins to see what will work, move or temporarily minimize the Telnet window to make sure you didn't miss an important message.

*If the remote system presents you with a login prompt but no information about what to enter, try typing **guest** and pressing Enter.*

4. Click OK in the message box. It disappears.
5. At the login prompt in the main Telnet window, type **nadb**. You are now logged in to the National Archeological Database, as shown in Figure 7-11.

```
Telnet - cast.uark.edu
Connect  Edit  Terminal  Help
    N A T I O N A L      A R C H E O L O G I C A L      D A T A B A S E
      N A T I O N A L      A R C H E O L O G I C A L      D A T A B A S E
    N A T I O N A L      A R C H E O L O G I C A L      D A T A B A S E
  N A T I O N A L      A R C H E O L O G I C A L      D A T A B A S E
N A T I O N A L      A R C H E O L O G I C A L      D A T A B A S E
N A T I O N A L      A R C H E O L O G I C A L      D A T A B A S E

                         NADB ONLINE SYSTEM
                  Archeological Assistance Program
                 Departmental Consulting Archeologist
         National Park Service, U.S. Department of the Interior

                        In Cooperation with the
    Center for Advanced Spatial Technologies, University of Arkansas
         Southwestern Division, U.S. Army Corps of Engineers
                          (Sat) Oct 28, 1995

Press RETURN to continue:
```

Figure 7-11: You're logged in to the National Archeological Database via Telnet.

6. As directed by the remote system, press Return (Enter) to continue. The NADB Connection Menu appears. Since you are connected via the Internet, select item 4, Internet to NADB, and press Return.
7. Continue following any directions that appear in the Telnet window. As is typical with research sites like this, you are asked to enter some information about yourself and to choose an ID number. Once you've gotten through this process, the NADB Main Menu appears, as shown in Figure 7-12.

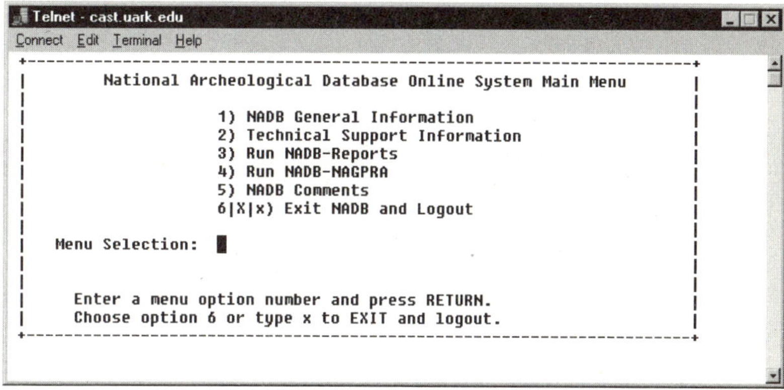

Figure 7-12: The NADB Main Menu.

TIP

Most Telnet programs let you copy text directly from the terminal window so that you can save it or paste it into other applications.

8. At this point, you can choose an item from the menu to get more information about the NADB or to access its search tools immediately. If you're interested in archeology, feel free to return to this site later, but for now let's select menu option 6 (or type the letter **x**), Exit NADB and Logout. If you are using the Windows 95 Telnet program, a message box pops up explaining that your connection to the host has been lost, as shown in Figure 7-13.

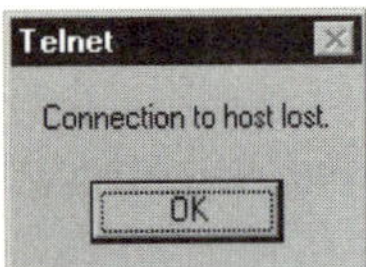

Figure 7-13: The Connection to host lost message.

Logging Off Remote Systems

Your Telnet program probably provides a way to disconnect from a remote site at any point, without even telling the remote host that you are leaving. In the Windows 95 Telnet program, you simply choose the Disconnect option from the Connect menu.

Whenever possible, however, you should end your session cleanly by logging out from the remote Telnet site, choosing the appropriate menu options, or following instructions for quitting. Otherwise, the software at the remote Telnet site may not immediately realize you are gone and may keep the connection open for several minutes, exacerbating Net traffic jams.

Unless you're having technical problems with the connection, disconnecting without logging out is considered poor online etiquette.

9. Once you are disconnected from the remote host, you can simply quit your Telnet program.

That's all there is to it. At first it may seem awkward that Netscape Navigator 3.0 needs to launch a separate helper application for Telnet access, but there are several advantages to this system. The most significant bonus is that you can use any Telnet application you want, including ones that are much more configurable and full-featured than the program included with Windows 95.

Speaking of configuration, let's take a quick look at some ways to tailor your Telnet application so that it works most efficiently for you.

Customizing Your Telnet Application

Most Telnet applications offer a variety of options to make your online life easier and more productive. Since the Windows 95 Telnet program is typical of the simple applications that are available, we'll use it as an example. If you're using a different program, you may have to look around a little for the configuration options we're examining, but they should be there somewhere.

1. Launch Telnet by clicking its icon on the desktop or by using the Windows 95 Run command. The main Telnet window appears, as shown in Figure 7-14.

Figure 7-14: The Windows 95 Telnet application.

Most Telnet applications don't require you to be connected to the Net to change preferences or configuration options.

2. Select Preferences from the Terminal menu. The Terminal Preferences dialog box appears, as shown in Figure 7-15.

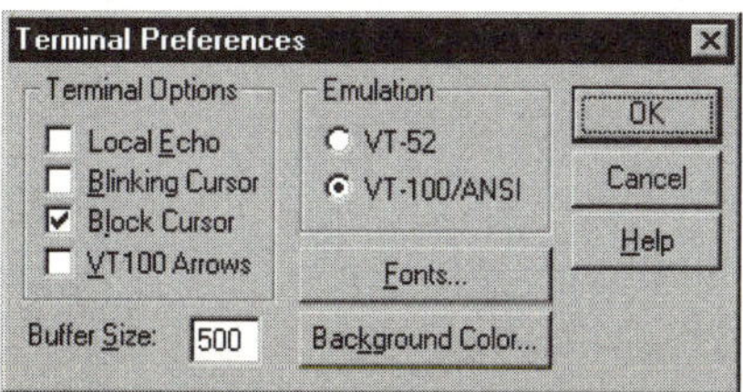

Figure 7-15: The Terminal Preferences dialog box.

The options in this dialog box are pretty typical of what's available in Telnet programs. Here are some tips for configuring these settings:

- **Local Echo**. Most remote Telnet sites echo back to you all the characters you type so that you can see what you are doing. Generally you should leave this check box unchecked; check it only if your typing is invisible to you.
- **Blinking Cursor**. Check this box if you want your cursor to blink while you are in Telnet. This can help you find the cursor on remote systems that include lots of lines or underscores in their screens.

- **Block Cursor**. Check this option if you want a block cursor instead of the usual cursor. This may be much easier to see on some systems.
- **VT100 Arrows**. The VT100 terminal emulation includes two different sets of character sequences ("mappings") that can be sent to the remote Telnet host when you press the arrow keys. Unless your arrow keys don't seem to be working properly at a particular site, leave this box unchecked. (For the propeller-heads out there, unchecked means Keypad Application Mode, and checked means Keypad Cursor Mode. The remote site may send sequences that temporarily change your default setting.)
- **Buffer Size**. This option lets you specify how many lines you can scroll back to see text that has scrolled out of the Telnet window. Since the VT100 terminal displays 25 lines of text at one time, this option should be set to 25 or greater.
- **Emulation**. Unless a remote Telnet host explicitly requires VT52 emulation, you should keep this set to VT100/ANSI. Other Telnet programs may let you choose from a wider variety of terminal emulations, but VT100 is the most commonly supported one on publicly accessible sites.
- **Fonts**. Click this button to change the font of the text that appears in your Telnet window.
- **Background Color**. Click this button to change the background color of your Telnet window.

Once you have made your configuration changes, click OK to return to the main Telnet window.

Moving On

This has been the "back to basics" chapter—a quick look at some of the older workhorse Net services available through Netscape Navigator 3.0. Now we're going to go in the other direction and explore Netscape Navigator 3.0's multimedia capabilities. In its support of Gopher and Telnet, Netscape Navigator 3.0 provides you with a dependable off-road utility vehicle. But as you'll see in Chapter 8, its forward-looking integration of graphics, sound, and video make it a true cyber-spaceship.

Graphics, Sound & Video

By now you have some idea what World Wide Web sites look like and have to offer. Unlike many other Internet services, the Web is not restricted to text. Web documents can contain images, sound, and even video clips. As a Web user, you have at your fingertips a vast assortment of multimedia documents that virtually come to life when you view them. Netscape Navigator 3.0 enables you to interact with these multimedia documents in a variety of ways.

Graphics on the Web

Pictures play an important role in our lives: we hang them on our walls; we pay money to stand and look at them in museums; we take snapshots of our loved ones and favorite places. Just as pictures are a common form of communication in our society, they are an important part of the World Wide Web. In fact, much of the growth and popularity of the Web is a result of people like you and me having a new way to gather and disseminate information in a colorful and creative way.

In the following sections, you'll read about the types of graphics that are available on the Web and how you can view and download them with Netscape Navigator 3.0.

What Kinds of Images Are Available?

Each month, thousands of new Web pages are created and placed online. Almost all of them contain some sort of graphic. Graphics can be small or large, colorful or black-and-white, tasteful or tasteless. You can probably find the exact image you're looking for on the Web if you look long enough. It may not be legally posted there, but it will be there (I discuss copyright infringement later in this chapter).

So what kinds of images can you expect to find on the Web? Almost anything. There are:

- Paintings by Renoir, Van Gogh, and little Jimmy from Ms. Wharton's first grade class.
- Publicity shots of your favorite movie and television stars, including Brad Pitt, Rosie O'Donnell, and Bill Gates.
- Detailed weather maps like the ones you see your local weather forecaster pointing at on the eleven o'clock news.
- More *Star Trek: Voyager* and *Deep Space Nine* photos than we care to know about.
- Business logos and advertisements, from IBM and Microsoft to Absolut and Ford Motor Company.
- Cartoons and animations.
- And yes, some pictures of naked people, if you look hard enough.

Graphics in Netscape Navigator 3.0: An Overview

Fortunately for all you picture lovers, Netscape Navigator 3.0 includes features that let you view the majority of graphics on the Web. Graphics appear in a variety of sizes, shapes, and formats. In one way or another, Netscape Navigator 3.0 can either display them or provide an easy way for you to view them in another application. The best way to understand the types of graphics and how they display on Netscape Navigator 3.0 is to link to a fairly typical site.

To view a graphic in Netscape Navigator 3.0:

1. Make sure you are connected to the Internet, either directly or through a SLIP or PPP connection with your access provider. If you are using a SLIP or PPP connection and are not currently connected, double-click the Dial-Up Networking icon for your access provider.

   If you are using Windows 3.1 rather than Windows 95, or if you are not using Windows 95's built-in networking, follow the instructions that came with your TCP/IP software for accessing the Internet.

2. Double-click the Netscape Navigator 3.0 icon to launch the program. The main window appears, and the Netscape home page starts loading.
3. Click your mouse inside the Location field at the top of the window to select the URL http://home.netscape.com/.
4. Replace the URL with the one for the Ventana Online page by typing **http://www.vmedia.com** (or simply **www.vmedia.com**). Then press Enter. Netscape Navigator 3.0 retrieves the Ventana Online page, as shown in Figure 8-1.

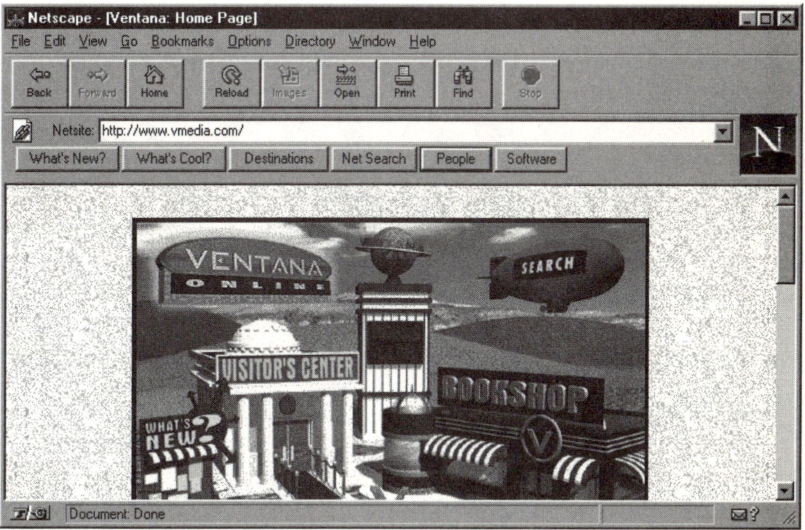

Figure 8-1: The Ventana Online page.

TIP

Notice that Navigator displays text first, then fills in the graphics. Sometimes you will see a description of the graphics, before the page starts loading, in the top left corner of its frame.

Have I Got the Entire Document?

Many Web pages take some time to download to your computer. How can you be sure you've received the whole thing? Netscape Navigator 3.0 provides several clues.

First, you can look at the status line at the bottom of the Netscape Navigator 3.0 window. This area indicates the transfer progress of the Web document. On the left side of the status line is a readout that displays the size, percentage downloaded, and the rate at which Netscape Navigator 3.0 is retrieving the document. You might have a difficult time reading this line because it's constantly changing, but it will give some idea of how fast your modem is transferring data. At the far right of the status line is a small graphical bar that represents the data transfer. The bar expands to the right as the new page transfers. When the document has completely transferred, this area goes blank, which tells you that no more data is being sent.

Another way to tell if a Web page is completely transferred is to look at the Stop button on the Netscape Navigator 3.0 toolbar. If it displays a red stop sign (which you can click to stop the transfer), the document is still transferring.

But probably the coolest way to see if a document is still transferring is to watch the animated Netscape logo in the top right corner of the Netscape Navigator 3.0 window. As the document transfers, a meteor shower streams across the big Netscape *N*. When the shower ends, the document has finished downloading and all the graphics are displayed.

On a Web page like the one shown in Figure 8-1, you may see several different graphics and notice that they're used in a variety of ways. By far the most prevalent type of image you encounter in Web pages is an *inline graphic*. Inline graphics are part of the Web document itself, and not a separate file; they appear alongside the text. Inline graphics can include photos, buttons, icons, cartoons, and many other types of pictures. They are commonly used for the following purposes:

- Logos
- Decorations
- Bullet points
- Illustrations
- Separators

Sometimes graphics are not inline, but exist only as a separate image file that you can download to your hard disk for later viewing, or one that you need to view in a separate application from Netscape Navigator 3.0. One common external viewer is LView Pro, which was used to display the graphic shown in Figure 8-2. You'll learn more about these types of images and how to view them in the section titled "Graphics on Demand," later in this chapter.

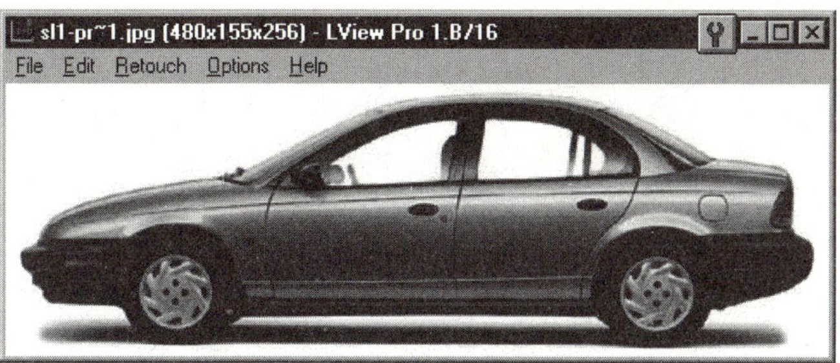

Figure 8-2: A graphic displayed in LView Pro.

When you connect to a site, such as http://www.vmedia.com (Ventana's Web site), the Web document begins to transfer to your computer and appears in Netscape Navigator 3.0. As the document displays, you usually see some text first, and then the graphics begin to appear. Depending on the speed of your connection, images may seem to flow in line by line or pop right up along with the text. It all has to do with the amount of data that your modem or phone line can transmit to your computer monitor. For example, high-speed connections, such as ISDN or T1 phone lines, can transmit more data per second than modem connections.

TIP

Tired of waiting for a document's images to display? Click the Stop button on the Netscape Navigator 3.0 toolbar to stop the transfer. If you want to complete the transfer later, click Reload.

Or turn off the automatic display of graphics entirely, as described later in this chapter under "Text-Only Mode."

To accommodate users with all kinds of connections, some sites now include two versions of the same page. One page usually includes a lot of graphics that a typical modem user will not want to wait to download to his or her computer. The other usually has very few images and mostly text. When you link to a site that has these options, such as the Internet Underground Music Archive (IUMA), you must make a choice to view the page with a lot of images, or one that has been toned down a little to avoid unnecessary waiting.

Figure 8-3 shows you the site when you choose to see the graphics-intensive pages. Figure 8-4 shows what you'll see if you choose the same pages with fewer graphics. Running with a 14.4 kbps modem, the graphics-intensive page took more than 2 minutes to display. The "lite" version took only 12 seconds!

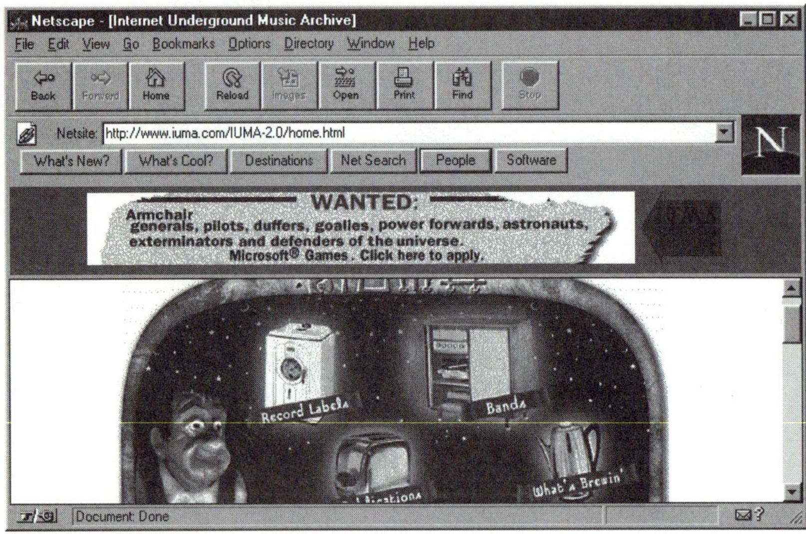

Figure 8-3: The IUMA site with lots of graphics.

Figure 8-4: The IUMA site with very few graphics.

TIP

Most sites include the same textual information in both their graphics version and their text-only pages—the only thing you'll miss is the images themselves.

You'll learn later how to optimize the display of graphics in Netscape Navigator 3.0, but let's first discuss a couple of special-purpose graphics often used on the World Wide Web: background images and icons.

Background Images

Background images do just what their name implies—they provide the background to the text and other graphics in a Web document. Background images typically are very small images that are repeated again and again—or tiled—over the entire background. (This technique sometimes is referred to as *texture mapping* in graphics design programs.) The images can be solid colors, textures, patterns, or whatever the Web author comes up with. For example, the Graphion home page pictured in Figure 8-5 shows a gray granite background. Some other backgrounds you may encounter include marble, wood grain, and metallic, but occasionally you'll even see some company's ugly logo repeated a hundred times across your screen.

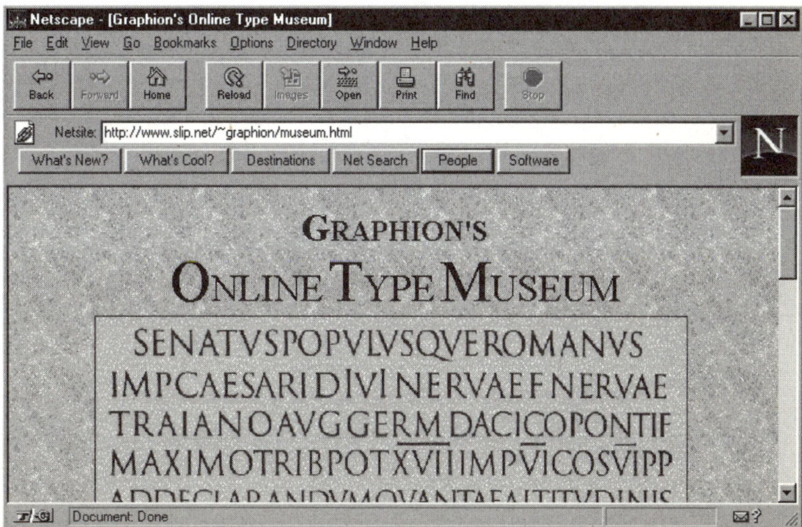

Figure 8-5: Graphion's home page, showing gray granite background.

When Web page authors create a page, they can enter HTML code (the language of Web pages) to include an image as the background. Not all Web sites use backgrounds, but these days it's becoming the norm. Backgrounds offer the Web author a way to set a standard color, texture, or image for the entire Web site. This eliminates the need to rely on the Web browser to provide a color (using the Options | General Preferences | Colors properties) for the Web page.

Icons

Icons are another type of graphic you'll encounter on almost all Web pages. Icons are small images or buttons, sometimes miniatures of larger images you can find at that site. Icons are used to highlight certain points on the page, lead you to another Web page or site, or let you view or download a larger image. Let's look at each of these uses.

In Figure 8-6, you see a set of icons to the left of some text on the Web page. These icons serve the same purpose that bullets do in a book or business document: to distinguish key points. Icons can also be used to highlight special text on a page.

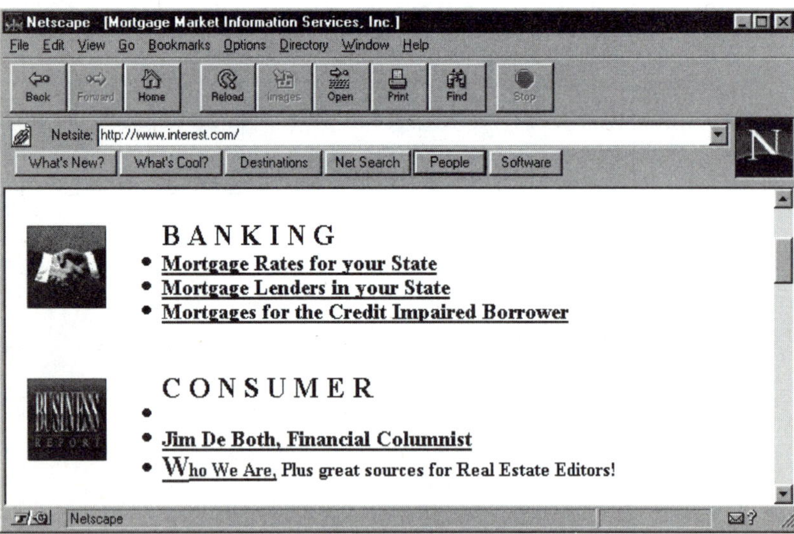

Figure 8-6: Icons emphasize important text on the page (© Mortgage Market Information Services, Inc.).

The second type of icon is actually a hot spot that links to another page or another site, sometimes to graphics of products or announcements. This type of icon works the same as linked text on a page—when you click it, you connect to that other site or page. Icons of this type often have a small blue border around them to indicate they are links. Figure 8-7 shows examples of icons that you click to advance to another related site.

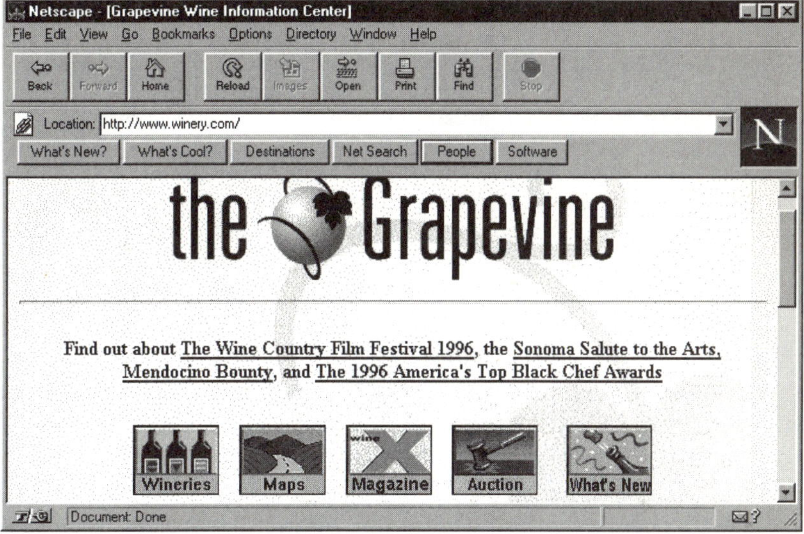

Figure 8-7: Icons that provide links.

What Is the Netscape Now Icon?

After your first 10 or 15 minutes on the Web, you're bound to run into a Web page that includes the Netscape Now icon (see Figure 8-8). Netscape provides this icon for Web page authors to include on pages designed especially for Netscape Navigator 3.0. This icon, or button, links the user to Netscape's home page so that users who don't have Netscape Navigator 3.0 installed can order or download a copy of it. For more information on obtaining permission to use this icon, see http://home.netscape.com/comprod/mirror/netscape_now_program.html.

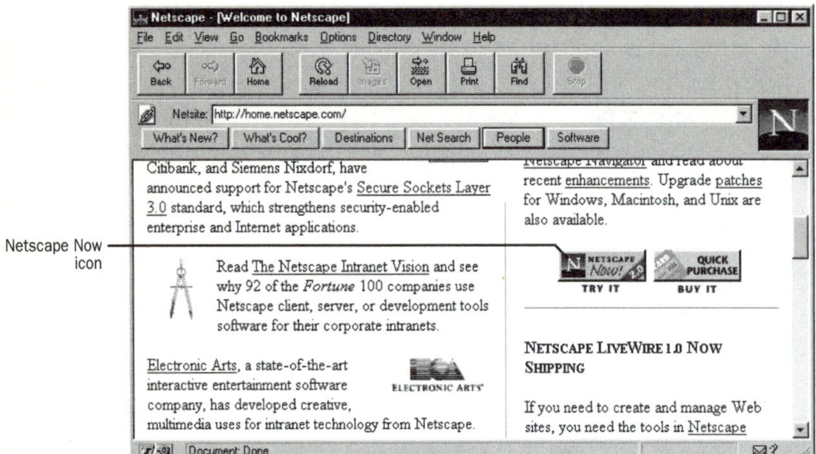

Figure 8-8: Web page authors can use the Netscape Now icon on pages designed for Netscape Navigator 3.0.

Icons are also used as small "try-before-you-download" versions of larger graphics. When you click this kind of icon, often called a *thumbnail*, the larger image begins to transfer. The advantage of this approach is obvious: the smaller thumbnails transfer to your machine much more quickly than full images you may not even be interested in.

For example, the Web page in Figure 8-9 shows small icons of Renoir paintings (http://sunsite.unc.edu/wm/paint/auth/renoir/). You can scroll down the page and click the painting you'd like to see in full size. Now a larger painting displays in Netscape Navigator 3.0, as shown in Figure 8-10.

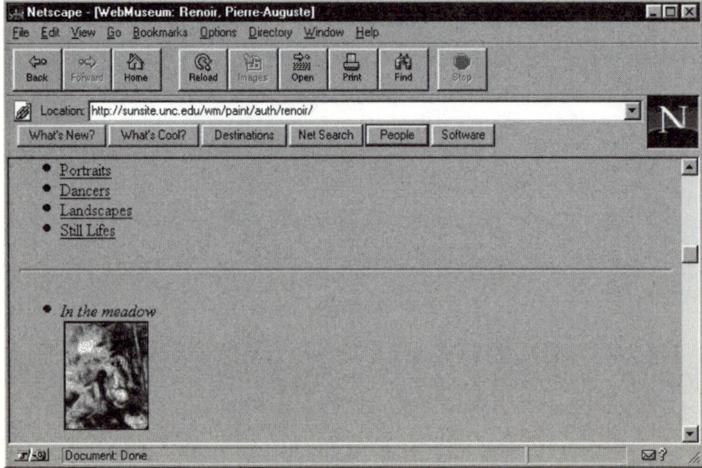

Figure 8-9: Thumbnail of a painting.

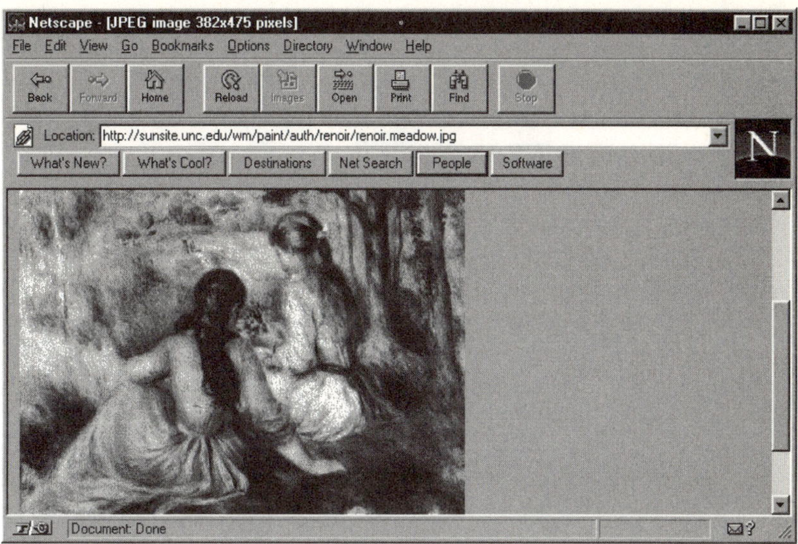

Figure 8-10: Full view of the same painting.

TIP

Conscientious Web page authors include file sizes and estimated transfer times next to icons or thumbnails. Use these estimates to determine if the wait is going to be worth it. When I am on these sites, I find the smallest file and download it first. If I don't like the quality, I probably will not download another one.

Graphics Formats Supported by Netscape Navigator 3.0

The graphics in Web documents typically come in standard file formats that most Web browsers, such as Netscape Navigator 3.0, can understand and display on your computer. The standard file formats include Graphics Interchange Format (GIF), Joint Photographic Experts Group (JPEG), and XBM. GIF and JPEG are the most common graphics you'll encounter in Web pages. XBM is a UNIX graphics format and is more likely to be found at university or research areas that generally work with high-speed computing applications.

Any Other Formats out There?

Many other types of graphics formats are available on the Web, including Macintosh PICT, BMP, PCX, TIFF, and encapsulated PostScript (EPS), but the most common image formats are GIF and JPEG.

Both GIF and JPEG files are compressed to save transmission time and to limit their storage size. It is beyond the scope of this book to get into the technical differences between JPEGs and GIFs, but the two formats excel in different areas. JPEG compression is often used for ultra-realistic photographic images, while GIF is used for colorful graphics. GIFs can start to display on your screen while they are still downloading, while with JPEG images you must wait for the entire image before it appears; a new standard called "progressive JPEG" is emerging, which displays images while they are loading, but it doesn't work with older versions of most browsers. GIF images may also be *transparent.* Transparent GIFs are graphic files that have been customized to eliminate the background color of the image. Thus they appear to "float" on top of the Web page instead of being stuck inside a rectangular prison.

TIP

JPEG files generally have an extension of .JPG; GIF files always have an extension of .GIF.

When authors create Web pages, they make sure the images they place as inline graphics can be displayed by the most popular Web browsers. Because Netscape Navigator is such a popular browser, Web authors almost always try to develop pages that are compatible with it. This means that they use GIFs and JPEGs. You should not have any problem viewing most Web pages.

Graphics on Demand

Some Web sites offer images you can download to your computer for subsequent viewing. These differ from inline graphics because they are not part of the text of the Web page display, but are only linked to the document. You can still view many of these files in Netscape Navigator 3.0, using it simply as a file viewer instead of a Web browser. Or, if you want to edit the file or save it in a different format, you can view it in a stand-alone graphics application such as Paint Shop Pro.

At the Saturn Web site shown in Figure 8-11, for example, you can download a picture of one of the automaker's new models and then view it in Netscape Navigator 3.0.

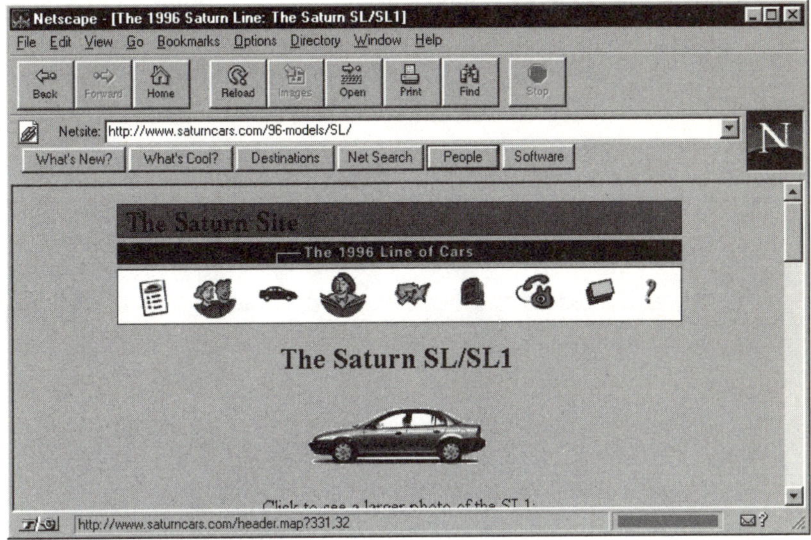

Figure 8-11: The Saturn Web site.

To download a picture:

1. Make sure you are connected to the Internet either directly or via your SLIP or PPP access provider. If Netscape Navigator 3.0 is not currently running, launch it by double-clicking its icon.
2. In the Location box at the top of the window, select the currently displayed URL and replace it with the address for the Saturn Web site, which is **http://www.saturncars.com/96-models/SL/**, and press Enter.

TIP

Remember, you can abbreviate URLs. You can leave off the ***http://*** *if you want.*

3. After the Web document transfers to your computer and displays, click on a link to a full-size picture. These are listed underneath the picture of the car on the home page. The links describe the view of the image, such as Front View or Rear View. Next to a hot link is the approximate size of the image in kilobytes. The larger the image, the more time it takes to display.
4. Click on the "A picture of the car in motion" link. Notice that Netscape Navigator 3.0 opens a new page where the image will display. Figure 8-12 shows the completed version of this picture.

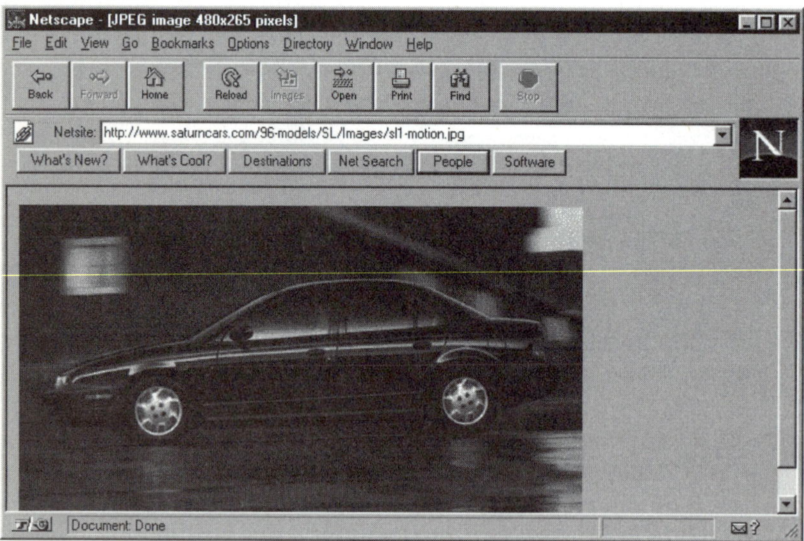

Figure 8-12: The Saturn SL/SL1 in motion.

Who Owns the Image?

The easy answer to this question is "probably not you." Almost every image on the World Wide Web and the Internet is owned by someone or by a legal corporation. Don't think that just because you can download an image to your computer's hard disk you own the rights to the file. In most cases, you do not. In fact, some images have been placed on the Web illegally, without permission from their owners. By downloading these images, you may also be breaking the law.

Fortunately, most sites comply with international copyright laws and make available only those images they own or have legally licensed from another party. These images are provided for you to view but not reuse or sell in any form.

Some sites legally allow you to download graphics for use in commercial or noncommercial ways. Clip art images, for example, fall into this category. Many sites offer downloadable images that you can incorporate in business documents, Web documents, and other sources. But remember, you are still responsible for making sure that the images you download are indeed owned or licensed by the person providing them.

Other sites require that you first pay a fee to acquire the rights to view and download images. Sites such as MTV, Sony, and Playboy offer repositories like this. Again, copyright laws restrict you from reselling these images as your own. You can only look at them; you can't plaster them all over Usenet newsgroups.

Now that the image is onscreen, what can you do with it? Not much, at this point. Netscape Navigator 3.0 is not designed to be a graphics editor, only a viewer of certain graphics types. What you can do is save the image to your hard disk for later viewing. If you enjoy a particular image and you've waited several minutes for it to transfer to your machine, you owe it to yourself to save it to disk.

To save an image to disk:

1. Select Save As from Netscape Navigator 3.0's File menu. The Save As dialog box appears, as shown in Figure 8-13.

Figure 8-13: The Save As dialog box.

To save a graphic quickly, you can also right-click the image and select Save This Image As from the context menu that appears.

2. Choose a location for the file and then click the Save button. The Saving Location dialog box appears, showing the progress of the file transfer.

   Because the file already has been downloaded to your computer (but not saved to disk), it takes only a few seconds to save it to disk.

3. Click on the Back button to return to the previous Web page.

Redecorating Your Desktop

Not only can you save any image you encounter on the Web, you can even set it as your Windows wallpaper. Netscape Navigator 3.0 makes this so easy that you might end up with all kinds of crazy designs on your screen!

To save an image as your Windows wallpaper:

1. Place your cursor over the image.
2. Click the right mouse button.
3. Select Set As Wallpaper from the context menu that appears.

Once you have set your new wallpaper, you might want to configure your system so that the image is tiled instead of centered. To make this change, click the Display icon in Control Panel.

Configuring Graphics Settings in Netscape Navigator 3.0

As you've already seen, Netscape Navigator 3.0 comes ready to display GIF, JPEG, and XBM graphics. Netscape Navigator 3.0 also includes customization options to configure the way graphics are viewed. These options are necessary because not all video display hardware is created equal. For example, you may be able to display 256 colors, while your 12-year-old son has configured his hot-rod machine to display 16 million. We all know that in carefully mixing his paints, Renoir used many more than 256 separate colors. So what does Netscape Navigator 3.0 do about images that were created with more colors than your machine can display? It uses two different approaches to solving the problem: *dithering* and *color substitution.*

Dithering is a process that arranges pixels (the little "dots" on your screen) of varying shades to achieve a visual effect, often a simulation of a different color. For instance, a pattern of black and white pixels can be used to simulate gray. By varying the ratio of white pixels to black pixels, you get different shades of gray. Since there is more information in this scenario, images that are displayed with dithering take slightly more time to display than images using simple color substitution.

Dithering often provides a pretty good approximation of colors that are not available on your display system. Sometimes, however, it can make an image look patchy or speckled, particularly at low resolutions. If you don't favor the speckled look, try switching to color substitution.

Color substitution does what you'd expect. As Netscape Navigator 3.0 reads in a graphics file and encounters a color not available on your display, it substitutes a color that *is* available. Color substitution may make a graphic's colors look slightly "off," but they will be textured the same as the original.

Let's take a look at the color options:

1. From the Netscape Navigator 3.0 Options menu, select General Preferences. The Preferences dialog box appears, as shown in Figure 8-14.

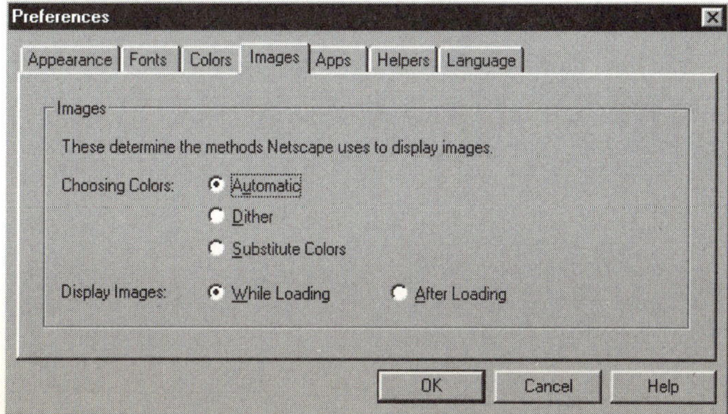

Figure 8-14: The Preferences dialog box with Images tab selected.

2. Click the Images tab to display it if it is not already displayed.
3. At Choosing Colors, select the way Netscape Navigator 3.0 handles graphics.

- **Automatic.** Lets Netscape Navigator 3.0 decide what colors to use when displaying a graphic. This is the default setting and should be OK for most users. With this setting selected, Netscape Navigator 3.0 makes up its own mind whether to dither or to substitute available colors.
- **Dither.** Tells Netscape Navigator 3.0 always to dither the computer's available colors to most closely match the image's colors. In Windows, JPEG images are dithered automatically.
- **Substitute Colors.** Instructs Netscape Navigator 3.0 to substitute an available color that most closely matches the image's colors.

TIP

By experimenting with these color settings, you can determine the best view for your system. Sometimes you may have to adjust a setting if your PC's monitor does not display an image properly.

There is one more setting in the Images tab. It specifies whether or not images will be displayed before they have been completely transferred. To change this setting, select from the following choices:

- **While Loading.** Instructs Netscape Navigator 3.0 to display partial images while they are being transferred. This is the default setting.
- **After Loading.** Tells Netscape Navigator 3.0 to wait until the entire image has transferred before displaying it. On very fast networks, this *may* be slightly faster than the other method, but I'm a child of the visual age and get anxious if I don't see something happening on my screen right away.

After you make changes to the Images tab, click OK to save them and return to the main Netscape Navigator 3.0 window. Or click Cancel if you want Netscape Navigator 3.0 to disregard any changes you have made.

Text-Only Mode

They say a picture is worth a thousand words, but we writers have never bought that. In spite of all the dire warnings of bow-tied professors, we have not degenerated into an illiterate society that worships only images. In fact, as technology gets better and better at surrounding us with imagery, more and more *words* get published!

You really see how important words are when you have a modem connection to the Net. If you have a slow modem and have been following the various links in this chapter, you're probably growing tired of waiting for some of the documents to transfer. In fact, if you have a modem that operates at less than 28.8 kbps, you may already be working on next year's letter to Santa. But besides speeding up your Internet connection, there is another approach: you can bypass graphics altogether.

Netscape Navigator 3.0 gives you the option of turning off the automatic display of graphics by deselecting the Auto Load Images option on the Options menu (see Figure 8-15). When this option is turned off, a small icon appears as a placeholder wherever an image is supposed to display. Figure 8-16 shows a Web document in text-only mode, with several placeholders for graphics.

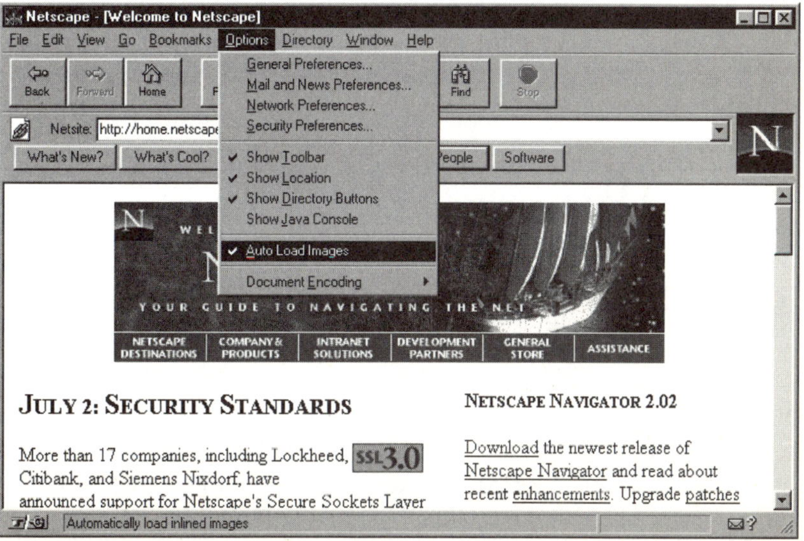

Figure 8-15: The Auto Load Images option.

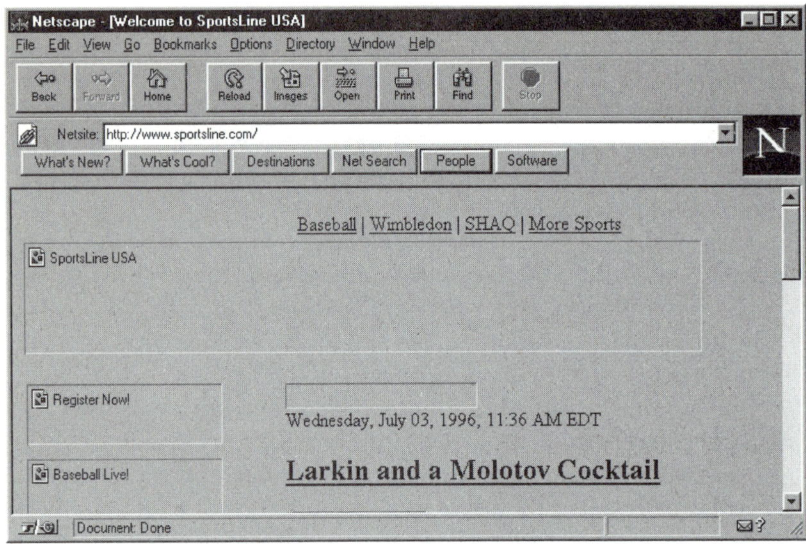

Figure 8-16: A Web page with Auto Load Images turned off.

If you then come across a particular document whose graphics you want to view, you can easily display them by clicking the Images button. This reloads the document with graphics displayed.

If you want to display graphics other than those supported directly by Netscape Navigator 3.0, there is one more configuration step: setting up helper applications.

Setting Up Helper Applications

You read earlier in this chapter about how you can download images to view in another application, such as LView or Paint Shop Pro. When configured to work with Netscape Navigator 3.0, these applications are called *helper applications*. To make them work with Netscape Navigator 3.0, you must set them up manually using the Helpers tab of the General Preferences dialog box.

First, obtain a helper application and install it on your system. Applications that let you view or edit graphics are available from various sources, including third-party books, software stores, FTP and Gopher sites, and World Wide Web sites. Some of the applications that you might want to obtain are listed in Table 8-1.

Viewer Name	Supports File Types
LView Pro	GIF, JPEG/JPG, TIFF, BMP
Paint Shop Pro	GIF, JPEG/JPG, TIFF, BMP
GhostView	PostScript

Table 8-1: Some graphics viewers that can be used as helper applications.

TIP

Virtually any *program that can run on your system can be used as a helper application in Netscape Navigator 3.0. In Chapter 9, "Power Navigator 3.0," you'll also learn about* plug-ins, *which are another type of application that can extend Navigator's graphics and sound capabilities.*

Netscape Navigator 3.0 natively displays GIF and JPEG files, so unless you're interested in editing or format conversion you won't gain much with a helper application that supports only these formats. You need one that offers the capabilities to read those formats and others, such as TIFF and BMP. These file types are fairly common, and some Web sites may include these types of graphics in their documents or file archives.

Once you acquire and install a helper application on your system, use the following steps to configure it to work with Netscape Navigator 3.0 to display any TIFF files you encounter:

1. Select General Preferences from the Options menu. The Preferences dialog box appears.
2. Click the Helpers tab, shown in Figure 8-17. If you feel overwhelmed by this screen, see the upcoming sidebar "What Are All Those Funny Settings?"

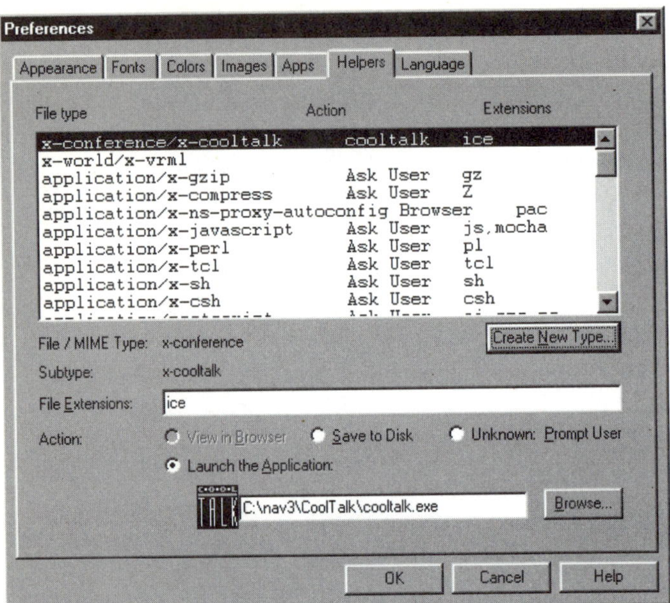

Figure 8-17: The Helpers tab.

What Are All Those Funny Settings?

The Helpers tab looks fairly complicated at first, but once you understand the concepts, using it is really pretty simple. The large scrolling list includes the names of different kinds of files you might encounter as you cruise the Net with Netscape Navigator 3.0. These file types are listed using a naming standard known as *MIME*. In MIME nomenclature, for instance, files with an .EXE or .BIN extension are classified as applications, with a subtype designation of "octet-stream." If you scroll down the list you'll see many different types of files, some familiar and some unfamiliar. Usually the MIME designations make sense, as in the case of GIF files, which are classified as images with a subtype of gif.

Here's where it gets interesting. For each type of file it encounters on the Internet, Netscape Navigator 3.0 has a default action that's listed in the Action column of the list. For image/gif files, for example, you can see that the default action is Browser. This means that GIF graphics will be displayed automatically by Netscape Navigator 3.0 itself, right within the browser window. And for application/octet-stream files, the default is Save. When you click on a link to an .EXE or .BIN file, it will be saved to your disk.

3. In the long scrolling list at the top of the tab, scroll down until you see the image/tiff entry. Click it. Notice in the File Extensions text box that the extensions .TIFF and .TIF automatically appear. These are the extensions for TIFF images Netscape Navigator 3.0 will recognize. Netscape Navigator 3.0 can then launch the associated helper application and tell it to load the TIFF image.
4. Click the Launch the Application radio button, which is below the File Extension box. This tells Netscape Navigator 3.0 to launch your helper application when it encounters a TIFF image.
5. Now you need to tell Netscape Navigator 3.0 where on your computer to find the helper application. In the text box below the radio button you just clicked, enter the full path and file name of the helper application. If you are using LView Pro, for instance, this will be something like **C:\LVIEW\LVIEWP1A.EXE.**

TIP

Use the Browse button to find helper applications on your system.

6. Click OK to save your changes and return to the main Netscape Navigator 3.0 window.

Now when you encounter a site that includes TIFF images, Netscape Navigator 3.0 automatically starts the helper application and lets you view and manipulate the image.

The subject of graphics on the Internet is a very large one, and we've covered only the basics in this chapter. Chapter 9, "Power Navigator 3.0," will go into more advanced uses of graphics through VRML and Netscape Navigator 3.0 *plug-ins* as well as Java and JavaScript, but for now let's see—or rather, hear—what's up with sound in Netscape Navigator 3.0.

Server Push & Simple Animation

Most Web pages require that you interact with them in some way. They usually include links to other pages, graphics to click, animation to view, or sound objects to download and listen to. All of these items are initiated in some way by the user, the person using the client application (Netscape Navigator 3.0, in this case).

Another type of HTML instruction enables Web authors to design pages that deliver an updated version of the page without interaction from the user. This technology is called *server push*. Using server push, the server transmits Web page instructions and information to your browser window. As you navigate to various Web sites that support server-push technology, the connection between you and the server on the other end remains open. The server can continue to "push" updated information and data to your computer continuously. By pushing several different images into the same location on a Web page, for instance, a server can give the impression of a single animated image. The connection between you and the server closes when you leave the site.

An example of a Web site that supports server push is the Word site at http://www.word.com. It uses server push in a variety of ways, often to display advertisements during the time you are moving from one page to another. The advertisement appears, gives you a few moments to read it, and then disappears so that you can continue on to the item that you originally selected.

Throughout Word, there are clever icons that rely on server push for animation. But there are all kinds of uses for server push. A sports site, for instance, can use server push to keep a scoreboard updated with the latest scores and team highlights.

Sound on the Web

Many computers you purchase today come with sound cards and speakers. This has fueled the growth of sound capabilities on the Web. Thousands of Web sites now include sound files that offer a new way to experience online content. Radio stations, public television stations, and network news shows are providing sites that feature sound recordings. Some sites even include *live* performances of rock bands or the play-by-play of weekly football games. As the Web matures, you'll be able to sit back and listen as you work on that marketing proposal or college term paper. The history of technology is a history of distractions, and the good folks at Netscape are doing their best to distract you by enabling Navigator 3.0 to play the sounds of the Net.

Why Can't I Use My PC's Speaker?

You can, but you'll be disappointed with the results. Every PC comes equipped with a tiny speaker in it that you may hear beep every once in awhile. You'll hear it beep a few times, for instance, when you start up your computer. You can make this speaker play some of the sound files you find on the Internet by acquiring a speaker driver from Microsoft (called SPEAKE.EXE) and loading it on your system. You also need to acquire an application that plays different sound files. For many users, the reigning champion during the past year or so has been WPLANY.EXE, which is short for "We Play Anything." You can download WPLANY.EXE from ftp://ftp.cam.org/systems/ms-windows/slip-ppp/viewers/wplny09b.zip.

SPEAKE.EXE is part of Microsoft's Windows Driver Library, an archive file that includes other drivers as well. The URL is ftp://ftp.microsoft.com/Softlib/softlib.exe.

Supported Sound Files in Netscape Navigator 3.0

Netscape Navigator 3.0 includes built-in support for the following sound file formats: AU, SND, AIF, AIFF, AIFC, MIDI, and WAV. It's not important to know what all these acronyms mean, but you *should* know that the three most popular sound types on the Web are AU, SND, and WAV. MIDI files are really music files rather than sound files, digital "scores" that can be played correctly on any electronic musical instrument that supports the General MIDI standard. And that probably includes your sound card.

What Is LiveAudio?

Until Netscape Navigator 3.0, Web browsers required special helper applications in order to play audio files. LiveAudio is what Netscape calls Navigator's ability to play audio files *without* any external helper application. Similarly, the built-in video features I cover later in this chapter are known as LiveVideo.

Listening to Sound in Netscape Navigator 3.0

When you connect to a Web site that contains sound files, you generally will see a speaker icon indicating that it is a sound file. If the sound file is of a type that Netscape Navigator 3.0 supports, you can click the icon. Netscape Navigator 3.0 automatically plays the file. If a sound file is embedded directly into an HTML page, you won't even have to click a link. Let's look at an example.

1. Make sure you are connected to the Internet either directly or via your SLIP or PPP access provider. If Netscape Navigator 3.0 is not currently running, launch it by double-clicking its icon.
2. In the Location box at the top of the window, select the currently displayed URL and replace it with **http://www.spottedantelope.com/wander.htm**. Press Enter. After a few moments, the Wandering Italy page appears, as shown in Figure 8-18.

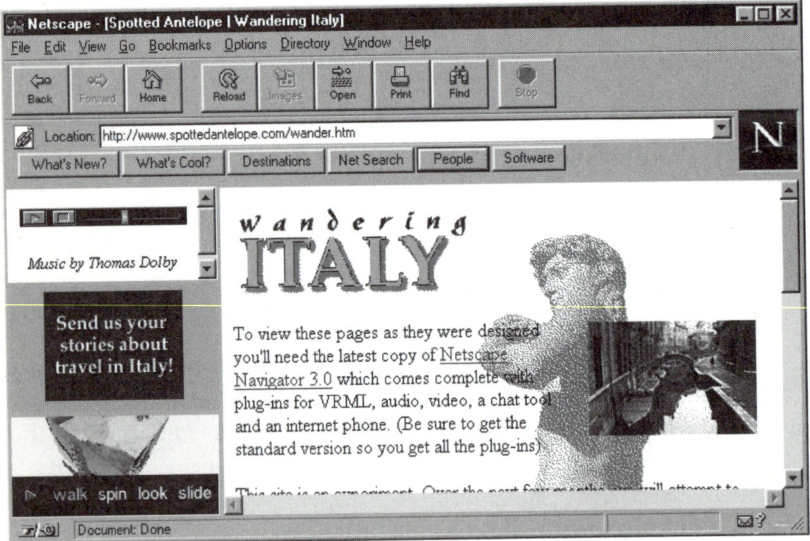

Figure 8-18: The Wandering Italy page.

Some pretty cool stuff here, no? Try to ignore the spinning image in the bottom left frame. That's VRML, and we get to that in the next chapter, "Power Navigator 3.0." What the heck, go ahead and play around with it before you read Chapter 9—I'm not your dad!

Notice the music playing—the soothing sounds of Thomas Dolby. (Or is it Tomaso Dolbinoni?) Notice also the sound control panel in the top left frame. That's what Netscape Navigator 3.0 displays whenever it encounters a sound file. The controls are pretty much like those on any electronic device: click the arrow button to start playing, click the other button to stop. You can adjust the volume of the selection by dragging the slider to the right or left.

When the sound file ends, it stops automatically and you can do one of two things: play it over and over again or get a life.

Using RealAudio With Netscape Navigator 3.0

As I'm sure you just discovered, sound files can take a while to download to your machine. But fortunately there are some new *streaming* standards that speed up the process. What do I mean by streaming? Suppose the sound file starts playing over your computer's speakers before it's completely downloaded. That's streaming. Instead of clicking a link and twiddling your thumbs, you can click a link and start shaking your booty. Not quite instant gratification, but close.

By far the most prominent streaming sound format on the Web is RealAudio. Using the RealAudio plug-in, which is available from the RealAudio Web site at http://www.realaudio.com, you can hear news, sporting events, music, and much more. The RealAudio format almost makes you feel as though you're listening to the radio, right on the Net. In fact, some traditional radio stations have started to supplement their broadcasts with RealAudio files on the Web.

The complete RealAudio system consists of two pieces. The first piece is one you'll probably never have to use unless you become a Web site administrator. The *RealAudio Server* is the software that enables Web sites to offer RealAudio files.

The other piece of the RealAudio puzzle is the client software that enables users like you to listen to RealAudio recordings. In this case it's a plug-in that works seamlessly with Netscape Navigator 3.0, just as if it were a built-in feature.

What's a Plug-in?

You've already learned about helper applications—programs that Netscape Navigator 3.0 can launch in order to display a particular graphics format or play a sound. Plug-ins are like helper applications in that they extend Navigator's abilities, but they do it seamlessly. When you install a plug-in, it almost becomes a part of Navigator. You can't tell that it isn't just another feature. For instance, a plug-in supporting an unusual graphics format might display images right within Navigator 3.0's browser window, just like a GIF or JPEG file. And once you install the RealAudio plug-in, it will behave very much like Navigator's built-in sound support.

Obtaining RealAudio

The RealAudio plug-in, which is what you want to install on your system, is currently free of charge. To get a copy of RealAudio, connect to RealAudio's Web site (**http://www.realaudio.com/**) and download the software to your computer. You will be asked to fill out a short form before downloading it.

Make sure to read the list of system requirements to run the program. The requirements include 2MB of free disk space and a sound card with a Windows Sound driver. (The RealAudio Player is not compatible with the PC Speaker program or other software programs that emulate a sound card.)

Installing & Configuring RealAudio

OK, you've completed the forms, chosen the correct version of RealAudio, and downloaded it to your computer. It's sitting on your computer and ready to install. Before you go any further, make sure that Netscape Navigator 3.0 is *NOT* running.

To install RealAudio, run the file you just downloaded by double-clicking it in the Windows Explorer (or in the File Manager if you are using Windows 3.1). RealAudio starts its installation program. Then simply follow the instructions that appear on your screen. When asked, make sure to indicate that you want to install the plug-in version of the program. At the conclusion of the setup process, the RealAudio player launches and plays a Welcome to RealAudio message. If the message sounds distorted, see the "Sound" section of the RealAudio Release Notes, which are stored on your system where you installed RealAudio.

Can I Create My Own RealAudio Files?

Yes, you can, but you'll need some extra software. Specifically, you must download a copy of the RealAudio Encoder from the Progressive Networks Web site. Using Encoder, you start with a WAV or AU audio file and convert it to the RealAudio file format, with the extension .RA. Within the RealAudio file you can insert a name of the file, author, and copyright information. This information is displayed on the user's machine when he or she is playing it back. Of course, the file you've created doesn't do you much good unless you have a way to distribute it to the public. You must copy it to a site that has the RealAudio server software. For more information on RealAudio servers, see the RealAudio Web site at http://www.realaudio.com/.

Trying Out RealAudio

When you connect to sites that contain RealAudio links, you can listen to a link by clicking it. It's that easy. The RealAudio player first contacts the host computer that contains the audio file. After a few moments during which it downloads the initial section of the file, it starts to play it over your system speakers. You can adjust the volume of the playback by using the slider control on the right side of the player.

TIP

RealAudio links are often indicated with an icon of a radio or boom box, sometimes with the letters "RA" on it. Take a look at Word magazine (http://www.word.com) for a typical use of iconized links like this, and for an example of RealAudio used effectively in conjunction with articles and stories.

So that you can try out RealAudio, Table 8-2 lists some sites that include RealAudio files. In the future, look for events such as football games, rock concerts, speeches, and the like to be simulcast as RealAudio events that you can listen to live.

Site Name	Address
National Public Radio	http://www.npr.org/
ABC Radio Network	http://www.abcradionet.com/
Delta Dream Vacations	http://pwr.com/LEISURE/DELTA.html
Advanced Digital Services	http://206.65.169.39/
Grace Hour	http://www. ggwo.org
Nightstand	http://www.nightstand.com/
Tabernacle Baptist Church	http://www.tabernacle.org/~tbc/
Toyota Motor	http://www.toyota.co.jp/
North Carolina News Network	http://www.capitolnet.com/ncnn/
Tech Talk Radio Network	http://ttn.nai.net/
BBC Radio 3: Facing the Radio	http://www.bbc.co.uk/ftr/
Black Cat Radio	http://www.memphiscat.com/
MusicNet	http://www.man.net/~musicnet/
OneWorld	http://www.oneworld.org/realaudio/index.html

Table 8-2: Some sites that have RealAudio files.

The RealAudio President

Politicians of every stripe are clamoring over the new telecommunications technologies, though they frequently misunderstand them. It is no surprise that several of President Clinton's speeches are available on the Web via RealAudio. Just point Navigator 3.0 to http://www.whitehouse.gov/WH/EOP/OP/html/OP_Speeches.html and start looking around—or listening around. If you have a good sound card and listen carefully enough, you might even hear Bill inhale.

Video in Netscape Navigator 3.0

We geeks spend so much time on the Web that sometimes we forget what Real Life is. Real Life is an operating environment that includes mountains, oceans, trees, crying babies, barking dogs, and Big Macs. It's not the greatest user interface, but it sure beats anything Bill Gates could come up with. And one of the most interesting features of Real Life is that things move! We do not experience life as a succession of still images such as those you usually encounter on the Net, but as a constant ebb and flow of matter through space.

Now you can come a little closer to Real Life on the Web. One of Netscape Navigator 3.0's most exciting new features is LiveVideo, the technology that lets you view video clips, often called movies, right within the browser window.

Let's give it a try:

1. Make sure you are connected to the Internet either directly or via your SLIP or PPP access provider. If Netscape Navigator 3.0 is not currently running, launch it by double-clicking its icon.
2. In the Location box at the top of the window, select the currently displayed URL and replace it with **http://www.wandering.com**. Press Enter. After a few moments, the Wandering Italy page appears, as shown in Figure 8-18.
3. In the large right-hand frame, scroll all the way down to the bottom of the page and click the "story index" link. A new page appears listing several available travel stories.
4. Scroll down and click the link "Part !: Arrival!" under The Adventures of Bill and Linda.

5. Once you're in Bill and Linda's story, scroll down and click the link "train station." A video clip starts downloading to your machine, and after about a minute it plays in the middle left-hand frame.

   Want to see it again? To replay the video clip, simply click it.

6. Now click your right mouse button on the video. A context menu appears, letting you rewind or fast forward the video, as shown in Figure 8-19.

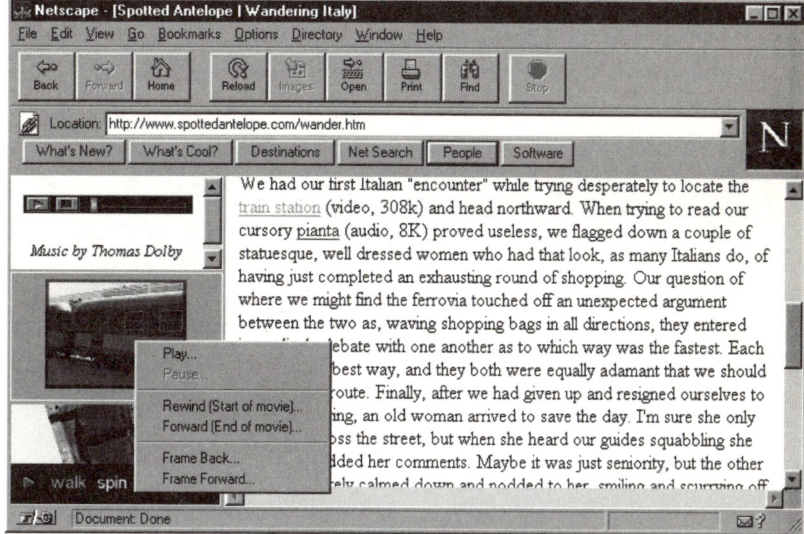

Figure 8-19: The LiveVideo context menu.

How does this work? When Netscape Navigator encounters what is known as an AVI file (AVI is Microsoft's format for video files), LiveVideo automatically kicks in and lets you view the image the way it was meant to be viewed. No need for external programs or helper applications—just sit back and enjoy.

Video With Sound

Wait a minute! Something is very wrong. Here we are using the slickest newest technology, and all we're getting is silent movies. Weren't talkies invented around 1927?

Not to worry: LiveVideo supports soundtracks as well as moving images. Not all AVI files include sound, but when you click on one that does, Netscape Navigator 3.0 will make you feel like you're sitting at Loew's Cineplex staring up at the big screen. (OK, so I exaggerate.)

Here's a nice example of an AVI clip that includes sound, put out by the government of Newfoundland and Labrador. Of course in order to hear the soundtrack, you'll need a sound card supported by your version of Windows.

1. Make sure you are connected to the Internet either directly or via your SLIP or PPP access provider. If Netscape Navigator 3.0 is not currently running, launch it by double-clicking its icon.
2. In the Location box at the top of the window, select the currently displayed URL and replace it with **http://www.gov.nf.ca/itt/business/people.avi**. Press Enter. After a few moments, the first image of an AVI file appears in your browser window, as shown in Figure 8-20.

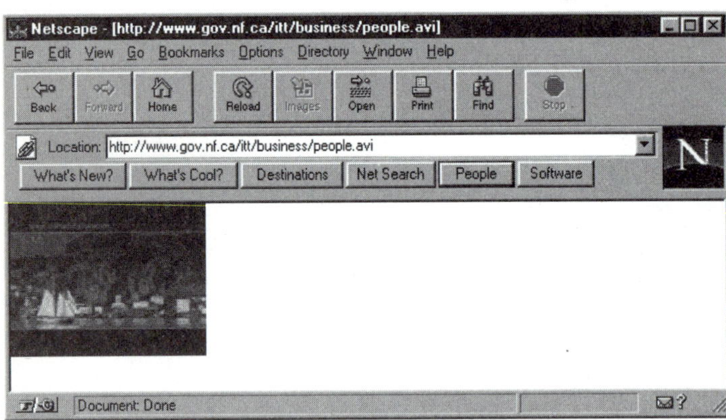

Figure 8-20: An AVI video clip by the government of Newfoundland and Labrador.

TIP

Large AVI files and AVI files that include sound may take a while to download. And I mean quite *a while. Keep that crossword puzzle and knitting project nearby.*

3. Click the image. Immediately it begins playing, complete with music and voice-over.

Other Video Formats

AVI is one of the most common video formats on the Web, but it's not the only one. As you venture into the far reaches of cyberspace you may encounter:

- QuickTime movies (with the extension .MOV or .QT)
- MPEG movies (with the extension .MPEG, .MPG, .MPE, or .MP2)
- Flick files (with the extension .FLI or .FLC)
- IFF/ILBM files (with the extension .IFF)

The current version of Navigator only plays AVI and QuickTime files automatically, but the Netscape developers were smart enough to make the program extensible. If you want Navigator 3.0 to play other animation formats right in the Browser window, all you have to do is find a plug-in for that particular media type. We've talked about plug-ins in the sections on RealAudio, and we'll come back to them in the next chapter, "Power Navigator 3.0."

TIP

To play QuickTime movies on your system, you need to have the latest version of Apple QuickTime for Windows installed. The software is available at http://quicktime.apple.com/qt/sw/sw.html.

Moving On

In this chapter, you've learned the basics of viewing graphics and listening to sound in Netscape Navigator 3.0. You've also learned how to play video clips, or movies, right in the browser window. By now you should have a sense of how vast the possibilities are when it comes to incorporating new media into Web pages. Advertising executives are jumping up and down with excitement, scheming all kinds of ways to inundate you with the latest multimedia innovations.

In the next chapter I cover some of the most powerful features of Netscape Navigator 3.0: VRML, plug-ins, Java, and JavaScript. This is where the ride gets wild, so hang on tight.

Power Navigator 3.0

As you learned in the last chapter, Netscape Navigator 3.0 is one of the most robust tools available for displaying a wide range of multimedia content. But the story doesn't end there. As new technologies develop, Netscape is quick to incorporate them. And Navigator 3.0 even includes methods by which developers can tack new modules onto the program, seamlessly integrating powerful new multimedia features. This open architecture ensures that Navigator 3.0 will keep looking young as the world at large comes up with ever more exciting ways to package information.

In this chapter we'll look at four ways in which Navigator 3.0 is keeping up with all the changes in multimedia presentation:

- VRML support, letting you navigate the three-dimensional virtual worlds that are starting to crop up all over the Net. VRML is the best legal way to get dizzy without leaving your desk chair.
- Plug-ins, which allow developers to extend Navigator 3.0's power in all kinds of imaginative ways. Thanks to a couple of plug-ins, my computer is now playing MIDI music files off the Net while it displays 3D models of agricultural chemicals. Did somebody say something about *work*?

- Support for the hundreds of Java applets available on the Web, as well as the thousands waiting to be written. Java is a full-featured, general-purpose programming language, and Navigator 3.0 is designed to execute any programs written in Java. This means that the ways to extend Navigator 3.0 are virtually limitless.
- JavaScript, a much simpler language that can be thrown right into HTML files to extend Navigator's capabilities. JavaScript can make sure you've entered a valid zip code in a Web form, make text scroll across your screen, or even replace the status information at the bottom of the browser window with a joke. I think of JavaScript as the tool of choice for "stupid Navigator tricks."

Feeling adventurous? Let's start right in with VRML.

VRML

First, how do you say it? Some people say V-R-M-L, carefully articulating each letter, but they're not the cool people. The cool people say *VER-MUHL*, with the stress on the first syllable, just as in *thermal*.

And what exactly does it stand for? **V**irtual **R**eality **M**odeling **L**anguage. It's really a pretty simple concept. Just as HTML is a markup language that tells a Web browser to display various elements such as headings, italic text, and links, VRML is an extension that tells a Web browser to display various components of three-dimensional virtual worlds. These include objects that rotate or otherwise move through space in a "realistic" way, as well as graphical backgrounds that make you feel as if *you're* moving as you manipulate your mouse. To get technical, VRML is a standard for encoding computer-generated graphics into a file format for transmission across the Internet or an intranet; it is also the standard a Web browser uses to interpret and display these graphics so that you can interact with them. Many people see VRML as an eventual replacement for HTML itself, offering a more intuitive and life-like way of navigating the Web.

Moving Worlds? Live3D?

Here's some more terminology you might encounter, but first a little history.

Originally, Silicon Graphics (SGI) came up with Open Inventor, a file format that became the basis for VRML; they also developed QvLib, which was the software component responsible for "understanding" and interpreting the file. Gavin Bell of SGI then wrote the proposal for the VRML 1.0 standard. The standard was adopted, and developers began implementing it.

Of course as soon as version 1 of any standard is accepted by the technology community, somebody starts working on version 2. There have been several rival proposals, but the one that really caught on is called *Moving Worlds*. Developed and supported by a broad consortium of software and hardware vendors, it provides many new features including full motion, live content and animation, enhanced audio, and the ability to connect with databases. Most importantly, it has strong support for multi-user interactivity. You won't need to get dizzy alone any more. At this point it looks like Moving Worlds will become VRML 2.0.

Just as the HTML standard doesn't specify exactly what headings or footnotes should look like in every Web browser, VRML doesn't specify exactly how to display graphical objects such as wire-frame models. Virtual worlds may look and feel a bit different from one VRML browser to another. *Live3D* is simply Netscape's own particular implementation of VRML, and it's widely considered one of the best available.

OK, let's go ahead and try some VRML navigation.

VRML Navigation

There are VRML sites you can get to right from the Netscape home page, but first we're going to try something even simpler. Netscape includes a sample VRML file with the program, so you can try your hand at exploring virtual worlds without even being connected to the Net.

1. From the Netscape Navigator 3.0 File menu, select Open File. Or you can simply press Ctrl+O. The Open dialog box appears.
2. In the "Files of type" drop-down list at the bottom of the dialog box, select VRML Worlds.
3. Now navigate to the Live3D folder under your main Netscape folder. For instance, if you're using Windows 95, your Live3D folder might be located in Program Files\Netscape\Navigator\.

4. Once you are in the correct folder, double-click the file Netscape.wrl. After a few seconds, a three-dimensional page appears, as shown in Figure 9-1.

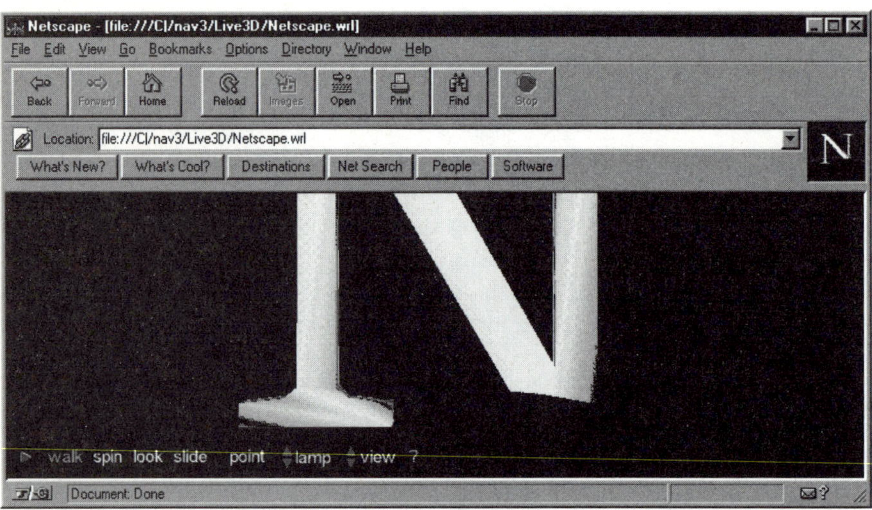

Figure 9-1: Navigator 3.0 with VRML page.

Let's take a few minutes to get oriented. There are eight clickable labels along the bottom of the window: Walk, Spin, Look, Slide, Point, Lamp, View, and ?. Each label represents a different operational mode for your controls. In other words, if you click Slide, your mouse and keyboard might act differently in the window than they do when you click Walk.

TIP

In addition to these labels, there's a small arrow button at the bottom left of the window. In the case of VRML pages that are animated when you first view them (a spinning globe, for instance), this button lets you start and stop the motion. It is like the Play button on a tape recorder or CD player.

Since you've got to walk before you can slide, let's start there:

1. Make sure the Walk button is depressed.
2. Move your mouse around the window. Notice that whenever your pointer rests on the large N, it becomes a hand and the word *Netscape* appears, as shown in Figure 9-2.

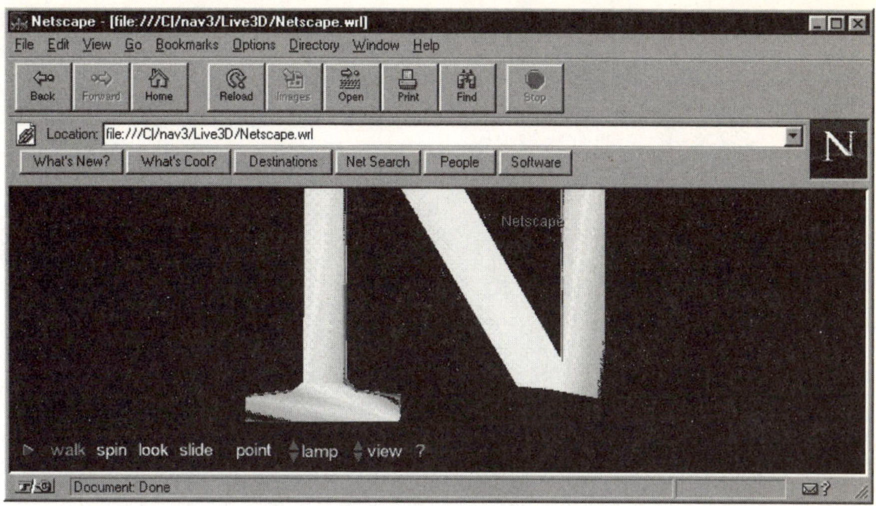

Figure 9-2: Link to Netscape site in the sample VRML page.

This is a simple link to the Netscape home page. Links in VRML do not appear as underlined text, but as a temporary element in the graphic.

3. If you are currently connected to the Net, try double-clicking your left mouse button while the link is displayed. You are transported to the regular old Netscape site, as shown in countless illustrations in this book. When you are done at the Netscape site, click the Back button to return to the VRML page.

TIP

At some VRML sites, you need to be in Point mode in order to see links to other URLs. For Point mode, simply click the Point label.

4. Now click your left mouse button and, while holding it down, drag your mouse slowly around the window. Notice that you seem to move in relation to the N, as shown in Figure 9-3.

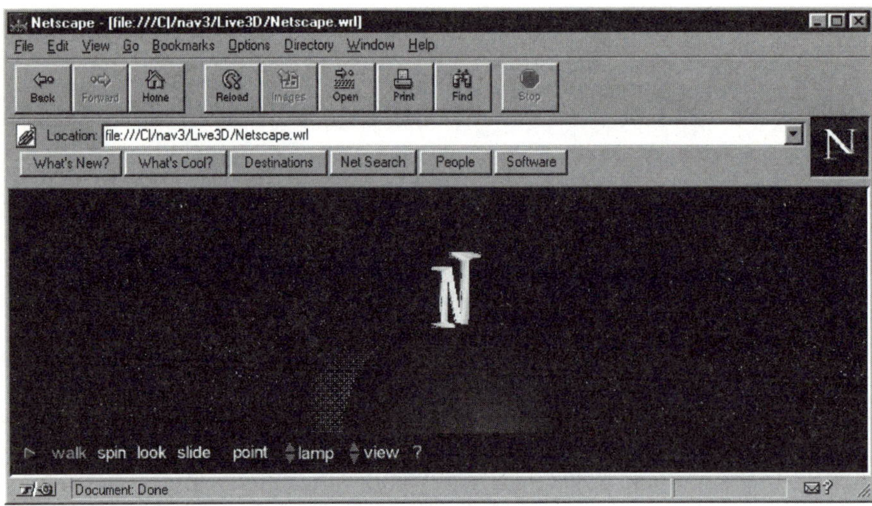

Figure 9-3: Moving around the sample VRML image.

- As you drag to the right or left, you seem to move right or left in relation to the object.
- As you drag up, you seem to move toward the object.
- As you drag down, you seem to move away from the object.

TIP

You can also use your arrow keys to move left, right, forward, and back.

5. Ready for some fun? Try dragging with your *right* mouse button instead of the left. Immediately you see the power of VRML: you are now moving around the object as if it's three-dimensional (see Figure 9-4).

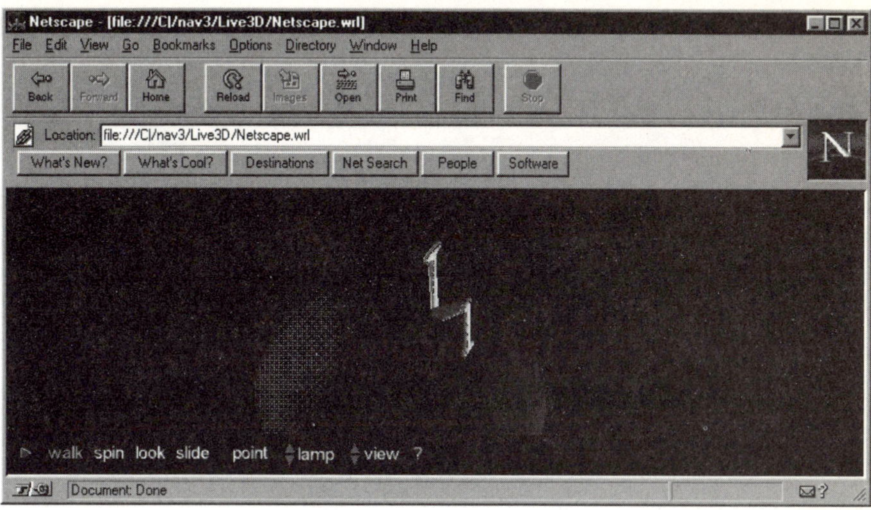

Figure 9-4: Three-dimensional movement.

6. One more move: hold down the Alt key while dragging with the left mouse button. The object "slides" in the window in a two-dimensional manner. In other words, the up-and-down component of your mouse movement does not change your apparent distance from the object.

TIP

In Walk mode, the A and Z keys slide you up and down.

7. OK, I was lying. There's still one more move I want to show you. Click the View label. The VRML window returns to its original state, as shown in Figure 9-1.

How do you remember all these navigational techniques? That's easy: just click the ? label. As shown in Figure 9-5, a convenient legend appears in the window, staying visible until you click the ? label again.

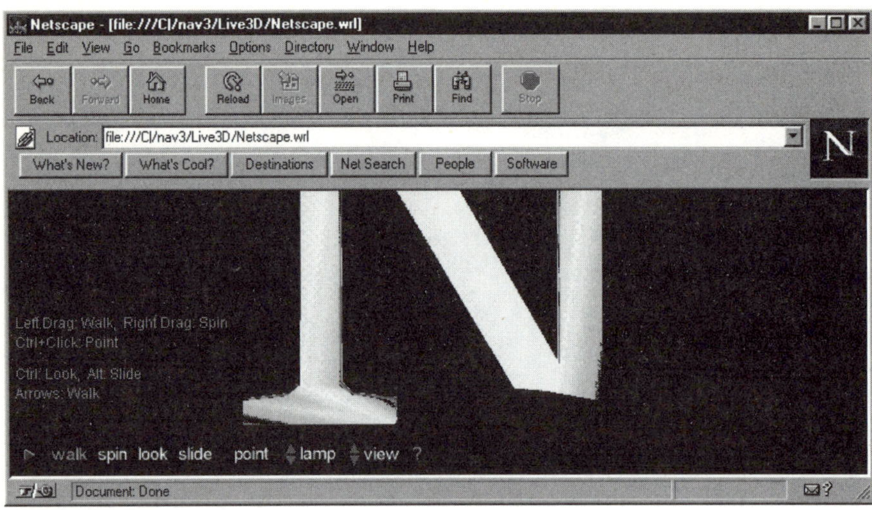

Figure 9-5: VRML Help.

Enough of the baby stuff. Are you ready for some motion sickness?

1. Click the Look label. The Help legend changes, indicating new functions for some of your controls as shown in Figure 9-6.

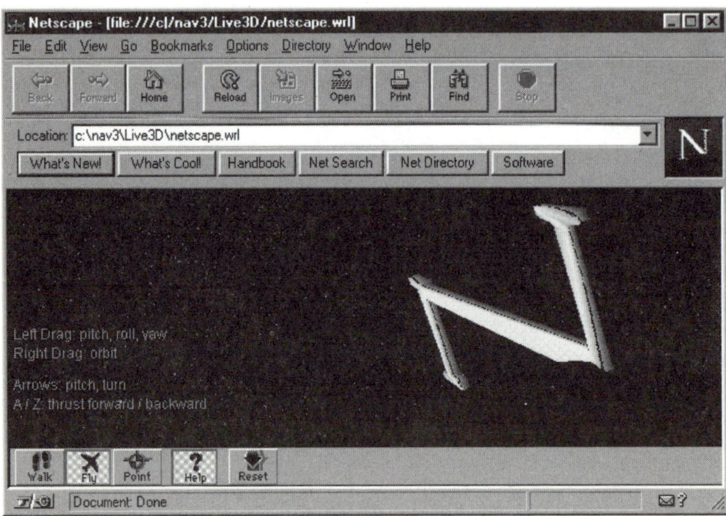

Figure 9-6: Help in Look mode.

2. Start looking around by dragging with the left mouse button. As you discover immediately, your imaginary spacecraft travels very quickly, and if you're not careful you'll spill Tang all over the place.

Lost in Cyberspace

Thank God for the View label. I was born in the early '50s and never saw a video game until I was an adult. My idea of fast-paced action was when the Lone Ranger and Tonto discovered a hideout, one that looked suspiciously like the hideout they found in the previous episode. Now drop me into a VRML page, and in a matter of seconds I'm hopelessly lost, wandering the far reaches of space looking for something—*anything*—recognizable.

My kids, on the other hand, seem to find virtual worlds utterly familiar, warm, and homey. So if you were born before the Kennedy assassination, here's my number-one hint for exploring VRML effectively: bring a kid along!

The way the labels work in different VRML worlds varies a bit. For example, try clicking the Lamp label and playing with the up and down arrows just to the left of it. In this particular 3D world you become the God of Light, making the sky glow or casting shadows across the universe. But in another virtual world, the Lamp label might simply turn underlining on and off! The only way to know what's going to happen is to click.

The VRML Context Menu

One of the most powerful features of VRML is that it lets *you* control the way the graphic information appears on your screen. You can do this by clicking your right mouse button anywhere within the browser window. A Context menu pops up, as shown in Figure 9-7.

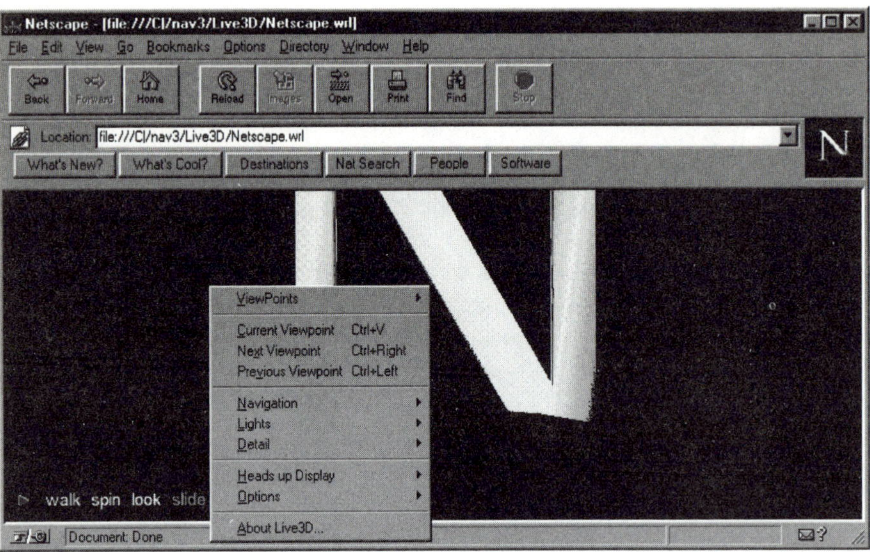

Figure 9-7: The Context menu.

From the Context menu there are a number of ways to reconfigure your navigation environment. I'm not going to cover all of these, mainly because they're a lot harder to describe than they are to explore. You can have some fun checking them out on your own, but here are a few things to try:

- Want to make your travels really wild? Select Fly mode from the Navigation submenu. Then select Bank when Flying. Your imaginary craft will tilt in the direction of your turns.
- Want to see what a 3D object looks like in wireframe instead of solid? Click Wireframe from the Detail menu.
- Want to turn off the buttons at the bottom of the window for a better view of your virtual world? Uncheck the Navigation Bar item on the Options submenu.

If you want to preserve the changes you have made, simply click Save All Settings As Default in the Options submenu.

What's the Point?

So far, VRML applications have concentrated on pretty, imaginative pictures. You can see some great examples of individual images, sometimes known as models, at http://www.tcp.ca/gsb/VRML/vrml-modelshop.html. (Don't miss the rotating zebra head!) But what about more serious applications?

Well, just about everything you can do with ordinary HTML you can do with VRML as well. Or at least you'll be able to when all the VRML 2.0 features are adopted. VRML pages can include links to other documents, enhance sites with sound and video, and even collect user information for online transactions. You can think of the added dimension as providing yet more ways to organize information.

In addition, VRML provides a visual analog for the "real" world. Imagine an online real estate company providing three-dimensional models of houses. You could check out the front yard, then the back yard, then go inside and wander through the rooms. You could click on various appliances to find out what brand they are, or how old they are. And think of the educational possibilities: kids in school wandering through three-dimensional depictions of the human body, clicking to get more information on their favorite organs.

No, we didn't see that in 1996, but it's quite likely by late 1997. VRML is just emerging from its "proof of concept" stage, and real-world applications haven't caught up with the technology yet. In addition, VRML pages are still pretty slow to load over modem connections. But for a taste of things to come, check out Netscape's own Media Showcase site at home.netscape.com/comprod/products/navigator/version_3.0/showcase/index.html.

Plug-ins

Right out of the box (or the CD sleeve), Netscape Navigator 3.0 lets you experience most of what is available on the Net. But as the Web becomes more popular and the technology improves, more sophisticated multimedia content is becoming available all the time. You just saw, for instance, how VRML is adding new dimensions to Web content—literally. Movies, desktop-published documents, and video conferencing are slowly making their way onto the Web as well. Not only are these new types of data putting strains on the infrastructure of the Internet, they are also forcing Web browsers to evolve from text and graphics displayers to real-time, interactive multimedia viewers.

Not to worry. Your investment in Netscape Navigator 3.0 is a good one. The Netscape developers have come up with an open-extendible architecture that lets the program evolve as technology itself evolves. Through plug-in applications developed by independent software vendors, Navigator 3.0 enables you to experience most of what is currently available online.

Plug-ins extend Netscape Navigator 3.0's capabilities so that it can display or play a wide variety of documents and file types, such as Adobe Acrobat .PDF (Portable Document Format) files, Macromedia Director movies, and MIDI music files. It uses what's known as its *Live Objects* technology to enable developers to create rich multimedia content for the Internet or office intranets.

Up until Netscape Navigator 2.0, Web users were required to configure separate helper applications that worked independently of their Web browsers to view and control most multimedia documents. Now when you download and configure plug-ins to work with Netscape Navigator 2.0 or later, the plug-ins become part of the browser itself. Movies, sound events, presentation graphics, and more display directly in the Netscape Navigator 3.0 window. In fact, plug-ins are so well integrated with the program that you'll quickly forget you're using them.

How Plug-ins Display in Netscape Navigator 3.0

When you use a plug-in with Netscape Navigator 3.0, it may not always be apparent that the plug-in is a separate application. With helper applications, you always know when a graphics program or a media player starts because you see it display in a separate window. Plug-ins, however, can interact with Netscape Navigator 3.0 in one of three modes of operation:

- **Full-screen plug-ins.** Full-screen plug-ins are just that—plug-ins that take up the entire Netscape Navigator 3.0 browser window. These are less common than embedded plug-ins.
- **Embedded plug-ins.** Embedded plug-ins are referenced in HTML documents so that when a user clicks on the reference, the plug-in activates and displays the object. Although this is similar to the way in which other objects, such as embedded graphics, are handled, embedded plug-ins can respond to user events, including mouse motions. Figure 9-8 shows a typical embedded plug-in, an interactive Shockwave tic-tac-toe game.

  As a Web author, you specify embedded plug-ins by using the <EMBED> HTML tag, as shown in the following syntax:

  ```
  <EMBED SRC="trailer.mpg", WIDTH=150, HEIGHT=250 CONTROLS=TRUE>
  ```

  In this example, when the user clicks on the plug-in reference on the Web page, an MPEG player activates automatically and plays a film clip named "trailer.mpg."
- **Hidden plug-ins.** Hidden plug-ins are ones that users cannot see or otherwise control, such as a plug-in that plays a music file in the background.

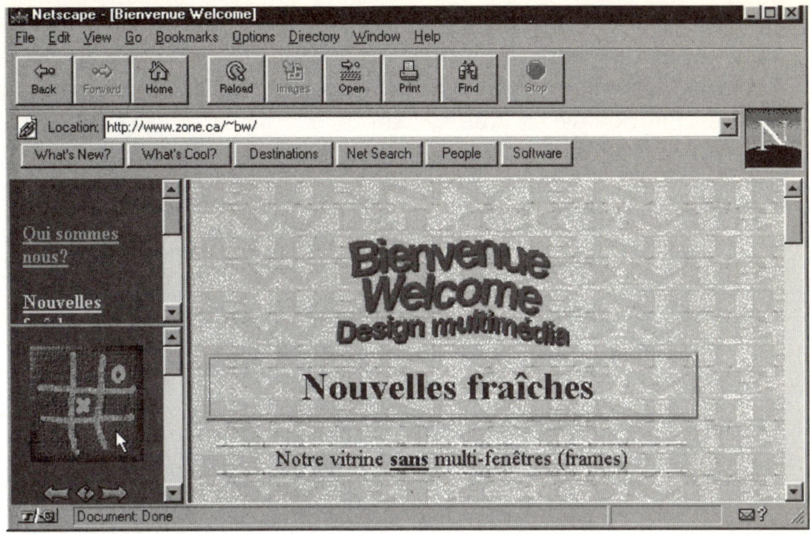

Figure 9-8: A plug-in tic-tac-toe game in the left-hand frame.

There are dozens of excellent plug-ins available for Netscape Navigator 3.0, and many of them are available in shareware or beta versions right on the Net.

Just to show you how easy it is to work with plug-ins, here's some more detailed information on one of the most exciting—the Macromedia Shockwave plug-in.

Shockwave & Netscape Navigator 3.0

The Shockwave plug-in lets you view Macromedia Director movies as well as FreeHand and Authorware multimedia files in Netscape Navigator 3.0. Developers can include this media in HTML documents by using the <EMBED> tag. Documents can even include more than one movie per HTML page.

When you access a site that includes a Director file, you can scroll through the Web page even while the movie is playing. You can interact with the movie by clicking on it, and you can enter text from the keyboard into text fields within the movie. And the movie itself can access information from the Internet and open URLs.

To download a copy of Shockwave, enter **http://www.macromedia.com/Tools/Shockwave/Plugin/plugin.cgi** in the Netscape Navigator 3.0 Location field and press Enter. Next, click the link Get the Shockwave Plug-in for Your Browser. On the next page, click the link for your appropriate operating system, such as Windows 95. You now can download the file by clicking one of the links provided.

After you download the Shockwave plug-in file, exit Netscape Navigator 3.0. This is very important. ***Plug-ins will not install properly if Navigator is running!*** Now double-click the downloaded file. This decompresses it and installs Shockwave on your system.

TIP

You may be asked during Shockwave's installation process if you want to install the plug-in for Director, FreeHand, Authorware, or all three. To experience the full range of graphics, multimedia, and interactive applications developed for the Web using Macromedia products, you should install all three.

Once Shockwave is installed, you can start Netscape Navigator 3.0 and test out its new capabilities. One site that uses a multimedia image to enhance its appeal is the Welcome To Netscape page for Shockwave. The URL for this page is: http://home. netscape.com/comprod/products/navigator/version_2.0/plugins/director_examples/director_example1.html. (Think they could have made that URL any longer?) Here's what it looks like:

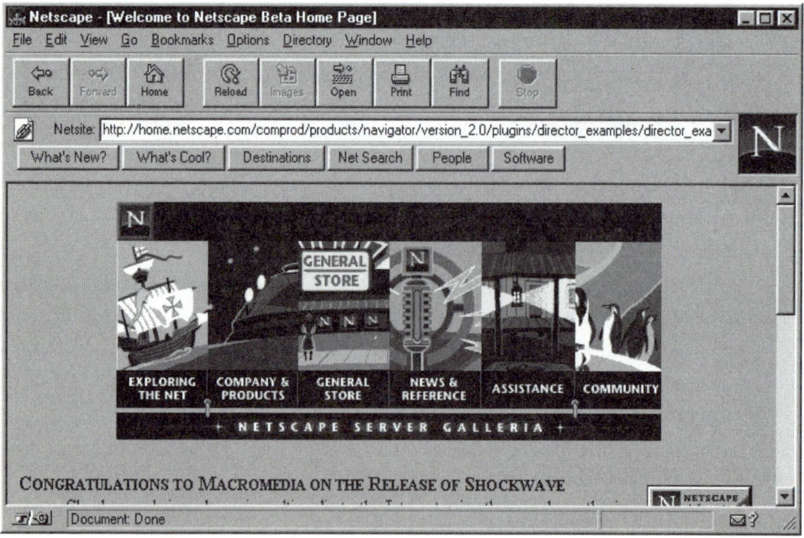

Figure 9-9: The Welcome to Shockwave page.

The interesting part of this page is that the normally static image at the top of Netscape's page is now animated. It includes a moving marquee, has hyperlinked buttons, and even highlights a button as you pass your mouse pointer over it.

You can see other uses of Shockwave at the Macromedia Shockwave Vanguard Gallery at http://www.macromedia.com/Tools/Shockwave/Gallery/Vanguard/index.html. Listed here are companies that are integrating Shockwave-compatible images into their Web sites, including *Advertising Age*, c|net, and the American Cancer Society.

Java

When you get older and your grandchildren ask you about the good old days of the World Wide Web, you'll tell them about Java. You'll tell them that Java was the technology that got us one step closer to bringing real-time interaction between people on the Internet. Java not only enhances Web pages with impressive graphics, it also enables software developers to create secure two-way Web applications in a straightforward fashion. These applications are called *Java applets*. Figure 9-10 shows an example of what a Java applet can do.

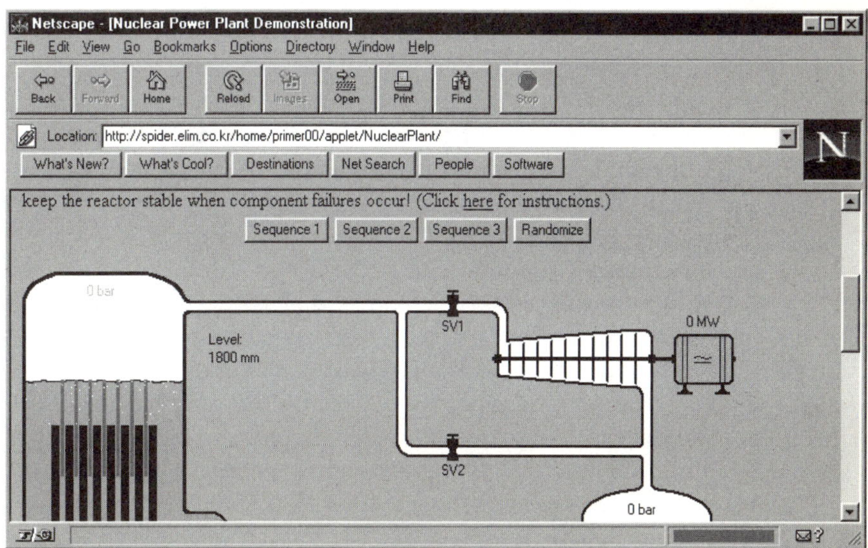

Figure 9-10: A Java applet in Netscape Navigator 3.0.

So What Are Applets?

Java applets are the hottest new eye-candy on the Web. But what exactly are they? They are simply small applications written in the Java programming language. Yes, Java is an entire programming language developed by Sun Microsystems, Inc. (For the propeller-heads reading this, it's similar to C++ but without pointers.) Java lets developers create platform-independent multimedia applications for distribution on the Web. With Netscape Navigator 3.0, you can visit sites that include Java applets (or even full-blown applications) and actually run them.

Since Java applets are cross-platform, you run the same code on a Mac as you do on a Windows 3.1 or Windows NT machine. When you get to a Web page that includes Java applets, you don't have to choose which version to link to. And since Netscape was in the technological vanguard in supporting Java, you don't need a special helper application to interpret the Java code—Navigator 3.0 does it all.

With traditional Internet and World Wide Web content, the focus is mainly only one-way—from the server to the user. It's similar to the cable television that comes into your house. You can receive data from this cable, but you cannot transmit data back through it. We've seen that forms allow for some two-way interactivity, but Java really opens up the possibilities. When Java applets are integrated with a Web browser, such as Netscape Navigator 3.0, you can experience live information updating, interaction with other users, and instant interaction with Internet servers.

Java applets are embedded in Web pages (using the APPLET HTML tag) and automatically downloaded by Netscape Navigator 3.0 to your computer. A Java run-time application included in Netscape Navigator 3.0 executes the Java applet and enables you to interact with the applet.

As more and more developers acquire Java programming skills, and more and more people start using browsers like Netscape Navigator 3.0 that support Java, Web sites will begin to include them. In fact, they may become as plentiful as graphics and other files you encounter on the Web now. For this reason, you need to know how to interact with Java applets when you encounter them.

Interacting With Java Applets

When you arrive at a site that includes a Java applet, you really don't have to do anything special. Netscape Navigator 3.0 does all the work. Information that Navigator needs for running the Java applet is embedded in the HTML documents using the <APPLET> tag. Netscape Navigator 3.0 automatically downloads and interprets the applet. A complete download may take several minutes. Once the applet arrives on your machine, you interact with it per the individual applet's instructions.

Figure 9-11 shows a Java crossword puzzle that lets you actually enter words.

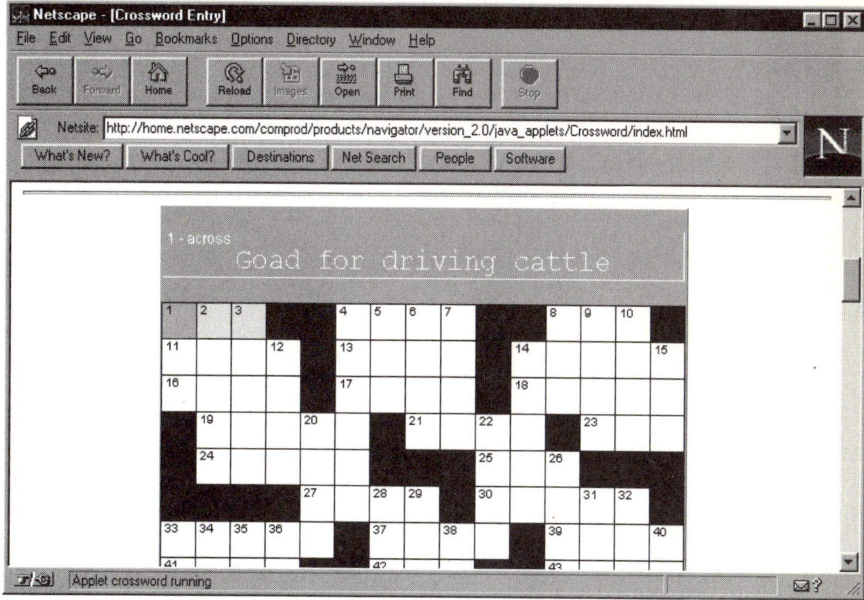

Figure 9-11: A Java crossword puzzle that enables real-time interaction.

If you scroll up the window you'll see that this Java applet, like many others, includes a list of instructions:

```
How to play:
1) The current word you are working on is highlighted in yellow.
2) The current letter is highlighted in cyan.
3) Click on any letter to move to that word.
4) <Spacebar> switches between across and down. It pivots around the current
letter.
5) <Back space> erases the current letter.
6) Incorrect letters are drawn in red.
```

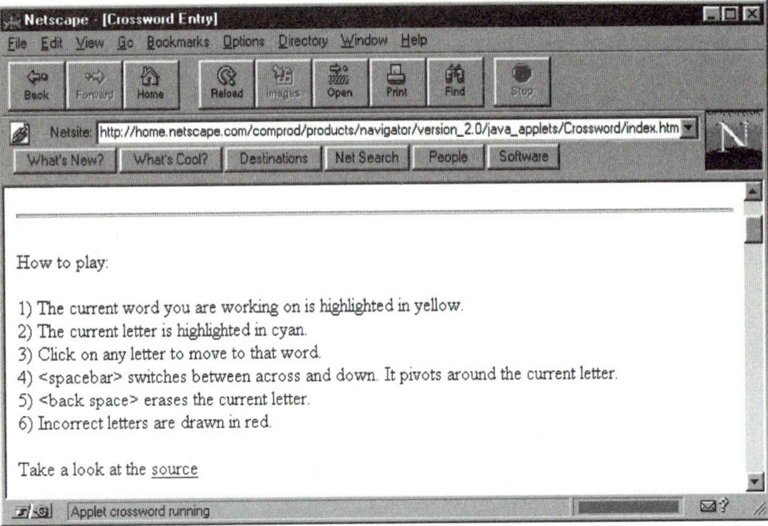

Figure 9-12: Instructions for the Crossword Puzzle applet.

As you can see, you fill out the crossword puzzle right while it's displayed in Netscape Navigator 3.0. You can type in letters, delete letters, and move from one box to another using your mouse and keyboard. The main difference between this type of application and a crossword puzzle that may have appeared earlier on the Internet is that the Java applet lets you interact with it directly in Netscape Navigator 3.0. Previously you would have had to download a file that runs separately from Netscape Navigator 3.0.

If you're interested in taking a look at some more Java applets, you can do so by visiting one of the sites listed in Table 9-1. These sites include one or several applets that automatically display in the Netscape Navigator 3.0 window. Remember that most Java applets are interactive, so get in there with your mouse.

Another great resource that has sprung up over the past few months is the Gamelan Java Directory at http://www.gamelan.com/. This Web site is full of links and resources to Java sites and development news. If you're serious about Java, either as a developer or end user, you need to check out this site every so often to see what's new on the Java front.

Applet	Where You Find It
Blinking Text	http://www.javasoft.com/applets/applets/Blink/example1.html
Curve	http://fas.sfu.ca:80/1/cs/people/GradStudents/heinrica/personal/curve.html
Crossword	http://home.netscape.com/comprod/products/navigator/version_2.0/java_applets/Crossword/index.html
Financial Portfolio Demo	http://www.javasoft.com/applets/applets/StockDemo/standalone.html
Imagemap	http://www.javasoft.com/applets/applets/ImageMap/example1.html
Modern Clock	http://www.wsrn.com/southern/java/DateClock.html
Pythagoras	http://home.netscape.com/comprod/products/navigator/version_2.0/java_applets/Pythagoras/index.html
Simple 3D Viewer	http://www.javasoft.com/applets/applets/WireFrame/example1.html
StarField	http://home.netscape.com/comprod/products/navigator/version_2.0/java_applets/StarField/index.html
Traditional Clock	http://www.javasoft.com/applets/applets/Clock/index.html

Table 9-1: Some Java applets and where to find them.

Are Java Applets Safe?

Yes, for the most part. Applets are written in a Java language subset that includes several security precautions. For instance, applets can't perform most file system access or file I/O routines. These precautions, however, do not absolutely guarantee that a developer intent on breaking into your system can't do so.

Another form of security is in the Netscape Navigator 3.0 browser itself. Select Network Preferences from the Options menu and then click the Languages tab, shown in Figure 9-13. Notice the Disable Java check box. Netscape Navigator 3.0 offers this option so that you can disable Java support for those times you want to download a Java applet to your machine but then cut off the network transactions back to the server (you can also disconnect from the Internet and run the applet locally). When you leave the option unchecked, this means you want full access to Java applets so you can initiate a two-way communication between your client and the server machine. By default, this setting is cleared to enable full Java access.

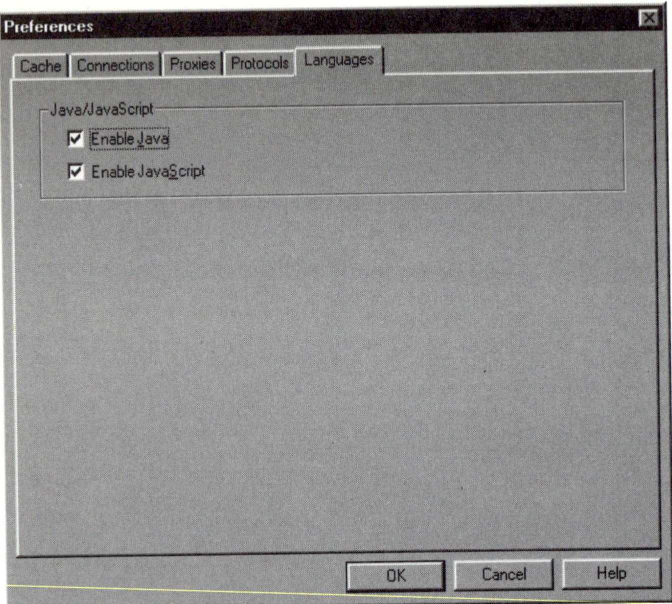

Figure 9-13: The Languages tab.

TIP

You can disable JavaScript here as well. Please refer to the upcoming section on JavaScript.

Creating Your Own Applets

For those interested in developing Java applets, you can obtain Sun's official documentation and the Java API (application programming interface) from http://java.sun.com/aboutJava/index.html. Remember, this is a serious programming language. If you don't have any previous experience with C++ or a similar object-oriented language, now's the time to go out and buy a book about programming in Java.

Java is what's known in the computer industry as a "cool new feature." It's not just something that's needed to perform a particular task—it also looks toward the future and has a strong element of fun to it. What you can do with Java is limited only by your imagination.

TIP

For detailed technical information on a particular Java applet, click the Show Java Console item in Netscape Navigator 3.0's Options menu.

JavaScript

As you travel around the Web, you may notice some user interface niceties that don't seem part of regular old HTML. For instance, there might be some text in your Navigator 3.0 status bar that ties in with the Web page you're viewing. Or words may scroll across the browser window. Or when you type a bogus area code into a form, a message pops up telling you your entry isn't valid. Some of the following material may be of interest to you only if you are planning to create your own Web pages. Once you have a basic understanding of what JavaScript is, feel free to skip over the technical stuff!

If you wonder how the author of the Web page is pulling off these tricks, a good guess would be JavaScript. You can think of JavaScript as "Java Lite": a language that's less powerful than Java but easier to use. While Java programs are independent binary files compiled using special Java programming tools, entire JavaScript programs may be entered directly into an HTML page with a simple text editor. Navigator 3.0 simply interprets the new commands on the fly. Table 9-2 points out some of the differences between Java and JavaScript.

JavaScript	Java
Code is human-readable and embedded right in HTML file.	Java applets are separate from HTML pages.
Interpreted by Navigator 3.0—not compiled.	Compiled on server.
Uses objects, but does not support classes or inheritance.	Completely object-oriented. Applets are made up of object classes that support inheritance.
No need to declare data type of variables.	Strong typing: data types need to be declared.
References to objects checked dynamically at run-time.	Static binding at compile time.

Table 9-2: Differences between Java and JavaScript.

Whoa! In case you're not a programmer, let me put that in plain English: Java is for the big stuff, JavaScript is for smaller effects. Java requires special development tools and a solid understanding of object-oriented programming concepts, while you can probably add some simple JavaScript to your own Web pages after a few hours of playing around.

LiveConnect

LiveConnect is a new Navigator 3.0 technology that lets plug-ins, JavaScripts, and Java applets interact with each other. For example, thanks to LiveConnect, clicking a button in a Web page could start up separate video and audio plug-in files that are perfectly synced. Or it might start a brief movie, which could then trigger a sound file. In other words, LiveConnect allows for real-time integration of various separate media files and interactive JavaScripts or applets.

JavaScript Nuts & Bolts

There are two ways that JavaScript can be embedded in HTML scripts. First, a Web author can use the <SCRIPT> tag. Here's a simple example:

```
<HTML>
<HEAD>
<SCRIPT LANGUAGE="JavaScript"> document.write("Everybody ? loves")
</SCRIPT>
</HEAD>
<BODY>
Netscape Navigator 3.0!
</BODY>
</HTML>
```

Yep, you guessed it: what appears on your screen is the phrase "Everybody loves Netscape Navigator 3.0!" OK, you would never really *do* it that way, but at least this gives you an idea of how it works. As you can see, the SCRIPT tag is inside the HEAD area of the document. Now just imagine that instead of using the predefined *document.write* function, we had used something more interesting. How about a function that scrolls the words across your browser window in rainbow colors?

Or here's a more practical example using a square function you define yourself:

```
<HTML>
<HEAD>
<SCRIPT LANGUAGE="JavaScript">
function square(i) {
```

```
    document.write("What number is to be squared: ", i,"<BR>")
      return i * i
    }
    document.write("The result of this calculation is: ? ",square(2),".")
</SCRIPT>
</HEAD>
<BODY>
<BR>
The script is all finished calculating the square.
</BODY>
</HTML>
```

The result?

```
What number is to be squared: 2
The result of this calculation is 4.
The script is all finished calculating the square.
```

If you study the code a little, you can see that it defines the square function as one that first prints the phrase "What number is to be squared?", then accepts a number from the user, then multiplies that number by itself and returns the result. Once defined like this, the function may be used anywhere later in the document.

The <SCRIPT> tag is pretty convenient, but there is also an even more powerful way of working with the language: *event handlers*. This sounds pretty techie, but it's actually quite simple. Netscape Navigator 3.0 obviously recognizes when a user performs some action such as clicking on a word or phrase. With JavaScript, you can associate chunks of code with actions (or events). In other words, when a user clicks on a word, JavaScript knows to do something. Take a look at this example:

```
<INPUT TYPE="button" VALUE="Add It Up Now" onClick="AddItUp(this.form)">
```

This snippet of code executes a function called AddItUp whenever you click on the button labeled "Add It Up." It could be used to add all the numbers you'd previously entered in a form.

JavaScript can use *properties* such as "visible" and "color" to return your specified response. You might, for example, design a Web page that includes listings and descriptions of your products. Let's say you sell countertops, and each model of countertop comes in various styles, textures, and colors. Customers to your site may want to design a virtual kitchen by mixing and matching colors and textures with different countertops and other fixtures. With JavaScript, you can include a selector that enables users to adjust the colors and textures of specific countertops. You could create the entire site as a Java applet, but why not use Java only where necessary (such as for creating the virtual kitchen and countertop and the selector). Then use JavaScript to change the colors and textures of the countertop in the applet.

What's New in JavaScript for Navigator 3.0

If you've already done some JavaScript programming with earlier versions of Netscape Navigator, you might be interested in what's changed for version 3.0. Besides general improvements in performance, here are two very exciting new features:

- JavaScript can now change JPEG and GIF images "on the fly." Imagine staring at a picture of Al Gore that suddenly turns into Madonna. (Frightening visual image, isn't it?) Graphics can change automatically at a particular interval or when the viewer clicks a button or icon.
- JavaScript can now detect whether or not a plug-in is available and adjust the Web page accordingly. For instance, suppose a page includes a fancy 3D-animated image that requires a plug-in you don't have. JavaScript could figure this out and substitute a plain old GIF or JPEG.

TIP

For a more comprehensive and up-to-date user reference on JavaScript, see the Netscape Navigator 3.0 reference at http://home.netscape.com/comprod/products/navigator/version_3.0/script/script_info/index.html. You can find the JavaScript Authoring Guide at that location.

In Conclusion

I hope that this book has helped guide you through the starting phase of your online journey; you've seen and heard much of what the Internet and the World Wide Web have to offer, and you've learned how to search for new sources of information, education, and entertainment throughout cyberspace.

The Internet and the Web, however, are constantly changing landscapes. As new technologies are born and cultivated, it's important to remember that site where we started—www.netscape.com—where you'll always find the latest version of Navigator, the newest and best links to other Web sites, and news on what's on the horizon.

Good luck and good exploring!

Glossary

access privileges—A user's rights on a host. Typically users are allowed to create or edit files only in their home directories, though they can run programs from public directories.

account—An agreement with an organization allowing you to take advantage of various services. For instance, an account on an e-mail server lets you log on to send and receive e-mail. Accounts are often protected by *authentication*, requiring that you type in a user name and password.

activate—To make a window the active one by clicking on it.

active window—The window with the highlighted title bar, where the user is currently interacting with a program.

ACU—*Automatic Call Unit.* Fancy word for a modem.

addressing—The assignment of unique names or numbers to every node on a network so that information doesn't get misdelivered.

agents—Search tool that automatically seeks out online information based on your queries. Also called intelligent agents, knowbots, and droids.

algorithm—The step-by-step process a software program uses to produce its results.

alias—An alternate name used in place of a "real" one. Rather than using your real name to log in to a system, you probably use a shorter alias. Commands can also have aliases. For instance, you can create command files on a UNIX system so that instead of typing **ls -al** to see all the files in your directory, you could just type **dir**.

American Standard Code for Information Interchange—*See* **ASCII**.

anchor—In HTML, the target of a link. It is sometimes also used to mean any link.

Apple menu—The menu which contains shortcut commands to any number of control panels, applications, system extensions, and desk accessories. The Apple menu can be configured to become your "mission control" point for efficient operation on your system. The menu is designed with the Apple symbol in the far left corner of the menu bar.

application protocol—A **protocol** that "sits on top of" the underlying transport layer of a communications system. For example, **FTP** and **Telnet** are application protocols that format data in particular ways and use the services of the lower-level **TCP/IP** transport layer.

Archie—A network service used for locating files available at **FTP** sites that accept anonymous logins.

ARP—*Address Resolution Protocol.* Protocol used on a network for mapping Ethernet addresses to IP addresses.

ARPAnet—A wide area network developed in the 1960s by the Advanced Research Projects Agency of the U.S. Department of Defense. It links government and academic networks around the world.

ASCII—*American Standard Code for Information Interchange.* This standard assigns a binary value to common text and control characters. ASCII is used for manipulating text in a program and for transmitting text to other devices or systems.

ASCII file—A human-readable file made up only of letters, numbers, and symbols. An ASCII file contains no formatting except tabs, linefeeds, and carriage returns. Also known as a *text file.*

assigned numbers—The usual port numbers for well-known Internet services such as **Telnet**, **FTP**, and so on. For instance, hosts usually wait for Telnet connections on TCP port 23, for World Wide Web connections on port 80, and for Usenet news connections on port 119. These assigned port numbers are how the host knows what kind of connection is being requested.

asynchronous transmission—The transmission of data without special timing information. Each character you transmit is made up of several bits of information. In asynchronous communications, the characters are "packaged," usually by special start and stop bits, so that the receiving hardware or software knows when it has received an entire character. This way, the interval *between* characters doesn't have to be fixed, and information can arrive at any time. *See also* **synchronous transmission**.

attribute (text)—The display characteristics of text. Text attributes include bold, italic, underlined, and so on. In **World Wide Web** documents, text may be tagged with a wide variety of attributes using **HTML**.

AU sound—Audio format developed by Sun and used for sound files on the Web. Netscape browsers play AU files using the helper program NAPLAYER.

authentication—The process of identifying a user to determine if he or she should have access to a particular computer system. Name and password prompts are a form of authentication.

authoring software—Any software that lets you create HTML or other multimedia documents.

bandwidth—The range of frequencies that can be transmitted over a network, limited by the hardware. Higher bandwidth allows more information on the network at one time.

baud rate—The number of signal changes per second as data is transmitted from one device to another. For instance, 110 transitions per second from a high frequency to a low frequency on a phone line would be 110 baud. Each signal change may signify one bit of data (for instance, high frequency to low could signify 1, low to high could signify 0); if a signal changes in multiple ways (frequency, amplitude, etc.), it may signify multiple bits of data. In the first case, baud rate would equal **bits per second**; in the second case, bits per second would be higher than the baud rate. The difference between baud rate and bits per second is a common icebreaker at nerd parties.

BBS—*See* **bulletin board system**.

binary—Numbers composed of combinations of two different digits, specifically 1 and 0. In the context of this book, binary data means information that may contain the full range of combinations of binary digits in a **byte**, as opposed to information that contains only the limited range of information that is displayable as text. Bytes of **ASCII** text contain only seven significant **data bits**, as in 1011001, while programs, graphics, spreadsheet files, and so on, contain eight significant data bits per byte, as in 10011011. Any files that cannot be read as text are considered binary files.

BIND—*Berkeley Internet Name Domain* server. This is the DNS server on BSD and related UNIX systems. *See also* **DNS**.

BinHex—A file format, used mainly in the Macintosh world, for storing and transmitting binary data as **ASCII** text. This format is useful for transferring 8-bit data over 7-bit networks or data paths, or for including binary files as part of mail messages. Among UNIX and PC users, **UUENCODING** is more common.

bit—A *b*inary dig*it*, the smallest piece of information that a computer can hold. A bit is always one of two values, written as 1 or 0 and corresponding to the on/off state of a digital switch or the high/low state of electrical impulses. Combinations of bits are used to represent more complex information, such as **ASCII** text or commands to the computer.

bitmap—A representation of an image as an array of bits.

bit rate—The rate at which bits are transmitted, usually expressed as a certain number of **bits per second**, or bps. *See also* **baud rate**.

bits per second—*See* **bit rate**.

bookmarks—In Netscape browsers, a means of permanently storing the **URL**s for sites you want to revisit.

bridge—(1) A device or a combination of hardware and software for connecting networks together. (2) Something that goes over troubled water. *See also* **Internet**.

bulk cipher—An **encryption** method used to encrypt large quantities of information.

bulletin board system (BBS)—An electronic version of the old cork bulletin—a place to leave and collect messages and files. A modern BBS is really like a whole collection of bulletin boards, with different sections covering different areas of interest. Users can generally exchange public as well as private messages, and many BBSes include extensive areas for distributing shareware or public domain software.

board—a place to leave and collect messages and files. A modern BBS is really like a whole collection of bulletin boards, with different sections covering different areas of interest. Users can generally exchange public as well as private messages, and many BBSes include extensive areas for distributing shareware or public domain software.

byte—A combination of **bits** used to represent a single character. In the world of personal computers, a byte is 8 bits long.

cable—A bundle of wires or fiber strands wrapped with insulation and used to connect devices.

cache—An area of memory or a file used to store frequently accessed instructions or data. A memory cache is used to reduce hard disk access time. Memory and file caches are also used by Web browsers and other online programs to store images or data that rarely change; thus, a large home page does not have to be re-sent each time a connection is established.

carrier—A steady background signal on a communication channel used to indicate that the system is ready for the transmission of data. The carrier is then modified to represent the data transmitted.

Certifying Authorities—Organizations that distribute **Digital Certificates**.

CGI—*Common Gateway Interface.* A standardized technique that lets Web clients pass information to Web servers, and then on to other programs that process the information. When a Web site accepts the information you enter into a form, it is using CGI.

character entities—In HTML, special symbols that stand for other characters. Character entities begin with an ampersand (&) and end with a semicolon (;). For example, *>* in an HTML document would appear on your screen as > (greater than).

check box—A Windows 95 and Windows NT control that lets you choose a particular option by clicking. Once you click, an X or checkmark appears in the check box; click again and it is cleared.

CIX—*Commercial Internet Exchange.* CIX is an agreement among Internet service providers allowing them to make the Internet available to commercial traffic.

Clear To Send—A signal from a **DCE** to a **DTE** indicating that circuits are ready for data transmission. *See also* **DCE**; **DTE**.

clickable image—In a Web page, an image you can click in order to access a different URL. *See also* **image map**.

client—A computer or a software program that can access particular services on a network. The machine or the software that provides the service for a client is called a **server**. For instance, an e-mail client would request received mail from an e-mail server.

client pull—A method specific to Netscape products whereby a Web client can request the Web server to send it a particular set of data. *See also* **server push**.

client/server architecture—A system in which a **client** program establishes a connection with a **server** and then requests information or services. *See also* **client**; **server**.

client write key—The software key used to encrypt data written or transmitted by the client in a **client/server** system.

Clipboard or clipboard—An area of memory where objects (data) are placed when a user carries out a Cut or Copy command or chooses a menu option. This data can then be passed to another program.

column heading—A Windows 95 and Windows NT control that displays data in a multicolumn list.

combo box—A standard Windows 95 and Windows NT control that combines a text box and a list box.

command button—A control used to initiate a command; also known as a push button.

command prompt—A set of characters or a symbol that indicates where you type in commands. The DOS C:\ prompt is an example of a command prompt.

computer name—On Microsoft networks, a unique name of up to 15 characters that identifies a particular computer on the network.

configuration registry—In Windows 95 and Windows NT, a database that stores information about a computer's configuration as well as the configuration of various software. The registry may be edited by using the program *regedit* in Windows 95 or *regedt32* in Windows NT.

connect time—The amount of time you're connected to a host or to a service provider.

connection—A link between two computers for the purpose of transferring or sharing information.

container—Any screen object that holds other objects; for instance, a folder.

content-type—The MIME name for particular types of files to be transferred by e-mail or the Web. For instance, the content-type for a GIF file is **image/gif**. *See also* **MIME**.

control—Any window object that lets you interact with a program by selecting an action, inputting data, and so on.

Control menu—The menu that pops up when you click the icon at the top left of a program's main window. It contains commands such as Move, Size, Maximize, Minimize, and Close.

crawler—*See* **spider**.

CSLIP—A common variant of the SLIP protocol that uses compressed IP headers. *See also* **SLIP**.

cyberspace—A slightly dated term referring to the entire world of online information and services. It was originally coined by the writer William Gibson.

daemon—UNIX-speak for a program that's always running on a server machine, waiting for requests for a particular service. For instance, an FTP server daemon sits and waits for an FTP client to connect and request files.

data—Information used or processed by a software program.

data bits—Bits that carry information as opposed to control information. For example, the bits in the middle of a **byte** might signify a text character and are, therefore, data bits, while the bits at the beginning and end of the byte merely mark the beginning and end of the data.

Data Carrier Detect (DCD or CD)—A signal from a **DCE**, such as a modem, to a **DTE**, such as a PC, indicating that a communication channel has been established with a remote device. *See also* **DCE**; **DTE**.

data-file object—An object representing a data file (spreadsheet, document, image, sound clip, etc.) in the file system.

Data Terminal Ready (DTR)—A signal from a DTE to a DCE indicating that it's ready to receive and transmit data. Usually, a modem keeps DTR high as long as it's turned on. *See also* **DCE**; **DTE**.

DCE—*Data Communication Equipment*. A device used by a **DTE** to transmit and receive information. Your modem is a DCE.

DDE—*See* **dynamic data exchange**.

default—In software, the "out of the box" value of a configuration option. The software will use this value unless the user explicitly indicates a different one in a setup program, property sheet, or .INI file.

desktop—The visual work area that fills your screen and holds the objects you interact with, such as icons, the task bar, and so on. The desktop is a container (or folder) that can also be used as a convenient place to access files.

destination directory—The directory to which you copy, move, or download a file or files.

device driver—A program used by the system to access devices such as video cards, printers, and mice.

dialog box—In Windows 95 and Windows NT, a box that appears on your screen requesting your input; it engages you in a *dialogue* with the software. It may contain edit fields, check boxes, list boxes, radio buttons, and so on, and it stays on your screen until you click its Cancel or OK button.

dial-up networking—A facility built into Windows 95 that allows users to link to a network or to the Internet using phone lines. Similar to **Remote Access Dialer** in Windows NT.

Digital Certificate—A unique electronic key that identifies you and authorizes you to access secure Web sites.

dimmed—A button, menu item, or other control is dimmed or *grayed* (displayed in light gray instead of black) to indicate it represents an option or command that is not currently available.

direct connection—A permanent connection between a computer and the Internet as opposed to a temporary dial-up or **SLIP/PPP** connection.

directory—A structure on a disk that contains files or other subdirectories. Also sometimes referred to as a folder.

directory tree—A hierarchical display of a disk's directories and subdirectories.

DNS—*Domain Name Service,* an Internet service that returns the appropriate **IP address** when queried with a **domain-name address**.

dock—To configure a toolbar so that it no longer floats, but lines up with the edge of a window or pane.

document (World Wide Web)—On the **World Wide Web**, a file or set of related files that can be transferred from a **Web server** to a Web **client.** The document may contain text, graphics, sound, or hyperlinks to other documents.

document encoding—*See* **encoding**.

document window—A window that lets you view the contents of a document.

domain—A collection of associated computers on the Internet, given a specific domain name that is used as part of the Internet address. For Windows NT Server, a domain is also a uniquely named collection of computers that share a domain database and security policy.

domain-name address—The "plain English" address of a computer on the Internet, as opposed to its numeric **IP address**. For instance, www.echonyc.com is a domain-name address.

download—To get a file or files from a remote computer; the opposite of **upload**.

drag—To move a mouse while pressing and holding one of its buttons. Dragging is used to move or resize objects on the screen.

droids—*See* **agents**.

drop-down combo box—A Windows 95 and Windows NT control that combines a text box with a drop-down list box.

drop-down list box—A Windows 95 and Windows NT control that displays a current text selection, but that can be opened to display the entire list of choices.

drop-down menu—A menu that is displayed from a menu bar.

DSU—*Digital Services Unit*. The piece of equipment that enables transmission of data in synchronous digital connections to the Net.

DTE—*Data Terminal Equipment*. A device that serves as the originating point or the final destination of information. Typically, a computer or a terminal is a DTE.

dynamic data exchange (DDE)—The exchange of data between programs such that any change in the data in one program affects that same data in the other program. For instance, if spreadsheet data are shared via DDE by Word and Excel, any changes made to the data in Excel will also appear in the Word document.

edit field—*See* **text box**.

electronic mail—A network service for transmitting messages from one computer to another. Also called *e-mail*.

ellipsis—The ". . ." added to a menu item or button label to show that the command needs more information to be completed. When you choose a command with an ellipsis, a dialog box appears so you can enter additional information.

encoding—The technique used for storing or expressing data. For instance, text may be stored via ASCII encoding or some form of encoding that uses compression (such as ZIP). In Web browsers, document encoding refers to the translation of incoming characters into display fonts. For instance, you may set Netscape browsers to Japanese encoding so that information in a Japanese HTML document will be correctly displayed.

encryption—A method of **encoding** information for secure transmission. The data can be read in its original form only after it has been decoded. *See also* **public-key encryption**.

environment variable—A symbolic name associated with a string of characters used by an operating system or programs for its own informational purposes. For instance, the environment variable GIF_DIRECTORY could be set to C:\GIF so that a graphics program knows where to look for GIF files. Typically, you set an environment variable by using the Set command at a command prompt or in a batch file. In Windows NT, you can use the System option in Control Panel to define environment variables.

Ethernet—A hardware system and a protocol that is commonly used to connect computers on a LAN.

external viewer—A separate program used by a **World Wide Web** browser to display graphics or to play sound or video files. After downloading a particular media file, the Web browser launches the external viewer program appropriate to the type of file. In order for this to work, you must configure your Web browser with the names of the external viewer programs you have on your system. Another term for external viewer is **helper application**.

extension—The period and characters at the end of a file or directory name, often used to indicate the type of file or directory. For instance, INDEX.HTML includes the .HTML extension to indicate it is an HTML document.

e-zine—A zine, or small non-mass-market magazine in electronic format. Some e-zines are text files distributed via electronic mail or posted on a BBS; others are Web pages with extensive graphics and even sounds.

FAQ—Abbreviation for *frequently asked question*. FAQs are lists of frequently asked questions (and their answers) in a particular topic area. For instance, a Windows NT FAQ would help users understand the basics of using Windows NT by providing answers to common questions. Most mailing lists and network newsgroups regularly provide updated FAQs. It is important to read the FAQ for a particular newsgroup before beginning to post messages.

file—A named collection of **ASCII** or **binary** information stored on a disk or other storage device. Files include text, programs, databases, spreadsheets, graphics, and so on.

file server—A computer that provides storage space for files and applications that may be shared by network users.

file system—In an operating system such as Windows 95 or Windows NT, the structure used for storing, organizing, and naming files.

file transfer protocol—Any **protocol** for transferring files from one computer to another. A file transfer protocol usually includes provisions for making sure the data was transferred without errors and for resending any blocks of information that were corrupt.

finger—A UNIX program that lets you retrieve basic information about an Internet user or host. Finger is available via the Web at various sites.

flag—A characteristic of a file that may restrict its use in particular ways. A file may be flagged read-only, for instance.

flame—A public message on any electronic forum, such as a **BBS** or online service, that personally attacks another user. Usually a flame is in response to an earlier message. If the user who has been flamed responds with another flame, or if other users jump into the fray, a "flame war" ensues. Flaming, though common in **Usenet** newsgroups, is generally considered an obnoxious waste of other users' time and of network bandwidth.

folder—A container that holds and organizes objects, typically files or other folders. On the desktop, a folder may represent a directory in the file system; other folders within it are equivalent to subdirectories.

font—A particular style for displayed or printed characters, including the shape, weight, slant, and so on.

font size—The size of a **font**; typically represented in units of measurement called *points*.

FQDN—*Fully Qualified Domain Name.* The full domain name of a computer on the Internet, including both the host name and the domain name. *See also* **domain-name address**.

frame—A portion of a Web browser window that may contain a different document from other frames within the same window.

FTP—Abbreviation for *File Transfer Protocol.* A particular file transfer protocol that is common on the Internet. It is also used as a verb, as in, "FTP me that file, wouldya?"

full duplex—A communications link in which both ends can transmit data simultaneously, as in a telephone conversation. In situations where you are working interactively online, full duplex communication lets a remote host echo back to you each character you type so that you can see what you're writing as you work. *See also* **half duplex**.

FYI—*For Your Information.* A series of technical documents on various Internet-related topics, available at many public FTP sites. *See also* **RFC**.

gateway—A device or the software that links networks that use different protocols. For instance, a Novell network might have an Internet gateway that "packages" information into the **TCP/IP** packets required for Internet communication. The term *gateway* is also used in a very specialized sense to mean a program on a **World Wide Web** host that accepts and processes information sent by a Web client. For instance, a document on a **Web server** might display a form in which you can type your name; the gateway program would then enter your name in a database.

GIF—(Pronounced "jiff.") Abbreviation for *Graphic Interchange Format*. This is a format for compressed graphic files developed by CompuServe and Unisys.

Gopher—A menu-based client/server system for exploring information resources on the Internet. A Gopher client is seamlessly built into Web browsers, so you don't need a separate Gopher client program.

GopherSpace—All of the information presented by a **Gopher** server, in the form of directory and file menus.

grayed—*See* **dimmed**.

half duplex—A communications link in which both ends can transmit and receive data, but not at the same time. Half duplex communication is like two-way radio or CB, where only one person speaks at a time. In situations where you are working interactively online in half duplex, you will not see characters you type echoed to the screen unless you set your communications program to echo them locally. *See also* **full duplex**.

handle—An interface element added to an object to enable the user to move, resize, or reshape it.

handshaking—The initial negotiation and the exchange of control information between a **DCE** and a **DTE** or between two DTEs in a communications link. Handshaking is necessary to make sure both devices are ready to transfer data and can "understand" each other. *See also* **Data Carrier Detect; Data Terminal Ready; XOFF; XON**.

hardware handshake—A protocol whereby a **DTE** tells the connected computer to start or stop sending data. Typically, hardware handshaking is implemented by raising and lowering the voltage on the DTR (**Data Terminal Ready**) line in the cable that connects the **DTE** and **DCE**. *See also* **XOFF; XON**.

helper applications—Programs that a Web browser such as Netscape Navigator 3.0 uses to perform tasks such as displaying particular types of graphics, playing sounds, or initiating Telnet sessions.

history list—In Netscape Navigator 3.0, the list of Web documents you've displayed during the current session.

home page—The **HTML** document you choose to display when you open a **Web browser** such as Netscape Navigator 3.0. It may be located on your own hard drive or on a remote **Web server**. Home page can also refer to the top-level document at a particular Web site.

host computer—A computer that a user can connect to in order to access information or run programs. A user may log in locally using a **terminal** or remotely using a computer and phone lines or the Internet.

host name—The name clients use to access your Web server or other Internet server. For instance, your Web server's host name might be www.acme.com.

hotlist—In a **Web browser**, a user-built list of frequently accessed **World Wide Web** sites. Also, an **HTML** document consisting of hotlinks to Web sites or other Internet resources.

HTML—Abbreviation for *Hypertext Markup Language*. A "markup language" for indicating attributes and links in a Web document. An HTML **tag** may tell a Web browser program how to display a piece of text or a graphic, or it may direct the browser to another file or document.

HTTP—*Hypertext Transfer Protocol*. The **protocol** that World Wide Web **clients** and **servers** use to communicate with each other.

hypermedia—**Hypertext** that also includes nontext information such as graphics, video, or sound.

hypertext—Text that is organized by means of links, or jumps, from one piece of information to another. The reader can move among related topics by clicking on tagged words or phrases.

IAB–*Internet Architecture Board*. The organization that decides on Internet standards.

icon—An image used to represent an object such as a file or program.

image map—A graphic in a Web document that lets you click on certain portions in order to activate particular **URLs**. It has an associated map file that identifies these hot spots. *See also* **clickable image**.

inactive window—A window with which you are not currently interacting. Its title bar is not highlighted, and it receives no keyboard or mouse input. *See also* **active window**.

inline images—Graphic images contained within **World Wide Web** documents. An inline image displays automatically as part of a document when it is retrieved; a non-inline image must be retrieved by clicking on a **hotlink**.

intelligent agents—*See* **agents**.

internet—A larger network made up of two or more connected LANs (**local area networks**) or WANs (**wide area networks**).

Internet—The huge worldwide Internet made up of cooperative networks and using **TCP/IP** protocols to offer a variety of services.

Internet access provider—A business or organization that provides Internet access to consumers, often via dial-up **SLIP** or **PPP** connections. Also known as an **ISP**, or Internet Service Provider.

Internet address—*See* **IP address**.

Internet presence provider—An Internet-connected business that provides equipment and services to customers without equipment or technical expertise.

IP address—Also called *Internet address*. The unique address for each computer on the Internet. The IP address appears as a set of four numbers separated by periods.

ISDN—*Integrated Services Digital Network.* The telecommunications standard that supports digital transmission of voice, video, and data over phone lines.

ISOC—*Internet Society.* Organization that was formed to support a worldwide information network. The ISOC sponsors the **IAB**.

ISP—*Internet Service Provider.* Another term for an **Internet access provider**.

IPP—*See* **Internet Presence Provider**.

Java—An object-oriented programming language developed by Sun Microsystems. It allows developers to create applications that may be run from within Web browsers such as Netscape Navigator 3.0.

JavaScript—A set of commands that can be added to HTML files to add functionality to Web documents. JavaScript is useful for scrolling text, data validation in forms, etc.

JPEG—A format for compressed graphics files. JPEG graphics are commonly used as part of **World Wide Web** documents.

kbyte—*See* **kilobyte**.

kilobyte (K)—1024 (2^{10}) **bytes** of data. Thus, a 64K file consists of 65,536 bytes.

knowbot—A software program that can retrieve information from a variety of electronic sources when you give it a set of search parameters. Same as **agent**.

LAN—*See* **local area network**.

link—A special hidden **tag** in an HTML document on the Web. It includes the **URL** for another file or document, or for another anchor point within the same document. When you click a word, phrase, or graphic that's tagged as a link, Netscape Navigator 3.0 automatically retrieves the appropriate target.

list box—A control that displays a scrollable list of choices.

Live3D—Netscape's **VRML** technology.

LiveConnect—Netscape technology that allows Navigator plug-ins, Java applets, and JavaScript to communicate with each other.

local area network (LAN)—A group of computers connected together by cable or wireless transceivers so that users can share resources such as database files, programs, printers, and so on. *See also* **wide area network**.

log file—A file that is automatically generated by software, indicating events that occurred such as errors, attempts to access your server, etc.

log in—To identify yourself to a remote system or network by typing in your login name and password.

login name—The name you use for security verification when you call into a remote system.

login prompt—The prompt (usually *login:* or *name:*) a remote host uses to tell you it's ready for you to type in your login name.

logon script—A file containing simple commands that automate the process of logging on to a server, **SLIP** or **PPP** account, or other computer. In Windows NT, the files SWITCH.INF and MODEM.INF are logon scripts that automate the process of logging on to a remote machine using the **Remote Access Dialer**. In Windows 95, logon scripts generally have a .SCP extension and are associated with particular **Dial-Up Networking** connections using Microsoft's Dial-Up Scripting utility.

log off—To tell a remote host system or a network, using the appropriate commands, that you are terminating interaction. In many cases, logging off will also break the communications link to the remote machine.

log on—To tell a remote system or network, using the appropriate commands, that you are initiating a session.

maximize—To expand a window to its maximum size. *See also* **minimize**.

maximize button—The button used to maximize a window. In Windows 95 and Windows NT 4.0, it is the second button from the right in the title bar.

megabyte (MB)—1024 **kilobytes**, or 1,048,576 bytes.

menu bar—A horizontal bar at the top of a window (between the title bar and the rest of the window) that contains menu choices. *See also* **drop-down menu**.

menu button—A command button that displays a menu.

menu item—A choice on a menu.

message box—A window that appears to inform you of something, for instance that a connection has been established or that an error has occurred.

MIME—*Multipurpose Internet Mail Extensions*. MIME is a convention for identifying different types of **binary** information, such as images or sounds, and thereby indicating the appropriate programs for viewing or playing this information. MIME is used in attaching binary files to e-mail messages so that they can be displayed or played automatically when received.

minimize—To minimize the size of a window; in some cases, this means to hide the window. *See also* **maximize**.

minimize button—The button used to minimize a window.

modem—Short for *mo*dulator/*dem*odulator. A hardware device that connects your computer to other computers using analog telephone lines.

modem command—An instruction, typed from the keyboard or transmitted automatically by a software program, that tells a modem to perform some action. For instance, the command ATH0 tells a modem to hang up the line.

Mozilla—This word stands for "Mosaic meets Godzilla." It is the name for the early Netscape products and for the Netscape-specific extensions to the HTML language. It has also become the Netscape mascot. The word and the associated image appear frequently in Netscape products.

MPEG—*Moving Pictures Expert Group*. MPEG is a standard format for compressed video files, sometimes known as "desktop movies." MPEG files may be part of **World Wide Web** documents, but they require a special **helper application** for viewing.

MUDs and MOOs—Text-based multiuser interactive games, accessed using specialized software or via **Telnet**.

multiple selection list box—A special list box that's used for multiple independent selections.

multiuser system—An operating system, such as UNIX, that lets more than one user at a time access services.

My Computer—A Windows 95 object (icon) that represents all of your local data storage.

NCSA—*National Center for Supercomputing Applications*. NCSA is the department of the University of Illinois where the Web browser Mosaic was developed. Mosaic was the forerunner of all modern graphically based Web browsers.

network—A collection of interconnected computers. Each attached computer runs its own software processes, whereas in an unnetworked **multiuser system**, users run all processes on the central host computer and use terminals simply to interact. A network lets users share information as well as devices such as printers, disks, and modems.

network administrator—In an organization, the individual who is responsible for configuring and maintaining the network. This is the person to talk to if you have problems with a direct "hard-wired" connection to the Internet.

Network Neighborhood—A Windows 95 folder that includes objects stored on a network file system.

NFS—*Network File System.* NFS is a set of protocols developed by Sun Microsystems for allowing computers running different operating systems to share files and disk storage.

NIC—*Network Information Center.* The organization responsible for supplying information about the Internet.

NOC—*Network Operations Center.* The organization in charge of the day-to-day operations of a network on the Internet.

node—Any computer or other device on a network that has its own unique network address.

NTFS—A **file system** that can be used under Windows NT. It supports a variety of advanced features including system recovery.

object—An entity that you manipulate in some way to perform a task. (Is that vague enough?) Typical objects are **icons** or **folders** on the **desktop**.

offline—Not currently connected to a remote computer.

online—Currently connected to a remote computer.

option button—A control that allows a user to select one choice from a set of mutually exclusive choices (also known as a *radio button*). *Compare* **check box**.

packet—A block of information that has been "packaged" with address information, error-checking information, and so on, for transmission on a **network** or on the **Internet**.

parameter—A variable that affects the results of a command. For instance, in the command *dir /p*, /p is a parameter.

parity—A crude system of error-checking used in data communications. For most scenarios these days, your communications software should be set to "no parity."

parsed HTML—HTML files that are read and manipulated by separate software on a server machine after the server software has answered a client request for the document. Using parsed HTML, for instance, a program could customize a Web document based on who requested it. Parsed HTML is also known as server-parsed HTML and SHTML. Often HTML files that will be parsed end with the extension .SHTML instead of .HTML.

Perl—*Practical Extraction and Report Language.* A programming language first developed by Larry Wall for UNIX systems. Because of its power in pattern matching and in handling strings, it is often the language of choice for creating **CGI** programs.

pixel—The smallest unit of graphic information on a computer screen. Graphic images are usually measured in pixels, and a pair of pixel coordinates can indicate an exact point within an image.

POP—*Point of Presence.* The local dial-up node an Internet access provider makes available for its customers.

POP3—*Post Office Protocol, version 3.* The protocol used by Netscape Navigator 3.0 and other e-mail programs to retrieve messages from your e-mail server. *See also* **SMTP**.

pop-up menu—A menu that appears right at the location of a selected object (sometimes called a *shortcut menu*). The menu contains items related to the selection.

pop-up window—A window with no title bar that appears next to an object and provides information about that object.

port—(1) A hardware connector on the back panel of a computer where you can plug in a serial, parallel, or network **cable**. (2) A unique number assigned to a particular Internet **service** on a host machine. For instance, most **MUDs** and **MOOs** require that you Telnet to a host using a specific port different from the standard Telnet port number. You can usually specify a port number as part of an Internet address, as in *lambda.parc.xerox.com 8888.*

POTS—*Plain Old Telephone Service.* What it sounds like—the current analog phone system, as distinguished from ISDN and other digital technologies.

PPP—*Point-to-Point Protocol.* This is a protocol that lets a computer link to the **Internet** by calling in to a service provider using a modem and a standard telephone line.

properties—Characteristics of an object defining its state, appearance, or value. Often used to mean a program's settings.

property inspector—A viewer that displays the properties of the current selection.

protocol—A set of rules for interaction between software programs on a network. Protocols may include requirements for formatting data, for passing control information back and forth, and for error checking.

public-key encryption—An **encryption** method that requires two unique software keys (one public and one private) for decrypting the data, making it secure across public networks. Pretty Good Privacy (PGP) is a well-known public-key encryption system.

query string—The word or phrase you pass to a Web search engine.

QuickTime—A multimedia file format developed by Apple. It is often used for video clips or "movies."

radio button—*See* **option button**.

random access memory (RAM)—Computer memory that temporarily stores information; for instance, software code that you've loaded by launching a program or data that you're processing. Generally, the more of it, the better!

read-only memory (ROM)—Computer memory containing data that cannot be changed by the user and that remains even when the computer is turned off. ROM is used for storing your computer's BIOS, for instance, which is the code that lets you boot up and that performs a variety of low-level functions.

refresh—In Netscape Web browsers such as Navigator 3.0, the command that reloads a document into the browser window from a disk or memory **cache**.

regedit—A program in Windows 95 for editing the **configuration registry**. In Windows NT this program is called regedt32.

registry—*See* **configuration registry**.

reload—In Netscape Web browsers such as Navigator 3.0, the command that reloads a document into the browser window from its original local or remote source.

remote—Any system that you can connect to by using only communications devices rather than just local wiring.

Remote Access Dialer—A Windows NT program for connecting via ordinary phone lines or **ISDN** to a remote computer, often used for **SLIP** or **PPP** connectivity.

remote computer—A computer you link to via telephone lines, satellite, or other communication links.

resolution—The density of an image, expressed in dots per inch.

restore button—The button that replaces the maximize button once a window has been maximized. It lets you return the window to the size it was before maximizing.

reverse lookup—The process of looking up the domain name of an Internet-connected computer when all that's known is the numeric IP address. For instance, you may have a numeric IP address assigned by a **SLIP** or **PPP** access provider, but no associated domain name. When you try to log in to certain security-conscious FTP sites, the host software looks up your domain name via DNS reverse lookup. If it can't find one, you are not allowed on the system. *See also* **domain-name address**.

RFC—*Request for Comments*. An RFC is a proposal or report electronically distributed via the Internet, usually for the purpose of elucidating or helping to define a new Internet technical standard.

robot—*See* **spider**.

root directory—The top-level **directory** on a disk such as your hard drive. For example, C:\ would be the root directory of your C: drive.

RS-232—The standard used by your serial port. RS-232 lines are the individual pins and wires that make up the hardware interface, such as the send data line, the receive data line, and the various hardware handshaking (or hardware flow control) lines.

RTF—*Rich Text Format.* A file format that can be read by many word processing programs across all platforms.

RTS/CTS—*Ready to Send/Clear to Send.* In an RS-232 serial port, the two lines that allow two devices to signal each other when they are ready to send or receive data. This process is known as **hardware handshaking** or hardware flow control. *See also* **RS-232**.

script—A software program that doesn't need to be compiled. It is run by another program "as is," in human-readable form. *See also* **logon script**.

scroll bar—The control that lets you move the image or text within a window either horizontally or vertically to view data that is not currently visible.

search engine—A program on the Net that lets users search for online information. Typical search engines include Infoseek and Alta Vista, both available from Netscape's Search page.

server—A computer or a program that provides a particular service on a network or on the Internet. Typical services include file access, printing, e-mail, **FTP**, and so on. The computers and software that access servers are called **clients**.

server—*See* **parsed HTML**.

server push—A technique specific to Netscape products whereby a Web server can initiate the transmission of data to the Web **client**. Server push is often used for animation or sound. *See also* **client pull**.

server write key—The software key used to encrypt data written or transmitted by the server in a **client/server** system. *See also* **client write key**.

service—A specialized function or utility provided by a **server**.

service provider—An organization, usually commercial, that provides connections to the Internet.

session—A connection between two machines on a network or on the Internet.

SGML—*Standard Generalized Markup Language*. A high-level standard for the electronic publication of information. **HTML** is a subset of SGML.

shell account—An account with an access provider that lets you access a text-based system for performing routine Internet tasks. You connect to a shell account via Telnet or a dial-up terminal emulation program. Some Internet access providers let you put your own Web pages on their server using a shell account.

shortcut—A desktop icon that can be used as a quick way to launch a program or document. Another word for *hotlink* in a WWW document.

SHTML—*See* **parsed HTML**.

signature—A text file that contains any information that you want to attach regularly to your e-mail messages and network news posts. A signature is usually less than five lines long and contains contact information.

single selection list box—A list box that lets you choose only a single item from a list.

slider—A control that displays a continuous range of values and lets you choose one.

SLIP—*Serial Line Internet Protocol*. Like **PPP**, this is a protocol that lets a computer link to the Internet by calling in to a service provider using a modem and a standard telephone line.

SMTP—*Simple Mail Transfer Protocol.* The most common protocol for sending e-mail messages over the Internet. *See also* **POP3**.

snail mail—A form of messaging that utilizes carbon-based materials to create and address human-readable data, which is then transmitted over a complex network of streets and air routes by human entities known as "postal employees."

sockets—A software mechanism that allows programs to communicate locally or remotely by setting up endpoints for sending and receiving data. The application programmer does not have to worry about the nuts-and-bolts details of how the data travels from one point to the other, as that is taken care of by the operating system or other resident software. The Windows Sockets API (**Winsock**) uses this concept.

spider—A program that wanders around the Web looking for new content. Links to new sites that it finds may then be added to large directory documents such as Yahoo. Spiders are also known as robots, wanderers, crawlers, and WebCrawlers.

spin box—A control that displays a limited range of values and lets you choose one.

SSL—*Secure Sockets Layer.* A version of the **HTTP** protocol that includes encryption. SSL allows for the secure transfer of sensitive information across the Net, as in financial transactions.

string—Geek-speak for a set of characters. Your name, for instance, is a string.

symbolic link—A name that does not refer to an actual object but points to another name. For instance, on an FTP site, a directory list might include the entry WINDOWS, even though there is no WINDOWS directory at this level. The WINDOWS entry could be a symbolic link to a directory buried much deeper in the file system, such as /pub/micro/pc/GUI/windows. Symbolic links provide convenient shortcuts to actual objects.

synchronous transmission—A method of transmitting data that uses a special timing signal to ensure a set time interval between any two characters. *See also* **asynchronous transmission**.

tag—A special code used in an **HTML** document to indicate how a piece of text or a graphic should be displayed by a Web browser; it may also establish a **hotlink** to another document.

TCP/IP—*Transmission Control Protocol/Internet Protocol.* TCP/IP is a set of protocols that applications use for communicating across networks or over the Internet. These protocols specify how packets of data should be constructed, addressed, checked for errors, and so on.

Telnet—A program that lets you log in to a remote **host computer** and access its data and services as if you were using a text-based **terminal** attached locally.

terminal—A keyboard and display screen used to access a **host computer**.

terminal emulation—A software program that lets you use a personal computer to communicate with a **host computer**. It transmits special commands and interprets incoming data as if it were a terminal directly connected to the host.

text box—A control that lets you enter and edit text.

text file—*See* **ASCII file**.

text-only—Containing no visual information other than human-readable **ASCII** text. When you **Telnet** into a UNIX system, for instance, your user interface is text-only, as distinguished from the graphical user interface of systems like Windows.

thread—A software process or task. Operating systems like Windows 95 and Windows NT allow for many threads to occur simultaneously.

title bar—The horizontal bar at the top of a window that includes the window name. The title bar also acts as a handle that can be used to drag the window.

title bar icon—The small icon at the top-left corner of the title bar. You can use it to display the pop-up menu. Double-clicking this icon closes the program.

toolbar—A control that provides a defined area for a set of other controls such as icon buttons, drop-down list boxes, and so on.

traffic—Data traveling across a network or across the Internet.

tree control—A control that lets you display a set of hierarchical objects in an expandable outline format.

upload—To send a file to a remote system; the opposite of **download**.

URL—*Uniform Resource Locator*. A URL is a specially formatted address that a Web browser uses to locate, retrieve, and display a document. The URL includes the Internet address of the data, where it is located on the Web server machine, and what kind of transport protocol is required to retrieve it. URLs are contained in the **hotlinks** within **HTML** documents; they may also be specified by the user of a Web browser "on the fly."

Usenet—A large collection of networked users who communicate using the UNIX-to-UNIX Copy Protocol (UUCP) rather than **TCP/IP**. Usenet is connected to the Internet by gateways, and many Internet users are familiar with its broad range of discussion forums known as newsgroups.

UUCP—*UNIX to UNIX copy.* An older set of network commands for sending and receiving data on dial-up networks.

UUENCODING—A standard for encoding binary data that allows it to be transmitted as 7-bit ASCII information; it is then *UUDECODED* into its original binary form.

virtual server—A server that appears like a separate server to clients, but which actually runs on the same machine and uses the same server software as other servers. For instance, the Netscape FastTrack server lets you set up www.server1.com, www.server2.com, and www.server3.com all at once. Somebody logging onto www.server2.com would access different information from somebody logging onto www.server1.com.

VRML—*Virtual Reality Modeling Language.* VRML is a specialized language that allows for the creation of three-dimensional user interfaces that can be accessed via Web browsers such as Netscape Navigator 3.0.

WAIS—*Wide-Area Information Server.* WAIS is a specialized Internet client/server system for researching information in Internet databases.

WAN—*See* **wide area network**.

wanderer—*See* **spider**.

Web—Short for **World Wide Web**.

Web browser—A program for retrieving and viewing **HTML** documents on the **World Wide Web**. Also known as a Web **client**.

WebCrawler—*See* **spider**.

Web document—Any document available on the **World Wide Web**.

Webmaster—The individual in charge of developing or administering a Web site.

Web server—A computer that stores Web documents and allows **Web browsers** to retrieve them over the Internet using the **HTTP** protocol. Also, the software that makes this possible.

wide area network—A group of computers and/or networks connected to one another by means of long-distance communication devices such as telephone lines and satellites, rather than just through local wiring. *See also* **local area network**.

widget—In HTML geek-speak, an object in a Web document that accepts user input. Examples are check boxes, radio buttons, drop-down lists, and so on.

wildcard character—A character used when you specify a filename; it is a variable that stands for any other valid character or characters. The question mark (?) stands for a single character, while the asterisk (*) stands for any string of characters in the filename. For instance, **.txt* means "any file that has the .TXT extension"; *??.txt* means "any file that has a two-letter name and the .TXT extension."

Windows NT Server—The version of the Windows NT operating system that provides centralized network management and security as well as additional connectivity options.

Windows NT Workstation—The version of the Windows NT operating system that provides operating and networking functionality, but without centralized management.

Winsock—*Windows Sockets API*. A software "toolkit" that lets Windows programmers access **TCP/IP** services using a standard interface. Any Internet programs that use this standard, such as e-mail clients, Web browsers, and so on, will work under Windows 95 and Windows NT.

workgroup—On Microsoft networks, a collection of grouped computers with a unique name.

workstation—In Windows NT, a computer running the **Windows NT Workstation** software.

World Wide Web (WWW)—An Internet service used for browsing hypermedia documents; the "Internet within the Internet" formed by all the Web servers and **HTML** documents currently online.

XOFF—A special character that's used to control the flow of information between a **DCE** and a **DTE**. When one device receives an XOFF character from the other, it stops transmitting until it receives an **XON**.

XON—A special character used to control the flow of data between a **DCE** and a **DTE**. *See also* **XOFF**.

APPENDIX
A

About the Companion CD-ROM

The Companion CD-ROM included with your copy of the *Official Netscape Internet Starter Kit* contains valuable Internet connectivity software from three sources: AT&T WorldNet Service, EarthLink, and Sprint.

Navigating the CD-ROM

To View the CD-ROM

Macintosh PPC:
Double-click on the "Launch Mac PPC" file.

Macintosh 68K:
Double-click on the "Launch Mac 68K" file.

Windows 95/NT:
Double-click on the "LAUNCH32.EXE" file, or go to START | RUN and type d:\(where d is the name of your CD-ROM drive)launch.exe in the space provided.

Windows 3.1x:
Double-click on the "LAUNCH16.EXE" file in File Manager, or go to FILE | RUN and type d:\(where d is the name of your CD-ROM drive)launch16.exe in the space provided.

You will see a small menu screen offering several button choices. You can navigate around the CD-ROM via these buttons.

EarthLink Network TotalAccess

TotalAccess provides a top-quality, easy-to-use Internet connection. It includes an Internet Dialer, Netscape Navigator 3, and registration software for opening an Internet account with EarthLink Network. For more information about using the software, consult the EarthLink vreadme on the CD-ROM or see Chapter 1 of this book. For EarthLink technical support, call 800-395-8410. For more information about other EarthLink Network products, visit http://www.earthlink.com.

AT&T WorldNet Service Software

Note: Please see Chapter 1 of this book for complete instructions for installation of AT&T WorldNet Service software and information about registering with AT&T WorldNet Service.

Currently AT&T WorldNet Service is available in the continental United States, Hawaii, Puerto Rico, and the U.S. Virgin Islands.

Windows 3.1:

Windows 3.1x Netscape Navigator v3.0 with Setup 1.1 16-bit international, exportable AT&T customized Netscape Navigator 3.0 Browser. This is to be integrated ONLY with Windows 3.1x software. This product includes an enhanced TCP/IP stack, a dialer, and integrated mail/news.

Windows 95:

Netscape Navigator v3.0 with Setup 1.2 32-bit international, exportable AT&T customized Netscape Navigator 3.0 Browser. This is to be integrated ONLY with Windows 95 software. This product uses Windows 95 Dial-up-Networking (included with Windows 95) and is intended to be used only on Windows 95 machines.

Macintosh:

Netscape v2.02 for the Macintosh International, exportable version of AT&T customized Netscape Navigator 2.02 Browser. This product includes the free TCP stack and is intended to be integrated with MAC software.

Registration Code Please note that you will need to use a registration code in order to activate your AT&T account. If AT&T is your long-distance carrier, your code is LAK79N6A4. If you are using a carrier other than AT&T, your registration code is LAK79N6A5. Please see Chapter 1 for more details about setting up an AT&T WorldNet Service account.

Sprint Internet Passport

- Full-service Internet access from Sprint.
- Friendly customer support on-line or by phone.
- Customer support available 24 hours/day, seven days/week.
- Netscape Navigator Personal Edition client software included for easy browsing around the World Wide Web.
- Includes one e-mail account to communicate with family, friends, and colleagues.
- Full access to more than 18,000 Usenet newsgroups.
- Local service from more than 200 U.S. cities (more planned in 1997). Reliable service from one of the Internet's largest carriers.

Pricing

$19.95 per month for unlimited use* or pay only for hours used at $1.50 per hour. For your convenience, we'll bill your VISA, Mastercard, or American Express.

Ordering Information

Just double-click the Sprint icon to start your Internet experience. Or to order additional copies, call toll-free at 1-800-359-3900.

* Nationwide Access Number includes surcharge of $4.80 per hour if local service is not available in your area.

System Requirements

Windows Users:

- CD-ROM drive required
- IBM-compatible computer with a 386sx or higher processor (486 or higher recommended)
- At least 8MB RAM and at least 11MB of free hard disk space needed
- 14.4 Kbps or faster modem (28.8 Kbps recommended)
- Windows 3.1 or Windows 95

Macintosh Users:

- CD-ROM drive required
- Macintosh Operating System 7.1 up to 7.5.5
- At least 16MB RAM and at least 12MB of free hard disk space needed
- Macintosh TCP 2.0.6 (or higher) or Open Transport 1.1 (or higher)
- FreePPP 2.5 (or higher)—included on this installation CD-ROM
- 14.4 Kbps or faster modem (28.8 Kbps recommended)
- If you are unsure whether you meet the system requirements, please consult your systems manual or contact your system manufacturer.

Customer Support

- Internet experts—so you don't have to be.
- Extensive help files available at Sprint Internet Passport site.
- Dedicated to helping you have more fun on the Internet.
- Load, click, and cruise on...

If you currently use Netscape Navigator as your Internet browser, Sprint Internet Passport will automatically overwrite that software. However, with just a little extra care and effort, Sprint Internet Passport will nicely coexist on your system with your current software. More information and details on the exact steps necessary to preserve your current configuration can be found at http://www.sprint.com/passport, or you may call us at 1-800-726-1400.

Registration and Instructions

Windows 3.1 Users:

1. Insert the Ventana Internet Starter Kit CD into your CD-ROM drive.
2. In Program Manager or File Manager, select File from the menu bar, and then select Run.
3. In the Command Line field, type D:\launch16.exe (where D: represents the drive letter of your CD-ROM).
4. When the Ventana Internet Starter Kit display comes on your screen, click on Software.
5. Click on Sprint Internet Passport, then click on Launch.
6. Click OK, then follow the on-screen prompts to complete the software setup. When you're prompted to do so, allow setup to restart Windows[a].
7. When restart is complete, double-click on the Sprint Internet Passport icon in the Netscape Personal Edition program group.
8. Follow the on-screen prompts to set up your Sprint Internet Passport account.
9. When registration is complete, exit out of the Ventana Internet Starter Kit program.
10. Double-click on the Sprint Internet Passport icon in the Netscape Personal Edition program group.
11. Click Connect.You're ready to begin!

Windows 95 Users:

1. If you have never been online before, be sure to have your Windows 95 diskettes or CD handy.
2. Insert the Ventana Internet Starter Kit CD into your CD-ROM drive. On most systems, the setup process will begin automatically within about 10 seconds.
3. If the setup program doesn't begin automatically, click the Start button on your Task Bar and then click Run. In the Run window, type D:\launch32.exe and click OK.
4. When the Ventana Internet Starter Kit display comes on your screen, click on Software.
5. Click on Sprint Internet Passport, then click on Launch.

6. Follow the on-screen prompts to complete the software setup. If you're prompted for a Windows 95 diskette, place the required diskette in Drive A:; if you're prompted for the Windows 95 CD, remove the Ventana Internet Starter Kit CD from your CD-ROM drive and insert your Windows® 95 CD. If you're prompted to do so, allow setup to restart your computer.
7. If necessary, double-click the Sprint Internet Passport Account Setup icon in the Navigator window.
8. Follow the on-screen prompts to set up your Sprint Internet Passport account.
9. When registration is complete, exit out of the Ventana Internet Starter Kit program.
10. Double-click on the Shortcut to Sprint Internet Passport Dialer icon on your desktop.
11. If the password field is blank (no stars), enter your password.
12. Click Connect. You're ready to begin!

Macintosh Users:

1. Turn off all extensions by starting your computer with the shift key held down.
2. Insert the Ventana Internet Starter Kit CD into your CD-ROM drive.
3. The Ventana Internet Starter Kit window will appear on your desktop. Inside this window, double-click the Launch PPC or Launch 68k icon (depending on whether your Macintosh is a PPC or a 68k machine).
4. When the Ventana Internet Starter Kit display comes on your screen, click on Software.
5. Click on Sprint Internet Passport, then click on Launch.
6. Follow the on-screen prompts to complete the software setup. Be sure to take the default settings.
7. When setup is complete, you will be prompted to restart your computer. Click on Restart.
8. When restart is complete, double-click on the Account Setup icon in the Sprint Internet Passport window.
9. Follow the on-screen prompts to set up your Sprint Internet Passport account.
10. When registration is complete, you will be prompted to restart your computer. Click on Restart..

11. When restart is complete, double-click on the Sprint Internet Passport icon in the Sprint Internet Passport window. FreePPP will connect you to Sprint Internet Services, and the Sprint Internet Passport browser will launch. You're ready to begin!

Exiting Sprint Internet Passport Account

Windows 3.1:

1. Close Sprint Internet Passport (Netscape Navigator) by clicking on File and then clicking on Exit.
2. Close any other open Internet client applications (e.g., IRC, FTP, and Telnet sessions).
3. Disconnect from Sprint Internet Passport by clicking the Disconnect button in the Sprint Internet Dialer dialog box.

Windows 95:

1. Close Sprint Internet Passport (Netscape Navigator) by clicking on File and then clicking on Exit.
2. Close any other open Internet client applications (e.g., IRC, FTP, and Telnet sessions).
3. To disconnect from Sprint Internet Services, locate and click on the Connected to Sprint Internet button on your Task Bar. This will bring the Sprint Dialer Dialogue box to the foreground. Click on the Disconnect button.

Macintosh:

1. Close Sprint Internet Passport (Netscape Navigator).
2. Double-click on the FreePPPSetup icon in the Sprint Internet Passport folder.
3. Click Disconnect.

Note: Be sure to record your Dial Access Number, Sprint Internet Passport password, e-mail address, and Sprint Internet Passport log-in ID.

A README file has been included on your Ventana Internet Starter Kit CD. It contains detailed installation instructions as well as general and trouble-shooting tips. For IBM-PC users, it is located in the DISK3 directory under the appropriate version of Windows:

D:\SOFTWARE\WIN\SPRINT\WIN.95\DISK1\README.TXT
D:\SOFTWARE\WIN\SPRINT\WIN.31\DISK1\README.TXT

For Macintosh users, the README alias can be found by clicking Internet Starter Kit, Software, Mac, Sprint Internet.

Your software will automatically search for and attempt to identify your modem; however, if setup encounters difficulties, you may need to identify your modem manually. See the README.TXT for more information.

Macintosh users may wish to install Live 3D. See the README file for more information.

Be sure to verify your pricing plan selection.

Be sure your registration address matches your credit card billing address. If you credit card company uses ZIP+4, it is important that you include the extra 4 digits.

If you live in an area where local calls can span two (or more) area codes, you may want to modify the 1+Area Code settings in your dialer. See the README.TXT for more information.

Please note that in some areas, a call may be considered long distance, even though it does not require dialing a "1" or "0". If you are unsure if a number is a local call, check with your local telephone company.

Technical Support

Technical support is available for installation-related problems only. The technical support office is open from 8:00 A.M. to 6:00 P.M. Monday through Friday and can be reached via the following methods:

- Phone: (919) 544-9404 extension 81
- Faxback Answer System: (919) 544-9404 extension 85
- E-mail: help@vmedia.com
- FAX: (919) 544-9472
- World Wide Web: **http://www.vmedia.com/support**
- America Online: keyword *Ventana*

Limits of Liability & Disclaimer of Warranty

The authors and publisher of this book have used their best efforts in preparing the CD-ROM and the programs contained in it. These efforts include the development, research, and testing of the theories and programs to determine their effectiveness. The authors and publisher make no warranty of any kind expressed or implied, with regard to these programs or the documentation contained in this book.

The authors and publisher shall not be liable in the event of incidental or consequential damages in connection with, or arising out of, the furnishing, performance, or use of the programs, associated instructions, and/or claims of productivity gains.

Index

F

G

H

I

O

P-Q

V

W-X-Y-Z

VENTANA

Official Netscape Messenger & Collabra Book

$39.99, 408 pages, part #: 1-56604-685-8

Windows, Macintosh • Intermediate to Advanced

The Power of Web-based Communications—Without a Web Site!
Stay in touch with customers; promote products and services visually; share the latest market trends—with simple Internet dial-up access! This step-by-step guide helps you harness Netscape Communicator's e-mail, newsreader, HTML authoring and real-time conference tools to achieve faster, more powerful business communications—without the effort or expense of a Web site. Learn how to:

- Integrate Messenger, Collabra, Conference and Composer for efficient business communications.
- Distribute eye-catching, HTML-based marketing materials without a Web site.
- Use the Net to gather, organize and share information efficiently.

Official Netscape Composer Book

$39.99, 600 pages, part #: 1-56604-674-2

Windows • Beginning to Intermediate

Forget about tedious tags and cumbersome code! Now you can create sophisticated, interactive Web pages using simple, drag-and-drop techniques. Whether you want to create your personal home page, promote your hobby, or launch your business on the Web, here's everything you need to know to get started:

- Step-by-step instructions for designing sophisticated Web sites with no previous experience.
- JavaScript basics and techniques for adding multimedia, including animation and interactivity.
- Tips for businesses on the Web, including creating forms, ensuring security and promoting a Web site.

The CD-ROM features a wide selection of Web tools for designing Web pages, adding multimedia, creating forms and building image maps.

Official Netscape Plug-in Book, Second Edition

$39.99, 700 pages, part #: 1-56604-612-2

Windows, Macintosh • All Users

Your One-Stop Plug-in Resource & Desktop Reference!
Why waste expensive online time searching the Net for the plug-ins you want? This handy one-stop reference includes in-depth reviews, easy-to-understand instructions and step-by-step tutorials. And you avoid costly download time—the hottest plug-ins are included! Includes:

- In-depth reviews & tutorials for most Netscape plug-ins.
- Professional tips on designing pages with plug-ins.
- Fundamentals of developing your own plug-ins.

The CD-ROM includes all the featured plug-ins available at press time.

VENTANA

The Comprehensive Guide to SmartSuite 97

James Meade

$34.99, 528 pages, illustrated, part #: 1-56604-651-3

Here's Suite relief for business users at all levels. Step by step, learn to use applications together, work collaboratively, and maximize Internet and intranet connectivity. Packed with tips and shortcuts.

For Windows 95/NT • Beginning to Intermediate

The Comprehensive Guide to Microsoft Office 97

Ned Snell

$39.99, 848 pages, illustrated, part #: 1-56604-646-7

The "right-size" guide to the world's hottest suite! Easy enough for beginners, yet in-depth enough for power users. Covers all five applications, plus tips, shortcuts, Internet techniques and more.

For Windows 95/NT • Beginning to Intermediate

VENTANA

Official HTML Publishing for Netscape, Second Edition

$39.99, 800 pages, part #: 1-56604-650-5

Windows 95/NT, Macintosh • Intermediate

Make the Most of the Latest Netscape Features!
Learn how the latest developments in Netscape Navigator and HTML enhance your ability to deliver eye-catching, interactive Web pages to a broad audience, and how to harness new technologies to create a compelling site. Includes:

- Playing to Navigator's hottest features, including tables, frames, plug-ins and support for Java applets.
- Guidelines for designing great Web pages.
- New material on style sheets, sound, multimedia and databases.

The CD-ROM contains an example Web site on the Net, sample JavaScript, clip objects, backgrounds and more.

Official Netscape JavaScript 1.2 Book, Second Edition

$29.99, 520 pages, part #: 1-56604-675-0

All platforms • Beginning to Intermediate

Brew up instant scripts—even if you're not a programmer!
Learn all the skills you need to perk up your Web pages with multimedia and interactivity. Fully updated for Netscape Communicator, this bestseller now includes:

- Basic programming techniques.
- Tips for using existing scripts and building your own from scratch.
- Nearly 200 script samples and interactive tutorials online.

Official Netscape FastTrack Server Book

$39.99, 600 pages, part #: 1-56604-483-9

Windows NT • Intermediate to Advanced

Turn your PC into an Internet/intranet powerhouse!
This step-by-step guide to the hottest server software on the Net provides all the instructions you need to launch your Internet or intranet site, from technical requirements to content creation and administration. Learn how to exploit FastTrack Server's high-performance server architecture to easily create and manage customized web sites. Plus, enhance your site with FTP and Telnet; ensure security for online transactions; and import and convert documents.

VENTANA

Web Publishing With Adobe PageMill 2

$34.99, 480 pages, illustrated, part #: 1-56604-458-8

Now, creating and designing professional pages on the Web is a simple, drag-and-drop function. Learn to pump up PageMill with tips, tricks and troubleshooting strategies in this step-by-step tutorial for designing professional pages. The CD-ROM features Netscape plug-ins, original textures, graphical and text-editing tools, sample backgrounds, icons, buttons, bars, GIF and JPEG images, Shockwave animations.

Web Publishing With QuarkImmedia

$39.99, 552 pages, illustrated, part #: 1-56604-525-8

Use multimedia to learn multimedia, building on the power of QuarkXPress. Step-by-step instructions introduce basic features and techniques, moving quickly to delivering dynamic documents for the Web and other electronic media. The CD-ROM features an interactive manual and sample movie gallery with displays showing settings and steps. Both are written in QuarkImmedia.

VENTANA

Exploring Moving Worlds

$24.99, 288 pages, illustrated, part #: 1-56604-467-7

Where will the Moving Worlds standard lead? This overview points the way, with specifications and software examples to help developers create live content, animation and full motion on the Web. Features detailed specifications and software examples.

Exploring ActiveX

$24.99, 320 pages, illustrated, part #: 1-56604-526-6

Web developers, take control! ActiveX is changing how you work, and this book tells you how to adapt. Thoroughly explains ActiveX controls, documents and scripting, with guidelines for effective use. Tips, tricks and shortcuts throughout help you make the most of this powerful new Microsoft technology.

Technical support for installation related issues only provided by Ventana. The Ventana technical support office is open from 8:00 A.M. to 6:00 P.M. (EST) Monday through Friday and can be reached via the following methods:

World Wide Web: http://www.netscapepress.com/support

E–mail: help@vmedia.com

Phone: (919) 544-9404 extension 81

FAX: (919) 544-9472

America Online: keyword **Ventana**

MACROMEDIA ®

End-User License Agreement for Shockwave ™ Run-Time Software (*"The Software"*)

PLEASE READ THIS DOCUMENT CAREFULLY BEFORE FIRST USING THE SOFTWARE. THIS DOCUMENT PROVIDES IMPORTANT INFORMATION CONCERNING THE SOFTWARE, PROVIDES YOU WITH A LICENSE TO USE THE SOFTWARE, AND CONTAINS WARRANTY AND LIABILITY INFORMATION. BY FIRST USING THE SOFTWARE, YOU ARE ACCEPTING THE SOFTWARE AND AGREEING TO BECOME BOUND BY THE TERMS OF THIS AGREEMENT. IF YOU DO NOT WISH TO DO SO, DO NOT USE THE SOFTWARE.

1. Important Notice

Shockwave software is a unique addition to Macromedia's Run-Time software library, allowing End-Users to play applications created with Macromedia's authoring software, available on the World Wide Web. The Software is an object code package that is designed to run with and will run only with an Internet browser which is licensed to contain and contains Macromedia Player software. If your browser is not one of these, the Software may not function properly.

2. License

This Agreement allows you to:

(a) Use the Software on a single computer.

(b) Make one copy of the Software in machine-readable form for backup purposes.

3. Restrictions

Unless Macromedia has authorized you to distribute the Software, you may not make or distribute copies of the Software or electronically transfer the Software from one computer to another. You may not decompile, reverse engineer, disassemble, or otherwise reduce the Software to a human-perceivable form. You may not modify, rent, resell for profit, distribute or create derivative works based upon the Software.

4. Ownership

This license gives you limited rights to use the Software. You do not own and Macromedia retains ownership of the Software and all copies of it. All rights not specifically granted in this Agreement, including Federal and International copyrights, are reserved by Macromedia.

5. Disclaimer of Warranties and Technical Support

The Software is provided to you free of charge, and on an "AS IS" basis, without any technical support or warranty of any kind from Macromedia, including, without limitation, a warranty of merchantability, fitness for a particular purpose and non-infringement. SOME STATES DO NOT ALLOW THE EXCLUSION OF IMPLIED WARRANTIES, SO THE ABOVE EXCLUSION MAY NOT APPLY TO YOU. YOU MAY ALSO HAVE OTHER LEGAL RIGHTS WHICH VARY FROM STATE TO STATE.

6. Limitation of Damages

MACROMEDIA SHALL NOT BE LIABLE FOR ANY INDIRECT, SPECIAL, INCIDENTAL OR CONSEQUENTIAL DAMAGE OR LOSS (INCLUDING DAMAGES FOR LOSS OF BUSINESS, LOSS OF PROFITS, OR THE LIKE), WHETHER BASED ON BREACH OF CONTRACT, TORT (INCLUDING NEGLIGENCE), PRODUCT LIABILITY OR OTHERWISE, EVEN IF MACROMEDIA OR ITS REPRESENTATIVES HAVE BEEN ADVISED OF THE POSSIBILITY OF SUCH DAMAGES. SOME STATES DO NOT ALLOW THE LIMITATION OR EXCLUSION OF LIABILITY FOR INCIDENTAL OR CONSEQUENTIAL DAMAGES, SO THIS LIMITATION OR EXCLUSION MAY NOT APPLY TO YOU. The limited warranty, exclusive remedies and limited liability set forth above are fundamental elements of the basis of the bargain between Macromedia and you. You agree that Macromedia would not be able to provide the Macromedia Software on an economic basis without such limitations.

7. Government End-Users RESTRICTED RIGHTS LEGEND

The Software is "Restricted Computer Software." Use, duplication, or disclosure by the Government is subject to restrictions as set forth in subparagraph (c)(1)(ii) of the Rights in Technical Data and Computer Software clause at DFARS 252.227-7013. Manufacturer: Macromedia, Inc., 600 Townsend St., San Francisco, CA, 94103.

8. General

This Agreement shall be governed by the internal laws of the State of California. This Agreement contains the complete agreement between the parties with respect to the subject matter hereof, and supersedes all prior or contemporaneous agreements or understandings, whether oral or written. All questions concerning this Agreement shall be directed to: Macromedia, Inc., 600 Townsend St., San Francisco, CA, 94103, Attention: Chief Financial Officer.